Contemporary Debates in Philosophy of Religion

Contemporary Debates in Philosophy

In teaching and research, philosophy makes progress through argumentation and debate. *Contemporary Debates in Philosophy* presents a forum for students and their teachers to follow and participate in the debates that animate philosophy today in the western world. Each volume presents pairs of opposing viewpoints on contested themes and topics in the central subfields of philosophy. Each volume is edited and introduced by an expert in the field, and also includes an index, bibliography, and suggestions for further reading. The opposing essays, commissioned especially for the volumes in the series, are thorough but accessible presentations of opposing points of view.

1. Contemporary Debates in Philosophy of Religion *edited by Michael L. Peterson and Raymond J. VanArragon*
2. Contemporary Debates in Philosophy of Science *edited by Christopher Hitchcock*

Forthcoming *Contemporary Debates* are in:

Aesthetics *edited by Matthew Kieran*
Applied Ethics *edited by Andrew Cohen and Christopher Heath Wellman*
Cognitive Science *edited by Robert Stainton*
Epistemology *edited by Matthias Steup and David Sosa*
Metaphysics *edited by Ted Sider, Dean Zimmerman, and John Hawthorne*
Moral Theory *edited by James Dreier*
Philosophy of Mind *edited by Brian McLaughlin and Jonathan Cohen*
Social Philosophy *edited by Laurence Thomas*

CONTEMPORARY DEBATES IN PHILOSOPHY OF RELIGION

Edited by

Michael L. Peterson

and

Raymond J. VanArragon

Blackwell
Publishing

BLACKWELL PUBLISHING
350 Main Street, Malden, MA 02148-5020, USA
9600 Garsington Road, Oxford OX4 2DQ, UK
550 Swanston Street, Carlton, Victoria 3053, Australia

First published 2004 by Blackwell Publishing Ltd

6 2008

Library of Congress Cataloging-in-Publication Data

Contemporary debates in the philosophy of religion / edited by Michael L. Peterson and Raymond J. VanArragon.
p. cm.—(Contemporary debates in philosophy ; 1)
Includes bibliographical references and index.
ISBN 978-0-631-20042-2 (hardcover : alk. paper)—ISBN 978-0-631-20043-7 (pbk. : alk. paper)
1. Religion—Philosophy. 2. Christianity—Philosophy. I. Peterson, Michael L., 1950–
II. VanArragon, Raymond J. III. Series.

BL51.C63682 2003
210—c21

2003005122

A catalogue record for this title is available from the British Library.

Set in 10/12½ pt Rotis serif
by SNP Best-set Typesetter Ltd., Hong Kong

For further information on
Blackwell Publishing, visit our website:
http://www.blackwellpublishing.com

Contents

PART II ARGUMENTS FOR RELIGIOUS BELIEF 95

Notes on Contributors

William P. Alston is Professor Emeritus in the Philosophy Department at Syracuse University. He is well known for his work in philosophy of language, epistemology, and philosophy of religion. He has written several books, including *Perceiving God: The Epistemology of Religious Experience* (1991).

Lynne Rudder Baker is Professor of Philosophy at the University of Massachusetts. Her areas of interest include metaphysics and philosophy of mind, and she is the author of *Persons and Bodies: A Constitution View* (2000).

David Basinger is Professor of Philosophy and Ethics at Roberts Wesleyan College. He specializes in philosophy of religion and ethics and publishes regularly on issues relating to divine providence.

Michael Bergmann is Assistant Professor of Philosophy at Purdue University. He has published many articles in the areas of metaphysics, epistemology, and philosophy of religion.

Craig A. Boyd is Associate Professor of Philosophy at Greenville College. His areas of interest include ethics and medieval philosophy, and he has published professional articles in both areas.

Peter Byrne is Professor of Ethics and the Philosophy of Religion at King's College, University of London. He has published books in both ethics and philosophy of religion, including *Prolegomena to Religious Pluralism: Reference and Realism in Religion* (1995).

Stephen T. Davis is Professor of Philosophy at Claremont McKenna College. His interests include philosophy of religion and the history of philosophy. He is the author of *Risen Indeed: Making Sense of the Resurrection* (1993).

Evan Fales is Associate Professor of Philosophy at the University of Iowa. He does work in several areas, including epistemology and philosophy of science; he is author of *A Defense of the Given* (1996).

Richard M. Gale is Professor of Philosophy at the University of Pittsburgh. He does work in metaphysics and has published widely in philosophy of religion, including the book *On the Nature and Existence of God* (1991).

William Hasker is Emeritus Professor of Philosophy at Huntington College. His areas of research include metaphysics and philosophy of religion. Among other books, he is the author of *God, Time, and Knowledge* (1989).

Paul Helm is the J. I. Packer Professor of Theology and Philosophy at Regent College. His primary area of interest is philosophy of religion, and he is author of several books, including *The Providence of God* (1994).

Daniel Howard-Snyder is Associate Professor of Philosophy at Western Washington University. His interests include philosophy of religion and epistemology, and he is editor of *The Evidential Argument from Evil* (1996).

Janine Marie Idziak is Professor of Philosophy at Loras College. Her interests include medieval philosophy and ethics. She is the editor of *Questions on an Ethics of Divine Commands* (1997).

Michael Martin is Emeritus Professor of Philosophy at Boston University. He has done work in philosophy of religion and philosophy of social science and is author of *The Case Against Christianity* (1991).

Paul K. Moser is Professor of Philosophy at Loyola University, Chicago. His specialties include epistemology and metaphilosophy. He is co-editor of *Divine Hiddenness: New Essays* (2002).

Michael J. Murray is Associate Professor of Philosophy at Franklin and Marshall College. His interests include Leibniz and philosophy of religion, and he is editor of the book, *Reason for the Hope Within* (1999).

Del Ratzsch is Professor of Philosophy at Calvin College. He specializes in philosophy of science of logic. Among other books, he has published *Nature, Design, and Science* (2001).

Bruce R. Reichenbach is Professor of Philosophy at Augsburg College. He has interests in philosophy of religion and Asian philosophy, and his most recent book is *Introduction to Critical Thinking* (2001).

William L. Rowe is Professor of Philosophy at Purdue University. He has published widely in philosophy of religion and metaphysics and is editor of *God and the Problem of Evil* (2002).

J. L. Schellenberg is Associate Professor of Philosophy at Mount Saint Vincent University. His interests include philosophy of religion, and he is the author of *Divine Hiddenness and Human Reason* (1993).

Thomas Talbott is Professor of Philosophy at Willamette University. He has interests in issues pertaining to free will and divine providence, and he is author of the book *The Inescapable Love of God* (1999).

Raymond J. VanArragon is Assistant Professor of Philosophy at Asbury College. His areas of interest include epistemology and philosophy of religion.

Jerry Walls is Professor of Philosophy at Asbury Theological Seminary. His areas of interest include philosophy of religion and philosophical theology, and he is author of *Heaven: The Logic of Eternal Joy* (2002).

John Worrall is Professor of Philosophy of Science at the London School of Economics and Political Science. He has numerous publications and is editor of *The Ontology of Science* (1994).

Keith E. Yandell is Professor of Philosophy at the University of Wisconsin. His interests include philosophy of religion and modern philosophy, and he is author of *Philosophy of Religion* (1999).

Dean W. Zimmerman is Associate Professor of Philosophy at Rutgers University. He has published many articles in the areas of metaphysics and philosophy of religion and is co-editor of *Metaphysics: The Big Questions* (1998).

Preface

This is the first book in Blackwell's "Contemporary Debates" textbook series. It is designed to feature some of the most important current controversies in the philosophy of religion. In the Western philosophical tradition, theism – the belief that an omnipotent, omniscient, wholly good God exists – has been the focus of much philosophical debate and discussion. Although not a living religion itself, theism forms a significant conceptual component of three living religions: Judaism, Christianity, and Islam. Moreover, beliefs within living religions – particularly beliefs of the historic Christian faith – have also occupied the attention of philosophers of religion. So, in staking out the territory for this book, we selected some issues related to classical theism and some related to Christian faith in particular.

Most Anglo-American philosophy is oriented toward the rigorous analysis of ideas, arguments, and positions – and this orientation certainly flourishes in the philosophical treatment of religion. Since the analytic approach lends itself to crisp, straightforward debate, we have made "debate" the central motif of the book. With its most notable origins in Socratic dialectic, debate is essentially the interplay between opposing positions. Each debate here is organized around a key question on which recognized experts take drastically different positions. For each question, one expert on the subject presents an affirmative position and develops his or her argument, and another presents a negative position with a corresponding argument. Brief responses are also included to allow writers to clarify further their own positions, identify weaknesses in the opposing position, and point out directions for further discussion. Each debate on a given question has a short editorial introduction, and then the following structure: affirmative essay, negative essay, reply to negative position, reply to positive position.

Teach the conflicts! We are convinced of the pedagogical value of teaching vigorous, well-argued debate for encouraging students to sharpen their own critical abilities and formulate their own points of view. The noteworthy growth and vibrancy of contemporary philosophy of religion provide a wide range of exciting topics for debate. From this rich vein of discussion, we have chosen topics that fall into three general categories: those involving attacks on religious belief, those involving arguments *for* religious belief, and those involving internal evaluation of the coherence or appropriateness of certain religious beliefs. In the first two categories, the debates are waged between theists and nontheists; in the last category, the debates are largely between religious believers who differ over the implications of their faith commitments. In all, these debates provide an ideal format not simply for students but also for professional philosophers and interested nonprofessionals to explore issues in the philosophy of religion.

M.L.P.
R.V.A.
Asbury College

PART I

ATTACKS ON RELIGIOUS BELIEF

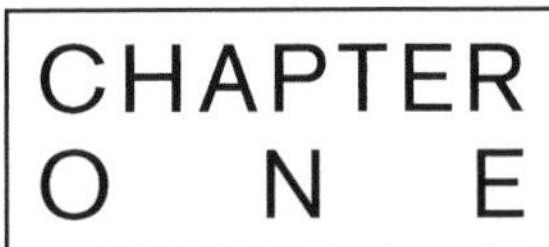

Is Evil Evidence against Belief in God?

In his essay, William Rowe claims that the existence of pervasive and horrendous evil provides strong evidence that God does not exist. He argues that we have good reason to think that at least some of the evils in our world are such that God would have no justifying reason for permitting them. Since God would only permit evils if he had a justifying reason for doing so, it follows that we have good reason for thinking that God does not exist. Daniel Howard-Snyder and Michael Bergmann argue that this is not so. They agree that God would only permit evils if he had a justifying reason for doing so, but they contend that our failure to see God's reasons does not constitute evidence that there are none.

Evil Is Evidence against Theistic Belief

William L. Rowe

1 The Issue

The specific question assigned to us for discussion is this: Grounds for belief in God aside, do the evils in our world make atheistic belief more reasonable than theistic belief? The initial clause in this question is important. For it is one thing to argue that the evils in our world provide such compelling reasons for atheism that the reasons for the existence of God are insufficient to swing the pendulum back in favor of the existence of God, and another thing to argue that, *putting aside* whatever reasons there may be for believing that God exists, the evils that occur in our world make belief in atheism more reasonable than belief in theism. If we put aside grounds for belief in the existence of God, the likelihood that God exists cannot reasonably be assigned any probability beyond 0.5 – where 1 represents God's existence as certain, and 0 represents certainty that God does not exist. So, if we start from an initial point of God's existence having a likelihood of 0.5 or less, and *restrict* ourselves to the evidence generated by the enormous amount of horrendous evil that occurs daily in our world, it should strike anyone that the likelihood of God's existence can only go downward from 0.5.[1] To reach such a judgment is perfectly consistent with holding that once the reasons supportive of the existence of God are brought into the equation, the likelihood of God's existence is in fact positive, somewhere between 0.5 and 1. So, we should not confuse arguing that the negative evidence of evil shows God's existence to be unlikely, *even taking into account* the positive reasons there are to think that God exists, with arguing that *putting aside* the positive reasons for thinking that God exists, the evils that occur in our world make atheistic belief more reasonable than theistic belief. The issue in this discussion is only the latter: Apart from taking into account the positive reasons for thinking that God exists, do the evils that occur in our world make atheistic belief more reasonable than theistic belief? I shall argue that they do.

Before proceeding to argue this point, however, it is important to be clear on what theism is. Theism is the view that there exists an all-powerful, all-knowing, perfectly good being (God). We can call this view *restricted theism.* It is *restricted* in that it does not include any claim that is not entailed by it.[2] So, theism itself does not include any of the following claims: God delivered the Ten Commandments to Moses, Jesus was the incarnation of God, Muhammad ascended into heaven. These are claims made in specific theistic religions; thus they are a part of an *expanded* form of theism: Judaic theism, Christian theism, and Islamic theism. The importance of not taking theism to include the claims held by only one particular religion among the three major theistic religions of the West is that the inclusion would make theism less likely; for if we identify theism with a particular one among the great theistic religions, then the truth of theism itself is made to depend on all the essential beliefs of that particular theistic religion. The other side of this coin is that philosophers who wish to defend theism ought not to suppose that the assumption of theism entitles them to assume any of the special claims associated with their own particular theistic religion. Since most of the philosophers in the Anglo-American tradition who defend theism are adherents of some version of Christian theism, they should beware of confusing the assumption that theism is true with the altogether different, and less likely, assumption that Christian theism is true.

1 At best it can but remain the same. For no reasonable person would argue that all the horrendous evils that occur daily in our world are to be counted as *evidence for* the existence of God.

2 Theism itself does not include the claim that God created a world. For theists hold that God was free not to create a world. They hold that there is a possible world in which God exists but creates nothing at all. What theism may be taken to include is the claim that any contingent things that exist depend for their existence on God's creative act.

2 The Argument

Do the evils that occur in our world significantly lower the likelihood of God's existence?[3] Let's begin thinking about this problem by considering a simple argument from the existence of some of the evils in our world to the nonexistence of God.

1 There exist horrendous evils that an all-powerful, all-knowing, perfectly good being would have no justifying reason to permit.
2 An all-powerful, all-knowing, perfectly good being would not permit an evil unless he had a justifying reason to permit it.

Therefore,

3 God does not exist.

If theists reject this argument for the nonexistence of God, they must reject either the first premise or the second premise. Most theists accept the second premise, as do nontheists. So, most theists must reject the first premise, holding instead that God has a justifying reason for permitting each and every horrendous evil that occurs. But what would be a justifying reason for God to permit some terrible evil he could prevent? Since an evil is something that by its very nature is bad, God's justifying reason for permitting it would have to include something else – either some outweighing good that, all things considered, he wishes to realize and cannot realize without permitting that evil,[4] or some equal or worse evil that, all things considered, he wishes to prevent and cannot prevent without permitting that evil. And the question we must ask ourselves is whether it is rational for us to believe that all the terrible evils that occur daily in our world are like that? Is it rational to believe that each evil is such that were an all-powerful, all-knowing being to prevent it, he would have to forfeit some outweighing good?[5]

Perhaps it will make the issue before us a bit more concrete if we focus on some examples of terrible evils, rather than just terrible evils in the abstract. Here are two examples.

> A fawn is horribly burned in a forest fire caused by lightning. It lies on the forest floor suffering terribly for five days before death relieves it of its suffering.

> A five-year-old girl is brutally beaten, raped, and strangled in Flint, Michigan, on New Year's day a few years ago.

3 Portions of the following are drawn from my essay "God and Evil," *Annual Proceedings of the Center for Philosophic Exchange*, 28 (1997–8), pp. 4–15.
4 It could be that the outweighing good cannot be realized by God without his permitting *that* evil or *some other* evil just as bad. But for ease of understanding the fundamental issue, I will ignore this complication.
5 To avoid needless complexity, I will not mention the other possibility: that God permits the evil in question so as to prevent some equal or greater evil.

The theist must believe that for each of these evils there is some greater good to which it leads, a good that an all-powerful being simply could not realize without permitting that evil. But is what the theist believes about these two evils really so? Is there really some great good that an all-powerful being could bring about only by permitting that fawn to be badly burned and to suffer intensely for five long days before death relieves its torment? And is there really some great good that an all-powerful being could bring about only by permitting that little five-year-old girl in Flint, Michigan, to be savagely beaten, raped, and strangled? And even if it should somehow be so in these two cases, is it true that *all* the instances of intense human and animal suffering occurring daily in our world lead to greater goods in such a way that even an *all-powerful, all-knowing* being could not have achieved *any* of those goods without permitting the instances of suffering that supposedly lead to them? In light of our knowledge of the scale of human and animal suffering occurring daily in our world, the idea that none of those instances of suffering could have been prevented by an all-powerful being without the loss of a greater good must strike us as an extraordinary idea, quite beyond our belief. And if it does strike us in this way, the first premise of the argument we are considering – that there exist horrendous evils that an all-powerful, all-knowing, perfectly good being would have no justifying reason to permit – is bound to strike us as plausible, as something quite likely to be true. But since the second premise is generally agreed to be true, we should then reason that it is likely that our conclusion is true, that God does not exist.

It is important here to understand two points about the argument just presented. First, the argument is not, nor is it meant to be, a *proof* that God does not exist. To be a *proof* of its conclusion, an argument must be such that its conclusion logically follows from its premises and its premises are known with certainty to be true. The argument we are considering meets the first condition, but not the second. The conclusion follows deductively from the two premises, but its first premise is not known with certainty to be true. The claim is only that the first premise is one that we are rationally justified in believing to be true. And since our confidence in the truth of the conclusion should not exceed our confidence in the premises from which it follows, the claim is only that the premises provide sufficient rational support for that conclusion. Second, the truth of the first premise does not logically depend on any claim about the two examples, of the fawn and the five-year-old girl. The examples are meant to *illustrate* the profound difficulty in really believing that an all-powerful, all-knowing being is incapable of achieving his noble ends without having to permit such horrendous, undeserved suffering. But if there were only a few such examples as these, perhaps it would not be unreasonable to believe that somehow even an infinitely intelligent, all-powerful being could not achieve his good ends without permitting them. But, of course, our world is not like that. It is the *enormous amount* of apparently pointless, horrendous suffering occurring daily in our world that grounds the claim in the first premise that there are pointless evils in our world, evils that an all-powerful being could have prevented without forfeiting some outweighing good. But, again, it is not being asserted that the existence of pointless evils is known with certainty, only that it is quite likely that pointless evils occur.

3 Evaluating Two Responses

3.1 First response

Having looked at a particular argument from evil against theistic belief, we can now consider and critically evaluate two theistic responses to this argument. The first response that the theist may put forth goes something like this:

> The first point I want to make is that thus far we have been given no reason at all to think that premise 1 is true. For all you have pointed out is that we don't know what the good is that justifies God in permitting any of these horrendous evils, like the fawn's suffering or the little girl's suffering. But to argue from the fact that we don't know what the good is that justifies God in permitting a certain evil to the conclusion that there is no such good is to engage in a fallacious argument from ignorance: we don't know of any justifying good, therefore there isn't any. So, you haven't really given any good reason at all to think that there are terrible evils for which there are no God-justifying goods. All you have shown, if you have shown anything, is that if these evils do serve some God-justifying goods, we don't know what they are. And the interesting question to ask about our ignorance of these justifying goods is this: Given that God's mind *infinitely transcends* ours, is it really at all likely that the goods for the sake of which he permits much horrendous suffering will be goods we comprehend? After all, isn't God in relation to us like good, loving parents in relation to their small child? Such parents may permit their very young child to suffer a painful surgical procedure for a good the child simply cannot comprehend. So, too, we should expect that if God exists, he may permit many instances of human or animal suffering so as to realize goods that our minds simply cannot comprehend. And if that is so, the fact that we don't know the goods that justify God in permitting much horrendous suffering cannot really be a reason for thinking he doesn't exist. For it is just what we should expect to be true if he does exist.[6]

What are we to make of this response by the theist? Are we really just arguing from ignorance? Perhaps we can come to see that we are not by first distinguishing between goods we know about (goods within our ken) and goods beyond our ken. Consider the suffering of the five-year-old girl as she was brutally beaten, raped, and strangled on New Year's Eve a few years ago in Flint, Michigan. I believe that no good we know about justifies God in permitting that suffering. By "goods we know about" I *mean* goods that we have some cognitive grasp of, even though we may have no knowledge at all that they have occurred or ever will occur. For example, consider the good of the little girl experiencing complete felicity in the everlasting presence of God. Theists consider this an enormous personal good, perhaps the greatest personal good possible for the little girl. So, even though we don't have a very clear grasp of what this great good involves, and even though we don't know that such a

6 This response has been elegantly developed by Stephen Wykstra in "The Humean Obstacle to Evidential Arguments from Suffering: On Avoiding the 'Evils of Appearance,'" *International Journal for Philosophy of Religion*, 16 (1984), pp. 73–93. See also William L. Rowe "Evil and the Theistic Hypothesis: A Response to Wykstra," *International Journal for Philosophy of Religion*, 16 (1984), pp. 95–100.

good will ever be actualized, I include the good of her experiencing complete felicity in the everlasting presence of God among *the goods we know about.* Of course, if some good we know about does justify God in permitting her suffering, that good must have already been actualized or be actualized at some point in the future. But the notion of a good we know about extends to many future goods and to goods that never have and never will occur. And what we have good reason to believe is that none of the goods we know about justifies God in permitting the horrendous suffering of that little girl. For with respect to each such good that we consider, we have reason to believe either that it isn't good enough to justify God in permitting that evil, or that it could likely be actualized by God without his having to permit the horrendous suffering of that little girl, or that some equal or better good could likely be actualized by God without his having to permit the horrendous suffering of that little girl.

Of course, even granting that we know of many great goods and have reason to think that none of these goods justifies God in permitting the little girl's suffering, there still remains the possibility that some good we cannot even conceive does so. And it is here that the theist may appeal to the analogy between the good parent and God. For we cannot deny that some good the child's mind cannot even conceive may justify the parents in permitting the child to suffer. And, by analogy, won't the same be true of God in relation to us as his children? Indeed, since the disparity between his mind and ours may greatly exceed that of the good parents' minds and the mind of their child, isn't it likely that the goods that justify him in permitting us to suffer will often be beyond our comprehension? But against this argument from analogy, two points need to be made.

First, although arguments from analogy are rather weak, the analogy in question has some merit if drawn between a good parent and a good deity of considerable, but nevertheless *finite*, power and knowledge. For, like the good parent, a deity with great but *finite* powers may reasonably believe that he cannot realize some important future good for some of his creatures without permitting a present evil to befall them. And there may be occasions when, like the good parent, the finite deity is simply unable to prevent a dreadful evil befalling his creatures even though there is no good at all served by it. But the theistic God has unlimited power and knowledge. A good parent may be unable to prevent some suffering that her child undergoes, or even the child's death from some painful disease. Can we seriously think that an *infinitely* powerful, all-knowing deity was powerless to prevent the horror of Auschwitz? A good parent may see that she cannot realize some important future good for her child without permitting some present evil to befall the child. Can we seriously think that there is some far-off future good for the victims of Auschwitz, a good that a deity of *infinite* power and knowledge judged to be worth the horror of Auschwitz, and was powerless to achieve without permitting that horror? Perhaps we can if we turn from reason to faith. But the infinite distance between the God of traditional theism and the good mother with the sick child doesn't, in my judgment, provide human reason with good grounds for thinking that such a being would be powerless to prevent many of the countless, seemingly pointless horrors in our world without losing some goods so distant from us that even the mere conception of them must elude our grasp.

But suppose we do reason from the good-parent analogy to the behavior of an all-powerful, all-knowing, infinitely good deity. I think we shall see that the good-parent analogy leads in a different direction from what its proposers desire. We know that when a good, loving parent permits her child to suffer severely in the present for some outweighing good which the child *cannot comprehend*, the loving parent then makes every effort to be present to their children's consciousness during their period of suffering, giving special assurances of her love, concern, and care. For the child may believe that the parent could prevent her present suffering. So the parent will be particularly careful to give her child special assurances of her love and concern during this period of permitted suffering for a distant good the child does not understand. And indeed, what we know about good, loving parents, especially when they permit their children to suffer intensely for goods the children cannot comprehend, is that they are almost always present to their children's consciousness during the period of their suffering, giving special assurances of their love and care. So, on the basis of the good-parent analogy, we should infer that it is likely that God, too, will almost always be consciously present to humans, if not other animals, when he permits them to suffer for goods they cannot comprehend, giving special assurances of his love for them. But since countless numbers of human beings undergo prolonged, horrendous suffering without being consciously aware of God's presence or any special assurances of his love and comfort, we can reasonably infer either that God does not exist or that the good-parent analogy is unable to help us understand why God permits all the horrendous suffering that occurs daily in our world.

Our conclusion about the theist's first response is this. The argument in support of premise 1 is not an argument from ignorance. It is an argument from our knowledge of many goods and our reasonable judgment that none of them justifies God in permitting instances of horrendous evil. It is also an argument from our knowledge of what a being of infinite power, intelligence, and goodness would be disposed to do and would be capable of doing. Of course, there remains the logical possibility both that some goods incomprehensible to us justify God in permitting all these horrendous evils that occur daily in our world and that some further goods incomprehensible to us justify God in not being consciously present to so many who endure these horrendous evils. So, we cannot *prove* that premise 1 is true. Nevertheless, the first response of the theist should, I believe, be judged insufficient to defeat our reasons for thinking that premise 1 is probably true.

Before turning to the theist's second response, we should note that some theists will protest the conclusion that we've come to about the first response. Here is what such a theist may say:

> Your distinction between goods we know about and goods beyond our ken is well-taken. Moreover, you are right to insist that your argument is not a flagrant example of an argument from ignorance. But there is one quite important point you have failed to establish. It is crucial to your argument that we should expect to know the goods for the sake of which God permits much terrible suffering or, failing such knowledge, be particularly aware of God's presence and his love for us during the period of intense suffering for goods we cannot comprehend. For if we have no good reason to expect to know these goods, or to experience God's presence and love during our suffering, then the fact that we don't know them and don't experience God's presence and love won't really count

> against the existence of God. And my point is that God may have good reasons (unknown to us) for not revealing these goods to us. And he also may have good reasons (unknown to us) for not disclosing himself and his love during the period when many suffer terribly for goods they cannot comprehend. How are you able to show that this point of mine is just a mere *logical possibility* and not the way things really are? I think you need to treat more seriously than you do the distinct possibility that God's reasons for permitting so much horrendous suffering, and his reasons for not being consciously present to us during our suffering, involve goods that are presently incomprehensible to us.

The theist here raises an important point. Using the theist's own good-parent analogy, I argued that there is reason to think that when we don't know the goods for the sake of which God permits some horrendous suffering, it is probable that, like the good parent, he would provide us, his children, with special assurances of his love and concern. Since many endure horrendous suffering without any such special assurances, I suggested that we have further reason to doubt God's existence. And the theist's only reply can be that there are still further unknown goods that justify God in not being consciously present to us when we endure terrible suffering for the sake of goods beyond our ken. And I've allowed that we cannot *prove* that this isn't so. It clearly remains a logical possibility. I've said, however, that we can conclude that premise 1 is probably true. But the theist says that I'm not justified in concluding that premise 1 is probably true unless I give a reason for thinking it likely that there are no unknown goods that justify God in permitting much horrendous suffering or no unknown goods that justify God in not being present to us when we endure suffering for the sake of unknown goods. The theist may grant me that no goods we know of play this justifying role. But before allowing me to conclude that it is probable that premise 1 is true and, therefore, probable that God does not exist, the theist says I must also provide some grounds for thinking that no unknown goods play that justifying role.

Suppose we are unsure whether Smith will be in town this evening. It is just as likely, say, that he will be out of town this evening as that he will be in town. Suppose, however, that we do know that *if* Smith is in town, it is just as likely that he will be at the concert this evening as that he won't be. Later we discover that he is not at the concert. I conclude that, given this further information (that he is not at the concert), it is now less likely that he's in town than that he's out of town, that given our information that he is not at the concert, it is more likely that he is out of town than that he is in town. I do admit, however, that I haven't done anything to show that he is not actually somewhere else in town. All I've established is that he is not at the concert. I acknowledge that it is logically possible that he's somewhere else in town. Nor do I know for certain that he is not somewhere else in town. All I claim is that it is *probable* that he is not in town, that it is *more likely* that he is not in town than that he is in town. Those who want to believe that Smith is in town may say that I'm not justified in concluding that it is *probable* that he's out of town *unless* I give some reason to think that he is not somewhere else in town. For, they may say, all I've done is exclude one of the places he will be if he is in town. Similarly, the theist says that if God exists, then either all the horrendous evils we consider serve unknown goods or some of them serve goods we know of. We might even agree that if God exists, it is equally likely that some of the justifying goods will be known to us as that all of the justifying goods will be beyond our ken. After all, when we understand why God may be permitting some terrible evils to occur, those evils will be easier to bear than if we haven't a clue as to why God is permitting them to occur. Suppose we then consider the goods we know of, and reasonably conclude that none of them justifies God in permitting any of these horrendous evils that abound in our world. The theist may even agree that this is true. I then say that it is *probable* that God does not exist. The theist says I'm not justified in drawing this conclusion *unless* I give some reason to think that no unknown goods justify God in permitting all these terrible evils. For, he says, all I've done is exclude one sort of good (goods known by us) as God's justification for permitting any of these terrible evils. Who is right here?

Let's go back to the claim that it is *probable* that Smith is not in town this evening. How can we be justified in making that claim if we've learned only that he is not at the concert? The reason is this. We originally knew that it was equally likely that he would be out of town as in town. We also agreed that *if* he is in town, it is equally likely that he will be at the concert as that he won't be. Once we learn that he is not at the concert, the likelihood that he is out of town must increase, as does the likelihood that he is somewhere else in town. But since it was equally likely that he is out of town as in town, if the likelihood that he is out of town goes up, it then becomes greater than 0.5, with the result that it is *probable* that he is not in town.

Turn now to the existence of God and the occurrence of horrendous evils. Either God exists or he does not. Suppose for a moment that, like the case of Smith being or not being in town, each of these (God exists, God does not exist) is equally likely on the information we have prior to considering the problem of evil.[7] Consider again the many horrendous evils that we know to occur in our world. Before we examine these evils and consider what sort of goods (known or unknown) might justify God (if he exists) in permitting them, let us suppose that it is as likely that the justifying goods for *some* of these evils are known to us as that the justifying goods for *all* of these evils are unknown to us. We then examine the known goods and those horrendous evils and come to the conclusion that no known good justifies God in permitting *any* of those horrendous evils. That discovery parallels our discovery that Smith is not at the concert. And the result is just the same: it is then more probable than not that God does not exist.

3.2 Second response

The second response which the theist can give to the challenge of the problem of evil is the following:

> It is a mistake to think that the goods for which God permits these horrendous evils are totally beyond our ken. For religious thinkers have developed very plausible *theodicies* that suggest a variety of goods that may well constitute God's reasons for permitting many of the horrendous evils that affect human and animal existence. When we seri-

7 As we noted earlier, given that we are putting aside reasons for the existence of God, the existence of God is, at best, no more likely than is the nonexistence of God.

ously consider these theodicies, we can see that we have good reason to think that premise 1 is false. For these theodicies provide us with plausible accounts of what may be God's justifying reasons for permitting the evils that occur in our world.

The theist's first response was to argue both that we have given no reason at all for thinking that premise 1 is true and that our ignorance of many goods that God's mind can comprehend prevents us from being able to establish that premise 1 is probably true. In the second response, the theist proposes to give a good reason for thinking that premise 1 is false. And, of course, to the extent that theodicies do provide a good reason for rejecting premise 1, to that extent the theist will have pointed the way to reconciling the existence of God with the fact that our world contains the horrendous evils that it does. But do these theodicies really succeed in providing a good reason for rejecting premise 1? I believe they do not. But to demonstrate this, we would have to show that these theodicies, taken together, are really unsuccessful in providing what could be God's reasons for permitting the horrendous evils in the world. Although I believe this can be done, I propose here to take just one of these theodicies, the one most commonly appealed to, and show how it fails to provide a good reason for rejecting premise 1. I refer to the *free will theodicy*, a theodicy that has played a central role in defense of theism in the theistic religions of the West.

Developed extensively by St Augustine (AD 354–430), the free will theodicy proposes to explain all the evils in the world as due either directly to evil acts of human free will or to divine punishment for evil acts of human free will. The basic idea is that, rather than create humans so that they behave like automatons, acting rightly of necessity, God created beings who have the power to act well or ill, free either to pursue the good and thereby enjoy God's eternal blessing or to pursue the bad and thereby experience God's punishment. As things turned out, many humans used their free will to turn away from God, freely choosing to do ill rather than good, rejecting God's purpose for their lives. Thus, the evils in the world that are not bad acts of human free will, or their causal effects, are due to God's own acts of punishment for wrongful exercise of human free will.

The cornerstone of this theodicy is that human free will is a good of such enormous value that God is justified in creating humans with free will even if, as Augustine held, God knew in advance of creating them that certain human beings would use their freedom to do ill rather than good, while knowing that others would use their freedom to do only (or mostly) what is good. So, all the horrendous evils occurring daily in our world are either evil acts of free human beings and their causal effects or divine punishments for those acts. And the implication of this theodicy is that the good of human free will justifies God in permitting all these horrendous acts of evil and their causal effects, as well as the other evils resulting from plagues, floods, hurricanes, etc., that are God's ways of punishing us for our evil acts.

While this theodicy may explain some of the evil in our world, it cannot account for the massive amount of human suffering that is not due to human acts of free will. Natural disasters (floods, earthquakes, hurricanes, etc.) bring about enormous amounts of human and animal suffering. But it is obvious that such suffering is not proportionate to the abuses of free will by humans. So, we cannot reasonably think that such disasters are God's way of punishing human free choices to do evil. Second, while being free to do evil may be essential to genuine freedom, no responsible person thinks that the good of human freedom is so great as to require that no steps be taken to prevent some of the more flagrant abuses of free choice that result in massive, undeserved suffering by human and animals. Any moral person who had power to do so would have intervened to prevent the evil free choices that resulted in the torture and death of six million Jews in the Holocaust. We commonly act to restrict egregious abuses of human freedom that result in massive, undeserved human and animal suffering. Any moral being, including God, if he exists, would likely do the same. And since the free will theodicy is representative of the other attempts to justify God's permission of the horrendous evils in our world, it is reasonably clear that these evils cannot be explained away by appeal to theodicies.

In this essay I have argued that, putting aside whatever reasons there may be to think that the theistic God exists, the facts about evil in our world provide good reason to think that God does not exist. While the argument is only one of probability, it provides a sound basis for an affirmative answer to the question that is the focus of this exchange.

Evil Does Not Make Atheism More Reasonable than Theism

Daniel Howard-Snyder and Michael Bergmann

Many people deny that evil makes belief in atheism more reasonable for us than belief in theism. After all, they say, the grounds for belief in God are much better than the evidence for atheism, including the evidence provided by evil. We will not join their ranks on this occasion. Rather, we wish to consider the proposition that, setting aside grounds for belief in God and relying only on the background knowledge shared in common by nontheists and theists, evil makes belief in atheism more reasonable for us than belief in theism. Our aim is to argue against this proposition. We recognize that in doing so, we face a formidable challenge. It's one thing to say that evil presents a reason for atheism that is, ultimately, overridden by arguments for theism. It's another to say that it doesn't so much as provide us with a reason for atheism in the first place. In order to make this latter claim seem initially more plausible, consider the apparent design of the mammalian eye or the apparent fine-tuning of the universe to support life. These are often proposed as reasons to believe in theism. Critics commonly argue *not* merely that these supposed reasons for theism are overridden by arguments for atheism, but *rather* that they aren't good reasons for theism in the first place. Our parallel proposal with respect to evil and atheism is, initially at least, no less plausible than this proposal with respect to apparent design and theism.

We begin by laying out what we will refer to as "the basic argument" for the conclusion that *grounds for belief in God aside, evil does not make belief in atheism more reasonable for us than belief in theism*:

1 Grounds for belief in God aside, evil makes belief in atheism more reasonable for us than belief in theism only if somebody has a good argument that displays how evil makes atheism more likely than theism.
2 Nobody has a good argument that displays how evil makes atheism more likely than theism.
3 So, grounds for belief in God aside, evil does not make belief in atheism more reasonable for us than belief in theism. (from 1 & 2)

Before we get down to work, we need to address several preliminary questions.

1 Preliminary Questions

What do we mean by "a good argument" here? We have nothing out of the ordinary in mind. A good argument conforms to the rules of logic, none of its premises is obviously false, and there are other standards as well. But for our purposes, it is important to single out one more *minimal standard*, namely:

> Every premise, inference, and assumption on which the argument depends must be more reasonable for us to affirm than to refrain from affirming.

The proponent of the basic argument says that nobody has a good argument that displays how evil makes atheism more likely than theism, because this minimal standard has not been satisfied.

Now, how can we tell that nobody has a good argument of the sort in question? While some have argued that there *couldn't* be such an argument, we think that a more promising strategy is to consider one by one each argument from evil, laboriously checking whether every premise, assumption, and inference is more reasonable to affirm than to refrain from affirming. If every argument put forward by recognized authorities on the topic were to have a premise, inference, or assumption that failed to pass the test, then we'd have pretty good reason to think that nobody has an argument of the sort in question. Unfortunately, to complete the work that this strategy requires would take a book. So we must rest content in this chapter with only a start at undertaking it.

But which arguments should we focus on here? It would be uncharitable to focus on lousy arguments. We will focus on two, both of which are recognizably identified with our friend and esteemed colleague – who also happens to be the most frequently anthologized proponent of an affirmative answer to our title question – William Rowe.

2 Noseeum Arguments

We begin with an analogy introduced to show how our minimal standard for a good argument works and to develop an important principle for assessing a certain popular kind of argument from evil.

Suppose we asked a friend who claimed that there is no extraterrestial life why he thought that, and he responded like this: "I don't have any way to *prove* that there is none. I am in no position to do that. But it is reasonable to think there is none. After all, so far as we can tell, there isn't any. We've never detected any other life forms, nor have we received any signals or codes from distant galaxies – and we've been searching pretty hard. While this doesn't add up to proof, surely it makes it *more* likely that there is no extraterrestrial life than that there is, even *significantly* more likely." What should we make of our friend's reasoning?

2.1 Noseeum arguments in general

Well, notice first of all that he argued for his claim like this:

A: So far as we can tell (detect), there is no extraterrestrial life.

So, it is more likely than not (perhaps significantly so) that

B: There is no extraterrestrial life.

This argument follows a general pattern:

So far as we can tell (detect), there is no x.

So, it is more likely than not (perhaps significantly so) that

There is no x.

Let's call this general pattern a *no-see-um* argument: we don't see 'um, so they ain't there![8]

Notice that our friend did not claim that (a) *guarantees* the truth of (b). He merely claimed that it makes it *more likely than its denial*, perhaps quite a bit more. So we can't just retort that there *could be* extraterrestrial life even if we don't detect any. That's true, but it's irrelevant. What is relevant, however, is that his noseeum argument relies on a certain assumption. To see it, consider some other noseeum arguments.

Suppose that, after rummaging around carefully in your refrigerator, you can't find a carton of milk. Naturally enough, you infer that there isn't one there. Or suppose that, on viewing a chess match between two novices, Kasparov says to himself, "So far as I can tell, there is no way for John to get out of check," and then infers that there is no way. These are clear cases in which the noseeum premise makes the conclusion more likely than its denial – significantly more likely.[9] On the other hand,

8 The "noseeum" lingo is Stephen Wykstra's. See his "Rowe's Noseeum Arguments from Evil," in Daniel Howard-Snyder (ed.), *The Evidential Argument from Evil* (Bloomington: Indiana University Press, 1996).
9 Another case of legitimate reliance on a noseeum premise is in the strategy recommended in the second to last paragraph of section 1.

suppose that, looking at a distant garden, so far as we can see, there are no slugs there. Should we infer that it is more likely that there are no slugs in the garden than that there are? Or imagine listening to the best physicists in the world discussing the mathematics used to describe quantum phenomena; so far as we can tell, they don't make any sense at all. Should we infer from this that it is more likely that they don't make any sense than that they do? Clearly not. So what accounts for the difference between these two pairs of cases?

Notice that it is more likely than not that you would see a milk carton in the refrigerator if one were there, and it is more likely than not that Kasparov would see a way out of check if there were one. That's because you and Kasparov have what it takes to discern the sorts of things in question. On the other hand, it is not more likely than not that we would see a slug in a distant garden if there were one there; and it is not more likely than not that we'd be able to understand quantum mathematics if it were understandable. That's because we don't have what it takes to discern the sorts of things in question, in those circumstances with the cognitive equipment we possess. A general principle about noseeum arguments is lurking here, namely:

> A noseeum premise makes its conclusion more likely than not only if *more likely than not we'd detect (see, discern) the item in question if it existed.*

Call the italicized portion the *Noseeum Assumption.* Anybody who uses a noseeum argument makes a noseeum assumption of this form. Let's return to our friend, the anti-extraterrestrialist.

2.2 The Anti-extraterrestrialist's Noseeum Assumption

He gave a noseeum argument and thereby made a noseeum assumption, namely this one:

> More likely than not we'd detect extraterrestrial life forms if there were any.

Our minimal standard for a good argument implies that his noseeum argument is a good argument only if it is more reasonable to *affirm* his noseeum assumption than to *refrain* from affirming it. Is it more reasonable to do that?

Clearly not. After all, if there were extraterrestrial life forms, how likely is it that some of them would be intelligent enough to attempt contact? And of those who are intelligent enough, how likely is it that any would care about it? And of those who are intelligent enough and care about it, how likely is it that they would have the means at their disposal to try? And of those with the intelligence, the desire, and the means, how likely is it that they would succeed? Nobody has a very good idea how to answer these questions. We can't begin to say with even the most minimal degree of confidence that the probabilities are low, or that they are middling, or that they are high. We just don't have enough to go on. For this reason we should be *in doubt* as to whether it is *more likely than not that we'd detect extraterrestrial life forms if there were any.* So it is *not* more reasonable to affirm our friend's noseeum assumption than to refrain from affirming it.

It is important to see that we are not saying that it is highly likely that we would *not* discern any extraterrestrial life forms; nor are we saying that it is more likely that we would not detect extraterrestrial life forms than that we would. Rather, our point is that it is not reasonable for us to make any judgment about the probability of our detecting extraterrestrial life forms if there were any. That's all it takes for it *not* to be more reasonable for us to affirm than to refrain from affirming this noseeum assumption.

3 Noseeum Arguments from Evil

In this section, we will apply the main points of section 2 to some popular noseeum arguments from evil.

3.1 Standard noseeum arguments from evil

Here's a standard argument from evil:

1 There is no reason that would justify God in permitting certain instances of intense suffering.
2 If God exists, then there is a reason that would justify God in permitting every instance of intense suffering.
3 So, God does not exist.

From the vantage of the title question, our main concern is whether noseeum arguments in defense of premise 1 make it more reasonable for us to believe it than to refrain from believing it. Let's look into the matter closely.[10]

Consider the case of the fawn, trapped in a forest fire occasioned by lightning, who suffers for several days before dying (call this case *E1*). Or consider the case of the five-year-old girl from Flint, Michigan, who, on January 1, 1986, was raped, severely beaten, and strangled to death by her mother's boyfriend (call this case *E2*). How could a God who loved this fawn and this child and who had the power to prevent their suffering permit them to suffer so horribly? Of course, God might permit *E1* and *E2* if doing so is necessary to achieve for the fawn and the child (or, perhaps, someone else) some benefit whose goodness outweighs the badness of their suffering. But what could the benefit be? When we try to answer this question, we draw a blank. We just can't think of a benefit that is both sufficiently great to outweigh the badness of their suffering and such that God can't obtain it without permitting *E1* and *E2*. So far as we can tell, there isn't one. While this doesn't *prove* that there is no reason, surely, says the atheistic objector, it makes it more likely than not that there is none, perhaps even a good deal more likely.

In short, the noseeum argument here goes like this:

10 The noseeum arguments we mention in this section are simplified versions of arguments in Rowe's work, especially his classic essay, "The Problem of Evil and Some Varieties of Atheism," collected in Howard-Snyder (ed.), *Evidential Argument from Evil.*

1a So far as we can tell, there is no reason that would justify God in permitting *E1* and *E2*.

So it is more likely than not that

1b There is no reason that would justify God in permitting *E1* and *E2*.

So it is more likely than not that

1 There is no reason that would justify God in permitting certain instances of intense suffering.

Other noseeum arguments from evil are just like this except that they focus on the *amount* of suffering rather than on particular instances of intense suffering or horrific evil. What should we make of these noseeum arguments? Many people think that we *do* see how God would be justified in permitting *E1* and *E2*, that we *do* see how he would be justified in permitting so much, rather than a lot less intense suffering. While this strategy is not wholly without merit, we will not pursue it here.[11] Rather, we begin by noting that each of these noseeum arguments from evil makes a noseeum assumption, specifically:

> More likely than not we'd detect a reason that would justify God in permitting . . . if there were one,

where the ellipsis is filled in with either "*E1* and *E2*" or "so much intense suffering rather than a lot less" or "so much intense suffering rather than just a little less." Nothing we have to say hangs on the difference, so we'll focus on the first. Call it the *Atheist's Noseeum Assumption*. Is it more reasonable to affirm it than to refrain from affirming it?

3.2 Considerations against the Atheist's Noseeum Assumption

Several considerations suggest that it is *not* more reasonable to affirm than to refrain from affirming the Atheist's Noseeum Assumption.[12]

1 Two aspects of the atheist's noseeum inference should make us wary. First, it takes "the insights attainable by finite, fallible human beings as an adequate indication of

11 This strategy, often called "giving a *theodicy*," has a venerable history. For literature on the topic, as well as other relevant issues, see Barry Whitney, *Theodicy: An Annotated Bibliography, 1960–1991*, 2nd edn (Bowling Green, Oh.: Philosophy Documentation Center, 1998), as well as the bibliographies in Michael Peterson (ed.), *The Problem of Evil* (Notre Dame, Ind.: University of Notre Dame Press, 1992) and Howard-Snyder (ed.), *Evidential Argument from Evil.*

12 The considerations we mention here are developed by William Alston. The first is in his "Some (Temporarily) Final Thoughts on Evidential Arguments from Evil," in Howard-Snyder (ed.), *Evidential Argument from Evil*, pp. 316–19. The second is in his "The Inductive Argument Evil and the Human Cognitive Condition," ibid., p. 109.

what is available in the way of reasons to an omniscient, omnipotent being." But this is like supposing that when you're confronted with the activity or productions of a master in a field in which you have little expertise, it is reasonable for you to draw inferences about the quality of her work just because you "don't get it." You've taken a year of high school physics. You're faced with some theory about quantum phenomena, and you can't make heads or tails of it. Certainly it is unreasonable for you to assume that more likely than not you'd be able to make sense of it. Similarly for other areas of expertise: painting, architectural design, chess, music, and so on. Second, the atheist's noseeum inference "involves trying to determine whether there is a so-and-so in a territory the extent and composition of which is largely unknown to us." It is like someone who is culturally and geographically isolated supposing that if there were something on earth beyond her forest, more likely than not she'd discern it. It is like a physicist supposing that if there were something beyond the temporal bounds of the universe, more likely than not she'd know about it (where those bounds are the big bang and the final crunch).

All these analogies and others like them point in the same direction: we should be of two minds about affirming the claim that more likely than not we'd be aware of some reason that would justify God in permitting *E1* and *E2*, if there were one.

2 Knowledge has progressed in a variety of fields of inquiry, especially the physical sciences. The periodic discovery of previously unknown aspects of reality strongly suggests that there will be further progress of a similar sort. Since future progress implies present ignorance, it wouldn't be surprising if there is much we are currently ignorant of. Now, what we have to go on in charting the progress of the discovery of fundamental goods (like freedom, love, and justice) by our ancestors is meager, to say the least. Indeed, given the scant archeological evidence we have, and given paleontological evidence regarding the evolutionary development of the human brain, it would not be surprising at all that humans discovered various fundamental goods over tens of thousands of years separated by several millennia-long gaps in which nothing was discovered. Hence, given what we have to go on, it would not be surprising if there has been the sort of periodic progress that strongly suggests that there remain goods to be discovered. Thus it would not be surprising if there are goods of which we are ignorant, goods of which God – in his omniscience – would not be ignorant.

3.3 Considerations in favor of the Atheist's Noseeum Assumption

So there is good reason to be in doubt about the Atheist's Noseeum Assumption. In addition, there are good reasons to reject the considerations that have been offered in its favor.

Consider, for example, the supposed fact that for thousands of years we have not discovered any new fundamental goods in addition to the old standbys – friendship, pleasure, freedom, knowledge, etc. One might think that the best explanation of this fact is that there are no new fundamental goods to be discovered. Hence, the argument goes, our inability to think of a reason that would justify God in permitting *E1* and *E2* makes it likely that there is no such reason.[13] But this ignores the live possibility that, due to our cognitive limitations, we are (permanently or at least currently) unable to discover certain of the fundamental goods there are. And we have no reason to think that this "cognitive limitation" hypothesis is a worse explanation of our lack of discovery than the hypothesis that there are no new goods to be discovered.

Others claim that if we confess skepticism about the Atheist's Noseeum Assumption, then we'll have to do the same thing in other areas as well, resulting in excessive and unpalatable skepticism in those other areas. They ask us to consider claims like these:

1 The earth is more than 100 years old.
2 You are not constantly dreaming.
3 There is no reason that justified Hitler in perpetrating the Holocaust.

They say that since doubts about (1)–(3) are unreasonable, excessive, and unpalatable, so is doubt about the Atheist's Noseeum Assumption.[14] What should we make of this argument?

It seems eminently sensible insofar as it recommends that we be consistent in our skepticism rather than apply it only when doing so serves our agenda. And we agree that doubts about (1)–(3) are unreasonable. But our main concern is whether the comparison is apt. Most of us think that doubts about (1)–(3) are unreasonable because we're pretty sure that we have what it takes to believe these things reasonably, even if we can't say exactly how, and even though we don't have a knockdown argument for them. Do any of us, however, have even a modicum of assurance that we've got what it takes to believe reasonably that there is no reason outside our ken that would justify God in permitting *E1* and *E2*? Think of it like this: To be in doubt about the Atheist's Noseeum Assumption involves being in doubt about whether there is a reason outside our ken that would justify God in permitting *E1* and *E2*. Is being in doubt about whether there is such a reason like being in doubt about (1)–(3) – unreasonable, excessive, unpalatable, a bit wacky, over the top? Or is it more like being in doubt about these three claims, claims that none of us is in a position to make reasonably?

4 There is no extraterrestrial life.
5 There will be no further developments in science as radical as quantum mechanics.
6 There is no atheistic explanation outside our ken for the apparent fine-tuning of the universe to support life.

In light of the considerations mentioned in section 3.2 (and others like them), we submit that doubts about whether there is a God-justifying reason outside our ken

13 See Michael Tooley, "The Argument from Evil," *Philosophical Perspectives*, 5 (1991), pp. 89–134.
14 Richard Gale, "Some Difficulties in Theistic Treatments of Evil," in Howard-Snyder (ed.), *Evidential Argument from Evil*, pp. 208–9; Bruce Russell, "Defenseless," ibid., pp. 196–8; Theodore Drange, *Nonbelief and Evil* (Amherst, NY: Prometheus, 1998), p. 207.

are more like doubts about (4)–(6) than like doubts about (1)–(3). We suggest, therefore, that since doubts about (4)–(6) are sensible, sane, fitting, reasonable, and otherwise in accordance with good mental hygiene, so are doubts about the Atheist's Noseeum Assumption.

It might seem that if we're going to be skeptical about the Atheist's Noseeum Assumption, then we're going to have to be skeptical about reasoning about God altogether. By our lights, that would be an unhappy consequence of our argument. Fortunately, however, we don't need to go that far. Our arguments support agnosticism only about what reasons there are that would justify God in permitting *E1* and *E2*, or, more generally, the horrific, undeserved suffering in our world. Such limited skepticism need not extend to every argument for theism or to all reflection on the nature of God.

3.4 Summing up

The Atheist's Noseeum Assumption says that, more likely than not, we'd see a God-justifying reason if there were one. We have argued that it is not reasonable to accept it. We aren't saying that it is highly likely that we would *not* see a reason; nor are we saying that our not seeing a reason is more likely than our seeing a reason. Rather, given the considerations mentioned in sections 3.2 and 3.3, we're saying that it is not more reasonable to affirm than to refrain from affirming the Atheist's Noseeum Assumption. In light of the minimal standard for a good argument mentioned in section 1, this is enough to show that arguments from evil depending on the Atheist's Noseeum Assumption are not good arguments.

4 Rowe's New Bayesian Argument

Rowe has come to recognize that noseeum arguments have some of the weaknesses discussed above. And, presumably because of this recognition, he has recently abandoned them in favor of another argument, relying on Bayes' theorem, a fundamental principle used in probabilistic reasoning.[15] In this new Bayesian argument, he aims to show that

P: No good we know of justifies God in permitting *E1* and *E2*.

provides us with a good reason for atheism – i.e., for not-*G* (where *G* is theism). We will note some flaws in this argument which, despite Rowe's efforts, include its dependence on noseeum assumptions.

The argument goes like this. Let k be the background knowledge shared in common by nontheists and theists alike, and let Pr (x/y) refer to the probability of x given the assumption that y is true (this probability will be a number greater than or equal to 0 and less than or equal to 1). According to Bayes' theorem:

15 Rowe, "The Evidential Argument from Evil: A Second Look," in Howard-Snyder (ed.), *Evidential Argument from Evil.*

$$\frac{\Pr(G/P \,\&\, k)}{\Pr(G/k)} = \frac{\Pr(P/G \,\&\, k)}{\Pr(P/k)}.$$

(The rough idea is that *P* makes *G* less likely than it would otherwise be – i.e., Pr (*G/P & k*) < Pr (*G/k*) – only if *G* makes *P* less likely than it would otherwise be.) A quick perusal of this equation shows us that if Pr (*P/G & k*) < Pr (*P/k*), then Pr (*G/ P & k*) < Pr (*G/k*). And if Pr (*G/P & k*) < Pr (*G/k*), then, as I said, *P* makes *G* less likely than it would otherwise be; i.e., *P* gives us a reason for atheism. Thus, if Rowe can show that Pr (*P/G & k*) < Pr (*P/k*), it looks like he will have established his conclusion.

Rowe thinks he can show that Pr (*P/G & k*) < Pr (*P/k*). We don't have the space to lay out his argument in any detail. But, as he acknowledges, his argument assumes that Pr (*P/G & k*) is less than 1. For if Pr (*P/G & k*) were equal to 1, it would be impossible for Pr (*P/G & k*) to be less than Pr (*P/k*) (since 1 is as high as probabilities go). Furthermore, if Pr (*P/G & k*) were only very slightly less than 1, then the right-hand side of the above equation would be equal to some number very slightly less than 1, such as 0.95. And of course the left-hand side will be equal to exactly the same number, which means that Pr (*G/P & k*) could be only slightly less than Pr (*G/k*). But that would mean that *P* provides us with only a very negligible reason for atheism instead of a moderate or good reason for atheism. So an important question arises: Why should we suppose that Pr (*P/G & k*) is not extremely high, perhaps even as high as 1?

As it turns out, Rowe doesn't answer this question. Instead, he argues that we have no good reason for thinking that Pr (*P/G & k*) is high.[16] But this isn't enough. Even if we have no good reason for thinking that it *is* high, this doesn't mean we have good reason for thinking that it is *not* extremely high. So our question remains.

The truth is that our question is enormously difficult to answer. In fact, by our lights, we presently have no good reason to think that Pr (*P/G & k*) is not extremely high, perhaps even as high as 1. We just aren't in a good position to judge that Pr (*P/G & k*) is low, or that it is middling, or that it is high. We should shrug our shoulders and admit that we don't have enough to go on here. So Rowe's new Bayesian argument is (at best) incomplete, because he hasn't given us a reason for thinking that Pr (*P/G & k*) isn't high.

There are two *further* troubles with his argument. The first additional trouble is that in order to give us a reason for thinking that Pr (*P/G & k*) isn't high, Rowe must explain why it isn't highly *un*likely, given *G* and *k*, that we would be aware of the goods that justify the permission of *E1* and *E2*. Unfortunately, many of the candidate reasons that come to mind here depend on illegitimate noseeum assumptions. For example, Rowe argues that if we were *not* aware of the goods that justify the permission of *E1* and *E2*, it is likely that we would be given comforting words from God telling us that he has reasons for such permission – reasons that are beyond our ken. But *k* includes the knowledge that very often we lack such comforting communication – that we experience divine silence instead. Thus, given *G* and *k*, Rowe thinks it is likely that we *would* know of the goods justifying permission of *E1* and *E2*.[17]

16 Ibid., pp. 274–6.

17 See ibid., p. 276. Rowe himself does *not* try to use this argument to show that Pr (P/*G & k*) is not high.

But notice that this argument depends on the assumption that:

If God exists and the goods that justify permission of *E1* and *E2* are beyond our ken, then it is unlikely that we would experience divine silence.

The problem with this assumption is that it takes for granted that it is unlikely that there is a good that justifies divine silence in the face of evils like *E1* and *E2*. But what reason do we have for thinking *that* unlikely? We can't rely on our inability to discern such a good. To do so would be to depend on a noseeum assumption – one that is illegitimate in ways analogous to those described in sections 3.2 and 3.3.

The second additional problem with Rowe's new Bayesian argument is that he presumes (as he does in his noseeum argument) that we reasonably believe that

P: No good we know of justifies God in permitting *E1* and *E2*.

But is that right? Let's focus on *E2*. Consider the good of both the little girl and her murderer living together completely reconciled (which involves genuine and deep repentance on the part of the murderer and genuine and deep forgiveness on the part of the little girl) and enjoying eternal felicity in the presence of God. That is a possible good we know of (which isn't to say that we know it will obtain). Is it reasonable for us to affirm that *that* good doesn't justify God in permitting *E2*? No. We aren't in a position to judge that its goodness doesn't outweigh the evil of *E2*. Nor are we in a position to determine that it (or something like it) doesn't require the permission of *E2* (or something as bad or worse). For it is not only our knowledge of what possible goods there are that may be limited. Our knowledge of the logical (i.e., omnipotence-constraining) connections between the obtaining of certain goods and the permission of evils like *E2* might also be limited (it wouldn't be the least bit surprising if it were). Just as we are in the dark about whether known goods are representative of the goods there are, so also we are in the dark about whether the omnipotence-constraining connections we know of are representative of the omnipotence-constraining connections there are. Consequently, our inability to discern such a connection doesn't give us a good reason to think there is none. Likewise, the fact that we can't intelligently compare the magnitude of the good mentioned above with the magnitude of *E2* doesn't give us a good reason for thinking the former does not outweigh the latter. Thus, even the acceptance of *P* seems to depend on our making certain questionable noseeum assumptions.[18]

5 Conclusion

We've raised some serious questions about explicit noseeum arguments from evil. And we've pointed out that Rowe's new Bayesian argument is incomplete, and that certain obvious attempts to complete it (as well as the acceptance of *P* itself) seem to depend, implicitly, on questionable noseeum assumptions. But we haven't shown that nobody

18 For more on the points in this section, see Michael Bergmann, "Skeptical Theism and Rowe's New Evidential Argument from Evil" (forthcoming).

has a good argument from evil. To show that, we would have to consider other arguments in the literature and other ways to complete Rowe's Bayesian argument or support *P*. In closing, we'll mention briefly two arguments that seem to refrain from depending on noseeum assumptions and which deserve serious reflection.

First, Paul Draper argues that atheism explains the actual pattern of pain and pleasure in the world better than theism does. The focus here is not on our inability to see a justifying reason, but on our supposed ability to see that an atheistic explanation is superior to a theistic one.[19] Second, Michael Tooley argues that since

1 Permission of suffering is justified only if it is, in some way, for the sake of the sufferer,

and

2 Animal suffering in cases like *E1* cannot benefit the sufferer,

there is suffering whose permission is unjustified and, hence, there is no God.[20] Notice that this argument does not depend on an inference from known goods to unknown goods. Instead, it takes for granted that we know a general moral principle (i.e., premise 1) which, together with certain information we supposedly have about animal capacities, enables us to make a generalization about *all* the goods there are (i.e., that none of them – even the ones we don't know of – could justify the permission of *E1*).

Draper's argument has received considerable discussion in the literature (much of which suggests that it doesn't satisfy the minimal standard for a good argument identified in section 1).[21] Tooley's has received virtually none. So let's ask ourselves, briefly: Are there any considerations that would lead us to think that *Tooley's* argument fails to satisfy our minimal standard? That's hard to say. But here are some pertinent questions. First, regarding premise 1: Is this a true general moral principle?[22] Can the state be justified in confiscating the land and home of one its citizens against her will in order to construct an irrigation canal required for the survival of many of its other citizens *provided it supplies compensation*? For that matter, is compensation even necessary? What if the state lacks the resources to supply compensation? Are these considerations about a state and its citizens relevant to our present worries about God and his suffering creatures? That is, could *God* be constrained (by the limits of logical possibility) in achieving his purposes in ways analogous to those in which the state is constrained? Regarding premise 2 (according to which dying fawns *can't* benefit from their final moments of suffering): Must the sufferer be able to appreciate fully

19 See Paul Draper, "Pain and Pleasure: An Evidential Problem for Theists," collected in Howard-Snyder (ed.), *Evidential Argument from Evil.*

20 See Tooley, "Argument from Evil," pp. 110–11.

21 See both essays by Peter van Inwagen, both essays by Draper, the second contribution by Alvin Plantinga, and Alston's concluding paper in Howard-Snyder (ed.), *Evidential Argument from Evil.* See also Howard-Snyder, "Theism, the Hypothesis of Indifference, and the Biological Role of Pain and Pleasure," *Faith and Philosophy*, 3 (1994), pp. 452–66.

22 For more on this question, see Peter van Inwagen, "The Magnitude, Duration, and Distribution of Evil: A Theodicy," in *God, Knowledge, and Mystery* (Ithaca, NY: Cornell University Press, 1995), pp. 121–2, and Alston, "Inductive Argument from Evil," pp. 111–12.

(or even partially) the sense in which he or she benefits from the suffering?[23] People take seriously the idea that humans (even the severely mentally handicapped) can experience postmortem goods – are we right not to take this possibility seriously with respect to animals?

Other arguments from evil deserve serious consideration before anyone can claim that the strategy recommended at the outset of this chapter is successful. We have only pointed the way toward a more extensive defense of it.[24]

Reply to Howard-Snyder and Bergmann

My friends Dan Howard-Snyder and Mike Bergmann think that the enormous amount of seemingly pointless, horrendous evil occurring daily in our world gives us no good reason at all to think it unlikely that God exists. For, on the assumption that God exists, they believe we have no good reason to think it probable either that there would be any less horrendous evil or that God would help us understand what are some of the justifying goods that he is powerless to bring about without permitting all this horrendous evil. In support of their view, they liken my argument for the probable nonexistence of God to the reasoning of someone who concludes that there is probably no extraterrestrial life because we don't detect any communications from extraterrestrials. I believe they are right to reject the inference to the likely nonexistence of extraterrestrials from our failure to detect communications from them. For, as they point out, we have no good reason to think that extraterrestrials would know that we exist, or would care about us enough to want to communicate with us, or would have anything like sufficient power and knowledge to devise a way to do so. Thus, given these considerations, we cannot reasonably infer the nonexistence of extraterrestrials from our not having detected any communications from them. As opposed to what we don't know about extraterrestrials, however, we do know that God, if he exists, most certainly knows that we exist, most certainly loves us and cares for us, and, being infinitely powerful, is able to prevent any of the horrendous evils that befall us. Furthermore, given his infinite knowledge, God would know how to achieve the very best lives possible for us with the minimum of horrible suffering. But my friends believe that we have no sufficient reason at all to think it *even likely* that God could achieve the very best for us (humans and animals) were he to have prevented the Holocaust, the terrible suffering of the fawn, the horrible suffering of the little girl, or any of the other countless evils that abound in this world. Why on earth do they believe this? The basic reason is this: *God's knowledge of goods and the conditions of their realization extends far beyond our own.* Because God's knowledge extends far beyond our own, they think it just may be that God would know that even he, with his infinite power, cannot achieve the best for us without permitting

23 See Alston, "Inductive Argument from Evil," p. 108.

24 Thanks to William Alston, Andrew Cortens, Del Kiernan-Lewis, Michael Murray, and Timothy O'Connor for comments on an earlier draft of this paper.

all the horrendous evils that occur daily in our world. And they also think it just may be that God can achieve the best for us only if he keeps us in the dark as to what the good is that justifies him in permitting any of these horrendous evils. But what their view comes to is this. Because we cannot rule out God's knowing goods we do not know, we cannot rule out there being goods that justify God in permitting *any amount of evil whatever* that might occur in our world. If human and animal life on earth were *nothing more than a series of agonizing moments from birth to death*, my friends' position would still require them to say that we cannot reasonably infer that it is even likely that God does not exist. For, since we don't know that the goods we know of are representative of the goods there are, we can't know that it is likely that there are no goods that justify God in permitting human and animal life on earth to be nothing more than a series of agonizing moments from birth to death. But surely such a view is unreasonable, if not absurd. Surely there must be some point at which the appalling agony of human and animal existence on earth would render it unlikely that God exists. And this must be so even though we all agree that God's knowledge would far exceed our own. I believe my theistic friends have gone considerably beyond that point when, in light of the enormous proliferation of horrendous evil in this world, they continue to insist that we are unjustified in concluding that it is unlikely that God exists.

They characterize my argument as a "noseeum" argument. But this is not quite correct. There are lots of things we can conceive of occurring in our world which we don't *see* occurring. My argument is basically a "noconceiveum" argument, not a "noseeum" argument. We cannot even *conceive* of goods that may occur and would justify God in permitting the terrible evils that afflict our world. Of course, being finite beings, we can't expect to know all the goods that God would know, any more than an amateur at chess should expect to know all the reasons for a particular move that Kasparov makes in a game. But, unlike Kasparov, who in a chess match has good reason not to tell us how a particular move fits into his plan to win the game, God, if he exists, isn't playing chess with our lives. In fact, since understanding the goods for the sake of which he permits terrible evils to befall us would itself enable us to better bear our suffering, God has a strong reason to help us understand those goods and how they require his permission of the terrible evils that befall us. My friends, however, do seem to think that we can conceive of goods that may require God to permit at least some of these awful evils. They suggest that for all we know the following complex good may occur: the little five-year-old girl meets up with her rapist-killer somewhere in the next life, and he then repents and begs her forgiveness for savagely beating, raping, and strangling her, and she then forgives him, with the result that both of them live happily ever after in the presence of God. What are we to make of this suggestion as to why God permitted the little girl to be brutally beaten, raped, and strangled? Well, they are right in holding that even God cannot bring about this complex good without permitting that individual to brutally beat, rape, and strangle the little girl. But that alone won't justify God in permitting that to happen to her. For it is eminently reasonable to believe that God could win the soul of the little girl's rapist-killer without having to permit him to do what he did to her. And even if he can't, is it right for any being to permit the little girl to be robbed of her life in that way just so that her killer could have something bad enough on his conscience to ultimately seek forgiveness? It is one thing to knowingly and freely give up one's life for the sake of another, and quite another to have it ripped away, against one's will, just so that someone else can later be led to repentance. If this is the best that can be done to find a good we know of that may justify God in permitting the little girl to be brutally beaten, raped, and strangled, the evidential argument from evil will surely remain a thorn in the side of theism for some time to come.

Reply to Rowe

We will limit our replies to Rowe's case to the following three points.[25]

1 Throughout Rowe's essay, one finds "the theist" rejecting his argument, *and nobody else.* No atheist objects; no agnostic. Just "the theist." This gives the misleading impression that you have to be a theist to reject it, or that only theists reject it, or that nontheists can't reject it, or mustn't, or in fact don't. None of this is true, however. Many intelligent nontheists do not find Rowe's argument persuasive. For example, many agnostics – those who neither believe there is a God nor believe there isn't – reject it for the kinds of reasons we laid out in our essay. In fact, everything we said there could be said by an agnostic or an atheist.

2 Rowe insists that his atheistic arguments from evil are not arguments from ignorance. Thus, he denies that his arguments depend on noseeum assumptions. We beg to differ. Here are two examples of his depending on a noseeum assumption.

First, at one point he says: "the idea that none of those instances of suffering could have been prevented by an all-powerful being without loss of a greater good must strike us as an extraordinary idea, quite beyond belief." But if we are in the dark about what goods there are and what omnipotence-constraining connections there are between such goods and the permission of such evils, how could that idea seem "extraordinary . . . quite beyond belief"? Only if we assume that there probably aren't any such goods or omnipotence-constraining connections if we don't detect any.

Second, Rowe says that each good we know of is such that "we have reason to believe either that it isn't good enough to justify God in permitting that evil, or that it could likely be actualized by God without his having to permit the horrendous suffering [in question]." But how could we have a reason to believe that "God could

25 An additional point that we haven't the space to develop is this. Rowe makes it clear, in the paragraph following his introduction of premise 2, that that premise should be understood as follows:

> An all-powerful, all-knowing, perfectly good being would prevent the occurrence of any terrible evil he could, unless he could not do so without thereby losing some greater good or permitting some evil equally bad or worse.

But this implies that there is a minimum amount of terrible evil that God must permit in order for the greater goods involved in his purposes to be secured. For a persuasive objection to this implication, see Peter van Inwagen, "The Problem of Evil, the Problem of Air, and the Problem of Silence," *Philosophical Perspectives*, 5 (1991), esp. p. 64 n.11, and *idem*, "Magnitude, Duration, and Distribution of Evil," pp. 121–2.

obtain the goods we know of without permitting the evils we see" if we are in the dark about what omnipotence-constraining connections there are between such goods and the permission of such evils? Here too Rowe seems to be assuming that there probably are no such connections if we don't detect any.

3 Rowe also considers one last attempt to defend what he calls 'the first response' to his argument from evil. In his reply to this last attempt, he uses the example of Smith and the concert. Let *T* signify "Smith is in town this evening," and let *C* signify "Smith is at the concert this evening." We can then state Rowe's example as follows:

$\Pr\left(T/k\right) = 0.5$

$\Pr\left(\text{not-}T/k\right) = 0.5$

$\Pr\left(C/T \mathbin{\&} k\right) = 0.5$

$\Pr\left(\text{not-}C/T \mathbin{\&} k\right) = 0.5$[26]

He sensibly concludes that if we know these things and then learn that not-*C*, we may conclude that T is less likely than not-*T*. So far, so good.[27] Next, Rowe tries to draw a parallel with the case of theism and evil. Let *G* signify "God exists," and let *A* signify "Some good we know of justifies God in permitting all the horrendous evils we see." We can, says Rowe, state the parallel case like this:

$\Pr\left(G/k\right) = 0.5$

$\Pr\left(\text{not-}G/k\right) = 0.5$

$\Pr\left(A/G \mathbin{\&} k\right) = 0.5$

$\Pr\left(\text{not-}A/G \mathbin{\&} k\right) = 0.5$

Again, he sensibly concludes that if we know these things and then learn that, not-*A*, we may conclude that *G* is less likely than not-*G*.[28]

What we've been given here is an easily digestible version of Rowe's new Bayesian argument from evil, the one we discussed in section 4 of our essay. Our response is essentially the same as the response we gave there.

The first thing to notice is that Rowe's argument about Smith's whereabouts could not get off the ground unless Pr (not-*C*/*T* & *k*) is not high. For if it is extremely high, then not-*C* will not significantly lower the likelihood of *T*. (If Pr (not-*C*/*T* & *k*) is as

26 In section 4 of our essay we explain our use of the symbol *k* and the notation Pr (*x*/*y*).

27 The idea here seems to be that since not-*T* entails not-*C*, we know that Pr (not-*C*/not-*T* & *k*) = 1 and that Pr (*C*/not-*T* & *k*) = 0. So we know that Pr (not-*C*/not-*T* & *k*) > Pr (not-*C*/*T* & *k*). This, we take it, is why Rowe concludes that learning not-*C* makes *T* less likely than not-*T*.

28 Rowe is assuming that just as not-*T* entails not-*C*, so also not-*G* entails not-*A*.

high as 1, not-*C* won't lower the likelihood of *T* at all!) In other words, if not-*C* is just what you would expect if *T* were true, then learning not-*C* won't make *T* less likely than it would otherwise be.

For similar reasons, Rowe's parallel argument about God and evil doesn't have a chance unless Pr (not-*A*/*G* & *k*) is not high. Rowe tries to avoid this problem by simply *asserting* that this latter probability is equal to 0.5. But why think that? In fact, why think Pr (not-*A*/*G* & *k*) isn't extremely high, perhaps as high as 1? These questions will be familiar to those who have read our essay. For not-*A* (i.e., no good we know of justifies God in permitting all the horrendous evils we see) is a lot like *P* in our essay (i.e., no good we know of justifies God in permitting *E1* and *E2*). And just as we are in no position to tell that Pr (*P*/*G* & *k*) is high or that it is low or that it is middling, so too we are in no position to tell that Pr (not-*A*/*G* & *k*) is high or that it is low or that it is middling. Rowe's argument simply takes for granted that we are in a position to assign a value of 0.5 here, when in fact we are in the dark about what probability to assign.

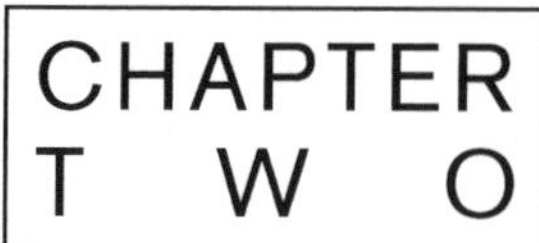

CHAPTER TWO

Does Divine Hiddenness Justify Atheism?

For many people, it is not at all obvious that God exists. They simply do not find the traditional arguments for God's existence compelling. What may be worse, some people search for God with apparent sincerity but come away feeling unfulfilled and disillusioned. "Divine hiddenness" is the label philosophers have given to these phenomena. Recently, nontheists have appealed to divine hiddenness as a basis for atheism. If God exists, the argument goes, God's existence would be more obvious to people than it is. In this debate, J. L. Schellenberg argues that divine hiddenness justifies atheism. Paul Moser argues, on the contrary, that divine hiddenness is just what the Judeo-Christian tradition leads us to expect, given the kind of God who is purportedly hidden.

Divine Hiddenness Justifies Atheism

J. L. Schellenberg

Arguments from divine hiddenness often go unnoticed in the consideration of arguments for and against the existence of God – where by "God" is meant the *traditional* God: a separate but infinite consciousness, a personal and perfect creator of the universe. Perhaps the most interesting variety of this oversight occurs when people find themselves unable to settle the question of God's existence and therefore inclined toward agnosticism without noticing that these facts are *themselves* relevant to their quest and may support atheism. Of course, we need to be careful here. If by "God is hidden" you mean "There is an actually existing God who hides from us," it will be short work proving that divine hiddenness provides no basis for atheism. For how could a premise asserting the *actual existence* of God lead to the conclusion that God *does not exist*? But perhaps the careful reader will be able to see that it is also possible to take the language of hiddenness less literally – as referring simply to the absence of convincing evidence for the existence of God, or, more specifically, to the absence of some kind of positive experiential result in the search for God. That is how it will be taken here. I begin with an argument from analogy focused on the latter, more specific form of hiddenness. The possibility of broadening and strengthening this argument through a closer look at the concept of divine love is then considered. The first argument will here be called "the Analogy Argument"; its sibling, naturally, is called "the Conceptual Argument."

1 The Analogy Argument

Imagine yourself in the following situation. You're a child playing hide-and-seek with your mother in the woods at the back of your house. You've been crouching for some time now behind a large oak tree, quite a fine hiding place but not undiscoverable – certainly not for someone as clever as your mother. However, she does not appear. The sun is setting, and it will soon be bedtime, but still no mother. Not only isn't she finding you, but, more disconcerting, you can't *hear* her anywhere: she's not beating the nearby bushes, making those exaggerated "looking for you" noises, and talking to you meanwhile as mothers playing this game usually do. Now imagine that you start *calling* for your mother. Coming out from behind the tree, you yell out her name, over and over again. "Mooooommmmm!" But no answer. You look everywhere: through the woods, in the house, down to the road. An hour passes, and you are growing hoarse from calling. Is she anywhere around? Would she fail to answer if she were around?

Now let's change the story a little. You're a child with amnesia – apparently because of a blow to the head (which of course you don't remember), your memory goes back only a few days – and you don't even know whether you *have* a mother. You see other children with their mothers and think it would sure be nice to have one. So you ask everyone you meet and look everywhere you can, but without forwarding your goal in the slightest. You take up the search anew each day, looking diligently, even though the strangers who took you in assure you that your mother must be dead. But to no avail. Is this what we should expect if you really have a mother and she is around, and aware of your search? When in the middle of the night you tentatively call out – "Mooooommmmm!" – would she not answer if she were really within earshot?

Let's change the story one more time. You're still a small child, and an amnesiac, but this time you're in the middle of a vast rain forest, dripping with dangers of various kinds. You've been stuck there for days, trying to figure out who you are and where you came from. You don't remember having a mother who accompanied you into this jungle, but in your moments of deepest pain and misery you call for her anyway: "MOOOOOMMMMM!" Over and over again. For days and days . . . the last time when a jaguar comes at you out of nowhere . . . but with no response. What should you think in this situation? In your dying moments, what should cross your mind? Would the thought that you have a mother who cares about you and hears your cry and *could* come to you but chooses *not* to even make it onto the list?

Now perhaps we could suppose, in each of these cases, that you *do* have a mother and that she *is* around, but that she simply *doesn't* care. We are inclined to think of mothers as almost by definition loving and caring, but just remember the mother of Hyde in *That 70s Show*, someone might say. Another possibility is that your mother has been prevented from doing what mothers tend naturally to do by factors external to her own desire and will: perhaps she fell into a deep well in the woods, or was kidnapped by that escaped convict who was spotted near town last week (from whose clutches you narrowly escaped, suffering only a memory-erasing blow to the head), or is fending off a crocodile even as you succumb to the jaguar. What we *can't* say is that a *loving* mother would in circumstances like these be hidden from her child *if she could help it.*

The first step in the Analogy Argument is the defense of this claim. As we might put it, our job is to find the proper filling for the blank at the end of the following sentence: "A loving mother would not be hidden from her child in circumstances like those mentioned if she could help it *because* —." What we need here are propositions specifying the properties of love *in virtue of which* the claim appearing in front of the "because" is true. These would, I suggest, include the following: (1) A loving mother would consider each of her child's serious requests important and seek to provide a quick response. (2) A loving mother would wish to spare her child needless trauma, or, more positively, would wish to foster her child's physical and emotional well-being. (3) A loving mother would seek to avoid encouraging in her child false or misleading thoughts about herself or about their relationship. (4) A loving mother would want personal interaction with her child whenever possible, for the joy it brings as well as for its own sake. (5) A loving mother would *miss* her child if separated from her. It is clear that each of these propositions is true. It is also clear that, *if* they are true, the claim we are defending is true – that no loving mother who could help it would be hidden from her child in circumstances like those mentioned. We may therefore conclude that the latter claim *is* true.

The next step in the Analogy Argument involves pointing out that there are, in the actual world, circumstances of *divine* hiddenness very similar to the circumstances we have highlighted in respect of our fictional mother and child. The relevant circumstances in our stories are those in which the mother is sought by the child but not found. Well, just so, God is (and has often been) hidden from many human beings: sought but not found. Some persons start out assured of the power and presence of God in their lives, and then *lose* all this – in the typical case because of reasoning that engenders doubt about the reliability of the support they have for theistic belief. And though they grieve what they have lost and seek to regain it, looking for God in all the old familiar places as well as in new, unfamiliar locales, they fail to do so: God seems simply absent, and their belief is gone. The situation of such individuals is relevantly similar to that of the child in the first story. Other persons don't start out in what they consider to be a relationship with God but, nonetheless, are, in their wanderings and in their attempts to determine where they belong, open to finding and being found by a divine parent; some of them seek long and hard for God, wishing to be related in love to God. But though they seek, they do not find. Their situation is relevantly similar to that of the second child. And many seekers, because of the inhospitable place this world can sometimes be, are at one time or another in a lot of *trouble*, and so have not only the usual and obvious reasons to seek to be united (or reunited) with a divine parent: they are also in serious need of divine help, calling out to God in conditions of great suffering and pain. But a divine answer to their calls is not forthcoming. What we see here is clearly relevantly similar to the situation of the third child.

Additional stories can be imagined, with features equally troubling from the perspective of motherly care, corresponding to other aspects of the form of divine hiddenness we are considering. We might have our first child, after many calls for her mother, hearing sounds in the woods that she is sure mark her mother's presence, but which turn out to come from nothing more than leaves rolling in the wind. This is like the experience of those who think they have detected traces of God in some happening or argument, only to have the former's theological significance undermined by convincing reinterpretation or the latter proved unsound. Our second child might come to be adopted by the strangers who take her in, and brought up in a manner that leaves her predisposed to be suspicious instead of trusting, calculatingly self-centered instead of generous and giving; or perhaps she comes to have experiences which cause her to deny the importance of personal relationship with a parent in the development of a child. This can be compared to what happens in the life of a seeker who, because of the influence of those who *do* answer her calls, is led to develop a character contrary to that which the God of traditional theism is said to desire for us, or whose search leads to religious experiences all right, but *nontheistic* ones. Clearly, the analogies between our fictional situations of parental hiddenness and the actual facts of divine hiddenness are very close.

So what can be done with these analogies? Well, the next step in the argument involves showing that what we have said about a mother's love applies to God as well. This is fairly easily done. For God, on the traditional theistic view we are challenging, is not only loving and caring, but *unsurpassably* loving and caring. Indeed, it seems that each of our propositions (1) to (5) above must specify a property that applies as much to God as to the mother. If God gives birth to the human race and is related to its members in a manner that is unimaginably close, caring, and loving, then surely: (1′) God would consider each serious request submitted by God's human children important and seek to provide a quick response; (2′) God would wish to spare human beings needless trauma or, more positively, would wish to foster their physical and emotional well-being; (3′) God would seek not to encourage in human beings false or misleading thoughts about God or about the divine–human relationship; (4′) God would want personal interaction with human beings whenever possible, for the joy it brings as well as for its own sake; and (5′) God would *miss* such personal interaction if it were absent.

Now perhaps someone will say that God might be totally different from ourselves, and thus unlike a human mother. But there are certain conceptual constraints that need to be respected here. Of course we don't mean that God should be conceptualized as physical and as biologically female. But situations of human interaction and discussions of human interaction, including interaction between mothers and their children, do represent the primary contexts in which such concepts as those of "closeness," "care," and "love" are used and acquire their meanings. What, then, could justify the supposition that God's closeness, caring, and loving would not be like those of the ideal mother, displayed in a manner appropriate to the divine nature (e.g., through religious experience instead of physical touching)? The question is rhetorical. Clearly what we have said about the best mother's love must in this way apply to God as well.

An important conclusion may now be reached quite easily. Let *P* be the conjunction of the various loving properties picked out by the original five propositions about a mother's love and the five propositions referring to God. We saw earlier that, in virtue of *P*, a loving mother who could help it would never be hidden from her child in the fictional circumstances we described. We also saw that the analogies between the latter circumstances and those of divine hiddenness are very close. But then we may infer that, very probably, *a God who could help it would never be hidden in those circumstances*: the operation of *P* would prevent this in the case of God, just as it would in the case of our fictional mother.

Thus far the Analogy Argument proper. Certain plausible additional moves may be made to bring us from this conclusion to atheism. In the case of the mother, we saw that there might be external actors that prevent her from responding to her child despite the presence of *P* – that she might be hidden and *not* able to help it. But if omnipotence means anything, it means that God couldn't *ever* be prevented from responding to the cries of God's human children. The disanalogy we see here, far from weakening the argument that starts out from the analogy, permits us to *complete* it. For it means that we may justifiably remove the little qualifier 'who could help it' from our earlier conclusion and say simply that *God would never be hidden in the circumstances in question.* In other words, the Analogy Argument in conjunction with what we know about divine resourcefulness gives us a powerful reason to say that, if God exists, this form of divine hiddenness does not occur. But it *does* occur. Therefore, we have a powerful reason to believe that God does *not* exist.

2 Is the Analogy Argument a Success?

Before getting too excited – or upset – about this argument, the reader should consider whether it can be defeated by counter-argument. It will, I think, be hard to question the claims we have made about how a loving mother would behave in our fictional scenarios. Most objections will quite naturally focus instead on questioning the closeness of the analogies we have drawn *between* those scenarios and the facts of divine hiddenness.

This can be done in various ways. One might argue, for example, that persons who seek God are not very much like *children* – the vulnerability and immaturity we attach to the latter and need to be able to transfer to the former if the argument is to succeed are in fact not transferable in this way. But this objection appears to assume that all who seek God in the relevant way are adult humans, and this is not at all obvious: actual children may (and do) seek God too, without in every case finding their search rewarded with positive results. More important, because of the evil we face and the evident frailty of our natures, even human grown-ups are not appropriately construed, theologically speaking, as mature adults. Theology has traditionally pictured us this way (while also referring to us as "God's children"), but a close look at the world suggests that a better picture would portray us as young and unformed, still needing a home – in particular, still in need of parental support and encouragement in the development of a character and self-esteem that can withstand the pressures toward fragmentation and despair that life presents and make the achievement of our full potential possible.

It might also be claimed that God is not appropriately thought of as mother – that in our application of human talk to the divine, non-motherly elements of human experience ought to predominate. Now it is clear that, traditionally, the notion of God as Father is much more common than that of God as Mother, but an appeal to "common practice" is always weak, especially when the practice in question has been (or can be) successfully challenged. Instead of getting into debates about feminism and patriarchy, though, let me simply point out that, whether presented under the label of "loving Father" or in some other way, such attributes as those of caring and closeness, compassion and empathy, are nonnegotiable in any theistic view that takes the moral perfection and worship-worthiness of God seriously. And these are the attributes at issue here. I have found it helpful to focus on the model of a mother because these attributes are still more closely linked in our experience and imagination with the notion of mother than with that of father. Indeed, the commonness in human experience of *distant* or *absent* fathers makes it possible for us to construe the connection between fatherhood and the attributes in question rather loosely. This fact, in conjunction with the tendency to think uncritically of God as Father, is, I think, a big part of the reason why so many are inclined to underestimate the force of arguments from divine hiddenness.

A third objection to our argument – a rather common sort – suggests that there is something presumptuous about *expecting* a response from God. God is not obligated to respond to our every whim; and if God responds, it will be in God's own way, not necessarily as we expect. Even if so-called seekers lack presumption, we ought still to consider that there may be some *other* human sin that prevents them from experiencing God. Perhaps God is hidden from us because of our *own* failings, instead of God's.

But the Analogy Argument, as you may have noticed, is not suggesting that God should satisfy our every *whim*, our every sudden, unreflective, unreasonable desire; only that God would respond to serious attempts to be united or reunited with God in a loving relationship. Observe how much more plausible the latter claim is than the former. The objection is here dealing with a caricature of our argument, not the real thing. As for presumption, the expectation of a seeker does not come in the form of a *demand*, but as anticipation or reasoned inference. Are we really to imagine seekers walking around demanding that God "show himself"? Some *philosophers* may do this, but these are usually individuals who have long since concluded that God does not exist and think the world is better off that way; it would be a mistake to confuse them with the earnest, hopeful seekers of our argument, or with those (perhaps the same individuals) who after careful reflection on all the available information conclude that it would be in the nature of God to be in some way revealed to anyone who calls upon God sincerely.

Turning now to the general reference to sin: this seems completely unsubstantiated – many who seek God seem in fact to be quite blameless in the relevant respects. It is important to notice here that beyond looking thoroughly and carefully for reason to believe in the existence of God and removing all observed impediments to success in the search, there is nothing the seeker *can do* to bring about belief. Belief as such is involuntary; it is something that happens to you when evidence adds up to a certain point, not something you can do directly (if you doubt this, just try to acquire right now, or to drop, as the case may be, the belief that God exists). Thus, if a search of the sort in question has been undertaken (as it often has), a nonbeliever cannot be "to blame" for not believing.

What about the possibility, also mentioned by the "sin" objection, that God *does* respond, and seekers simply miss the response, expecting something else – something other than what God has in mind? Well, what else might God have in mind? If the request is for the beginning or resumption of a loving relationship, and what is needed for this is, among other things, some measure of belief that there is someone there to relate *to*, what *could* count both as *loving* and as a *response* apart from some noticeable indication of God's presence? Certainly in the case of the unencumbered mother and her child, nothing apart from the mother actually coming to her child in a manner recognized by the child would qualify as a loving response. What makes us think that something else would do in the case of God's immeasurably greater love? Perhaps it will be said that God, unlike the mother, is able to be present to us all the time without us noticing it and is, moreover, responsible for every single good thing we experience. This is indeed true, if God exists. But it still doesn't qualify as a *response* to the cry of those who seek God. And we need to recognize that the absence of love in one respect is not compensated for by *other* forms of love when what we're dealing with is not the love of a finite being but the perfect love of an unlimited God. Indeed, it's starting to look as though the relevant differences between God and ourselves make it *harder* to mount an "other response" objection, not easier.

But maybe we can press this notion of differences between ourselves and God a little further, in a different direction. Perhaps there is some *great good* for the seeker that depends on the continuation of her search, and thus prevents God from responding. Perhaps no loving human mother would ever have reason to consider continued separation from her child, in circumstances like those we have described, to be "for his own good," but God, the critic will say, is aware of so many more forms of goodness than we are, and has a design plan that spans incomprehensible distances in time and space. We are therefore not justified in concluding that God would do what the mother does, even if they share the loving properties we have discussed.

Now various possible goods we know of might be enumerated and discussed in response to this objection, but the objector would only reply by saying that the relevant goods may be *unknown* to us. Fortunately, there is a way around all this. First, let's notice that if the ultimate spiritual reality is a personal God, then all serious spiritual development must begin in personal relationship with God. And if God is infinitely deep and rich, then any such relationship must be multileveled and developmental – indeed, the development of it would surely be potentially unending. Third, such relationship with a perfect and infinitely rich personal reality would have to be the greatest good that any human being could experience, if God exists – certainly this is the claim of all theistic traditions. But then why this talk of some *other* good, for which God would *sacrifice* such relationship?

Perhaps it will be replied that God sacrifices only *some time* in the relationship, not the whole relationship, and that what is gained thereby may contribute to the *flourishing* of a *future* relationship with God. But it is hard to see how someone seeking God, desiring a loving personal relationship, could possibly be in a state such that experience of God or evidence of some other sort would inhibit or prevent the success of the relationship in the long term, as this point requires. Indeed, such individuals would seem to be in just the *right* position in this respect – a position emphasized as eminently desirable by theistic traditions. Certainly their state is no less appropriate to relationship with God than that of many who would be declared by those traditions to be enjoying it already.

Consider also, in this connection, the infinite *resourcefulness* of God. If God indeed possesses this attribute and is, moreover, unsurpassably deep and rich, then there must at any juncture be literally an *infinite number* of ways of developing in relationship with God, which omnipotence and omniscience could facilitate, despite obstacles to continuing relationship that might seem to present themselves. To say less than this, a theist must surely contradict what she believes about the greatness of God! Hence, even if we were *not* dealing with seekers, individuals optimally placed to benefit from God's presence, we would *still* lack reason to maintain the present objection.

One particular form that the exercise of God's resourcefulness might take may be highlighted here. Strange as it may seem, there is an important form of "hiddenness" that is quite compatible with – and indeed *requires* – a situation in which God is revealed to every seeker. To see this, suppose that God exists, and that our seeker finds reason to believe in God and responds by entering into a personal relationship with God ("conversing" with God in prayer, feeling God's presence, living her whole life in the context of divine–human communion). Suppose also that she subsequently lapses into some inappropriate state – say, arrogance or presumption. What can God do? Well, there is still the possibility of a sort of divine withdrawal *within* the relationship. What I have in mind here is analogous to what has traditionally been called "the dark night of the soul" – a state in which there is evidence for God's existence on which the believer may rely, but in which God is not felt as directly present to her experience, and may indeed feel absent. While not removing the conditions of relationship, such a "withdrawal" would severely test the believer's faith, and, in particular, work against the sort of arrogance and presumption we have mentioned. Indeed, this form of hiddenness would seem capable of accomplishing much, perhaps all, of what theists sometimes say the *other* sort of hiddenness is designed to do! John Macquarrie, a Christian theologian, puts it nicely:

> As happens also in some of our deepest human relationships, the lover reveals himself enough to awaken the love of the beloved, yet veils himself enough to draw the beloved into an even deeper exploration of that love. In the love affair with God . . . there is an

> alternation of consolation and desolation and it is in this way that the finite being is constantly drawn beyond self into the depths of the divine.[1]

If this sort of hiddenness can produce the goods in question and is compatible with God having been revealed to the seeker, what possible reason could we have for insisting that God would leave the seeker in *doubt and nonbelief* in order to further those goods?

A final objection, significantly different from the rest, should briefly be mentioned. This is the claim that there are *other* reasons *for* belief in God which counterbalance or outweigh the reason *against* such belief that our argument represents. Our Analogy Argument, it should be emphasized, is broadly inductive, claiming only that its conclusion is very probable (i.e., much more probable than not). So it is always at least conceivable that the probability we assess for our conclusion on the basis of analogy may need to be adjusted when arguments *supporting* God's existence are taken into account. Someone, for example, who was deeply convinced of the soundness of a simple *de*ductive argument for God's existence (an argument with premises *entailing* the claim that God exists) and had only our Analogy Argument to consider on the side of atheism might well justifiably conclude, on the strength of her apparent proof of God's existence, that despite the closeness and persuasive force of the analogies, there must be *something* wrong with our argument and that God certainly exists, even if she can not put her finger on what the mistake in our reasoning is.

For how many will this sort of move function as a successful defeater? It is hard to say: everything depends on how the independent evidence is assessed, and whether it is properly assessed. Even if we had the space for an exhaustive discussion of other evidence (and of course we do not), it would be possible for others to justifiably disagree with our assessment of it, given facts of personality, experience, time, intelligence, opportunity, and so on that nonculpably incline them in another direction. But some general points can be made, that are not without interest or effect. Most readers, it must be said, are likely to be *without* such proofs of God as were earlier mentioned – indeed, that such proofs are in short supply is one of the circumstances that helps to generate the problem of divine hiddenness in the first place! Certainly, anyone who finds that the other evidence for and against God's existence leaves her thinking that theism and atheism are about equally probable should find the balance tipping toward atheism when this *new* evidence is considered. And it is interesting to note that even those who came to this discussion convinced of the truth of theism may find their epistemic situation changing because of the apparent force of our argument. This is because its apparent force may *affect* – and *negatively* affect – the confidence with which other arguments or experiences are taken to support theism, especially in cases where this other evidence has not previously been carefully examined. We should therefore not suppose that just anyone who comes to these discussions justified in theistic belief will leave that way.

That concludes our discussion of objections to the Analogy Argument. Nothing we have seen takes away from its initial persuasiveness (even the last defeater we discussed must concede this much). Indeed, we have encountered points in this discus-

1 John Macquarrie, *In Search of Deity* (London: SCM Press, 1984), p. 198.

sion that add to its force. Does the divine hiddenness referred to in its premises therefore justify atheism? Does it justify *you, the reader,* in believing atheism? Well, it seems plausible and would be accepted by most philosophers that the following proposition refers to conditions necessary and sufficient for justification of the relevant sort.

> An individual *S* is epistemically justified in believing that *p* in response to evidence *e* if and only if (i) *S* does to some degree believe that *p* on *e*, (ii) has considered all available epistemic reasons for not believing that *p* on *e*, (iii) finds none to be a good reason, and (iv) has fulfilled all relevant epistemic duties in the course of her investigation.

Thinking of yourself as *S*, of *p* as atheism, of *e* as the form of divine hiddenness we have discussed, of the defeaters we have considered (including the defeater relying on independent evidence) and any others known to you as the available reasons for *not* believing atheism because of divine hiddenness, and of the relevant epistemic duties as including such things as care, thoroughness, and openness to the truth, you may, by reference to this standard, work out for *yourself* whether our argument justifies you in believing that God does not exist.

3 The Conceptual Argument

The Analogy Argument is not the only argument from divine hiddenness. Indeed, in my previous work on this topic it is only alluded to, and another form of argumentation is utilized instead.[2] I wanted to develop the Analogy Argument here, and had thought to leave the other aside. But after proceeding, I realized that in developing the former argument, a natural basis for an abbreviated but still forceful presentation of the latter would be laid. So let us briefly consider the additional moves which the latter argument requires.

The Conceptual Argument takes further a theme already touched upon: namely, the proper understanding of the concept of divine love. In examining this concept, developing our understanding of it as we must, by reference to what is best in human love, we are led to endorse claims from which it follows that, if God exists, evidence sufficient to form belief in God is available to everyone capable of a personal relationship with God and not inclined to resist such evidence. As can be seen, this argument not only focuses more closely on the concept of divine love (while drawing information from what we know of human love, including a mother's love) but embraces a wider range of nonbelievers in its premises. In this new argument, the notion of divine hiddenness is, as it were, *expanded* to include events (or the absence of certain events) in the lives of people who, without being closed toward the tradi-

2 See my *Divine Hiddenness and Human Reason* (Ithaca, NY: Cornell University Press, 1993). See also my "Response to Howard-Snyder" (and the paper to which it is a response), in *Canadian Journal of Philosophy*, 26/3 (1996), pp. 455–62, and my "What the Hiddenness of God Reveals: A Collaborative Discussion," in Daniel Howard-Snyder and Paul Moser (eds), *Divine Hiddenness* (Cambridge: Cambridge University Press, 2001), pp. 33–61.

tional God, are for one reason or another not aware of any need to seek God. If a label is desired, we may call all those belonging to this new and broader category of nonbelievers *nonresisters*. Nonresisters might include, in addition to seekers, individuals in the West whose upbringing has been completely secular. They certainly include the vast number of persons in both past and present living in parts of the world where the very *idea* of such a God is distant from human thought and imagination.

Now why should we suppose that the absence of evidence sufficient to form belief in God in the lives of nonresisters presents a problem for theism? Well, because reflection on the concept of divine love shows that a perfectly loving God would necessarily seek personal relationship with *all* individuals belonging to this type, and because such seeking entails the provision of evidence sufficient for belief in the existence of God. (As can be seen, here the emphasis is not on human seekers but on *God* as seeker.)

In defense of the first of these claims, we may point out that the seeking of a personal relationship is an essential part of the best human love. The best human lover encourages her beloved to draw from relationship with herself what he may need to flourish, but also quite naturally aspires to a kind of closeness between herself and her beloved: she reaches out to the one she loves immediately and spontaneously, and not only because of some prior calculation of advantages or disadvantages for either party. Something similar must apply to God's love for us: clearly an explicit divine–human relationship must do much to promote human flourishing, in which case God would seek it for that reason; and clearly God would also value personal relationship with human beings – creatures created in God's own image – for its own sake. No doubt God would not *force* such a loving relationship on anyone (the notion is logically contradictory and, in any case, contrary to love's respect for freedom), but surely a God who did not at least make such a relationship *available* to those who are *nonresisting* would not be perfectly loving.

This point sometimes has a hard time getting through. Due to a variety of social and religious factors, we seem to have got used to thinking of even God's love in a limited and limiting fashion, contrary to what all philosophical methods for working out an explication of the divine nature would indicate. But why suppose that if God exists there will be times when personal relationship with God will not be available to us? While a perfectly good and loving parent might occasionally stand to one side and let her child make the first move, and refuse to suffocate the child with her attentions, or even withdraw for a time to make a point, these are moments *within* the relationship, which *add* to its meaning. And while she might with deep sadness acknowledge that her child had completely cut himself off from the relationship, and not actively seek its resumption, it *would take* such resistance on the part of the child for the relationship to be put out of his immediate reach. What loving parent would ever willingly participate in bringing about such a state of affairs? And similar points apply to love as it occurs in the context of friendship and marriage relationships. So there seems no escaping this point: some form of personal relationship with God is always going to be available to nonresisters, if God is indeed loving.

A defense of our second claim – that for such relationship to be available, evidence sufficient for belief in God's existence would have to be similarly available – may now be added. The key point here is that it is logically impossible for you to hear God speaking to you or consciously to experience divine forgiveness and support or feel grateful to God or experience God's loving presence and respond thereto in love and obedience and worship or participate in any *other* element of a personal relationship with God while *not believing that there is a God.* Simply by looking at what it *means* to be in personal relationship with God, we can see that this is so. Since belief is involuntary, it follows that without evidence sufficient for belief in the existence of God, nonresisters are not in a position to relate personally to God. But where nonresisters are not in such a position, relationship with God has not been made available to them in the above sense. It follows that if relationship with God is to be made available to them, nonresisters must be provided with evidence sufficient for belief in God. This evidence, notice, would not need to be some thunderbolt from the sky or miracle or devastating theoretical proof. The quiet evidence of religious experience would do, and might also be most appropriate to the aims of any would-be divine relationship partner. But *some* such evidence must be available to nonresisters if they are to have the possibility of responding in love to God.

Taken in conjunction, the two points we have defended imply that if God exists, evidence sufficient for belief in God is *much more widely available than is in fact the case.* And from this it follows that God does *not* exist. Now this argument, like the other, has of course got to deal with objections. But as it turns out, the objections are pretty much the same ones, tailored to address the specifics of the new argument. And so are the replies. The reader is invited to go over the objections and replies again, this time with the Conceptual Argument in mind. She or he will see, I think, that the resources are there for a fully satisfying defense of the latter argument too. If so, we have not just the probable grounds of analogy but the more certain grounds of conceptual analysis for concluding that God does not exist.

4 Consequences for the Philosophy of Religion

Suppose I am right and that the arguments we have discussed can be used to justify atheism. What should those who are convinced by them conclude with respect to God and religion? That neither matters, and that any reasonably intelligent inquirer will arrive at a place where concerns about such things no longer enter her head? That nature is all there is, and that we should limit our intellectual attention to the methods and results of the various sciences? Hardly. The perceptive reader will notice that our discussion has been restricted to the epistemic status of *traditional* theism. And anyone who thinks that traditional theism and naturalistic atheism are the only options worth exploring here has a woefully inadequate grasp of the range and diversity and complexity of religion. Indeed, there are intriguing religious possibilities that are only now beginning to receive the attention they deserve from Western philosophers. And as human beings continue to develop, intellectually and morally, as well as emotionally and socially, it may well be that new possibilities will come to light. The philosophy of religion is potentially far richer and far more wide-ranging in its explorations than it is at present. And so I conclude by suggesting that the hiddenness of the traditional God may ultimately only have the effect of allowing the *real* God – ultimate reality as it really is – to be more clearly revealed.

Chapter Two

Divine Hiddenness Does Not Justify Atheism

Paul K. Moser

> *There is a sense in which God hides himself. Sometimes it is because we are looking for him in the wrong place . . . or among things that we can see, until one dull morning we seem to lose him entirely because he refuses to do our bidding. Sometimes it is because we carefully avoid looking for him in the right place. Over and over again he is where we are quite sure he is not.*
>
> – Paul Scherer[3]

1 Clarifying the Question

Someone once asked Bertrand Russell what he would say if after his death he met God. Russell's proposed reply: "God, you gave us insufficient evidence."[4] This reply reflects an attitude of many people, including theists as well as atheists and agnostics. Why isn't God more obvious? If God exists, why doesn't God give us "sufficient evidence" of God's existence? God, I shall argue, does indeed supply sufficient decisive evidence. The decisive evidence supplied is, however, profoundly different from what we naturally expect. So a key issue is: Who has the proper authority to decide what *kind* of evidence God must supply? God or humans? Russell does not say what kind of evidence God failed to supply, but he assumes nonetheless that some kind of evidence is lacking, or "insufficient," regarding God's existence.

Our question is whether God's hiddenness justifies atheism. This question calls for some clarification of its key terms: "God," "hiddenness," and "justifies." The term "God" represents a wide range of notions in ordinary parlance. Its ambiguity is severe, but often unnoticed. Let's use the term "God" not as a personal name but as a *supreme title*, in keeping with one long-standing use. This use of the term requires of any possible holder: (a) worthiness of worship and full life commitment and thus (b) moral perfection and (c) an all-loving character. One might use the term in a different manner, but then one would not be talking about the kind of personal God central to the monotheistic traditions of Judaism, Christianity, and Islam. Lacking a better candidate for title-holder, let's consider the God of Abraham, Isaac, Jacob, and Jesus. We thus shall speak of "the Hebraic God." We shall also speak of "Hebraic theism" as the view that the Hebraic God actually exists. Is Hebraic theism true? In addition, is it adequately grounded in evidence indicating that it is true? Or does our available evidence indicate, as Russell suggested, that Hebraic theism is false, or at least unreasonable? Such questions motivate this essay.

3 Paul Scherer, *Love Is a Spendthrift* (New York: Harper and Row, 1961), pp. 4–5.

4 See Bertrand Russell, "The Talk of the Town," *New Yorker*, February 21, 1970, p. 29; cited in Al Seckel (ed.), *Bertrand Russell on God and Religion* (Buffalo: Prometheus, 1986), p. 11.

In the absence of elaboration, the term "justifies" is nearly as unclear as the term "God." Philosophers and others use the term with different meanings, and this often blocks progress toward understanding and true belief. Justifiers, broadly characterized, are *truth-indicators*; they are evidence indicating that a proposition is true.[5] They can be *fallible*; thus a justifier can yield a justified *false* belief. Justifiers can also be *defeasible*; thus they can cease to confer justification once one's evidence base is expanded. My evidence for believing that a table is before me, for instance, can be defeated by my acquiring evidence that a holographic image of a table is being projected before me. Justifiers, then, need not guarantee truth or certainty, and they can confer justification in various strengths or degrees. In addition, justifiers can vary from person to person; my justifiers need not be yours. Whether justifiers must be reproducible or showable is controversial in some quarters. Some people assume that if you cannot *show* your justification, then you do not actually *have* it. This, however, is doubtful. Showing justification requires a certain skill in formulation that goes beyond the mere *having* of justification. As for the reproducibility of justification, I can reproduce only what I can control, but evidence (for example, from experience) need not be under one's control. We must be careful, then, not to build into justification something extraneous.

The proposal that a factor (for example, divine hiddenness) "justifies atheism" implies that this factor *makes it reasonable* to endorse the truth of atheism. One might take this to imply that the justifying factor makes atheism *more likely to be true* than theism. At any rate, our question becomes: Does our evidence regarding God, subtle and easily rejectable as it is, make it reasonable to believe that the Hebraic God does not exist? Any answer would be altogether premature in advance of reflection on the nature and announced intentions of the God in question. Many atheists and agnostics jump to a nontheistic conclusion without adequate attention to such reflection. As a result, their nontheism is altogether premature.

2 The Kind of God in Question

It's a waste of time to ask about God's existence if we lack understanding of the *kind* of God in question. If we leave the notion of God amorphous, our question about God's existence will be similarly obscure and resistant to worthwhile reflection. We would then not know what *kind of evidence* for God to expect if God does in fact exist. Many philosophers of religion are in exactly this disadvantaged position. They do expect a certain kind of evidence for God, as we shall see, but their expectation lacks a cogent basis in the notion or character of God, at least if the Hebraic God is our concern. The notion of God and God's purposes suggests what kind of evidence for God one should expect. It is odd, therefore, that philosophers of religion rarely attend adequately to that notion.

5 For detailed discussion of truth-indicators, see Paul K. Moser, *Knowledge and Evidence* (New York: Cambridge University Press, 1989), and *idem*, *Philosophy after Objectivity* (New York: Oxford University Press, 1993), ch. 4.

Anything but amorphous, the Hebraic God is famous for hiding at times. The theme of divine hiding recurs throughout the Hebrew Scriptures and the New Testament.[6] So we are confronted by an all-loving God who sometimes hides from people. Many people assume that an all-loving God's existence, if real, would be *obvious* to all normal humans. God's existence is not, however, obvious to all normal humans. So, according to many people, we may reasonably (or justifiably) deny that God actually exists. These people ask, rhetorically: How could an all-loving God fail to manifest God's reality in a way that removes all serious doubt about God's existence? Some normal humans, of course, do not believe that God exists. They claim *not* to have adequate evidence (for reasonable belief) that God exists. Would an all-loving God permit such doubt about God's existence? How could this be permitted if God is indeed all-loving? Many atheists and agnostics deny that this could be permitted by an all-loving God. They thus recommend against belief that God exists.

Does divine hiding support a recommendation against Hebraic theism? The kind of hiding characteristic of the Hebraic God entails neither the nonexistence nor the unavailability of God. In addition, such hiding does not entail either that God hides always or that humans have no evidence of God's reality. Hebraic theism acknowledges that divine hiding occurs not always but at some times for God's own purposes. The Hebrew Scriptures present God's hiding as *at times* a response to human disobedience and morally significant indifference toward God (Deuteronomy 31:16–19, 32:19–20; Psalm 89:46; Isaiah 59:2; Micah 3:4). This is not, however, the full account of divine hiding. God hides at times for *various* purposes in interacting with humans. Divine hiding is *not* always a judgment on human disobedience or indifference. It is, according to Hebraic theism, often a constructive effort on God's part to encourage (deeper) human focus, longing, and gratitude toward God. God thus aims to take us, even if painfully, to our own deepest resources and their inadequacy, where we become aware of our needing and already depending on God. In apprehending God's *absence*, one can achieve a deeper, more profound appreciation of God's *presence*. Human experience of a contrast between God's presence and absence can highlight the preeminent value of God's presence.

Hebraic theism places divine hiding in the context of God's primary desire to have people lovingly know God and thereby become loving as God is loving. God's *primary* aim is not to hide from people, but rather to include all people in God's kingdom family as beloved children under God's lovingly righteous guidance. A loving filial relationship with God is God's main goal for every human, according to Hebraic theism. This means that God wants us to love God and thus to treasure God, not just to believe that God exists (see Deuteronomy 6:5; Mark 12:30; James 2:19). The Hebraic God wants all people to enter lovingly into God's life, in action as well as thought. So production of mere reasonable belief that God exists does not meet God's higher aim for humans. For our own good, God is after something more profound and more transforming than simple reasonable belief. As all-loving, God will not settle for anything less.

6 On the scriptural data, see Samuel Balentine, *The Hidden God* (Oxford: Clarendon Press, 1983), and Samuel Terrien, *The Elusive Presence* (San Fransisco: Harper and Row, 1978). For broader discussion, see Daniel Howard-Snyder and Paul Moser (eds), *Divine Hiddenness* (Cambridge: Cambridge University Press, 2001).

Divine hiding typically results from a deficiency of some sort on the human side of the divine–human relationship. If God is hiding from us, according to Hebraic theism, we should assess our standing before God. We may then need to change something in our lives, perhaps certain attitudes and practices incompatible with the ways of God. Even in a case such as that of "blameless and upright" Job, a certain presumptuous attitude regarding knowledge of God needed revision (Job 38–42). Similarly, many people today boldly presume to know how a loving God *should* or *must* intervene in the world, allegedly if God is to be genuinely loving. A loving God, however, will not, and should not, be bound by superficial human expectations. Rather, human expectations must be transformed, for the good of humans, toward the profoundly loving character of God. This disturbing and humbling lesson is central to Hebraic theism.

According to Hebraic theism, human "wisdom" falls short of God's wisdom, and human expectations are typically superficial and even misplaced in comparison with God's loving intentions and character. Due humility is thus the order of the day, relative to the ways of the Hebraic God. This should be no surprise, once we reflect on the significant differences between an all-loving morally perfect God and self-centered humans. Even so, according to Hebraic theism, God takes no pleasure in staying away from humans or being rejected by them (see Ezekiel 18:23, 32; 33:11). The epistle of James puts decisive responsibility on us humans: "Come near to God and God will come near to you" (4:8; cf. Jeremiah 29:13; Malachi 3:7). The key issue is thus: How may humans acquire knowledge of the Hebraic God?

3 Proper Knowledge of the Hebraic God

Jesus prays as follows regarding the lessons of his mission to inaugurate the kingdom of God:

> I thank you, Father, Lord of heaven and earth, because you have hidden these things from the wise and the intelligent and have revealed them to infants; yes, Father, for such was your gracious will. All things have been handed over to me by my Father; and no one knows the Son except the Father, and no one knows the Father except the Son and anyone to whom the Son chooses to reveal him. (Matthew 11:25–6, NRSV/Luke 10:21–2; cf. Psalm 8:2)

Proper knowledge of God, according to Jesus, requires one's humbly, faithfully, and lovingly standing in a child–parent, or *filial*, relationship to God as one's righteously gracious Father. Such *filial knowledge* rarely surfaces in philosophy of religion, or even in Jewish-Christian approaches to knowledge of God. This omission is regrettable indeed.

Jesus's awareness of being God's beloved son was not a matter of mere intellectual assent. It was a profound experiential relationship that called for talk of God as *Father*, in keeping with the Hebrew Scriptures.[7] Jesus was gripped, even overwhelmed,

7 For helpful discussion of this theme, see Bernard Cooke, *God's Beloved: Jesus' Experience of the Transcendent* (Philadelphia: Trinity Press International, 1992), esp. pp. 1–24, 103–9.

by his Father's love and its effects. His experience of being God's son is clearly expressed in his prayers. Indeed, Jesus seems to have regarded filial prayer toward God as an ideal avenue to proper, filial knowledge of God. Such prayer is primarily a matter of asking what God wants from us rather than what we want from God. This kind of humility figures importantly in the issue of what kind of evidence of God we should expect.

Proper knowledge of the Hebraic God is inherently *person*-relational. We come to know other human persons by actively relating to them in personal interaction with them. Likewise, we come to know God via *personal* interaction whereby we become personally accountable to God. Through conscience, for example, one can be personally convicted on moral grounds by the personal will of God. One could not responsibly apprehend the reality of a parent's or a spouse's love for one apart from a sincere personal relationship with that parent or spouse. An analogous point holds for one's responsibly apprehending the reality of God's love. So Hebraic filial knowledge of God is irreducible to knowledge that a particular object in the universe exists. Such filial knowledge, in keeping with God's preeminence, requires that one know God not as a mere *object* but as the supreme *personal subject* who is Lord of all, including one's own life. Knowledge of this kind results from God's gracious self-revelation, not from human ways that are self-crediting, manipulative, or exclusive.

For our own good, we cannot know God on our own self-serving terms. Instead, we must be amenable to God's better terms for filial knowledge, and this requires genuine humility. It challenges our presumed epistemological autonomy. We must *enter into*, and *participate in*, a loving filial relationship with God in response to God's drawing us toward God through conscience and other means. This, of course, is no matter of mere intellectual assent to a proposition. It demands that one put the Hebraic God at the center of one's life, in terms of whom one values, loves, and follows.

Divine hiding arises from God's upholding the supreme value of God's invaluable loving ways. God sustains the value of God's gracious ways of human renewal in the presence of all people who would compromise the value of those ways to their own detriment. Having preeminent value, God's loving ways must remain sacred and not be diminished in value. God's primary goal in self-revelation is transformation of its recipients toward God's loving character. This goal will not be satisfied by God's achieving our reasonably believing that God exists. A person can reasonably believe that God exists but loathe God. So God must be careful, even subtle at times, to have God's loving self-manifestation elicit a freely given response of humble love rather than fear, indifference, or arrogance. God cares mainly about what and how we *love*, not just what we *believe*. For our own good, God aims that we love God above all else.

Proper moral education toward God's kind of sacrificial love and reconciliation is difficult, noncoercive business. Its important lessons must be *shown* to us in action rather than simply *stated* to us in sentences or arguments. We must learn such lessons in *living* them rather than merely *thinking* them, for the lessons concern *who we are*, not just *what we think*. This holds true especially when our moral educator is God.

Accordingly, the crucifixion of Jesus, as God's unique son, offers a noncoercive demonstration of God's self-giving love toward humans.[8] Given the important reality of human free will (a requirement for genuine love), such moral education has no guarantee of success, even when God is the loving educator. Not even God can force genuine loving reconciliation.

We must attune ourselves to evidence of God's self-revelation. Consider an instance of non-English language:

Abba yithqaddash shemakh. Tethe malkuthakh. Lakhman delimkhar, habh lan yoma dhen.

(An English translation: Father, hallowed be your name. Your kingdom come. Our bread for tomorrow, give us today.) Perhaps you did not initially apprehend the meaning of this (transliteration of an) instance of Palestinian Aramaic. Perhaps you were not even confident initially that this inscription actually has meaning. The problem, however, lies not in the Aramaic token. It lies rather in the overall perspective of beliefs and other attitudes you bring to this inscription. Call this perspective your *receptive attitude.* The problem of perceiving meaning lies in your lack of appropriate exposure and sensitivity to Palestinian Aramaic. Clearly, then, the reception of significant evidence sometimes depends on the receptive attitude of people. In particular, failure to receive some evidence stems from psychological facts about the intended *recipients*, rather than from flaws in the available evidence itself.

The analogy, in brief, is this: People whose receptive attitude is closed to God's program of all-inclusive renewal by grace may be blinded from the available evidence for the reality of God. The evidence may be readily available, just as our Aramaic inscription is meaningful. We need, however, appropriate "ears to hear and eyes to see" the available evidence. We need a change of receptive attitude to apprehend the available evidence in the right way. This change involves the direction of our lives, including our settled priorities, not just our intellectual assent.

The needed change includes acknowledgment that on our own we humans, individually and collectively, have failed dismally at manifesting God's all-loving character. This failure occurs in the face of serious challenges to our existence (for example, death), to our well-being (for example, physical and mental decline), and to our moral standing (for example, our tendency to selfishness). These challenges constitute our *human predicament.* We have no self-made or even self-discovered solution to this predicament. This humbling acknowledgment is significant for our knowing God. It calls for our beginning and continuing a humble *filial* relationship of acknowledged dependence toward God. Such a relationship demands a renunciation of our supposed independence of God, even in the cognitive domain.

Without suitable openness to transformation toward God's character, we may be blinded by our own counterfeit "intelligence" and "wisdom." We will then lack the kind of openness, humility, and filial obedience appropriate to relating, cognitively and otherwise, to the God of the universe. We will have then arrogated the author-

8 On this theme, see D. M. Ross, *The Cross of Christ* (Garden City, NY: Doubleday, 1928), and Timothy Jackson, *Love Disconsoled* (New York: Cambridge University Press, 1999).

ity of God to ourselves or to some other part of creation. In that case, we would be guilty of *idolatry*, perhaps even a kind of *cognitive* idolatry where we demand a certain sort of knowledge or evidence for God inappropriate to a filial relationship with God. To the extent that we violate God's program of human volitional transformation, we are slaves to selfishness and need to be set free. Cognitive idolatry can keep us from the needed transformation toward freedom. It often rests on a principle of this sort: Unless God (if God exists) supplies evidence of kind *K*, God's existence is too hidden to merit reasonable endorsement. The problem is not with a principle of this form; it is rather with the specification of kind *K*. If we specify *K* in a way that disregards the character and intentions of the Hebraic God, thereby protecting ourselves from the divine challenge of transformation, we manifest cognitive idolatry. We then wield a cognitive commitment designed to exclude God. This is the heart of cognitive idolatry.

Our self-protective fear typically yields antipathy toward God. Candidly, philosopher Thomas Nagel reports his fearful hope that God does not exist.[9] He avowedly wants a universe without God. Nagel has a "cosmic authority problem" with God. A highly educated atheist acquaintance of mine has a similar attitude toward God. When asked how he would respond if after death he met God directly, he replied that he would immediately kill himself. These are sad cases of our self-protective fears banishing God from human lives. All humans suffer from this problem to some degree. It is the problem of ultimate authority for our lives. We typically want to be, or at least to appoint, the ultimate authority for our lives, as if we had a right to this. We thereby deceive ourselves, blinding ourselves to the supreme reality and authority over our lives.

The extent to which we know God depends on the extent to which we are gratefully willing to acknowledge God's authority and, as a result, to participate in God's program of all-inclusive redemption. So it becomes obvious why we humans (*not* just atheists and agnostics) have difficulty in knowing God. The difficulty stems from our resisting transformation toward God's morally perfect all-loving character. So it is simply presumptuous for us humans to approach the question whether God exists as if we were automatically in an appropriate moral and cognitive position to handle it reliably. God is, after all, a very special kind of agent with distinctive purposes, not a household object or a laboratory specimen. We humans cannot easily abide a gracious Being who evades our self-approving cognitive nets.

God cares about how we handle evidence for God's existence. We are to become, in the image of God's character, more loving in handling it. So, contrary to a typical philosophical attitude, knowledge of God is not a spectator sport. It is rather part of a process of God's thorough makeover of a person. It is, from our side of the process, akin to an *active commitment* to a morally transforming *personal* relationship rather than to a mere subjective state or disposition. We come to know God only as God becomes *our God*, the Lord of our lives, rather than just an object of our contemplation, self-indulgence, or amusement. God refuses, for our own good, to become a mere idol of our speculation or entertainment. We manifest dangerous arrogance in assum-

9 See Thomas Nagel, *The Last Word* (New York: Oxford University Press, 1997), p. 130.

ing that we can have proper knowledge of God without undergoing profound transformation. In proper knowledge of God, knowers must be transformed to become *like the known* in character.

Proper knowledge of the Hebraic God is inherently ethical and practical, rather than simply reflective. Spectators complaining from afar may in fact remain afar by their own self-isolating choice. Knowing God requires one's apprehending a call to come in from afar and gratefully join in God's all-inclusive plan of gracious redemption. This plan is no mere intellectual puzzle for philosophers. God is more serious than our mental gymnastics, for our own good. We have *lives* to form and to live, not just thoughts to think or intellectual puzzles to solve. God's call, in keeping with the call to Abraham, Jeremiah, Jesus, and Saul of Tarsus, requires that we commit to using our *whole lives* for the advancement of God's kingdom of sacrificial love. So proper knowledge of God extends to our deepest attitudes and convictions, not just to our thoughts.

The Hebraic God is anything but cognitively "safe," or controllable. We cannot control either God or God's hiding on occasion. So we cannot remove God's hiding with our self-made recipes. The Hebraic God leaves us empty-handed when we insist on seeking with our self-made tools, including familiar recipe-like religious practices. We therefore cannot "solve" the problem of divine hiding if a solution requires a self-made tool to remove such hiding. We are, after all, neither God nor God's advisers (Isaiah 40:13–14). At best we are God's obedient children. So we should not be surprised at all that we lack our own devices to banish, or even to explain fully, all cases of God's occasional hiding.

4 Evidence of God

We have touched on two kinds of knowledge: (i) *propositional* knowledge that God exists and (ii) *filial* knowledge as one's humbly, faithfully, and lovingly standing in a relationship to God as righteously gracious Father. Filial knowledge of God requires propositional knowledge that God exists, but it exceeds propositional knowledge. One can know that God exists, as we noted, but hate God. Filial knowledge of God, in contrast, includes our being reconciled to God (at least to some degree) through a loving filial relationship with God. It requires our entrusting ourselves as children to God in grateful love, thereby being transformed in *who we are* and in *how we exist*, not just in what we believe.

Filial knowing of God is knowing God as Lord *in the second person*, as supreme "You." Divine lordship entails supreme *moral leadership*, and moral leadership entails a call to moral accountability and direction. When self-centered humans are the recipients of God's call, the call is for moral redirection and transformation toward God's character of sacrificial love. Knowing God *as Lord* requires our surrendering to God as follows: "Not my will, but Your will"; "Not my kingdom, but Your kingdom." Filial knowing of God thus involves Gethsemane, as the way to the cross, in that it depends on our volitional sensitivity and submission to the will of God. Such knowing requires a genuine commitment to obey God's call, even if the call is to give up one's life in sacrificial love on a criminal's cross. We thus come truly to know God not in our prideful cognitive glory but rather in our own volitional weakness relative to the priority of God's will.[10]

Are we *entitled* to know God? In particular, are we entitled to know that God exists without knowing God *as Lord*, as the morally supreme agent for our lives? Some people uncritically assume an affirmative answer, but this will not settle the issue. An even prior question is: *Who* is entitled to decide how one may know God – we humans or God? Given our moral and intellectual inferiority relative to God, can *we* reasonably make demands on God in favor of *our* preferred ways of knowing God? Perhaps God's dispensing of knowledge of God is truly gracious, a genuine gift calling for grateful reception. Many people presume that we have a *right* to know God, even on our preferred terms. In virtue of what, however, does God owe us revelation and knowledge of God on our preferred terms? God actually owes us no such thing, despite our bold expectations.

God does not owe us any kind of hands-off, personally abstract confirmation of God's reality, contrary to what Russell apparently assumed. Indeed, God owes us nothing beyond fidelity to a loving character and to the promises stemming from such a character. On due reflection we see that we are in no position to make evidential demands on God beyond such fidelity. Nothing requires that God allow for (i) our propositional knowledge that God exists apart from (ii) our filial knowledge of God. Ideally, God promotes the two together. God can be all-loving in supplying evidence of God's existence in a manner sensitive to human receptivity to filial knowledge of God. God's loving character does not require that God offer evidence of God susceptible to our trivializing God without being challenged toward volitional transformation. So God's elusiveness, or hiddenness, does not recommend atheism.

God's ways of imparting knowledge of God may differ significantly from our natural expectations regarding God. *How* we may know God depends perhaps on what God lovingly wants *for us* and *from us*. As knowers, we are responsible *to God*, and not just to ourselves and our antecedent cognitive commitments. Perhaps, moreover, we can truly come to know God only if we acknowledge our unworthiness of knowing God. It may thus be illuminating to ask about the attitudes of people inquiring about God. What are our *intentions* in wanting knowledge of God? Do we have a bias against filial knowledge of God? Do we resist knowing God as personal Lord who lovingly holds us morally accountable and expects grateful obedience from us as children of God? Hebraic theism disallows God being trivialized in the cognitive domain. In filial knowledge of God, we have knowledge of a supreme *personal* subject, not of a mere object for casual reflection. This is not knowledge of a vague First Cause, Ultimate Power, Ground of Being, or even a Best Explanation. It is rather *convicting* knowledge of a personal, communicating Lord who demands full, grateful commitment from all recipients. Such convicting knowledge includes our being *judged*, and *found unworthy*, by God's morally profound love.

Critics will object that God's presence is too ambiguous, at best, to merit reasonable acknowledgment. Surely, God owes us more miraculous signs and wonders, what-

10 On the important theme of volitional weakness, see Timothy Savage, *Power Through Weakness* (New York: Cambridge University Press, 1996), and Gene Davenport, *Into the Darkness* (Nashville, Tenn.: Abingdon, 1988).

ever God's redemptive aims. Why does not God entertain us, once and for all, with some decisive manifestations of God's awesome power? It would not cost God anything, and it might vanquish nagging doubts about God's existence. Surely, a truly loving God would use miraculous powers to free us from our doubts. God's redemptive purposes, many will therefore object, do not exonerate God from the charge of excessive restraint in manifestation. If God exists, God is blameworthy for inadequate self-revelation.

N. R. Hanson complains about the absence of observable happenings that would establish God's existence. "There is no single natural happening, nor any constellation of such happenings, which establishes God's existence. . . . If the heavens cracked open and [a] Zeus-like figure . . . made his presence and nature known to the world, *that* would establish such a happening."[11] Hanson observes that nothing like the Zeus-event has ever occurred so as to recommend theism to all reasonable people. He thus concludes that theism lacks adequate warrant for universal acceptance.

We should distinguish *morally impotent* and *morally transforming* miraculous signs. Morally impotent miraculous signs can surprise and entertain people but cannot transform their moral character. Morally transforming signs, by contrast, change one's moral character toward the moral character of God. People often seek mere entertainment from visible phenomena, whereas God seeks our moral transformation from the inside out. For our own good, God is not in the entertainment business regarding our coming to know God. Isaiah 58:2 portrays the Hebraic God as complaining about the Israelites that "day after day they seek me and delight to know my ways, as if they were a nation that practiced righteousness and did not forsake the ordinance of their God" (NRSV). The New Testament likewise discourages our seeking after morally impotent signs from God. It promises, however, a morally transforming sign to genuine seekers after God, seekers actively open to moral transformation toward God's moral character. Since such a sign is a definitive sign from the God of morally serious love, we should expect it to manifest the character of God: namely, God's morally serious love. The New Testament confirms this expectation, explicitly and repeatedly. Paul, for example, notes: "Hope [in God] does not disappoint, because God's love has been poured out in our hearts via the Holy Spirit given to us" (Romans 5:5). (See 1 Corinthians 2:4–16 on the role of the Spirit in Paul's epistemology.[12])

The presence of God's morally transforming love is the key *cognitive* foundation for genuine filial knowledge of God. Such love is a foundational source of knowledge of God (cf. Colossians 2:2; 1 Corinthians 8:2–3; Ephesians 3:17–18). It is real *evidence* of God's reality and presence. This love is a matter of personal intervention by God and the basis of a personal relationship with God. It is the distinctive presence of a personal God. So the filial knowledge in question rests on morally transforming divine love that produces a loving character in genuine children of God, even if at times such people obstruct God's transformation. This transformation *happens*

11 N. R. Hanson, *What I Do Not Believe and Other Essays* (Dordrecht: Reidel, 1971), p. 322.

12 See the discussion of this passage in Richard Hays, *First Corinthians* (Louisville, Ky.: John Knox, 1997). See also the broader epistemological discussion in Paul K. Moser, *Why Isn't God More Obvious?* (Atlanta: RZIM, 2000), and *idem*, "Cognitive Idolatry and Divine Hiding," in Howard-Snyder and Moser (eds), *Divine Hiddenness*, pp. 120–48.

to one, in part, and thus is neither purely self-made nor simply the by-product of a self-help strategy. (I say "in part" given the role of human free will in seeking and responding to God.) This widely neglected supernatural sign is available (at God's appointed time) to anyone who turns to God with moral seriousness. It transforms one's will not only to have gratitude, trust, and love toward God, but also to love others unselfishly. Thus, "We *know* that we have passed from death to life because we love one another. . . . Whoever does not love does not know God, for God is love" (1 John 3:14, 4:8, NRSV). So we need to learn how to apprehend, and be captured by, *God's love for all of us*, not just truths about God's love. Neither God nor God's love, being personal, is a proposition or an argument. God and God's love are much deeper, even inexhaustible mysteries.

The evidence of God's presence offered by character transformation in God's children merits serious attention. It goes much deeper than the comparatively superficial evidence found in entertaining signs, wonders, visions, ecstatic experiences, and philosophical arguments. We could consistently dismiss any such sign, wonder, vision, ecstatic experience, or argument as illusory or indecisive, given certain alterations in our beliefs. In contrast, genuine character transformation toward God's all-inclusive love does not admit of easy dismissal. It bears directly on *who one really is*, the kind of person one actually is. Such transformation cuts too deeply against our natural tendencies toward selfishness to qualify as a self-help gimmick. It thus offers a kind of firm evidence resistant to quick dismissal.

An all-loving God would make God's presence *available* to humans at God's appointed time. God's presence, however, need not exceed the presence of God's morally serious love or be available apart from morally serious inquiry and seeking. In particular, God's presence need not include miracles irrelevant to moral transformation toward a character of morally serious love, even though God may use such miracles as attention-getters. An all-loving God can properly make confident knowledge of God's existence arise simultaneously with filial knowledge of God. Accordingly, God is exonerated from the charge of irresponsibly refraining from entertaining signs, so long as God reveals God's presence to anyone suitably receptive. Hanson's use of the Zeus-example overlooks these considerations. In fact, it trivializes God's actual aim. As all-loving, God aims to bring unloving people to love God and others, even enemies. One could not have a more difficult, or more important, task.

God's self-revelation of transforming love will take us beyond mere historical and scientific probabilities to a firm foundation of *personal acquaintance* with God. As Paul remarks, in our sincerely crying out "Abba, Father" to God (note the Jesus-inspired filial content of this cry), God's Spirit confirms to our spirit that we are indeed children of God (Romans 8:16). We thereby receive God's personal assurance of our filial relationship with God. This assurance is more robust than any kind of theoretical certainty offered by philosophers or theologians. It liberates a person from dependence merely on the quagmire of speculation, hypothesis formation, probabilistic inference, or guesswork about God. Such assurance yields a distinctive kind of grounded firm confidence in God unavailable in any other way. God thus merits credit even for proper human confidence in God (cf. Ephesians 2:8). So humans who boast of their own intellectual resources in knowing God are guilty of misplaced boasting. God as gift-giver offers the proper confidence we cannot muster on our own.

5 Hiding, Seeking, and Theodicy

Hebraic theism can now assume the burden of support for its commitment to a God of morally serious love. This commitment not only is testable now in a morally serious manner but also *should* be tested now by every person. Each person must test for himself or herself by seeking God with due humility and moral seriousness, as pride and frivolity will automatically blind one to seeing God and our genuine need of God. The appropriate test cannot be accomplished by "neutral" examination of evidence, whatever that might be; it requires one's willingness to forsake all diversions for the required moral transformation. Filial knowledge of God is by grace, not by earning, but the grace is available (at God's appointed time) to all who call on God with sincere humility and due moral seriousness.

We can "reconcile" divine hiddenness and a perfectly loving God at a personal *evidential* level, but not at a comprehensive *explanatory* level. So we need a sharp distinction between: (a) "When you seek God aright, you will find God," and (b) "When you seek God aright, you will find an adequate, comprehensive explanation of why God hides at times." Promise (a) does not rely on promise (b), and thus does not underwrite a theodicy or any comprehensive explanation of divine hiddenness. Promise (a) is limited to the issue of one's acquiring evidence of God's reality.

Even though a theodicy for divine hiddenness is unavailable to us, promise (a) can hold good and be valuable to humans. In demanding human seeking, God upholds the value of divine revelation, thereby saving it from becoming "cheap and easy" to humans. God's aim is to have humans appreciate, and be transformed by, divine love, not just to think about it. Human seeking, even when followed by one's finding God, does not produce a theodicy for divine hiddenness, because it does not yield an adequate, comprehensive explanation of God's hiddenness. Even when such seeking delivers evidence of God, one can be ignorant of the specific intentions motivating God's hiding at times. This should be no surprise given the differences between God and humans. The important point, however, is that our lacking an adequate explanation of divine hiding does not challenge anyone's having good evidence of God's reality and love. Having such evidence is one thing; explaining God's intentions in hiding is quite another.

It would be question begging to portray divine hiddenness as falsifying widespread religious experience of God's reality. Divine hiddenness facing some people at some times, or even some people at all past and present times, does not underwrite divine hiddenness relative to all people at all times. So there is no clear, defensible way to generalize on actual cases of divine hiddenness to encompass all people. A generalized argument for atheism or agnosticism, then, seems not to emerge from divine hiddenness. Any such argument would require specific premises independent of divine hiddenness. It is unclear, however, what such premises would be. Their absence suggests a special problem of hiddenness facing a generalized case for atheism or agnosticism from divine hiddenness.

Why, then, isn't God more obvious? The question suffers from a misplaced emphasis. It should be redirected. Why do *we* fail to apprehend God's loving reality and presence? God is hidden only in God's unique superhuman love. Recall our opening statement of Russell's reply to God: "God, you gave us insufficient evidence." In God's presence, we do well to question *ourselves* rather than to blame God. In our pride, we often overlook God's ways of humble love. If our hearts are willingly attuned to God's self-giving transformative love, God will be obvious enough. We thus need proper eyes to see and ears to hear the reality of God. To that end, we need to call on the Lord, who alone can empower our cognitive and moral appropriation of the things of God. The Hebraic God of love will then answer in love. All things will then become new, under God's powerful transforming love. Instead of embracing atheism, then, the wise person will seek God with all due diligence and self-sacrifice. So "taste and see that the Lord is good" indeed.

Reply to Moser

I agree with Paul Moser that there is no reason to expect a God of the sort whose existence is at issue here to "be obvious to all normal humans," or to encourage "mere intellectual assent" to theistic claims, or to provide "morally impotent" proof or "entertaining signs" or "decisive manifestations of God's awesome power" to individuals who "resist knowing God as personal Lord." I also agree that there is something deeply wrong with the "kind of cognitive idolatry where we demand a certain sort of knowledge or evidence of God inappropriate to a filial relationship with God," or where we seek to make God "cognitively 'safe,' or controllable." But I do not agree that significant arguments from divine hiddenness against theism are to be associated with such expectations and demands. It is true that one can discern in some relevant comments of philosophers like Russell and Hanson assumptions and dispositions not unlike those mentioned here. But it is important for students of our subject to recognize that the work of these philosophers contains considerably less than a careful and thorough discussion of the problem of divine hiddenness. (Indeed, those old discussions are nearly as frivolous as the demands they embody.[13]) And it is equally important to note that contemporary atheistic discussion – which happens to provide the impetus for this debate! – is much more thorough and serious, and endorses none of the aforementioned assumptions and dispositions. (Indeed, readers should by now be able to tell that an atheist may – albeit with opposite results – place quite as much emphasis on "filial" relationship with God as does Moser.) A main point to be made in reply to Moser, therefore, is that his discussion has limited applicability, and in particular, little relevance to arguments of the sort that have been put forward more recently, on the basis of which I would defend atheism. Indeed, the more challenging arguments from divine hiddenness can accept most of what he says, beginning where he *ends* by, for example, pointing out that many of those whose "hearts are willingly attuned to God's self-giving transformative love" and who by any relevant standard "seek God aright" do not find themselves with evidence sufficient for theistic belief.

13 Russell, "Talk of the Town"; Hanson, *What I Do Not Believe.*

Another way of putting this point involves making a distinction between what we might call "easy" and "hard" problems of divine hiddenness. While Moser has, I think, solved some of the former, the latter are untouched by what he says.[14]

Now a tempting strategy for theists, and one Moser at times suggests he would endorse, involves *extending* the solutions offered for what I am calling the easy problems so as to make them apply to the harder ones as well. Thus we might say, for example, that the individuals referred to by my Analogy Argument who apparently are seeking God aright in fact are (or may well be) *prevented* from doing so by some hidden flaw, maybe a well-disguised self-seeking agenda. Or perhaps we will say, as Moser does in his piece, that it is in God's "appointed time" that the evidence will appear, not necessarily when we demand to have it. But the former reply ignores the fact that in the case of many who seek God, all our direct evidence – and strong evidence it is – supports the integrity of the search. Where, given such circumstances, critics continue to claim that an inhibiting culpability may well be present, the influence of a previously acquired theism is generally unmistakable, and the claim can therefore be seen to be one that nontheists have no reason to accept.[15] The latter reply neglects to notice, as already suggested, that many who seek God do so *humbly*, and that when we have established a theologically sensitive criterion for determining when and how God's presence will be felt – "a morally transforming sign [will be available to] seekers actively open to moral transformation toward God's moral character" – we are not in a position to say to those who *satisfy* it that it may not yet be God's appointed time.

I therefore find nothing either explicit or suggested in Moser's essay to show that the *hard* problems of hiddenness may not generate arguments justifying atheistic belief in certain circumstances. Of course, as he points out, "a *generalized* argument for atheism . . . seems not to emerge from divine hiddenness" (my emphasis). But here again we have only a solution to an *easy* problem: namely, the problem of showing how at any rate some individuals – theists convinced of the reality of God's presence in their lives – may evade the force of such an argument. (That the argument may in certain circumstances be thus evaded is admitted in my essay.) It does not follow at all, as he also claims, that *no one* has reason to become an atheist because of divine hiddenness. Perhaps the idea is that, given the seriousness of the issue, individuals investigating the existence of the God of traditional theism need to continue in this indefinitely, at *various* levels of life (emotional, moral, spiritual, intellectual), without succumbing to the belief that God does not exist. The underlying point here about thoroughness and conscientiousness is well taken. But, considered as a whole, this view is flawed; for it neglects the fact that belief is not a voluntary affair – indeed,

14 I do not mean to imply that there is nothing of value in Moser's discussion. *Within its limits*, his points are often insightful, and may well prove useful, especially for those who are already theists. But they do not seem to me to come to grips with any but the less difficult problems for theism posed by divine hiddenness.

15 Here we see another way (to which I allude in n. 14) in which Moser's arguments are sometimes limited. At times a "confessional" tone is evident: e.g., "God is hidden only in God's unique superhuman love" – and the argument or claim turns out to be one that only those who are *already theists* could conceivably have reason to accept without further defense.

such investigation as this view recommends may *itself* at some stage produce the belief in question, without the investigator being able to do anything (short of self-deception) to change it. Further, given the impartial interest in the truth that ought to be the motive for any such investigation, it is hard to see how – without assuming that the traditional God exists – investigators may avoid the obligation of equally scrupulous investigation of *other* serious conceptions of the Ultimate. Such investigation may of course turn up evidence that produces religious belief of *another* kind, and the truth of atheistic claims may be seen to follow by implication. (That traditional atheism may be produced in this manner is often neglected by contemporary philosophers of religion, whose own main interests and investigations are often restricted to Western perspectives.) Given these facts, and given that the arguments concealed by Moser's discussion can seem very forceful, and his own understanding of justification ("justifiers can vary from person to person; my justifiers need not be yours"), which I endorse – given all these things, I say, it seems evident that atheism may, in certain (commonly realized) circumstances, be justified by an argument from divine hiddenness.[16]

Reply to Schellenberg

Schellenberg characterizes his talk of divine hiddenness "as referring simply . . . to the absence of some kind of positive experiential result in the search for God." The absence of such an experiential result, he suggests, illustrates the absence of convincing evidence for the existence of God. Schellenberg contends that there is in fact an absence of the required positive experiential result in the search for God. So he recommends atheism regarding "the *traditional* God: a separate but infinite consciousness, a personal and perfect creator of the universe." Two arguments underwrite his atheism: the Analogy Argument and the Conceptual Argument. I shall explain why each argument fails to justify atheism.

1 The Analogy Argument

The argument begins with some imaginary cases where a small child seeks his mother but fails to find her. Schellenberg draws the following analogy:

> God is (and has often been) hidden from many human beings: sought but not found. Some persons start out assured of the power and presence of God in their lives, and then *lose* all this – in the typical case because of reasoning that engenders doubt about the reliability of the support they have for theistic belief. And though they grieve what they have lost and seek to regain it, looking for God in all the old familiar places as well as

16 I do not say that Moser has intentionally concealed the harder problems. I am sure he has not. For one reason or another, however, they are still frequently given short shrift by theistic philosophers.

> in new, unfamiliar locales, they fail to do so: God seems simply absent, and their belief is gone. . . . [A] divine answer to their calls is not forthcoming.

Schellenberg assumes, in addition, that a loving God would "seek to provide a quick response" to every serious request made of God by human seekers. His analogical inference is that "very probably, a God who could help it would never be hidden" in the circumstances in question. Such hiddenness seems real, however, for some seekers; so, Schellenberg concludes, "we have a powerful reason to believe that God does not exist."

The argument fails on at least two counts. First, we have no evidence available for the key assumption that "a divine answer to [some seekers'] calls is not forthcoming." Even *if* a divine answer has not come *yet*, it's an altogether open question whether a divine answer is *forthcoming*. The claim that a divine answer is not *forthcoming* makes obvious reference to the future. It implies that such an answer is not *approaching* the seekers in question, that the future does not hold such an answer for them. Schellenberg, however, gives no evidence whatever in support of such a future-referring assumption; nor is the needed evidence for such an assumption otherwise available to us.

For all we know, and for all Schellenberg's Analogy Argument shows, God *could* decisively answer all sincere seekers within a short time of your reflecting on this idea. Perhaps God actually has no reason to do this, but God (*so far as we know*) could do this. This objection involves no general Humean criticism of inductive inference. It rather involves Schellenberg's failure to supply evidence concerning a response *forthcoming* from God. Many sane, sincere people have received, after due seeking, a response from God. Schellenberg offers no evidence to suppose that his unanswered seekers will not be similarly answered by God. So Schellenberg's Analogy Argument does not deliver its atheistic conclusion even as a probabilistic inference. The Analogy Argument is thus rationally unconvincing.

The second defect concerns the assumption that a loving God would "seek to provide a quick response" to every serious seeker. Schellenberg offers no good evidence in support of this questionable assumption; nor is any such evidence otherwise available to us. God may want to develop deeper yearning for God in all seekers and therefore delay response for a while. An all-loving God could, moreover, have other reasons for avoiding a quick response. So God would not have to meet our hasty schedules. Schellenberg's case, at any rate, lacks needed support for the questionable requirement of a quick response from God. Even if a loving human mother would seek a quick response to her lost child, God could have loving purposes that go beyond those of the human mother. God can anticipate and influence ultimate outcomes in a way that a human mother cannot. So, with an eye toward human character transformation, God can exhibit effective patience and subtlety in a manner foreign to a human mother. Schellenberg neglects this important *disanalogy* between God and human mothers. As a result, the Analogy Argument fails to be rationally convincing on a second count.

At most, the Analogy Argument supports a *limited agnosticism*, the view that some (but not all) people should withhold judgment for now on God's existence (i.e., believe neither that God exists nor that God does not exist). Since the argument does not entail the probability that no future response from God will come, it does not support atheism at all. So, from the standpoint of the Analogy Argument, Schellenberg's atheism is altogether unwarranted.

2 The Conceptual Argument

This argument assumes that the concept of divine love implies that "if God exists, evidence sufficient to form belief in God is available to everyone capable of a personal relationship with God and not inclined to resist such evidence." An all-loving God would "necessarily seek personal relationship with *all* individuals [who are suitably receptive], and . . . such seeking entails the provision of evidence sufficient for belief in the existence of God." In supporting this position, Schellenberg claims that "it is logically impossible for you to hear God speak to you . . . while *not believing that there is a God.*" This is false. It rests on a confusion of (a) hearing God and (b) hearing God *as* (interpreted as) God. We have no reason whatever to think that (a) requires (b). Likewise, ordinary hearing of a human person does not require hearing that person *as* (interpreted as) that person. One can hear a voice, for instance, without (correctly) identifying the source of that voice. So people may actually hear God through conscience without correctly identifying the "voice" of conscience as God.

At least two additional problems undermine the Conceptual Argument. First, Schellenberg's requirement that evidence of God be *available* to all sincere seekers is interpreted in such a way that it falls prey to the second defect of the Analogy Argument. The Conceptual Argument assumes that God must give a quick response to seekers, but we have no reason whatever to accept this assumption. An all-loving God can reply, at an opportune time, with patience and subtlety so as to foster certain desirable traits in human seekers (e.g., humility, patience). God can be all-loving while being free of many of the anxieties found in human seekers. Second, the kind of evidence, or "positive experiential result," demanded by Schellenberg is too vague to warrant atheism. My essay referred to a kind of character transformation in relationship with God. This is evidence of God possessed by many sane and sincere people. The Conceptual Argument does not show, either deductively or inductively, that such evidence will not be received, at an opportune time, by Schellenberg's unanswered seekers. Hence, the Conceptual Argument does not warrant atheism.

3 Conclusion

Jewish-Christian theism does not yield answers to all available questions about God's subtle ways with humans; nor should we expect it to do so. Even so, in our broad ignorance of God's ways, we can see that neither the Analogy Argument nor the Conceptual Argument warrants atheism. So far as those arguments go, divine hiddenness offers no real threat to reasonable belief that the Jewish-Christian God actually exists and loves us all.

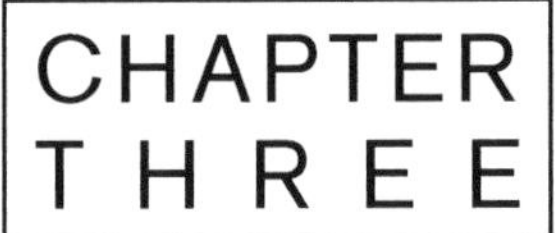

Does Science Discredit Religion?

In this debate, John Worrall argues that there are irreconcilable differences between science and religion. A fundamental difference pertains to methodology: science evaluates candidates for belief only on the basis of evidence, while religion patently does not. So, Worrall concludes that a properly scientifically minded person cannot give credence to religious belief. Del Ratzsch argues that the relation between religion and science is much less clear than that, and that the arguments that science discredits religion are not nearly so powerful as some have believed.

Science Discredits Religion

John Worrall

> *We get the ages of rock, and they get the rock of ages; we work out how the heavens go and they work out how to get to heaven.*
>
> – Old saying amongst *some* scientists

> *Strong Son of God, immortal love,*
> *Whom we, who have not seen Thy face,*
> *By faith, and faith alone, embrace,*
> *Believing where we cannot prove.*
>
> – Tennyson, *In Memoriam*

1 Introduction

Science and religion are in irreconcilable conflict – or so I shall argue in this chapter. There is no way in which you can be *both* properly scientifically minded *and* a true religious believer.

This might seem a surprising thesis in view of the undoubted fact that many scientists (even some of the most eminent ones) were or are also religious believers of one sort or another. But this results, I hold, from a mixture of three factors: (i) a simple failure to think things through fully; (ii) a failure to be properly scientific (as I shall explain, this involves more than simply giving due weight to well-accredited scientific results and theories, it also involves bringing a scientific attitude to the appraisal of claims and the weighing of evidence in general); (iii) adopting the attitude hinted at in the first of my epigraphs – one that holds that science and religion not only do not conflict, they *cannot* conflict, because they cover quite different domains.

The structure of my argument is very simple. I begin by analyzing the attitude just mentioned in (iii), arguing that, when properly understood, that attitude is (essentially) untenable for a religious person – the cost of adopting it is too high. This entails that both the scientist and the religious believer are playing the same game; they are both making substantive, descriptive, "explanatory" claims about the way the world is. But then they must surely also play by the same rules – all such claims must be judged by how well they stand up to the evidence. This, of course, is indeed how claims in science are appraised and accredited. When religious claims are appraised in this way, however, they all turn out to be untenable. Science, or rather a scientific attitude, is incompatible with religious belief.

2 Two Separate Domains?

The view is perhaps increasing in popularity that science and religion are about different domains, are two different "non-overlapping magisteria" (NOMA), as the eminent biologist Stephen Jay Gould recently put it,[1] and hence that, when properly understood, there can be no conflict between them. I can see three ways in which that view might be interpreted.

On one interpretation the view simply attempts to legislate away any clash by creating a separate, "spiritual reality," alongside ordinary "material reality" – science teaches us about the latter, religion about the former. But this is based on a confusion – it elevates a (perhaps natural, but clearly sloppy) way of speaking into an obviously untenable ontological doctrine. There is only one reality; that reality either does or does not contain a god, an afterlife, or whatever, just as it either does or does not contain quarks or superstrings or whatever; and the question that needs to be addressed about both sets of equally unobservable (alleged) entities is what evidence

1 See S. J. Gould, *Rocks of Ages: Science and Religion in the Fullness of Life* (London: Jonathan Cape, 2001).

we have for their existence.[2] To take an analogy: defenders of the paranormal, like Uri Geller, may speak loosely of "another reality" beyond the mundane one, but what they really mean of course is that extrasensory perception and psychokinetic powers are aspects of *this* reality – what else could they mean? If what they claim to be true is true, then ESP and psychokinetic powers are parts of this reality (what else?). The question is simply whether what they say *is* true (or rather, since they are talking about (alleged) things that are not directly observable, whether there is good evidence that what they say is true). If religion is committed to making allegedly factual assertions about the world, whether about its material *or* (supposed) spiritual aspects, then science and religion seem to be two competing "magisteria," not distinct ones.

Or are they? On a second way of understanding the NOMA view (perhaps to be thought of as a refinement of the first), religion does indeed make descriptive, factual assertions about the universe – even about some of its "material" aspects – but there is no conflict because religion kicks in only once science has gone as far as it can. Newton's theory may have given a perfect explanation of the movements of the planets (let's suppose), but of course it gives no explanation of how those planets were created. Religion should avoid interfering in the law-governed "mundane" reality of planetary motions (religious sentiments led even Newton himself to make a mistake here), but it comes into its own at the level of creation. One problem with this version of the view, as the example illustrates, is that the line between what science can explain and what it cannot has a habit of shifting – we do now have well-accredited theories of the formation of the solar system, ones radically at odds with those invented earlier by theists.

But, shifting or not, there always *is* a line – at any stage in science, there will be features of the universe (those described by the most fundamental theories then available) that science treats as "bottom line": being most fundamental exactly means that those theories cannot (to repeat: cannot *at that stage in science*) themselves be explained. The suggestion, then, might be that religion can penetrate to a deeper level, by explaining why those scientifically basic theories are true; and that there is no clash because, by definition, science has nothing to say at that deeper level. But think what such a claim would entail. Surely, in order to count not as mere speculative assertions, but as genuine *explanations*, any such ideas presented by religion would have to carry some rational warrant. But, on the assumption that there is only one set of standards for appraising substantive explanatory claims about the world in the light of evidence, this makes this second interpretation of the NOMA view incoherent. If all explanations involving substantive, synthetic claims about the world must satisfy the same criteria, then it is simply nonsense to claim that religion can explain the scientifically inexplicable. To deny the assumption and assert instead that there are different standards of explanation in the different fields is simple relativism. And I assume that this is acceptable to no one in this debate. For one thing, if we allow

2 Those of you who may have heard of "multi-universe" interpretations of quantum mechanics should not be confused. According to such interpretations (which, by the way, have precious little to recommend them), *the* universe has many (causally non-connected) sub-parts. (Again, there is nothing else they could mean!)

different standards for explanations in religion, why not also in the study of the paranormal, or voodoo or scientology or . . . and so the list goes on? (I will address this view again, from a somewhat different angle, later.)

I take it, then, that the only coherent version of the NOMA doctrine, the only one that thoughtful commentators might really want to defend, is quite different from the two so far considered. This third version sees religion as advancing no *descriptive* doctrine at all, as making no real claims about the way the world really is, but "only" as making claims about what is and what is not valuable, what is and what is not a worthwhile life. This view concedes to science exclusive rights to inform us about the world of fact (understood in the broad sense to include general structural features) and accepts that religion is restricted to the world of value. This is certainly the version advocated by Gould:

> Science tries to document the factual character of the natural world, and to develop theories that coordinate and explain these facts. Religion, on the other hand, operates in the equally important, but utterly different realm of human purposes, meanings and values – subjects that the factual domain of science might illuminate, but can never resolve.[3]

Obviously, this view of religion does indeed eliminate any possibility of a clash between it and science.[4] But at what a price! (My advice here to religious people would be to avoid scientists bearing gifts.) For one thing, the religious person who adopts this view cannot call on any of the usual justifications for whatever value system she endorses. She cannot, for example, claim that one ought to "love thy neighbor as thyself" *because* this is what pleases our loving creator. This justification, of course, along with any of its ilk, involves a claim of exactly the sort from which she must now abstain. Avoiding the conflict in this way means abstaining from asserting *any* descriptive claim – not just specific claims about Adam and Eve or the Virgin Birth or the like that thoughtful religious people often have difficulty with in any case, but also more general ones about our possessing souls, or even about the universe being the creation of a superhuman "entity" or "force" – and treating all such claims as, at best, merely metaphorical.

I concede to no one in my appreciation of the importance of issues about what sorts of lives are valuable, and about ethical issues more generally. But coming to a view on such issues is surely not the exclusive prerogative of religious people. (Gould acknowledges this and in fact quietly takes the "magisterium" of "religion" to consist in the discussion of ethical issues, whether or not based on religion in the more usual sense.[5]) More centrally for current purposes, it seems very doubtful that a religious faith stripped of any substantive descriptive claim about the universe, its history, and its creation can really count as a religious *belief*. The theologian Ian Barbour surely has it right:

3. Gould, *Rocks of Ages*, p. 4.

4 Actually it isn't *so* obvious – there is a substantial literature examining the issue of whether the domains of fact and value are logically distinct. Nonetheless, it is true.

5 "[I] construe as fundamentally religious (literally, binding us together) all moral discourse on principles that might activate the ideal of universal fellowship among people" (Gould, *Rocks of Ages*, p. 62).

> [R]eligious language does indeed express and evoke distinctive attitudes. It does encourage self-commitment to a way of life; it acknowledges allegiance to ethical principles and affirms the intention to act in particular ways. But . . . these *non-cognitive uses* presuppose *cognitive beliefs*. . . . [R]eligious faith is not simply assent to the truth of propositions; but it does require the assumption that certain propositions are true. It would be unreasonable to adopt or recommend a way of life unless one believes that the universe is of such a character that this way of life is appropriate.[6]

And once a religious faith "requires" such beliefs about the universe, then the clash with science (or more accurately the scientific attitude) is inevitable. Or so I now go on to argue.

3 Three Types of Religious Belief, Three Types of Clash with Science

Many beliefs about the world, its origins, and structure have been, and are, held in the name of religion. In order to examine carefully the issue of whether science and religion clash, we need to differentiate at least three types.

Into the *first* category fall quite specific beliefs about the universe and its history that some believers have certainly held (and in some cases presently hold) on the basis of their religion, but which are directly inconsistent with well-accredited scientific theories. One example is the claim that the earth is stationary in absolute space and that the sun and other planets orbit it; another is the claim that there were two humans, Adam and Eve, who had no ancestors, either human or human-like, and of whom all humans are descendants (or, more generally, the claim that the universe was created with essentially the same flora and fauna it presently exhibits in 4004 BC). I shall take it that no one seriously disputes that such claims are indeed inconsistent with well-accredited scientific theories.[7] However, no serious thinker any longer feels the need to defend the first claim on biblical grounds – even the Vatican now thinks that its attack on Galileo, and his Copernican allies, was a mistake (though it did take it until 1820 to remove Copernicus's *De Revolutionibus* from its Index of forbidden books). And none but a few (though very noisy) fundamentalists still feel the need to defend the second claim on biblical grounds. Again, even the Vatican seems to have reconciled itself to the idea that evolutionary theory is more than a mere "hypothesis."

I shall not go into details about either of these particular claims or others of similar status. There is, of course, an enormous literature on such matters. I shall simply assume that the upshot of this literature is that,

(1) on the one hand, such claims *are* directly inconsistent with well-accredited scientific theories (and indeed that where this is true it is the erstwhile religious claim that must, from a rational point of view, give way);

6 Ian G. Barbour, *Myths, Models and Paradigms: A Comparative Study in Science and Religion* (San Francisco: Harper and Ran, 1974), p. 58.

7 Anyone in any remaining doubt about the ineradicable clash between so-called scientific creationism and real science should consult Philip Kitcher, *Abusing Science* (Cambridge, Mass.: MIT Press, 1982).

(2) while on the other hand, there is no need for a religious person to commit herself to any such precise claim. A person may remain, in a clear sense, a religious believer without committing herself to any such claim that is (or at any rate is so obviously) inconsistent with well-accredited scientific theories.

While having seemingly reconciled itself to the (likely) truth of Darwinism, the Vatican, if I have understood its position correctly, continues to insist that there is some point along the branch of the evolutionary tree from chemical molecules to current humans at which "souls" were "infused" into some organism.[8] Such a belief, along with other relatively general beliefs about souls and like "entities," falls into a *second* category. This, I suggest, is the category of beliefs that while not, perhaps, directly inconsistent with any well-accredited theory in science nonetheless seem to be in a clear and strong sense contraindicated by science.[9]

Nothing in neurophysiology is directly inconsistent with the claim that alongside the 10^{11} or so neurons in the human central nervous system with their chemically governed activity there is another entity called the "soul." (Any more than that Newtonian gravitational theory is directly inconsistent with the claim that the reason why every particle of matter in the universe attracts every other with a force proportional to the product of their masses and inversely proportional to the square of the distance between them is that each such particle possesses an immaterial mind which happens to will this to be the case.) It is just that neurophysiology has no need for such a hypothesis – the "soul" simply and increasingly has no role to play (any more than those particulate "minds" would have any role to play in gravitation theory). Neurophysiology is, of course, a science still very much in its infancy, but it has already made impressive strides in explaining, in its own – "purely material" – terms, phenomena such as memories and pains that earlier thinkers held were in some irreducible sense "mental" and hence required some sort of "mind" or "spirit" whose properties and states they were. The religiously inclined could, then, readily identify the "soul" with such a "mind" or "spirit." But minds or spirits separate from bodies are no longer seriously available. There remain interesting and challenging issues about whether or not human psychology is fully "reducible" to the laws of nature governing matter. But these are to do with whether or not mental *properties* can be reduced to material properties – no serious scientist (even if religiously inclined) still holds any version of the Cartesian dualist view of a mental *substance* that is separate from the matter of the brain and central nervous system.

The reason why the soul can play no role, and why the idea of it gets in the way of proper scientific theorizing, is that the idea not only has no empirical support, it inevitably – in principle – can have no such support. There is reason to think (from the way that progressive science is going) that all the observable effects here are produced by neurophysiology, and that the "soul" can therefore itself have no observ-

8 See again the sympathetic treatment in Gould, *Rocks of Ages*.

9 Of course, I take it here that talk of souls and the like is to be understood in some "literal" sense – one that, if true, would make a factual difference to the way the world is – and not in any "metaphorical" sense, or sense that makes claims about the existence of souls some sort of hidden moral injunction. As already indicated, I readily concede that all "conflict" between science and religion can be eliminated by going fully "metaphorical" or restricting religious claims entirely to claims about values.

able causal effects. There is a principle of good scientific reasoning, sometimes called "Occam's razor," that is incorporated in one form or other into every sensible system of scientific confirmation, and which states that if some notion plays no role in – if it can be excised without cognitive loss from – our system of knowledge, then it should be so excised. This principle is uniformly applied within science itself. The nineteenth-century idea of a space-filling aether – a mechanical medium that was alleged to be the seat of the electromagnetic field (and earlier the carrier of the disturbances that constitute light) – is now rejected by physics. But the notion was rejected not because it is actually inconsistent with any new, well-accredited scientific theory, but rather because it is – provably – otiose. Once we have the real science, in this case the special and general theories of relativity, then further postulating the aether makes no empirical difference – not only is there no empirical evidence of its existence, there *cannot be* any such evidence. The same applies to this sort of intermediate second category of religious claim, exemplified by the idea of the soul.

This second category of religious belief slides over into a third. Beliefs in this third category are the most general of all. One example would be a general belief that the universe was created by (whatever that might actually mean) a superhuman power (whatever that might actually be). A retreat to claims in this third category may bring with it, for the religious person, the advantage of avoiding the need to account for why two religious persons selected at random from the world's population are likely to have apparently quite different specific beliefs – those differences being clearly correlated with accidents of birth, culture, and geography. What you are likely to believe about the speed of light or the half-life of particular isotopes of uranium, if you hold any such beliefs at all, is unlikely to depend on whether you were born and educated in Shanghai, Sydney, or Suez. But what *specific* religious beliefs you are likely to hold, assuming you hold any, *are* highly dependent on where you were born and educated. This fact, which surely ought to be disturbing for the thinking believer, may, perhaps, be nullified if one resorts to the very general level of belief – perhaps all religious people agree that the universe is the creation of some sort of superhuman power, and perhaps all the more specific claims should be thought of as merely metaphorical (and it must be said, then, pretty misleading) ways of endorsing that general one. (I take it that something like this is what J. S. Haldane had in mind when he claimed that "behind the recognized churches, there is an unrecognised church to which all may belong."[10])

A general claim of this kind not only fails to be inconsistent with any scientific claim, the structure of science itself guarantees its consistency. Let me first explain why this is so, and then why I, nonetheless, hold that belief in even such general claims is unscientific.

Explanation in science is essentially derivative. In order to avoid unnecessary complexities, assume we are back in the nineteenth century before relativity theory superseded Newtonian "classical" physics. If you had asked a scientist at that time why it is that the planets move in the way they do – why, for example, they move in (somewhat perturbed) elliptical orbits around the sun – he would have had a ready answer. He could show that the assertion that the planets move in that way follows logically

10 Gifford Lecture, 1927; quoted from Gould, *Rocks of Ages*, p. 92.

from Newton's theory of mechanics plus universal gravitation (actually together with an "initial condition" about the planet's velocity). *Given* that every material particle in the universe attracts every other with a force proportional to the product of their masses and inversely proportional to the square of the distance between them, then it follows that a planet must move in a (roughly) elliptical orbit around the sun. But suppose you asked such a nineteenth century scientist to explain in turn the "given" in that initial explanation – to explain why Newton's theory itself is true, not why he *thought* it was true (a question about evidence) but, assuming for the sake of argument that it is true, why the universe obeys Newton's theory rather than any other. Why, for example, is the gravitational force inversely proportional to the square of the distance rather than, say, to the cube of the distance? Our nineteenth-century physicist would be nonplussed by this question. Again, he can readily explain how he "*knows*" that it's the square of the distance – that assumption and only that assumption yields the right observational results – but we are now considering an ontological question, not an epistemological one: that of why the universe happens to obey this particular law (assuming that it does) rather than any other. And the only answer to that question that our physicist could give would be some variation on the theme of "that's the way the cookie crumbles." Relative to the state of science at the time, it had to be taken as just a "brute fact" that the universe instantiates Newton's theory.

Nothing, of course, prevents a scientist from *attempting* to go deeper, from attempting to explain why Newton's theory holds. Indeed, one eminent scientist who endorsed that attempt was Isaac Newton himself – he famously denied that gravity could be an "essential property" of matter, and hence denied that his theory could be the *ultimate* explanatory "bottom line." Newton was tempted by a Cartesian-style explanation of gravity in terms of some pressure gradient in an all-pervading elastic aether (though he himself established that Descartes's own particular explanation along these lines was hopeless). Suppose that Newton had succeeded, that he had produced a theory about the constitution of a space-filling plenum, pressures in which gave bodies a tendency to move towards one another in accordance with his principle of universal gravitation. The logical point would of course remain: while we would then have an explanation for the state of affairs described by Newton's theory, the facts about this plenum and its properties that did the explaining would then themselves be unexplained; *those* facts would be – as science would then have stood – unexplained explainers. Explanation must always start somewhere, no matter what stage science has achieved. Yesterday's "brute facts" may indeed become today's explained facts – if so, then science has made progress; but the logic of scientific explanation makes the existence of some "brute facts" inevitable at any stage.

This is what provides the (logically inevitable) latitude for the religiously inclined. Since the attempt to reduce gravity to the actions of an aether failed, the poor scientist cannot explain why the force of gravity between two bodies happens to be inversely proportional to the square of the distance between them; but the religious person, it seems, has no problem – that's how the creator willed it to be. Or, to take a more up-to-date example, the scientific cosmologist cannot explain why it was that the so-called escape velocity of matter at "Planck time" shortly after the Big Bang had the value it did – she must just take it as a "brute fact" (in that case a brute fact reflecting an "initial condition" rather than a law of nature). The religious person can, as always, "explain" that value by invoking a creator and his wishes – and indeed can, in that case, add a little more to the story, as we "know" on scientific grounds that if the value of that escape velocity had been just a little different than it in fact was, then galaxies (and hence humans) could never have formed. God fixed the value of the escape velocity because he wanted it to be possible for humans to evolve.

Although the structure of science inevitably leaves religion free to *claim* it can give "deeper" explanations than science, what could *warrant* such claims? As I explained earlier, a version of the "no conflict" (NOMA) account can be developed by allowing different standards for explanations in the two fields. But only, as we saw, at the surely unacceptable cost of adopting a purely relativistic viewpoint. If, as I urge, we refuse to pay that cost, then the credentials of these alleged religious explanations must be examined in the same way, by the same standards, as are scientific explanations; but if judged in that way, then those alleged explanations fail.

Notice, first, that once everyone is playing by the same (exacting) rules, then any claim that religion is in a superior position from the point of view of explaining the world is logically misplaced. A religious explanation in terms of a creator and his intentions is just another (attempted) explanation, and, even were it accepted, then, exactly as the request for an explanation of the latest scientific theory can always be made, so we can request an explanation of the religious claim: Why did the creator choose an inverse square law rather than, say, an inverse cube one? Why was the possibility of human evolution part of the creator's plan? The idea that religion can do what science cannot by "explaining everything" is an illusion.

This shows that the religious "explanation" can, at best, achieve parity – in fact, parity is far beyond its reach. Let's retreat just a little and ask why it was, for example, that the attempt to explain the law of gravity in terms of pressure gradients in a plenum was eventually deemed to be a failure. It could obviously and trivially simply have been claimed that there is an all-pervading medium and that – without specifying exactly how – there just happen to be pressure gradients set up in it that account for the gravitational attraction. But such an "explanation" would never be accepted in science because it is entirely *ad hoc* (in the pejorative sense) – it permits no independent test. All the alleged explanation does is to deliver what we already know – indeed, in the form I gave it, it was precisely designed so as to deliver that and only that.

A successful explanation, one that will be accepted in science, on the contrary, is independently testable and passes independent tests – that is, it not only entails the results it set out to entail, it also makes, often surprising, and hitherto unsuspected, empirical predictions which turn out to be correct. Independent testability and success in independent tests are the key to scientific progress.[11] The explanation of Kepler's laws of planetary motion by Newton's theory was a scientific success (and the theory was correspondingly regarded as empirically highly confirmed), because that theory turned out to entail not only those laws (or rather, in fact, a modified version of them) but also a range of other testable predictions – about the precession of the equinoxes,

11 See, e.g., Lakatos, "Falsification and the Methodology of Scientific Research Programmes," repr. in *Philosophical Papers*, vol. 1 (Cambridge: Cambridge University Press, 1974).

the return of Halley's comet, and so on (and later of the existence of a hitherto unsuspected planet), all of which turned out to be correct. The wave theory of light, developed by the French physicist Fresnel in the early nineteenth century, not only explained known optical effects, like reflection and refraction, it also turned out correctly to predict the existence of hitherto unsuspected and surprising phenomena – such as that the center of the (geometrical) shadow of a small opaque disc held in light diverging from a point source is illuminated, and illuminated just as strongly as if no obstacle were held in the light's path.

The "explanation" of, say, the facts revealed by Newton's theory or the value of the "escape velocity" of matter (or, of course, of any other feature of the universe) by the postulation that those facts reflect the wishes of a creator is, on the contrary, essentially non-independently testable. It is not just that such postulations happen to fail to be independently testable as yet. They can never in principle be subjected to independent tests – precisely because, unlike real successful explanations, they are explicitly designed to yield the already known facts (inverse square attraction, value of the "escape velocity") *and nothing more.*

Science not only declines to accept theories that fail to be independently testable, it positively rejects them. When a whole series of investigators, including, as I mentioned, Newton himself, consistently failed to produce any deeper account of gravity in terms of pressure gradients in a mechanical medium that was independently testable, then science adopted the view that there was no such deeper account to be had, and, despite initial reservations, accepted that matter just does act on other matter at a distance. Similarly, the initial reaction to Maxwell's postulation of the electromagnetic field was that such a field could not simply be a mysterious, primitive feature of the universe; the electric and magnetic field strengths at each point of space had to reflect the contortions of some underlying mechanical space-filling medium (our old friend, the aether). But when a whole series of investigators (again including, interestingly enough, the chief scientific innovator, in this case Maxwell) tried and failed to produce "mechanical models" of the field that were independently testable and independently confirmed, science came reluctantly to the view that the field is indeed a *sui generis*, independent, primitive part of the furniture of the universe – that is, the mechanical aether, at least as an underpinning of the electromagnetic field, was rejected.

I conclude that this third and most general type of religious belief, although not actually inconsistent with any substantive scientific theories, nonetheless runs counter to the practices that have informed successful science; and hence such beliefs, too, are unscientific. Some particular religious beliefs are inconsistent with well-accredited scientific theories, but all are inconsistent with a scientific attitude. Religious belief must, as Tennyson so eloquently reminds us in the second of my two epigraphs, rely on faith; and faith is unscientific.

4 Objections, Complexities, and Some Food for Further Thought

Not everyone who has contributed to the – very extensive – literature on the relationship between science and religion is likely to be convinced by the above argument. (Indeed, this may count as one of the all-time understatements, even by customary English standards!) In a longer treatment, objections would need to be met, complexities unraveled, and, above all, further confusions exposed and clarified. Let me end by indicating – in rough outline – some of the necessary elaborations, if only in an attempt to facilitate further thinking about the issue.

4.1 Belief in science

I have talked so far as if science and religion were two (conflicting) ways of generating beliefs about the world. In fact, however, the relationship between science and (outright) belief is not at all straightforward. As recent studies have underlined, it would be a bold thinker who, in view of the history of radical theory change in science, believed that our currently accepted best fundamental theories are true. If any sort of belief concerning those fundamental theories is rationally mandated, it is at best a belief in their *approximate* truth, which really amounts to the meta-level belief that those theories will be retained in "limiting-case form" in any future replacement theories. (Einstein's relativity theory is logically inconsistent with Newtonian theory, but yields the latter as a fully adequate approximation for cases of bodies moving at velocities small compared to that of light.) Outright belief – if reasonable at all – would be reserved for statements of evidence and, perhaps, for lower-level theories (such as that matter has *some sort* of atomic structure) that seem so firmly entrenched that their replacement is inconceivable. (This is reflected in the currently most popular formal account of the relationship between theory and evidence in science – personalist Bayesianism. This sees rational agents as assigning probabilities (short of 1) to explanatory theories – probability 1 (effective certainty) being reserved for statements of evidence and of "background knowledge."[12]) I need hardly say perhaps that this, if correct, *sharpens* the clash between science and religion: if outright belief at least in fundamental, explanatory theories is not rational – that is, not scientific – even in science, despite their enormous empirical success, then the same must apply *a fortiori* to religious explanatory claims, which have no empirical success at all.

4.2 Kuhnian "commitment" in science

In his interesting book *Myths, Models and Paradigms*, Ian Barbour suggests that developments in the philosophy of science – notably in Thomas Kuhn's *The Structure of Scientific Revolutions* (1962) – have reduced the differences between science and religion to differences of degree, rather than kind. Barbour's argument merits a more systematic rebuttal than can be given here. My response, however, is that it relies on

12 See, e.g., C. Howson and P. M. Urbach, *Scientific Reasoning: The Bayesian Approach*, 2nd edn (La Salle, Ill.: Open Court, 1993). I should add that there are a number of Bayesian, probabilistic arguments for religious claims that I lack space to consider here – see, e.g., R. Swinburne, "Argument from the Fine-tuning of the Universe," in J. Leslie (ed.), *Physical Cosmology and Philosophy* (New York: Macmillan, 1990). (Swinburne's argument is subjected to heavyweight criticism by Adolf Grünbaum in "A New Critique of Theological Interpretations of Cosmology," *British Journal for the Philosophy Science*, 51 (2000), pp. 1–43. See also Swinburne's reply in "Comments on Grünbaum," *British Journal for the Philosophy of Science*, 51 (2000), pp. 481–5. The arguments are tied to ideas about what can, and cannot, possibly count as an unexplained "brute fact." Those ideas are considered briefly below.

overinterpretation of Kuhn's views. Kuhn *does* suggest that successful, mature science requires "faith" in basic, paradigm-forming theories. Scientists must have faith in those theories in order, for example, not to promote "anomalies" into outright falsifications – holding that work within the paradigm will eventually solve them. However, nothing like religious faith is necessary here. Scientists' "commitments" are temporary, pragmatic, and defeasible. One needn't have believed in the absolute truth of Newton's theory in the nineteenth century to see that the anomalies for it posed by observations of Uranus's orbit were probably best dealt with within the Newtonian paradigm – ideas associated with that paradigm provided ways of approaching the problems with Uranus's orbit (perhaps, for example, there was another planet in the heavens, so far misidentified, and once its gravitational action on Uranus was taken into account, the anomaly would disappear). Whereas had a mid-nineteenth century scientist proposed to "abandon" Newtonian theory, he would have been left with absolutely no idea about how to proceed. Moreover, anomalies must eventually be resolved, and what counts as a resolution is clear and a fixed feature of science – scientific "faith" is temporary and eventually called to account (in this life!).

4.3 Worries about independent testability

My argument is oversimplified as it currently stands: not all accepted scientific explanations are independently testable. For example (there are many), the explanation of the failure to observe any stellar parallax that was (surely correctly) accepted in the seventeenth and eighteenth centuries was that there is indeed parallactic motion but available telescopes were not sufficiently powerful to observe it. (If we are on a moving observatory, the earth, then pairs of "fixed stars" ought to seem at least slightly further apart when we are at our nearest point to them than they do when we are furthest away.) This explanation itself was certainly not independently testable – it simply explained away the problem it was introduced to deal with. Is this not exactly like the religious "explanations" I have castigated as unscientific? But notice two things. First, the basic theories involved here – the Newtonian version of the Copernican view – were (massively) independently confirmed *in other areas, by other phenomena*. So the "faith" is underwritten. Moreover, the lack of independent testability of even the specific theory is again of temporary duration – if telescopes had continued to improve in accuracy and still no parallax was observed, then the Newtonian/Copernican view would have been in unambiguous trouble. The point about the difference between scientific and religious explanations therefore remains in tact.

4.4 Explanation as "understanding" or "making sense"

The discussion of the idea of scientific explanation has, in my view, been dogged from the beginning by certain associations of the word "explanation" that ought to be excised. It is natural to think that explanation has something to do with (human) understanding, or "making sense" of, the universe. The whole structure of scientific explanation surely shows, however, that this is a mistake – all such explanation is derivative, and that means that we don't ever really understand anything about the universe (why should we?). Instead, we simply attempt to describe it – eliminating minor mysteries (why do the planets move in ellipses?) in favor of major mysteries (why do all bodies attract one another in a certain way?).

An objection to this that certainly merits consideration is that even scientists allow that some theoretical claims "make sense" (reflect what can reasonably be taken as "natural" states of the universe), while others cannot be simply accepted as "brute facts" but *demand* explanation. It can then be argued that there are certain claims that must always remain brute facts on any scientific account (one much discussed contender is the fact that "there is something rather than nothing"[13]), but which cannot rationally be taken as brute, and that this therefore gives rational credit to religious claims which can explain them (and hence remove their erstwhile brutish character).

I can in response here only state my own view: namely, that all conceptions about what "makes sense" or what are plausibly "natural" states of the universe are historically conditioned by the successful research programs at the time, and hence are themselves subject to change in the light of the always dominant criterion of independent empirical support. Aristotelians demanded an explanation for any motion, Newtonians only for any *change* in motion; pre-quantum theory explanation in physics demanded a determinist theory, now that is no longer taken for granted; once Newtonian theory was established (and the aether-reductionist approach had failed), scientists were happy (for a while!) to take hitherto barely thinkable, action-at-a-distance as a brute fact. I hold, then, that there is no such thing as a fact that "cannot be taken as brute" – the sort of assumption that a scientist is happy to take as reflecting a brute fact is historically conditioned and historically variable.

4.5 Am I the victim of an evidentialist prejudice?

Finally, I have made it clear that my whole argument rests on the assumption that a rational, scientific person needs good evidence before admitting God into her world view, just as she would before admitting, say, electrons into it. Alvin Plantinga has mounted a well-known defense of the striking claim that belief in God can be "properly basic" – that is, taken to require no evidence.[14] Although again it requires detailed treatment which I cannot give here, I should at least indicate my response. This is that, on analysis, Plantinga's view amounts to no more than the obviously true descriptive claim that *some people as a matter of fact take* belief in God as basic. But this is no news, the question of course is whether or not they are *justified* in doing so; and, insofar as Plantinga has anything to say about this issue, it seems to rest on the sort of simple-minded relativism that I have throughout taken to be eschewed. His response, for example, to the obvious question of why in that case one couldn't take belief in a flat earth (or come to that, the innate superiority of the "Aryan" race) as "properly basic" seems to be simply that no Christian would in fact take – or is under any obligation to take – such beliefs as "properly basic." This, however, is plainly not the issue. The question is what such a Christian would say to someone

13 I cannot resist here citing Adolf Grunbaum's response to Richard Swinburne on this issue: "Surprisingly, Swinburne deems the existence of something or other to be 'extraordinary', i.e., literally out of the ordinary. To the contrary, surely, the most pervasively ordinary feature of our experience is that we are immersed in an ambiance of existence." ("New Critique," p. 3)

14 See, e.g., A. Plantinga, "Is Belief in God Properly Basic?", *Nous*, 15 (1981), pp. 41–51.

who *did* assert as "properly basic" (that is, on no basis at all) a claim that she, the Christian, found abhorrent – and, assuming that she would want to challenge that claim, how she would deal with the *tu quoque* objection. Long live evidentialism![15]

The Demise of Religion: Greatly Exaggerated Reports from the Science/Religion "Wars"

Del Ratzsch

> *The supernatural is being swept out of the universe in the flood of new knowledge of what is natural. It will soon be as impossible for an intelligent, educated man or woman to believe in a god as it is now to believe that the earth is flat, that flies can be spontaneously generated . . . or that death is always due to witchcraft.*
>
> – Julian Huxley[16]

This statement reflects a widespread intuition that the continuing triumphal march of science has resulted in religion gradually dissolving toward rational oblivion. In one of my earlier questing phases, that intuition seemed a welcome weapon against the demands of the particular religious beliefs I had been raised with. After a (sometimes rocky) reconciliation with the core of those beliefs, that intuition constituted a constant threat stalking the periphery of my world view. But neither weapon nor threat is genuine unless the picture of science inexorably destabilizing religious rationality is accurate. In what follows, I shall examine some of the justifications for that picture and will argue that they are inadequate. I come to this exploration with convictions contrary to, but not deeply hostile toward, that picture. I too have felt its force.

15 S. Wykstra, "Toward a Sensible Evidentialism: On the Notion of 'Needing Evidence'," in W. L. Rave and W. J. Wainwright (eds), *Philosophy of Religion: Selected Readings*, 3rd edn (Fort Worth, Tex.: Harcourt Brace, 1998), argues in response that Plantinga at least shows that we need a modified, more "sensible" evidentialism, because while everyone accepts that our access to electrons (if indeed they exist) is necessarily via inference, believers claim to have *direct access* to God. The important word here is "claim": what they are really saying is that, given their – clearly theoretical beliefs – they *take themselves* to be, in certain circumstances, in direct contact with God. But, contrary to Wykstra, the situation is precisely analogous in science, at least with respect to some theoretical entities: because of theories we accept (both about the nature of light and about our physiology), we take ourselves to be in regular (pretty well) direct contact with photons of various frequencies. In both cases the "access" is, whatever someone might believe, inferential; it relies on accepting a theoretical premise, and reasonable acceptance of such a premise requires an inference from evidence.

16 Julian Huxley, *Religion wihout Revelation* (New York: Mentor, 1957), p. 62.

1 Refutation: Some Preliminaries

The direst difficulty science could pose for religious belief would be direct scientific refutation of essential religious principles.[17] But refutation can emerge only out of genuine conflict, and that fact imposes some boundaries. For instance, many believe that science and religion operate in different domains or levels. If such positions are correct, there can be no genuine conflict. Any apparent conflict would represent trespassing or confusion. Furthermore, serious conflict between science and religious belief is possible only if *both* purport to be true. Consequently, if religious commitment is noncognitive or nonpropositional, genuine conflict seems impossible. It also follows that science taken anti-realistically (as in instrumentalism, social constructivism, etc.) poses minimal challenge. If the ultimate intent shaping science is mere empirical adequacy, or if the underlying engine of science is sexual dominance or the suppression of one's social competitors (as some allege), then whatever science says will have little rational force.

Suppose, however, that science can conflict with religion. Where would conflicts occur? For present purposes, we can separate religious claims into two rough categories: core beliefs shared by nearly every religion, and the more varied outlying beliefs constituting the specialized, characteristic beliefs of particular religious groups. The core usually includes the following:

1 A supernatural person – God – created the cosmos.
2 God cares about humans.
3 God ultimately controls cosmic and human history.
4 God can intervene in earthly events.
5 There is objective meaning/significance to human life, both now and after death.

There are only limited prospects of science contradicting that core. Plate tectonics, stellar and biological evolution, the periodic table, relativity, quantum mechanics, or other such results of science do not have even the appearance of contradicting any of the above. Evolution, for example, could be the means God used to achieve certain desired results, or the world could be quantum-mechanical because that is the way God wanted the cosmos to operate. If those claims are *coherent* (whether scientific or true), then the theories in question do not contradict (1)–(5).[18]

The typically cited "conflict" episodes nearly always involve specialized beliefs outside the core, such beliefs often being ascribed to special sources of information (e.g., revelation). For instance, many believers historically took the earth to be stationary, at the center of the cosmos. Some contemporary religious groups see the

17 Additional discussion of several relevant points can be found in my *Science and its Limits* (Downers Grove, Ill.: InterVarsity Press, 2000), and "Space Exploration and Challenges to Religion," *Monist*, 70/4 (Oct. 1987), pp. 101–13.

18 It might be countered that this sort of reference to God is empirically empty and adds no *content* to the scientific claims in question. That may or may not be true, but if it is true, then the proposition that *God made the world to be quantum-mechanical* is logically consistent if the claim that *the world is quantum-mechanical* is consistent. Religious claims cannot be simultaneously empirically empty *and* empirically refuted.

earth as quite young. Others take the basic kinds of organisms to be unchanged since the creation. These and other specialized religion-inspired claims are widely perceived as having been discredited by science. But would that be problematic for deeper religious belief? How would an anti-religious argument proceed from there? One line of thought is that such refutations undermine the claims to "revealed truth," and that since even the deeper core religious principles rest on that same source, they are thus rationally unsupported. A different line is that multiple consistent failures even of peripheral religious beliefs support an inductive case for the falsehood of religious principles in general, including the more fundamental core beliefs. Both will be discussed later.

2 Foundations: Deep Conflict?

Science would challenge religious belief were there principles essential to scientific method, scientific explanations, etc. which were thus presupposed in the very existence of science, and which conflicted with essential components of religion. For instance, Norman and Lucia Hall claim that there is a "fundamental incompatibility between the supernaturalism of traditional religion and the experimental method of science."[19] Is that correct?

2.1 The larger web

First, some cautions. Since most scientists historically were religious believers, we have to attribute intellectual blindness, self-deception, or hypocrisy to those scientists who missed this "fundamental incompatibility." But classifying Copernicus, Galileo, Newton, Kepler, Boyle, Maxwell, Faraday, Herschel, etc. as imperceptive or as religious hypocrites violates substantial historical evidence.[20] And since about 40 percent of current scientists classify themselves as believers, and even many who do not nonetheless see no fundamental *conflict* here, the present charge would indict the majority of scientists who ever lived as not fully grasping what they were doing. That seems implausible.

Furthermore, any science-based case against the rationality of religion must presume the rational justification of science itself, including its foundational presuppositions – the uniformity of nature, the basic reliability of human observation, the appropriateness of human conceptual and cognitive resources, etc. But science cannot straightforwardly establish the legitimacy of the foundations upon which it itself rests. If science is the only source of rational justification, then the foundational principles upon which science itself rests must be simply accepted on brute faith – effectively undermining a key purported distinction between science and religion. Otherwise, science's foundational presuppositions must obtain rational legitimation elsewhere.

19 Norman F. and Lucia K. B. Hall, "Is the War between Science and Religion Over?" *The Humanist*, May/June 1986, pp. 26–8: p. 27.

20 We cannot just let these scientists off the hook by claiming that the specific scientific facts and theories which generated problems were not yet known in their day, if the conflict flowed out of the very structure and necessary presuppositions of the scientific project itself in which they were intensely engaged.

Two things ensue. First, science could not be the *only* source of rational justification. Second, one question becomes inescapable: How does one give a non-circular *naturalistic* justification for the cognitive faculties we employ in science – that is, a justification, recognition of the rational adequacy of which does not itself rely on precisely the cognitive faculties whose justification is at issue?[21] Christian scientists in the past proposed religiously based solutions to justification problems. For instance, human observation and intellection could be trusted if properly employed, *given* that those faculties had been deliberately created in us for cognition of this cosmos. Although there are debates over details, historians of science no longer question the foundational role which religion – specifically, the doctrines of divine creation and divine voluntarism – played in the birth of modern science itself.[22]

Those foundations may be of more than merely historical interest. Despite centuries of development, science may not be disengaged from those roots even now. Physicist Paul Davies remarks that "Science began as an outgrowth of theology, and all scientists, whether atheists or theists . . . accept an essentially theological worldview."[23]

If Davies is right, prospects for anti-religious cases of the present sort are not promising, since science *still depends* upon foundational structures appropriated from its religious world view heritage, and thus seems unlikely to constitute a refutation of them.

2.2 Cases

Let us nonetheless look at two examples.

2.2.1 Naturalism: philosophical and methodological

Again, the Halls: "Science . . . assumes that there are no transcendent, immaterial forces and that all forces which do exist within the universe behave in an ultimately objective or random fashion. . . . [N]aturalism is the unifying theory for all of science."[24] But does science require philosophical naturalism? Many scientists – believers and nonbelievers – argue that science requires only *methodological* naturalism (sometimes called "methodological materialism," or "methodological atheism"). Advocates of this position argue that whether or not reality includes more than the natural realm, science by its very nature can deal only with the purely natural and must rigidly restrict itself to that realm. For instance, Eugenie Scott: "Science has made a little deal with itself; because you can't put God in a test tube (or keep it [sic] out of one) science acts as if the supernatural did not exist. This methodological material-

21 Darwin himself worried about this. See his July 3, 1881, letter to William Graham, in *The Life and Letters of Charles Darwin*, ed. Francis Darwin (New York: n.p., 1889).

22 In fact, some historians of science believe that scientific method was developed *as* empirical and experimental precisely *because*, as early scientists saw it, given the doctrine that God had created *freely*, unhampered by substantive constraints, science had to actually *look* to see how the cosmos was structured and governed.

23 Paul Davies, *Are We Alone?* (New York: Basic Books, 1995), p. 138.

24 Hall and Hall, "Is the War between Science and Religion Over," pp. 26–7 (lengthy ellipsis).

ism is the cornerstone of modern science."[25] On this version of methodological naturalism, science must pretend that what it cannot control does not exist, and so must operate *as if* there is no supernatural realm.[26]

It is evident that whether or not there is a nonnatural realm, the methods that science would employ and the results that science would obtain presupposing philosophical naturalism would be identical to those it would obtain employing methodological naturalism of this sort.[27] There is thus no *scientific* reason for insisting on philosophical, as opposed to this methodological, naturalism – whatever the *philosophical* rewards might be.

The critic might take a different tack here, claiming that science does require methodological naturalism, but that the continued success that science has achieved by thus insistently ignoring any alleged nonnatural realm constitutes indirect confirmation that the natural realm is, after all, the only reality – that is, that philosophical naturalism is true.

That move is sensible but not completely simple. First, science may not *require* even *methodological* naturalism. Science historically sometimes employed a non-naturalistic conception of *law* as regularities in God's immediate governance of the cosmos. Such views may even offer the *only* available explanation of unique logical characteristics of "natural laws."[28] A second reason involves what *success* means in this context. Most scientists do take methodological naturalism as a working prescription. This means that methodological naturalism defines the terms in which acceptability of scientific theories is assessed. Thus, if a theory is inadequate, it will *as a matter of methodological policy* be replaced only by some alternative theory which also meets methodological naturalistic criteria. Nonnaturalistic theories – regardless of how explanatorily powerful – will simply be ruled out of consideration by fiat. Given this procedure, only "naturalistic" theories – whatever their problems

25 Engenie Scott, "Darwin Prosecuted," *Creation/Evolution*, 13/2 (Winter 1993), p. 43. It is interesting that the deal that science purportedly makes is with *itself.* Shouldn't science be making deals with *nature*?

A particularly forceful statement of methodological (at least) naturalism as a faith claim comes from Harvard biologist Richard Lewontin:

> Our willingness to accept scientific claims that are against common sense is the key to an understanding of the real struggle between science and the supernatural. We take the side of science . . . because we have a prior commitment, a commitment to materialism. It is not that the methods and institutions of science somehow compel us to accept a material explanation of the phenomenal world, but, on the contrary, that we are forced by our a priori adherence to material causes to create an apparatus of investigation and a set of concepts that produce material explanations, no matter how counter-intuitive, no matter how mystifying to the uninitiated. Moreover, that materialism is absolute, for we cannot allow a Divine Foot in the door. ("Billions and Billions of Demons," *New York Review of Books*, January 9, 1997, p. 44 (1))

26 As Steven Wykstra has pointed out to me, the range of what is considered "natural" could be different in theistic and nontheistic universes. That would imply that a principle that science can involve only what is *natural* is *not* equivalent to the principle that science must proceed as if the natural is all that exists, as Scott and others seem to believe. Wykstra is developing this point in a manuscript currently in progress.

27 Of course, if philosophical naturalism is not true, then assuming either philosophical or methodological naturalism in science may well lead science irretrievably off track, but that is a different issue.

28 See my "Nomo(theo)logical Necessity," *Faith and Philosophy*, 4 (1987), pp. 383–402. Those unique characteristics include their being located between material generalizations and necessities, their support of counterfactuals, etc.

– can ever be candidates for "success." The claim, then, that naturalism has a monopoly on scientific success is both unsurprising and of restricted evidential force. That is not to say that it has *no* force. But the situation resembles that of the ruling party in a one-party country citing its unbroken history of electoral success – where only party members are even eligible to appear on a ballot – as evidence of the voters' high regard.[29]

In any case, conflict does not automatically entail that religion is in trouble without additional principles – for example, that science and its presuppositions take precedence over religion and its presuppositions. That is a philosophical – not a scientific – assertion and will be discussed later.[30]

2.2.2 The larger conceptual matrix

Richard Dawkins believes that religion's foundational outlook is profoundly misoriented. Religion does have empirical content:

> [Y]ou can't escape the scientific implications of religion. A universe with a God would look quite different from a universe without one. A physics, a biology where there is a God is bound to look different. So the most basic claims of religion *are* scientific. Religion *is* a scientific theory.[31]

But, unfortunately for religion, the empirical expectations it generates are precisely wrong:

> [I]f the universe were just electrons and selfish genes, meaningless tragedies . . . are exactly what we should expect, along with equally meaningless *good* fortune. . . . In a universe of blind physical forces and genetic replication, some people are going to get hurt, other people are going to get lucky, and you won't find any rhyme or reason in it, nor any justice. The universe we observe has precisely the properties we should expect if there is, at bottom, no design, no purpose, no evil and no good, nothing but blind, pitiless indifference.[32]

29 It is worth keeping in mind that the evidence in question (the claimed success of naturalism in science) is not only contingent, historical, and problematic, but that the conclusion it is supposed to support – philosophical naturalism – is *philosophical*. Such cross-categorial moves are not straightforward even under the best of circumstances.

30 It is often argued that methodological naturalism acts as an important safeguard against scientific investigation being short-circuited by scientists being too ready to take the easy way out by citing supernatural explanations for phenomena for which genuine scientific explanations could be found were investigations to continue. This might be true, but even if it is, that justifies methodological naturalism only as a *pragmatic* strategy, which has no substantive implications in the present context.

31 Richard Dawkins, *The Nullifidian*, 1/8 (Dec 1994). (*The Nullifidian* is an e-journal). And Julian Huxley again:

> The supernatural hypothesis, taken as involving both the god hypothesis and the spirit hypothesis and the various consequences drawn from them, appears to have reached the limits of its usefulness as an interpretation of the universe and of human destiny, and as a satisfactory basis for religion. It is no longer adequate to deal with phenomena, as disclosed by the advance of knowledge and discovery. (*Religion without Revelation*, p. 185)

32 Richard Dawkins, *River out of Eden* (Cambridge, Mass.: Perseus Publishing, 1996), pp. 132–3. See also Peter Atkins, *The Creation* (San Francisco: W. H. Freeman, 1981), pp. 17, 23.

The problem is not just that some specific scientific theory associated with religion is mistaken, but that the whole base orientation of religion is orthogonal to scientifically revealed reality.

It is not obvious that Dawkins is right. (Even many scientists disagree with him.) Some would deny that *empirical* results bear upon issues of *meaning* at all. In any case, we have experienced exactly one universe. Is this universe *precisely* what we'd expect of an undesigned, purposeless, blind, and pitiless one? I doubt that we know. Could we even reliably distinguish purposeless universes from designed, purposeful universes in which something has gone badly wrong (a familiar religious claim)? While Dawkins's intuitions here may be understandable, they are not rationally obligatory.

In any case, if we do form such expectations, and if we observe aspects of the world which clash with those expectations, the problems *may* lie in our expectations. It is worth noting that nearly every scientific revolution has involved reality itself violating our previous best *scientific* expectations concerning the natural. Our human expectations concerning the *super*natural may be far off the mark. But if our expectations *do* bear some weight here, it must be kept in mind that the world also exhibits characteristics we would not expect *unless* it were supernaturally created. Science itself may have something to say on this side of the issue. Although controversial, cosmological fine-tuning is at least suggestive.[33]

3 Epistemic Undertows: Dissolving Rationality

A number of "scientific" critiques of religious belief consist of

(a) citing purported causes of such belief,

then

(b) claiming that those causes are not rationally legitimate.

While such considerations would not show the *falsehood* of religious belief, wouldn't they undercut the *rationality* of religious belief?[34] Let us look briefly at two popular versions of this critique – roughly Freudian and Marxist respectively.

According to the Freudian proposal, religious belief represents wish fulfillment. We have deep, hidden psychological needs and terrors, and we construct emotionally comforting religious beliefs in response to them. But nonconscious, need-driven processes of forming beliefs are nonrational procedures for generating beliefs of any sort, represent profound immaturity (indeed, neurosis), and have no prospect of generating beliefs connected to the actualities of the world and ourselves. For Marx, religion is a reality-fleeing, empty promise of future compensation for present suffering whose

33 None of this is to say that there is not a problem here for religious believers. In any case, religious believers, far from ducking this and related problems historically, have been among those most insistent on coming to grips with them.

34 There are a number of technical qualifications that would be required even for that more modest project, but I shall bypass most of them.

true (societal) causes it deliberately conceals – an "opium," as he famously labeled it. In both cases, the belief-generating process is oriented toward something other than truth. The governing aim of Freud's wish fulfillment is psychological insulation. The governing aim of Marx's opium is psychological compensation. Both processes involve belief misorientation, and consequently do not deliver rational justification.

Success, for this critique, requires two things. First, there must be a plausible case that the proposed source of belief is in fact its actual source. Such cases are not easy to come by. Freud produced speculative stories involving a hypothetical domineering prehistoric father and his conscience-ridden cannibal sons.[35] It is not clear that such unverifiable speculations constitute a scientific threat to religious rationality.

Second, such critiques require a case for thinking that the proposed religion-producing tendencies are indeed unreliable – that they were not, for instance, placed in us by God exactly for the purpose of alerting us to spiritual matters. Showing that is not trivial.

Several additional points are worth noting. This criticism cuts in both directions. Some people may embrace religion because of fear of death, etc. But it is equally possible that some people embrace anti-religion because they fear ultimate accountability, have difficulty dealing with the idea of some Being immeasurably superior to them, cannot cope with being mere dependent creatures, etc.

Furthermore, if Darwin is right – as most critics believe – then natural selection produced the faculties and cognitive structures with which we form beliefs and pursue science. The governing aim of natural selection is reproductive success – *not* theoretical truth.[36] But if the governing aim of a belief-production mechanism being other than truth undercuts the rational legitimacy of the beliefs so produced – as Marxist and Freudian critiques presuppose – then *exactly* the same principle poses potential problems for scientific beliefs *and for anti-religious arguments* produced by cognitive faculties developed by Darwinian processes ultimately directed toward enhancing reproductive fitness.

Finally, the present criticism categorizes religion as an explanatory hypothesis competing with other hypotheses, answering to scientific criteria appropriate to such hypotheses. Later I will discuss one ground for questioning that.[37]

35 Freud, *Moses and Monotheism* (New York: Vintage, 1958), pp. 102ff.

36 Thus, Patricia Churchland:

> There is a fatal tendency to think of the brain . . . as a device whose primary function is to acquire propositional knowledge. . . . From a biological perspective, however, this does not make much sense. Looked at from an evolutionary point of view . . . [t]he principle chore of nervous systems is to get the body parts where they should be in order that the organism may survive. . . . Improvements in sensorimotor control confer an evolutionary advantage: a fancier style of representing is advantageous *so long as it is geared to the organism's way of life and enhances the organism's chances of survival.* Truth, whatever that is, definitely takes the hindmost. ("Epistemology in the Age of Neuroscience," *Journal of Philosophy*, 84/10 (Oct. 1987), pp. 544–53: pp. 548–9, emphasis original.)

37 Indeed, the implications apply even to the faculties Darwin employed in forming his own beliefs that evolution explained the existence of those same faculties. One might claim that the successful track record of the Darwinian-produced faculties has established their reliability, but that is not completely unproblematic, given that the judgment of "successfulness" essentially employs and depends upon *precisely* the cognitive faculties in question. Also, the recent dismal fates of both Freudian and Marxist systems might be worth pondering here as well. Other similar deconstructive critiques – e.g., postmodernism – also seem well on their way to dismal fates.

4 Conflicting Mind-Sets

Some cases involve psychological contrasts. For instance, Darwin's cousin Francis Galton remarked that "the pursuit of science is uncongenial to the priestly character."[38] The claim is not obviously true – at least, there are important exceptions (Copernicus and LeMaître, for instance). But what is it about scientific and religious mind-sets which is supposed to generate tension? The usual claim is that science requires an open, tentative, inquiring – even skeptical – mind-set, whereas religious belief requires a closed, dogmatic, authority-accepting, blinkered mind-set. One mind, it is claimed, cannot easily be of both sorts. Nobel physicist Richard Feynman describes as "a kind of conflict between science and religion" the "human difficulty that happens when you are educated two ways."[39]

If different mind-sets operated in different areas, there would need be no conflict. The objection thus suggests that, ideally, one consistent mind-set should dominate one's character – especially if one is not to be riddled with inner tensions. But obviously, rational people have different traits in different areas. The first collection of traits might be inappropriate and even irrational in the interpersonal relationships even of a scientist. The second set might be inappropriate and even irrational in the practical pursuits even of a fervent religious believer. The exaggerated dichotomy may thus misrepresent both sides of the discussion.

Furthermore, the mind-sets are not as distinct as critics would have it. Kuhn and others have taught us that certain degrees of dogmatism and similar traits are absolutely essential to the effective operation of science itself. Many scientists accept what they see as scientifically essential presuppositions as virtually nonnegotiable faith commitments. Some hold specific theories pretty dogmatically – e.g., Richard Dawkins: "The theory of evolution by cumulative natural selection is the only theory we know that is in principle *capable* of explaining the existence of organized complexity. Even if the evidence did not favor it, it would *still* be the best theory available."[40]

On the other hand, numerous religious traditions have valued – and devoted enormous effort to – reasoned justifications for their beliefs. In fact, basic theistic belief seems to be perfectly consistent with a "scientific" mind-set. There were those in the natural theology movement who refused to accept religious authority and revelation as legitimate and who undertook to accept beliefs about the supernatural *only* to the extent that such beliefs could be empirically substantiated, but who were convinced that God's existence and some of his properties could be so discovered. Perhaps their arguments were defective, but they were believers with no evident inconsistency within their overall mind-set.

38 Francis Galton, *English Men of Science: Their Nurture and Nature* (London: Macmillan, 1874), p. 24.
39 Richard Feynman, *The Meaning of it All* (Cambridge, Mass.: Perseus Publishing, 1999), p. 38. Even John Wesley noted this sort of difficulty (at least for some, including himself) in his sermon, "The Use of Money": "I am convinced, from many experiments, I could not study, to any degree of perfection, either mathematics, arithmetic, or algebra, without being a Deist, if not an Atheist."
40 Richard Dawkins, *The Blind Watchmaker* (New York: W. W. Norton, 1996), p. 317, emphasis original.

5 Historical Erosion

The problem which science purportedly presents for religion is perhaps most often seen not in terms of episodes of decisive confrontation between the two, but as a gradual historical erosion. Religion, the story goes, supplied prescientific explanations for otherwise inexplicable aspects of human experiences. Such purported explanations rested on religious conceptual foundations, constructed religious explanatory resources, and applied them to phenomena – both real and otherwise – countenanced within religious outlooks. These explanations might in their time have been rationally defensible, but, the story continues, science has progressively undermined all of those areas – religious conceptual foundations, explanatory resources, proposed explanations, and in some cases even the alleged phenomena "explained." Science has irreversibly eroded the conceptual foundations by revealing a cosmos ever more strikingly out of sync with the expectations those religious conceptual foundations generate. The "substance" of explanatory resources harvested from such foundations has progressively evaporated, and there is increasingly little within scientifically revealed reality for them to apply to. The alleged explanations of even those phenomena which are real (e.g., diseases) have exhibited a growing causal irrelevance. And some of the "explained" phenomena themselves have simply melted away under objective scientific scrutiny.

5.1 Dissolution by induction

One continuation of this story goes as follows. The various bits and pieces which have crumbled away from the religious conceptual scheme might not, *individually*, have been essential to religious belief, but, added together over the longer haul, they constitute a track record of serial failure substantive, persistent, and consistent enough to establish that whatever religious beliefs in general might be alleged to reflect, they do not reflect anything remotely resembling reality or truth. As such, religion is now at best a free-floating irrelevance, at worst, worse.

Such objections are quite popular. Stephen Hawking suggests that explanatory appeal to God may no longer be appropriate even for the bare existence of the cosmos:

> [T]he quantum theory of gravity has opened up a new possibility, in which there would be no boundary to space-time . . . The universe would be completely self-contained . . . But if the universe is really completely self-contained, having no boundary or edge, it would have neither beginning nor end; it would simply be. What place, then, for a creator?[41]

5.1.1 Imploding the gaps

One common way of packaging this "What place?" challenge is the "God-of-the-gaps" picture. According to this picture, religious explanations flourished before science

41 Stephen Hawking, *A Brief History of Time* (New York: Bantam Books, 1988), pp. 136, 141. See also Atkins, *Creation*, p. 17.

began to conquer the vast plains of human ignorance. But, as that conquest got under way, religious "explanations" simply could not compete with the confirmable explanations produced by science and were increasingly displaced by them. The available field of operations for religious explanations inevitably shrank, reducing religion to fighting for its life in doomed rearguard actions from within whatever gaps in the broader scientific picture happened to be (as yet) unclosed. But even those temporary shelters are, if not exhausted, well within the current gun sights of scientific inevitability.

Such objections are not without surface plausibility, but they may be less powerful than their advocates believe. First, there still are gaps in our scientific pictures. Although there are recurrent claims that we finally have in hand all the necessary materials for completing the scientific picture (and such claims have a long and, to this point, unsuccessful history[42]), such promises rest upon optimistic induction at best and prior philosophical commitments at worst, and share the hazards such processes embody. Second, Kuhn argued that revolutions and advances sometimes reopen scientific issues previously thought to be settled. Since there is no guarantee that closed gaps will stay closed, closed gaps may be an unstable launching platform for critiques.

Third, it is not clear that religion exhibits an unbroken record of being driven into gaps. For nearly two centuries, some scientists have argued that the fundamental empirically discovered structure of nature (governing laws, etc.) can best – maybe *only* – be sensibly explained in terms of deliberate design and adjustment. Indeed, theistic sympathies raised by "fine-tuning" considerations get progressively more pronounced, the *more* we know about nomic structures, incredibly tightly constrained natural constants, and so forth. Such positions have become noticeably stronger recently, and have attracted even some scientists who cannot by any stretch be classified as traditional religious believers.[43] There are, of course, proposed cosmologies which militate in the opposite direction – Hawking's view above, many-worlds theories, etc. But such cosmologies are currently largely speculative, and speculative cosmologies have been quite unstable historically.[44] And it should not be overlooked that some cosmologies – perhaps including some many-world theories – have been embraced by some precisely *for* the purpose of escaping what otherwise look like broadly religious implications of competing cosmologies.

5.1.2 Creeping marginalization

I am all in favor of a dialogue between science and religion, but not a constructive dialogue. One of the great achievements of science has been, if not to make it

42 e.g., Atkins, *Creation*, p. 127, says: "Complete knowledge is just within our grasp."

43 Furthermore, the initial emergence of this focus not on objects in nature but on design-friendly law structures underlying nature was not part of a retreat from Darwin (as it is frequently characterized), but predated Darwin by a number of decades.

44 The physicist John Archibald Wheeler reports one of his colleagues as advising people not to chase after a bus, a member of the opposite sex, or a cosmological theory – since, after all, in each case there will be another one along in about three minutes.

impossible for intelligent people to be religious, then at least to make it possible for them not to be religious. We should not retreat from this accomplishment.

– Steven Weinberg[45]

The perception expressed here by Nobel physicist Steven Weinberg represents a variant erosion theme. Perhaps science has not rendered religious belief epistemologically pathological, but it does make explanatory appeal to any supernatural agency unnecessary if not downright pointless. Religion is superfluous because (a) its primary purported function is explanatory, and (b) any domain of actual reality it might lay claim to will ultimately be covered by science. That is guaranteed by science's potential explanatory completeness – a potential inductively supported by its continually expanding track record to this point. So perhaps one can still believe if one wants, but one should not be under the illusion that religious belief does any essential explanatory work or is otherwise rationally indispensable.

Contention (a) will be addressed shortly. Concerning (b), we may need to be a bit circumspect. We must appreciate the power which science has and the incredible things it has achieved. But we must not overlook the fact that perceptions of science's potential completeness are at this point projections involving surprising leaps, and some of the remaining gaps are worth reflection. For instance, few things are more familiar than the fall of a raindrop. Yet no scientist anywhere has ever accurately predicted – let alone observed, measured, and confirmed – the path of a single descending raindrop. There are, of course, readily proposed, perhaps perfectly correct, explanations for that. But the *fact* is that assertions of global scientific capabilities constitute an unfulfilled promissory note even for vast stretches of the most familiar, directly observable physical events.

One other point for reflection here. Those who advance an "erosion" picture assume that science drove the process. But that is a historical claim and may not be totally accurate. On a closely related issue, historian John Henry says: "Far from being the predominant driving force in secularization, the practice of science itself was secularized as a result of influence from the wider culture."[46] The "credit" for the erosion may not be science's to claim – other, perhaps less than epistemically upright factors may have been driving the evolution of science itself.

5.2 Revelation

The claimed erosion also factors into another popular critique. Suppose that some person claims to have a special source of supernaturally revealed truth, but that the alleged revelation has a track record of frequent mistakes in readily testable areas. Suspicion of the claim to special access would certainly be understandable – maybe even proper. (There is, of course, the possibility that the mistakes result from misinterpretation of genuine revelation – not to mention the possibility that the alleged refuting scientific results are where the mistake lies.) But suppose that the revelation

45 Steven Weinberg, "A Designer Universe?" *New York Review of Books*, Oct. 21, 1999, p. 48.

46 John Henry, "Atheism," in Gary B. Ferngren (ed.), *The History of Science and Religion in the Western Tradition* (New York: Garland, 2000) pp. 182–8: p. 186.

– even all revelation – were shown to be spurious. Would not religion have to abandon all pretense of rational justification?

That follows only if the core rests solely on purported revelation – now discredited – and is devoid of other possible rational justification. By "rational justification," critics typically mean argumentation, evidence, experiences, observations, explanatory hypotheses, and the like. Of course, some believers (e.g., mystics) have cited special sorts of direct experience. Others, during nearly every historical period, have constructed formal arguments. Such attempts are generally rejected by critics as being either logically inadequate or somehow of the wrong sort – the experiences are non-reproducible; the arguments are contrived, fallacious, or rest upon empirically ambiguous foundations. The usual tacit presupposition is that any rational justification deserving of the title must conform to something like a scientific, explanatory, predictive model of rationality.[47] But is that presupposition correct? That question will be addressed momentarily.

6 Conflict and Rational Justification

6.1 Conflict: limited significance

As noted earlier, some argue that science and religion operate in different arenas and cannot even in principle conflict, meaning that science cannot possibly undercut religion. Perhaps that is true. But suppose that there is genuine, irresolvable conflict. What would the significance of that be? As noted, conflict would inexorably undo religious belief only given the epistemic priority of science – and establishing that may not be straightforward, for several reasons.

(1) Although we often speak of "scientific proof," the logical structure of scientific investigation and confirmation precludes rigorous proof of scientific theories and results. That well-known fact is one reason why science is typically described as provisional and is always willing to give up specific positions when necessary. The possibility that specific scientific beliefs involved in science/religion conflict are mistaken should not be overlooked.

(2) Science is done by humans and reflects human limitations. For instance, scientific theories and results are of necessity limited to reasonings, concepts, observations, measurements, and other resources which native human faculties can, either directly or indirectly, connect to. Regardless of how far instruments, computers, and other aids can extend humanity's scientific reach, that reach must have traceable ties ultimately to a fundamentally human bedrock. The anchors of human science must catch there, because our human faculties and capabilities are the only ones we have, and without such connections, we could neither grasp nor pursue our own science. Although we try – via the "scientific method" – rigorously to govern, correct, and

47 Some – e.g., Nancey Murphy and Michael Banner – have argued that there are significant formal parallels between science and religious belief.

test our faculties, reasonings, concepts, and theories, we have no alternative but to employ – and ultimately to trust – inescapably human capacities and insights. Claiming that we subject them to *nature*'s verdicts does not circumvent the loop. After all, we must ultimately rely on *our* convictions concerning what constitutes a *test*, what constitutes *passing* such a test, what the *evidence* of such passing does or does not include, what proper *evaluation* of such an attempt involves – and none of these matters are just dictated to us by nature. Careful, methodical, and responsible as we might try to be, those matters *inevitably* have human fingerprints all over them.

(3) Ultimately, then, we have no choice but to accept some deliverances of some basic human faculties as cognitive bedrock for any human enterprise. But the cognitive faculties and intuitions underlying science are not the only ones we humans have – or if they are, they also underlie other characteristic human projects which may thus have ultimate foundations just as legitimate as science's. If, then, there *is* any deep conflict between science and religion, each side may rest upon fundamental aspects of human nature, and each may have equally legitimate claims on us. In that case, science would have no more inherent claim to deeper allegiance than does religious belief. It may be that other dimensions of broader human existence – faith, loyalty, perseverance, love, religious commitment – *should* sometimes outweigh commitment to the abstract, provisional, inductive, theoretical, highly indirect, only partially confirmed theories and hypotheses of the scientific dimension of human existence – and on precisely the same ultimate grounds that science ought sometimes to overrule specific religious beliefs. That seems at least *possible*, and if so, then the mere fact of even genuine and irresolvable conflict would not automatically imply that religious belief should always give way to science.

(4) The history of science itself provides a caution here. Historically, the bulk of all scientific theories ever proposed or accepted by scientists have turned out to be incorrect, at least in detail. Anyone who risked all for nearly any scientific theory in the past would have lost all. Future generations may well say exactly the same about our present science. If so, then those who advocate the absolute primacy of science must either argue that at last, fortunately, *we* happen to be the lucky generation that finally got things right (which seems both unlikely and overly self-congratulatory), or else must base that claim on the prediction that although science has not yet gotten things quite right, it will someday. This means that theory-based scientific cases against religious belief rest partially upon faith in a promise for the future.

(5) The implications of inconsistency are not always straightforward even within science itself. (i) *Theory/data conflict*: nearly every successful scientific theory is proposed, developed, and accepted in the context of *known* contradicting data. That has been so prevalent historically that one historian of science remarked that *every* theory is *born* refuted. *Were* problematic data an automatic reason to reject scientific theories, we'd have to reject them all. (ii) *Theory/theory conflict*: General relativity and quantum mechanics – two of the best theories contemporary science owns – are mathematically inconsistent with each other. But science has so far – *perfectly properly* – refused to part with either. Logical ambiguity is where we flesh-and-blood humans – scientists included – must sometimes live.

6.2 Rational justification: sources

The conception of religious belief as constituting an explanatory hypothesis competing with science, whose rational credentials depend upon successfully meeting the criteria for such hypotheses, has arisen repeatedly in the foregoing. Is that conception correct? Very recently, some scholars have been struck by the fact that virtually none of our truly fundamental, commonsense, life-governing beliefs are generated by argumentation; nor are they merely provisional explanatory hypotheses or anything of the sort. Nor do we acquire or justify beliefs that those around us have minds, that there has been a past, that our reason applies to reality, or that there is an external world, on some 'scientific' model of argumentation, hypothesis, testing, and confirmation. *We could not do so were we to try* – as the long history of failed philosophical attempts amply attests. And belief that one's spouse loves one is neither a hypothesis to explain otherwise puzzling behavior, some sort of induction, nor an empty irrelevancy. Furthermore, centuries of serious *skeptical* arguments from various philosophical movements have failed to make the slightest dent in commitment to such pervasive and persistent beliefs as that we know that there is a real external world. Yet, despite their lack of formal support and their unruffled immunity to contrary argumentation, such fundamental beliefs are surely rational if any of our beliefs are. Rational justification here must thus have some different and deeper source, and artificially limiting acceptable grounds to explanatory hypotheses, argumentation, and the like does serious violence to human rationality. That has led some "reformed epistemologists" to suggest analogously that artificially limiting possible grounds for rational justification of religious beliefs to a set of "scientific" procedures which is demonstrably inadequate, even for the world of ordinary experience, may be equally misguided. We may, they argue, have deep inbuilt faculties which generate religious belief, just as we apparently have deep inbuilt faculties which generate the bulk of our commonsense beliefs. (Indeed, the indispensable presuppositions of science itself may ultimately rest upon an exactly similar foundation.) Relevant assessments of rationality may in each case require an approach very different from more formal 'scientific' ones.

If that proves correct, then some common demands – e.g., that religious believers produce science-shaped arguments or hypotheses, or identify empirical arenas in which religion withstands all empirical comers – may simply be inappropriate. Any inability of believers to meet such demands may be of as little rational significance as the inability of everyone to produce arguments for the existence of the external world, the minds of their colleagues, the reality of the past – or for the legitimacy of bedrock presuppositions of science. In none of these areas would any such inability alone establish lack of rational justification.

7 Conclusion

I have not tried to show that a theistic world view is correct, that science supports such a world view, that there have not been historical tensions, that there is no present ferment, or anything of the sort. In fact, ferment seems to be the natural condition of most truly open human projects – intellectual or otherwise. But making the case that science destabilizes fundamental religious belief is not so easy as some claims would make it seem. Furthermore, the force even of those critiques which may have substance is less than is often attributed to them. And if science really *is* to be our intellectual model here, as some critics suggest, then, given standard claims that science differs from blind religious dogma in being tentative, provisional, and always prepared to revise in the face of new information and insight, it would appear that some critics of religious belief are engaged in an existential inconsistency.[48]

Reply to Ratzsch

Del Ratzsch alludes to any number of arguments. I think it is fair, however, to take his paper's central claims to be: (i) the clash between science and religion is by no means as clear-cut as is often supposed, and (ii) even where there is, let's say, *tension* between the two fields, it is not obvious that epistemic considerations unambiguously dictate that it is religion that should give way.

Since I already conceded that religious believers can – though with more difficulty than Ratzsch's treatment suggests – avoid outright inconsistency with the "results" of science, I concentrate on part (ii) of his argument. His most challenging points seem to be these. First, there is not even the appearance of a clash between science and religion unless we take it that science provides rational warrant for belief in the truth, or approximate truth, of its *theories*. And there are widely defended views of scientific theories that deny this. Secondly, the thesis that our beliefs (or degrees of belief) should be governed by the scientific method is itself a philosophical, rather than a scientific, claim. This implies – point three – that even those who support the epistemic priority of science cannot hold that science is the only source of knowledge. Are the nonscientifically endorsed beliefs that underpin the scientific method really any different from the nonscientifically endorsed beliefs that underpin religion? Fourth, and finally, he claims that there are things that everyone would accept that we know – such as that there exists a world external to our consciousness – that we do not know via the scientific method; but then we may know religious truths in this same "alternative" way.

1 Anti-Realism and Religious Belief

Even the standard conflicts between science and particular commitments inspired by religious views – for example, over Copernican or Darwinian theory – undoubtedly depend on taking a "realist" view of those theories. If, instead, theories are regarded simply as tools for organizing empirical data, then there can be no conflict.

48 I wish to thank my colleagues in the Calvin College Philosophy Department, especially Steve Wykstra and Kelly Clark, and David Van Baak.

Now, whatever may be the case concerning "fundamental" theories, it is difficult to take seriously an anti-realist attitude to less-frontier, more well-entrenched theoretical claims such as that matter has *some sort* of atomic structure, the earth is not stationary, the fossil record is indeed a collection of the imprints or bones of now extinct species, and so on. But aside from this, it surely seems odd, to say the least, for someone defending religious faith to appeal to anti-realism. (Though it is, I admit, an oddity that frequently occurs.) After all, the motivation for that anti-realist view is the desire to go as little as possible beyond the evidence, beyond what we can reasonably take as certain. No matter how strongly our evidence from, say, cloud-chamber photographs and the like may seem to indicate the existence of electrons, that evidence can never be logically conclusive – so, the suggestion goes, stick to what *is* conclusive (namely, that electron theory makes true empirical predictions) and avoid commitment to the *truth* of electron theory. But this hard-headed, skeptical attitude is entirely at odds with the sort of credulousness required of religious believers, who advocate belief in substantive claims about the universe on the basis of no evidence at all. The anti-realist deist, having strained at a gnat, promptly swallows a camel with gusto.

2 *Tu quoque*? No Thank You

Believers through the ages have used the "tu quoque" response to those who try to use scientific rationality against them. The claim is that, when carefully analyzed, the principles that underwrite the canons of scientific rationality cannot themselves be defended rationally or scientifically, and hence that the defender of scientific rationality herself appeals to principles which must ultimately have the status of unproven (because basic) dogmas.

I agree with Ratzsch that the principles of scientific method cannot themselves be defended scientifically – all attempts to "naturalize epistemology" are circular.[49] Indeed, as Lewis Carroll showed,[50] – any attempt to justify even the simple principles of *deductive* logic, such as the rule of *modus ponens,* will inevitably presuppose those principles themselves. It follows that the principles of logic and of evidence underpinning science can ultimately only be defended "dogmatically": we just know that the rule of *modus ponens*, for example, transmits truth; we just know that it's a good idea to test claims against plausible rivals before accepting them, and so on.

This does not, however, entail, as Ratzsch asserts it does, that scientific "naturalism" is self-certifying. First, I cannot see, as explained in my essay, that it is coherent to contrast "naturalism" and "supernaturalism": there is what there is, and *if* what there is includes *so-called* supernatural entities, then those entities are really natural – they are parts of the universe as a whole (again, what else could they be?). Secondly, science has no inbuilt prejudice against God (or against psychic forces or teleportation or whatever). The scientific approach is not inherently "naturalist," but

49 John Worrall, "Two Cheers for Naturalised Philosophy of Science – or Why Naturalised Philosophy of Science Is Not the Cat's Whiskers," *Science and Education*, 8 (1999), pp. 339–61.
50 Lewis Carroll, "What the Tortoise Said to Achilles," *Mind*, New Series, 4/14 (1895), pp. 278–80.

rather inherently evidentialist: it accredits claims about features of the structure of reality exactly to the extent that there is evidence for the existence of those features. The problem with God is *not* that there is no room for her in physics – the problem is that there is no room for her in physics *because* there is no evidence of her physical (what else?) reality.

I do accept, though, that the principles of evidentialism have to be "taken as read." There is no way that someone could be rationally convinced that logic and evidence are essential parts of rationality unless they had already accepted logic and evidence! Does that mean, as Ratzsch intimates (without quite saying so), that in the end the pro-science and the pro-religion person are "equally dogmatic"? This would be like arguing that, because they both acted immorally, the hungry little old lady who steals a lamb chop from the supermarket stands on a par with Adolf Hitler. There are grades of wickedness, and there are grades of dogmatism – not all sins are equal, and neither are all "dogmas." There is an obvious difference between, on the one hand, asserting that it is just a basic truth, one that cannot be justified on the basis of anything simpler, that if, if p then q, and p are both true, then so also must be q, and, on the other hand, asserting that it is just a basic truth, not one that can be justified on the basis of anything simpler, that there exists an omnipotent, omniscient, omnibenevolent god who "created" the universe. The "dogmas" that underpin the scientific method are formal, intuitive, of minimal content, and, once understood, universally accepted by all serious parties; the dogmas of religion make enormously contentful claims and are matters of heated and continued dispute between serious parties – hence they surely cry out for (but fail) evidential assessment. As it says in "the good book," "Why beholdest thou the mote that is in thy brother's eye, but considerest not the beam that is in thine own eye?" (*Matthew* 7:3, KJV).

3 Different Ways of Knowing?

Del Ratzsch echoes the view of the 'reformed epistemologists' that there are features of the universe (such as its existence independently of human consciousness) that we (i) know as firmly as we could possibly know anything and (ii) do not know on the basis of any scientific reasoning. Hence there are nonscientific ways of knowing, and who is to say that we cannot know religious truths in some such nonscientific way?

One way in which this sort of thesis can be argued relies on the sort of outright relativism that I am taking to be rejected on all sides: if there is a "religious way of knowing" alongside the scientific, why not a parapsychological or a scientological or a . . . way of knowing? Ratzsch is not endorsing such easy (and clearly unacceptable) relativism, but rather is claiming that *anyone* serious must acknowledge that we know certain things in a way not dependent on the procedures of science, as well (or better) than we know things through science.

Surely, however, we *do* know that there exists a world independent of our consciousnesses precisely on scientific grounds. That claim is so fundamental, such a core assumption in all our scientific theories, that we may not think of it this way, but we accept it because of its (immense) predictive success (unlike its idealist rivals, it successfully predicts that the tree that appeared to be there before we closed our eyes will still appear to be there when we reopen them; we accept it because it is the best explanation of the evidence). Similar considerations of course apply to the case of the existence of other minds. Indeed, I would argue that all of our so-called commonsense knowledge is *either* flawed (and therefore not really knowledge at all) *or* based on scientific reasoning, very broadly construed (and hence in effect consists of well-confirmed hypotheses). I would certainly include here Ratzsch's example of the person who "knows" that his spouse loves him: *if* he knows this at all – and, sadly, the divorce courts churn out thousands of counterexamples a day – he knows it as a well-confirmed hypothesis (without of course formally thinking of it this way).

Notice that Ratzsch's argument for our not knowing of the external world or other minds in a scientific way is confused. He correctly remarks that *philosophical* attempts to *prove* the existence of the real world (and of other minds) fail. But the point is that we should never have expected a proof (science never offers these) even though the claims seem so evidently true. Exactly when we replace philosophy with science, we get the right answer: these claims are extremely well-confirmed hypotheses. Ratzsch's suggestion that all findings of science are "provisional," while the external world claim is not, again rests on concentrating – as much recent philosophy of science has done – on *fundamental* scientific theories. These, as cases of "scientific revolutions" have shown, are seriously fallible; but the same cannot be said of "lower-level" claims such as that the heart pumps blood around the body, that the earth is in motion, that DNA has a helical structure, and so on. The "external world" claim is even lower-level, even more deeply entrenched. Of course, being a synthetic claim, it is fallible *in principle*, but there is no reason to take its fallibility seriously.

The central thesis remains in tact: everything that we can legitimately claim to know about the world (as opposed to our methods) is based on the methods and rules of evidence employed in science, and there is no evidence for the existence of a god.

Reply to Worrall

Worrall has developed very clearly some intuitions which often underlie criticisms of religious belief but which are seldom explicated in such perspicuous form. Some of his views I agree with – for example, suspicion of NOMA, and that religious belief doesn't come to much if metaphorized out of all genuine substance. Furthermore, some of our disagreements do not involve matters of principle and could probably be resolved through further discussion.[51] But we do have significant differences.

Fundamental to Worrall's case is the view that one single set of criteria defines *rational justification* and that (on pain of an invidious relativism) all substantive beliefs must meet those same criteria to be rationally justified. But it is surely possible that sufficiently different substantive facets of the world require appropriately

51 For instance, I read Alvin Plantinga quite differently than does Worrall, and I am not convinced that the demographics of religious belief have the negative implications that Worrall suggests.

distinct approaches.[52] Were that the case, the demand that all evaluation be in identical lockstep terms might avoid relativism but produce conceptual chaos (or conceptual impoverishment). However, Worrall's initial candidate for this single evaluative structure is the plausible-sounding principle that substantive claims must be evaluated ultimately by reference to *evidence*.[53] Although that principle is actually controversial, one might accept it as a *general* evaluative requirement, then argue that different types of beliefs might be rationally justified in terms of appropriately different types of evidence. That would give a unitary underlying structure to rational justification (certainly plausible) while allowing specific sub-types of justification to reflect (sensibly enough) characteristic uniquenesses of distinct facets of reality. Such recognition of uniquenesses seems potentially crucial in the present case, since religious explanations are ultimately *agent* (person) explanations – involving God's actions, wishes, purposes, commands. Agent explanations are widely seen as having unique characteristics, and evidence concerning the wishes and purposes of other agents is often of a special sort – deliberate agent communication.

However, midway through his essay, Worrall's principle, with neither notice nor stated justification, mutates to the principle that such evaluation must be in terms not just of evidence, but of *empirical* or *observable* evidence. So not only is there only one admissible structure for rationality (that being a broad evidentialism), there is only one category of admissible evidence – the empirical. (Direct supernatural agent communication – e.g., revelation – is evidently ruled out by stipulation.) As Worrall sees it, then, all *rational* evaluation of substantive claims about the world becomes *scientific* evaluation[54] – the norms of empirical science simply *become* the norms of rationality, which substantive religious belief must then meet to be rational.

But extreme care is required here. Most scientists have believed that simplicity, mathematical beauty, explanatory power, systematizing capability, etc. – none of which constitute *empirical* aspects *of nature* – were essential evaluative criteria for scientific theories. Indeed, given the underdetermination of theory by empirical data, no realist conception of science can avoid nonempirical evaluative criteria, and thus evaluation could not be just in terms of *empirical* evidence, in any straightforward sense.[55]

52 By "substantive," Worrall may just *mean* "empirical." If so, that would seem to involve an ontological presupposition which would require support.

53 Although I will not pursue the matter here, that principle requires great care. My belief that I have consciousness is a substantive, factual matter – the world would be importantly (I think) different were it not true. But that belief does not rest upon *evidence* which I note, evaluate, and test, only then accepting that belief.

54 That equating can be seen in such statements as: "If all explanations involving substantive, synthetic claims about the world must satisfy the same criteria, then it is simply nonsense to claim that religion can explain the scientifically inexplicable" and the phrase "not rational, that is, not scientific."

55 Simplicity, for instance, is often taken as *evidence*, in some broad sense, for the simpler of two empirically equivalent theories. I am not sure whether Worrall would call that "evidence" – it surely isn't *empirical* evidence. Anyway, I am not at all sure that Worrall would disagree with the overall point here. Much would depend upon details of his view of the nature and exact role of the empirical, which, given length constraints, were understandably not covered in his main essay.

In any case, is this sort of evidentialism rationally fatal for religion? Couldn't a believer propose God's creative activity as *explaining* some observable phenomenon, then cite that as empirical evidence for God's existence and activity? Worrall's reply is that an *invariable* requirement of scientific method is the *rejection* of any explanatory proposal having no (possible) 'independent empirical support.'[56] A principle, purported fact, or theory proposed or hypothesized to explain some empirical phenomenon must not only successfully explain it, but must also have *additional* empirical implications beyond those it was specifically tailored to handle. Otherwise, it will be merely ad hoc. Thus, a proposed explanation offering no prospect of further corroboration of the hypothesized matters (e.g., novel predictions) is not genuinely scientific. Religious "explanations" of empirical matters, Worrall holds, invariably fail this invariable requirement of scientific practice.

Is that true? Long before the Big Bang theory, the doctrine of creation was taken as implying a beginning of the cosmos at a finite time in the past. That empirical implication is apparently right. (Some scientists *resisted* Big Bang cosmology precisely *because* it looked suspiciously like creation.) Furthermore, prominent early scientists insisted that investigation of nature must be empirical, because nature was *freely* created by God, and the only way to determine what God had done was to *look*. Scientifically essential confidence in the intelligibility of nature, and in the uniformity of nature, were historically given theological justifications. Does the subsequent success of science, and science's continuing corroboration of those implications of the doctrine of creation (which, long *predating* science, manifestly were not proposed just to explain science and its success) constitute independent support? Science as we conceive it certainly did not *have* to succeed – its success is a decidedly contingent, decidedly substantive fact. (As these issues suggest, religious explanations often focus not merely upon internal scientific matters, but on conditions essential for the very existence of science – matters which science itself is unequipped to address.[57] Worrall's examples of religious explanations of substantive matters (e.g., gravity operates by an inverse square because that's the way God wanted it) give a far too constricted view of the varying types of explanations involved – explanations which, again, are agent explanations.)

But is the stipulated "independent empirical support" requirement really invariable anyway? Contrary to Worrall's contention, even in broadly "scientific" contexts, it is not absolute. Suppose that you were the first human on Mars, and discovered an exact, full-scale replica of the Eiffel Tower, or a sign saying "Welcome, Delicious Earthling." The most *rational* explanation would be an agent explanation – aliens. And the absence of any additional "independent empirical support" for alien existence, activity, etc., would not have the *slightest* effect on the cogency of that explanation. Nor would our inability to tell – or even understand – why the aliens had done it. Nor would the fact that aliens were proposed specifically to explain only that

56 Whether or not there is such a thing as 'the' scientific method which is historically invariant is a matter of dispute among historians and philosophers of science. Prof. Worrall's reference to "the always dominant criterion of independent empirical support" suggests he believes there to be at least a core of invariability.

57 See my initial essay, especially the section entitled "The Larger Web."

one bit of empirical evidence render the proposal ad hoc.[58] The alien explanation would be an agent explanation designed to explain something made by that agent. Religious explanations are frequently, of course, of exactly that general type as well.

But suppose that Worrall had shown that religious belief did not conform to "the scientific attitude." If religion *is* religion and not science, wouldn't one expect it not to conform to norms definitive of something else – science? More importantly, why should that nonconformity be worrisome for religious believers? Should scientists worry if told that science does not conform to "the religious attitude"? Recall, furthermore, that Worrall warns us against thinking that *even our best* fundamental scientific theories are true, and says that not only does science not *logically* refute basic theistic beliefs, but that "outright belief at least in fundamental explanatory theories *is not rational*, that is, not scientific, even in science" (my emphasis). So why, we might ask Worrall, *should* science epistemologically rule all?

Superficially, Worrall's answer might seem to be that, regardless of its limitations, science is still the best we've got – it has had "enormous empirical success," whereas religion has had "no empirical success at all." But his reason goes deeper than that. Recall that Worrall's position constitutes an identification of the rational with the scientific – a form of scient*ism*. (Note Worrall's telling phrase: "not rational, *that is*, not scientific" (my emphasis).) Thus, if religious belief clashes either with well-accredited results of science or with the scientific attitude, it is thereby automatically in *rational* difficulty. In effect, if religious belief has *any* distinctive character *different* from that of science, it virtually *thereby* fails to conform to the requirements of rationality – making genuine religion rationally unacceptable almost by definition. In particular, "religious belief must . . . rely on faith; and faith is unscientific."[59] It *must* rely on faith – that is purportedly essential to its character *as* religious belief. And faith evidently cannot demand independent empirical support – that is presumably essential to its character as *faith*.[60] And belief despite failure of independent empirical support constitutes failure to be *scientific* – that is, failure to be rational. Science trumps and triumphs because it very nearly just *is* rationality, and anything purportedly substantive but not scientific is *a fortiori* not rational. With the boundaries thus drawn, religion's "clashes with science (or more accurately the scientific attitude) is inevitable," and (at least when in conflict with established scientific theory) religious claims "*must*, from a rational point of view, give way" (my emphasis).[61]

Worrall's argument, then, rests upon reduction of all evaluation of substantive matters to one preferred structure of evaluation (evidentialism), all legitimate evidence to one preferred sort of evidence (empirical), and all rationality to one preferred model of rationality (science). It seems to me that not only has Worrall not given adequate

58 This example might be far-fetched, but, as David Van Baak remarked to me, the *scientific* analysis of the first radio message recovered by a SETI program would have *precisely* this logical structure.

59 The reference here is to Tennyson, but Worrall clearly endorses the position.

60 This conception of faith would be deeply disputed by many believers.

61 So, as Worrall structures the issue, evaluation is stipulated as empirical, but religion will not get credit even when it happens to be empirically right. If a religious belief does have the proper empirical credentials, then it is *ipso facto science*, and not religion after all, and religion, again, does not get credit. One upshot here is that belief based just on, e.g., revelation is, by definition, not rationally justified – natural theology is in effect the only even possible justification for substantive religious belief.

support for that series of reductions, but that the specific picture of science presupposed may not be rich enough to accommodate either the history or the structure of science itself. And rather than declaring all that to characterize 'the scientific attitude,' the *true* scientific attitude might be to treat scientifically things discovered to fall within the proper domain of science's competence and *qua scientist* to remain silent (versus blanket rejection) on issues (if any) beyond that domain – leaving the extent of that domain as a matter for discovery, rather than stipulation.[62]

Worrall began by describing religious scientists as muddled in various ways. But that perception rests at least in part on Worrall's philosophical preferences. Those philosophical preferences may or may not be defensible – but they are surely not rationally obligatory.[63]

62 Some of Worrall's own views may generate difficulties here. For instance, his key principle that any acceptable scientific explanation must be *independently empirically testable* seems substantive – neither empty nor necessary – but it is unclear what *observable* evidence that principle rests upon. For that matter, what is the *empirical* evidence for Occam's razor?

63 I am indebted to David Van Baak and Stephen Wykstra for extremely helpful discussion of a number of issues raised here.

PART II

ARGUMENTS FOR RELIGIOUS BELIEF

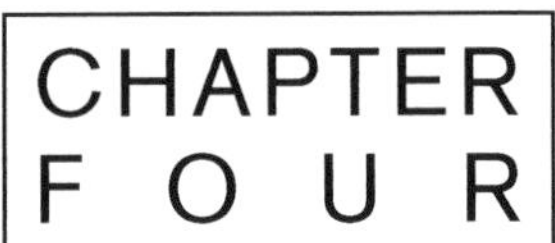

CHAPTER FOUR

Is God's Existence the Best Explanation of the Universe?

Theists have often claimed that God's existence best explains the existence of our contingent universe. One famous argument (or family of arguments) offered in support of this claim is known as "the cosmological argument." In his essay, Bruce Reichenbach presents and defends several sophisticated versions of this argument, including one of his own. Richard Gale offers some broad objections to cosmological arguments generally and then attacks Reichenbach's version of it. Gale goes on to present his own rendition of the argument, one which purports to establish the existence of a contingent, limited being who is responsible for the existence of the universe, rather than the existence of the omnipotent, omniscient, perfectly good, and necessarily existent Being of classical theism.

Explanation and the Cosmological Argument

Bruce R. Reichenbach

Theists are in good company when they look for explanations either of the universe or of particular phenomena within it. Historians search for explanations of why Hitler invaded Russia, economists of fluctuations in the GDP, psychologists for why some teens commit suicide, and natural scientists for why Eastern songbirds have reduced breeding. Some invoke personal explanations, others natural or scientific explanations;

yet all strive for the best explanation of what exists or happens or what they experience. In what follows I will say something about the nature of explanation, discuss what in the universe needs explanation that is best provided by the activity of God, and suggest why it is that God provides the best explanation of specific things or events.

1 The Need for Explanation

Explanatory reasoning that infers God's existence and activity has a long and distinguished career. Although Thomas Aquinas's thirteenth-century *Summae* contain the classical Western formulations, his arguments are firmly rooted in Aristotelian physics. Aristotle held that to understand or explain why something exists as it does, one must appeal to the three principles (form, matter, privation) and the four causes. Aquinas uses this structure, especially efficient and final causes, to construct his arguments for God's existence. For Aquinas, the existence of things in motion, of effects, and of contingent beings requires the causal activity of other things, for something must already be actual to realize another's potency, and if what is actual is itself an effect, it too requires a causal explanation for its existence and causal efficacy (for example, as an intermediate mover). The process proceeds until we must invoke the existence of something that causes but is itself not an effect.

Subsequent Enlightenment versions of this argument gradually depart from Aristotelian physics and instead appeal to a more general principle called the Principle of Sufficient Reason, according to which "no fact can be real or existing and no statement true unless it has a sufficient reason why it should be thus and not otherwise."[1] The contingent has causes, which themselves stand in need of causal explanation. Since an explanation in terms of other things that need explanation cannot sufficiently account for the existent if the series of explanations proceeds to infinity, that which ultimately explains any contingent fact must stand outside this infinity of contingent causes; the ultimate cause must be a necessary being that "has the reason for its existence in itself."[2]

Contemporary philosophers have distinguished among versions of the Principle of Sufficient Reason. On the one hand, William Rowe questions the rational defense, intuitiveness, and necessary truth of Leibniz's strong version of the principle, according to which all existents must have a cause of their existence.[3] However, this version of the principle is stronger than the cosmological argument actually requires. On the other hand, the very weak version suggested by Richard Gale – namely, that it is *possible* that every fact has an explanation – is too weak to sustain the deductive cosmological argument, for since this weak version would not require an explanation for the contingent, it could at best lead to the conclusion that if the contingent has an explanation, the best explanation would be based on God's activity.[4] The cosmolog-

1 Gottfried Leibniz, *Monadology*, tr. George Hendrix (Chicago: Open Court, 1992), p. 32.

2 Ibid., p. 45.

3 William Rowe, *The Cosmological Argument* (Princeton: Princeton University Press, 1975), pp. 73–94.

4 Richard Gale, *On the Nature and Existence of God* (Cambridge: Cambridge University Press, 1991), pp. 279–80. In the essay that follows mine, Gale disputes this claim, arguing that this weak version of the Principle of Sufficient Reason is sufficient to generate a sound deductive argument for a finite God's existence.

ical argument requires a moderate version of the principle, which holds that what is contingent or what comes into being requires a sufficient reason for why it exists or comes into being. The *contingent* needs an explanation because, although it exists, it could have not existed, and hence an explanation of why it exists rather than not is a reasonable demand. *What comes into existence* needs an explanation because, since things cannot bring themselves into existence or spring out of nothing, they must have a cause for their coming to be.

The moderate version of the Principle of Sufficient Reason is not derivable from more basic principles; an argument to derive it would ultimately invoke the principle itself, and hence beg the question. However, this is not to say that the principle is unjustified; its justification is located not only in the pragmatics of explanation[5] but also in the metaphysics of contingency. When so placed in metaphysics, it is perhaps better to speak about the Principle of Causation, according to which whatever exists contingently cannot have its existence from itself but is dependent upon something else for its existence, either at the moment of its conception or continuously. Since dependency is a causal notion, contingency itself requires that the cause be sufficient to bring about the effect.[6]

The classic argument against the necessity of the Principle of Causation is found in David Hume, who argues that "as all distinct ideas are separable from each other, and as the ideas of cause and effect are evidently distinct, 'twill be easy for us to conceive any object to be non-existent this moment, and existent the next, without conjoining to it the distinct idea of a cause or productive principle. The separation, therefore, of the idea of a cause from that of a beginning of existence, is plainly possible for the imagination; and consequently the actual separation of these objects is so far possible, that it implies no contradiction nor absurdity."[7] Hume's argument is that whatever items are distinguishable can be conceived to be separate from each other. Since cause and effect are distinguishable, they can be conceived to be separate. Since whatever is conceivable is possible in reality, cause and effect are separable, and the Principle of Causation is not necessarily true. For Hume, the criterion for deciding whether two things are distinguishable is whether we can entertain separate impressions of them. Distinguishability, therefore, is an epistemic category. Separability, however, is an ontological category, meaning that one thing can exist entirely independent of the other thing. But, so understood, Hume's critical premise that what is distinguishable is separable confuses epistemic with ontological conditions, and hence is not sound. The fact that we can have distinct impressions of things does not mean that those things are more than conceptually separable.[8]

In sum, there are two possible grounds for the Principle of Sufficient Reason: epistemic requirements for explanation and the ontology of contingency. Since reality need not meet subjective demands, an explanation grounded in ontological considerations leads to a stronger justification than that which places explanation merely

5 Richard Taylor, *Metaphysics*, 4th edn (Englewood Cliffs, NJ: Prentice-Hall, 1992), pp. 88–9.

6 Joseph Owens, "The Causal Proposition – Principle or Conclusion?" *Modern Schoolman*, 32 (1955), pp. 159–71, 257–70, 323–39.

7 David Hume, *Treatise of Human Nature* (Oxford: Clarendon Press, 1888), p. 79.

8 Bruce R. Reichenbach, *The Cosmological Argument: A Reassessment* (Springfield, Ill.: Charles Thomas, 1972), pp. 56–60.

within the subjective demand of rational endeavors. At the same time, an ontological grounding makes metaphysical commitments beyond those needed when grounding the principle in epistemic considerations.

2 Partial and Full Explanations

Theists construct both cosmological and teleological arguments around causal explanations for particular phenomena. Explanation contains two components: a description of what brought about the effect (the cause) and why the effect occurred. The causal factors are independent of the effect; otherwise there is no bringing about. A partial explanation appeals to some, often notable, causal condition that is partly responsible for the effect. That the boy played with matches partially but satisfactorily accounts for why the building burned, all things being equal (that the building was constructed of flammable material, oxygen was present, etc.). But a partial explanation, though often adequate from an epistemic or interest point of view, is inadequate when one wants to discover the ontology of the situation. Such requires a full explanation, which includes a *full* cause (the set of causal conditions that were individually necessary and jointly sufficient for the effect to occur) and "the reason why the cause, under the specified conditions, had the effect that it had."[9] The theistic arguments demand that whatever exists contingently or arises have a full explanation; otherwise there is no reason why something would exist or arise rather than not exist or arise.[10]

3 Scientific Explanation and Personal Explanation

Richard Swinburne distinguishes two types of explanation, the scientific and the personal. In a scientific explanation, the causes are natural features, events, processes, or conditions, and the "whys" are natural laws stating that events or things of a certain sort under specified conditions bring about effects of a certain sort. In a scientific explanation, given the causal conditions and the scientific laws operative at the time, the effect will – or perhaps better, given quantum and chaotic indeterminacy, probably will – occur.

A personal explanation, on the other hand, provides an "explanation in terms of the intentional action of a person."[11] It is appropriately invoked when scientific explanations do not suffice or when the personal explanation is simpler and no explanatory power is lost. Yet a personal explanation provides as legitimate an explanation as a scientific one.

Swinburne argues that personal explanations are not reducible to scientific explanations. That an action results from an agent having a specific intention is not equiv-

9 Richard Swinburne, *The Existence of God* (Oxford: Oxford University Press, 1979), p. 24.

10 The fact that often it is impossible to specify the full cause in any given case does not affect the ontological requirement that there be such a full cause in order to bring about the effect.

11 Swinburne, *Existence of God*, p. 22.

alent to the action being brought about by a person's brain states, for a brain state could bring about an event without the person intending to bring it about. Intention does not belong to the "what" of the explanation but to why persons act as they do.[12] Yet, "the fact that personal explanation cannot be analyzed in terms of scientific explanation does not mean that its operation on a particular occasion cannot be given a scientific explanation."[13] In the case of certain phenomena, this inability to give a scientific explanation, or the unsatisfactoriness or incompleteness of such explanations, is crucial to inferring the existence and activity of God from a particular effect.

4 What Needs Theistic Explanation?

In the history of the cosmological/teleological arguments, theists have contended that a variety of things cannot satisfactorily receive their needed explanation from a fully naturalistic account. In general, theists have used two types of things in the initial premises of the cosmological argument. One is the *existence* of certain things – individual contingent beings, the universe, natural laws, or principles that govern events; the other, the *coming to be* of certain things, either the universe itself or its contents. This has led to two types of cosmological argument: arguments for a sustaining cause and arguments for an initiating cause.

With regard to the first type of argument, Thomas Aquinas held that among the things that need explanation for their existence are contingent beings, for such beings are dependent for their existence upon other beings. Richard Taylor and others argue that the universe (meaning everything that ever existed) as contingent needs explanation. William Rowe, arguing that the term "universe" refers to an abstract entity or set, rephrases the issue, "Why does that set (the universe) have the members that it does rather than some other members or none at all?"[14] That is, "Why is there something rather than nothing?"

With regard to the second type of argument, theists focus on the coming to be of the universe or of certain of its features. William Craig, for example, in his version of the Islamic Kalam argument, argues that since whatever begins to exist must have a cause, and since the universe began to exist, the universe had a cause.[15] Theists such as John Polkinghorne and Robert John Russell see the fundamental openness of quantum events as both evidence of and the locus for God's activity in the world.[16] There must be something outside the deterministic, naturalistic schema that makes a quantum cause result in a specific effect. Others argue that the genesis of life and human consciousness need explanation, and that this explanation is best provided by the existence and intervention of God. With respect to the former, how could the information chains found in RNA develop out of basic, inorganic physical elements?

12 For a fuller defense of these theses, see ibid., pp. 36–42.

13 Ibid., p. 47.

14 Rowe, *Cosmological Argument*, p. 136.

15 William Craig, *The Kalam Cosmological Argument* (London: Macmillan, 1979), p. 63.

16 John Polkinghorne, "The Nature of Physical Reality," *Zygon*, 26/2 (June 1991), pp. 221–36; Robert John Russell, "Cosmology from Alpha to Omega," *Zygon*, 29/4 (Dec. 1994), pp. 557–78.

Once RNA sequences exist, we can understand how they combine and recombine. But prior to the existence of a processor and interpreter of such data, what reason would there be for information-neutral, physical/chemical elements to transform into information-bearing nucleotides, be preserved, and reproduce themselves?[17] With respect to human consciousness, some argue that the correlation of mental events and intentions with brain events cannot have a fully naturalistic explanation, that the development of the conceptual out of the non-conceptual and the intentional out of the non-intentional involve a qualitative change that cannot be explained merely in terms of quantitative complexity.[18]

Still others note that the arrival and development of beings capable of witnessing and understanding the very conditions of their existence requires the occurrence of certain conditions that, by themselves and collectively, have an extremely low antecedent probability.[19] It is not that the existence of conscious beings is a requirement for the existence of such improbable conditions, but the fact that these extraordinarily unlikely but highly significant events occurred at all and in a way that gave rise to beings who can witness them, that requires explanation.

The danger in the versions of the theistic argument that commence from specific natural phenomena is that they smack of the appeal to a god of the gaps. The history of rational theology is fraught with examples where individuals invoke the activity of God to explain events for which scientific reasoning at the time could not account. As scientific knowledge progressed, however, explanations were forthcoming, and the invocation of God as an explanatory hypothesis was no longer necessary. If the above arguments are to avoid this troubled past, the events in question must be intrinsically, and not merely accidentally, completely inexplicable by scientific or naturalistic accounts. For example, Russell and Polkinghorne argue that it is not the case that we merely do not yet possess enough information to understand how particular effects arise from quantum causes; the indeterminacy resides in nature itself. Any quantum explanation has "intrinsic gaps."[20] Similarly, Craig argues that it is not simply our limited knowledge that prevents us from exploring the cause of the universe at the moment of its inception at the Big Bang. For the universe to develop out of infinite density is for it to develop out of nothing, and out of nothing, nothing comes.[21]

The point (and problem) here is to determine whether one has encountered an intrinsic gap in our ontology or whether the gap lies in our epistemic state. In this sense, Gale wisely warns the theist about developing arguments where the explana-

17 J. J. C. Smart and J. J. Haldane, *Atheism and Theism* (Oxford: Blackwell, 1996), pp. 98–106; L. Stafford Betty with Bruce Cordell, "God and Modern Science: New Life for the Teleological Argument," *International Philosophical Quarterly*, 27/4 (Dec. 1987), pp. 409–35.

18 Swinburne, *Existence of God*, pp. 160–75; Smart and Haldane, *Atheism and Theism*, p. 117.

19 John Leslie, "The Anthropic Principle, World Ensemble, Design," *American Philosophical Quarterly*, 19/2 (Apr. 1982), pp. 141–51.

20 John Polkinghorne, "Theological Notions of Creation and Divine Causality," in Murray Rae, Hilary Regan, and John Stenhouse (eds), *Science and Theology* (Grand Rapids, Mich.: William B. Eerdmans, 1994), p. 237.

21 William Lane Craig and Quentin Smith, *Theism, Atheism, and Big Bang Cosmology* (New York: Oxford University Press, 1993), pp. 43–4.

tion in terms of God competes with that of science.[22] At the same time, it is not clear that explaining in terms of divine intention the origin of the Big Bang, the origin of life from nonliving physical/chemical elements, or why particular events arise out of quantum events competes with science, provided one can show ontological incongruity at these junctures. Lack of space prevents us from developing the relevant arguments here.

5 Deductive and Inductive Inferences

The classical versions of the cosmological argument, which hold that the sufficient explanation for the existence or arising of contingencies necessitates the existence and activity of God, are deductive. The conclusion that God (or a necessary being) exists follows necessarily from either the existence or arising of contingent beings (whether individual contingent beings or the universe as a whole), the invocation of the Principle of Sufficient Reason in one of its forms (e.g., Aristotelian act/potency, the Leibnizian strong version, or the Principle of Causation), and the denial that an infinity of contingent beings or causal conditions can supply the requisite sufficient explanation.

Some contemporary versions of the cosmological argument are weaker. For one thing, the claim is not that the existence of God provides the *only* explanation, but rather that it provides the *best* explanation of the things or events in question. God's existence is simpler and has greater explanatory power.[23] For another, theists appeal not to one particular event requiring nonnatural explanation, but rather to a variety of phenomena for which the best explanation is a personal, intelligent supernatural being. From such a cumulative case that combines cosmological and teleological arguments with religious experience, they conclude that it is probable or more likely than not that God exists, given the total data. Should some of the data find their explanation elsewhere, the argument is not significantly affected, since sufficient other data point to the theistic conclusion as the best explanation.

In what follows we first consider the approach that the existence of a necessary being (what we will term God, though one need not use that term[24]) follows deductively from certain premises. Later we briefly explore the inductive approach, arguing that certain contingent phenomena find their best explanation in an appeal to the existence and activity of a supernatural being.

6 The Deductive Cosmological Argument from Contingency

Although the cosmological argument appears in various writers with different first premises, the fundamental structure and resulting issues are basically the same.

22 Gale, *On the Nature and Existence of God*, pp. 240–1.

23 Swinburne, *Existence of God*, ch. 7.

24 One must carefully distinguish between the contention that x exists and what x is, although the second is related to the first in that certain properties of x are required to make the cosmological argument work. See Smart and Haldane, *Atheism and Theism*, pp. 140–8.

1 A contingent being (a being which, if it exists, can not-exist) exists.
2 This contingent being has a cause or explanation[25] of its existence.
3 The cause or explanation of its existence is something other than the contingent being itself.
4 What causes or explains the existence of this contingent being must either be solely other contingent beings or include a non-contingent (necessary) being.
5 Contingent beings alone cannot cause or explain the existence of a contingent being.
6 Therefore, what causes or explains the existence of this contingent being must include a non-contingent (necessary) being.
7 Therefore, a necessary being (a being which, if it exists, cannot not-exist) exists.

Premises 1 and 3 seem true, although objection has been raised to 3 on the grounds that certain complex things can be explained in terms of their components. We will look at this objection shortly. Premise 2 is seen by many to follow from the moderate version of the Principles of Sufficient Reason and Causation. If something is contingent, there must be a cause of its existence or a reason why it exists rather than not-exists. Premise 4 is true by virtue of the Principle of Excluded Middle. Premises 6 and 7 follow validly from the respective premises.

For many critics, premise 5 is the key to the argument's success or failure. Whether it is true depends upon the requirements for an adequate explanation. We have already noted that, according to the Principle of Sufficient Reason, at a minimum what is required is a *full explanation* – that is, an explanation that includes a full cause and the reason why the cause had the effect it did. If the contingent being in premise 1 is the universe, then a full explanation would require something beyond the contingent factors that, as part of the universe, are what are to be explained. That there has always been a magnetic field around the earth does not explain why there is a magnetic field. Similarly, that contingent or dependent things (a universe) have always existed fails to provide a sufficient reason for why the universe exists rather than not. A full explanation of the universe, then, would require the existence of a non-contingent causal condition – namely, a necessary being.

Finally, it should be noted in 7 that if the contingent being identified in 1 is the universe, the necessary being cannot provide a natural explanation for it, for no natural, non-contingent causes and laws or principles exist from which the existence of the universe follows. What remains is a personal explanation in terms of the intentional acts of some supernatural being that is eternal and *a sei*, properties that follow necessarily from its being essentially non-contingent.

6.1 First objection: the universe just is

Of the many objections to the argument, we will consider three major ones. First, over the centuries philosophers have suggested various instantiations for the contingent

25 I include the disjunct "cause or explanation" because not all versions of the cosmological argument invoke the Principle of Sufficient Reason expressed in the Enlightenment sense. The Thomistic arguments emphasize a causal account. Since an explanation is usually (but not always) given in causal language, we will not exploit the difference.

being noted in premise 1. The Thomistic form of the argument focuses on providing a causal explanation for particular contingent beings: something in motion, something caused, and a contingent being. Others, such as Samuel Clarke, suppose that the contingent being referred to in premise 1 is the universe. Due to considerations of space, we will focus on the second of these options.[26]

Bertrand Russell denies that the universe needs an explanation; it just is. His argument takes two forms. In the first version, Russell contends that since we derive the concept of cause from our observation of particular things, we cannot ask about the cause of the universe, which we cannot experience. The universe is "just there, and that's all."[27] Those who reason that we can apply the causal principle (that every contingent being requires a cause of its existence) to the universe commit the Fallacy of Composition, which mistakenly concludes that since the parts have a certain property, the whole likewise has that property. Applied to the cosmological argument, Russell contends that the move from the contingency of the elements of the universe to that of the universe is likewise fallacious. Hence, whereas we can ask for the cause of particular things, there is no reason to think we can ask for the cause of the universe or the set of all contingent beings.

Russell correctly notes that arguments of the part–whole type can commit the Fallacy of Composition. For example, the argument that since all the bricks in the wall are small, the wall is small, is fallacious. Yet sometimes the totality has the same character as the parts on account of the parts – the wall is brick because we built it out of bricks. The universe's contingency, theists argue, resembles the second case. If all the contingent things in the universe, including matter and energy, ceased to exist simultaneously, the universe itself, as the totality of these things, would cease to exist. But if the universe can cease to exist, it is contingent and requires an explanation for its existence.[28]

Some reply that this argument for the contingency of the universe is still fallacious, for even if every contingent being fails to exist in some possible world, it may be the case that there is no possible world that lacks a contingent being. That is, though no being would exist in every possible world, every world would possess at least one contingent being. Rowe gives the example of a horse race. "We know that although no horse in a given horse race necessarily will be the winner, it is, nevertheless, necessary that some horse in the race will be the winner."[29]

Rowe's example fails, however, for it is possible that all the horses break a leg and none finishes the race. That is, the necessity that some horse will win follows only if there is some reason to think that some horse must finish the race. Similarly, the objection to the universe's contingency will hold only if there is some reason to think that the existence of something is necessary. One reason given is that the existence

26 For a more detailed consideration of the Thomistic version of the argument, see Michael Peterson et al., *Reason and Religious Belief* (New York: Oxford University Press, 1991), pp. 76–9; Reichenbach, *Cosmological Argument*; Swinburne, *Existence of God*, pp. 87–9; Anthony Kenny, *The Five Ways* (Boston: Schocken Books, 1969).

27 Bertrand Russell and Frederick Copleston, "A Debate on the Existence of God," in John Hick (ed.), *The Existence of God* (New York: Macmillan, 1964), p. 175.

28 Reichenbach, *Cosmological Argument*, ch. 6.

29 Rowe, *Cosmological Argument*, p. 164.

of one contingent being may be necessary for the nonexistence of some other contingent being.[30]

But though the fact that something's existence is necessary for the existence of something else holds for certain properties (for example, the existence of siblings is necessary for someone not to be an only child), it is doubtful that something's existence is necessary for something else's nonexistence *per se*, which claim is needed to support the argument denying the contingency of the universe. Hence, with no good reason to the contrary, given the contingency of everything in the universe, it remains that there is a possible world without any contingent beings.[31]

Further, given contemporary accounts both of the origin of the universe and, in some quarters, its probable demise, it is reasonable to think that the universe is the sort of thing that is contingent (it could conceivably not be) and hence requires an explanation. The very meaningfulness of the discussion mutes the view that the universe is an abstraction, like the human race. Behind Russell's denial of causal predicates to the universe lies a positivism that presumes that the only meaningful causal accounts are those that invoke natural or scientific explanations. But such a presumption begs the question, especially if we admit personal explanations as genuine explanations. In short, contrary to Russell, the theist commits neither a fallacy nor a category mistake in asking for an explanation of the existence of the universe.[32]

Russell's second version appeals to quantum physics.[33] He notes that physicists find indetermination on the subatomic level. For example, it appears that electrons can pass out of existence at one point and then come back into existence elsewhere. One cannot trace their intermediate existence or determine what causes them to come into existence at one point rather than another. Their location is only statistically probable.[34] Since the singular event of the Big Bang is a microscopic event on the level where quantum principles apply, the cosmological argument cannot defend premise 2, and hence the argument fails.

30 This reason was suggested to me by James Sadowsky.

31 The theist need not establish that in fact this is the case, only that it is possible. William Rowe (*Cosmological Argument*, p. 166) develops a different argument to support the thesis that the universe must be contingent. He argues that it is necessary that if God exists, then it is possible that no dependent beings exist. Since it is possible that God exists, it is possible that no dependent beings exist, and hence the universe is contingent. Rowe takes the conditional as necessarily true in virtue of the concept of God. That is, given who God is, it is up to God whether dependent beings exist or not.

32 Rowe suggests a different argument for the inapplicability of cause to the universe. "Many collections of physical things cannot possibly be themselves *concrete* entities. Think, for example, of the collection whose members are the largest prehistoric beast, Socrates, and the Empire State Building. By any stretch of the imagination can we view this collection as itself a concrete thing? Clearly we cannot. Such a collection must be construed as an *abstract* entity, a class or set" (Rowe, *Cosmological Argument*, p. 135). From here Rowe reconstructs the cosmological argument to ask not why the universe exists in terms of a cause, but why it has the members it has rather than others or none at all. But there is no reason to think that collections of concrete entities cannot themselves be concrete objects or systems or aggregates of concrete objects, themselves needing an explanation for their existence. Indeed, Socrates is precisely the sort of thing about which one can mount a causal inquiry. (Though we do not have space to develop it here, the argument is presented cogently and clearly in Gale, *On the Nature and Existence of God*, pp. 248–50.)

33 See also Paul Davies, *Superforce* (New York: Simon and Schuster, 1984), p. 200.

34 Craig and Smith, *Theism, Atheism, and Big Bang Cosmology*, pp. 182, 121–3.

Given our present knowledge, it is difficult to know what to say about this argument from quantum physics. As some wag quipped, "one who claims to understand quantum physics does not understand quantum physics."[35] Some argue that the phenomenon of indeterminacy results from the limits of our investigative equipment. We simply are unable at this time to discern the intermediate states of the electron's existence. According to a second view, termed "the Copenhagen interpretation" of quantum physics, the very introduction of the observer into the arena so affects what is observed that it gives the appearance that effects exist without causes. But one cannot know what is happening without introducing observers and the changes they bring. A third view is that the indeterminacy is real, but that the evidence of particles or energy coming into existence out of vacuum fluctuation is not equivalent to showing that they are uncaused. "Virtual particles do not literally come into existence spontaneously out of nothing. . . . 'The quantum vacuum states . . . are defined simply as local, or global, energy minima.' The microstructure of the quantum vacuum is a sea of continually forming and dissolving particles which borrow energy from the vacuum for their brief existence. . . . Thus vacuum fluctuations do not constitute an exception to the principle that whatever begins to exist has a cause."[36] In each of these three explanations of quantum phenomena, premise 2 holds. A fourth view is that we have no idea what laws of physics applied in the very early stages of the universe, and hence no reason to deny that the Causal Principle applied at that stage.

At the same time, it should be recognized that showing that indeterminacy is a real feature of the world at the quantum level would have significant negative implications for the more general Causal Principle that underlies the deductive cosmological argument.[37] Quantum accounts allow for additional speculation regarding origins and structures of universes (for example, Hawking's theory that the finite universe has no space-time boundaries and hence, without an initial singularity, requires no cause[38]).

6.2 Second objection: explaining the individual constituents is sufficient

A second objection, originally raised by David Hume, is that the whole is explained when the parts are explained. "But the *whole*, you say, wants a cause. I answer that the uniting of these parts into a whole . . . is performed merely by an arbitrary act of the mind, and has no influence on the nature of things. Did I show you the particular causes of each individual in a collection of twenty particles of matter, I should think it very unreasonable should you afterwards ask me what was the cause of the whole twenty. This is sufficiently explained in explaining the parts."[39]

35 "The greatest paradox about quantum theory is that after more than fifty years of successful exploitation of its techniques its interpretation still remains a matter of dispute" (John Polkinghorne, *One World* (London: SPCK, 1986), p. 47).

36 Craig and Smith, *Theism, Atheism, and Big Bang Cosmology*, pp. 143–4.

37 Mark William Worthing, *God, Creation, and Contemporary Physics* (Minneapolis: Fortress, 1996), p. 50.

38 Stephen Hawking, *A Brief History of Time* (New York: Bantam Books, 1988), p. 136.

39 David Hume, *Dialogues Concerning Natural Religion*, part IX.

On the one hand, it is not always true that the whole is sufficiently explained in explaining its parts. An explanation of the parts may provide a partial but incomplete explanation; what remains unexplained is why these parts exist rather than others, why they exist rather than not, or why the parts are arranged as they are. With respect to the latter, Gale gives the example of a heap of rocks. While a prisoner swinging a sledgehammer may explain the existence of each individual rock in the pile, it does not explain the existence of the heap assembled by another prisoner.[40]

However, although this shows that Hume's principle that the whole is explained in explaining the parts is sometimes false, it does not show that it is false in the case under consideration: namely, that of the universe treated as a set rather than as an aggregate. But suppose one invokes the explanation of the parts to explain the whole. In terms of what are the parts themselves explained? Each is explained either in terms of itself or in terms of something else. The former would make them necessary beings, contrary to their contingency. If they are explained in terms of something else, the entire collection still remains unaccounted for. "When the existence of each member of a collection is explained by reference to some other member *of that very same collection* then it does not follow that the collection itself has an explanation. For it is one thing for there to be an explanation of the existence of each dependent being and quite another thing for there to be an explanation of why there are dependent beings at all."[41] Swinburne notes that an explanation is complete when "any attempt to go beyond the factors which we have would result in no gain of explanatory power or prior probability."[42] But explaining why something exists rather than nothing, and why it is as it is, gives additional explanatory power in explaining why a universe exists at all. Hence, to explain the parts of the universe and their particular concatenation, appeal must be made to something other than those parts.[43]

6.3 Third objection: the conclusion is contradictory

Some, like Immanuel Kant and, more recently, Richard Gale, object to the conclusion that a necessary being exists. They contend that when the cosmological argument concludes to the existence of a necessary being, it argues for the existence of a being whose nonexistence is absolutely inconceivable. But the only being that meets this condition is the most real or maximally excellent being, the concept that lies at the heart of the ontological argument. Accordingly, they claim, the cosmological argument presupposes the cogency of the ontological argument. But since the ontological argument is suspect, the cosmological argument that depends on it must likewise

40 Gale, *On the Nature and Existence of God*, pp. 253–4.

41 Rowe, *Cosmological Argument*, p. 264.

42 Swinburne, *Existence of God*, p. 86.

43 Gale, *On the Nature and Existence of God*, pp. 257–8. A different kind of explanation is provided by Frank Tipler, who holds that many worlds exist, so that the universe realizes all possibilities. On this view nothing is contingent. The many-worlds view of Tipler and Withrow, however interesting, is intrinsically incapable of being confirmed.

be suspect.[44] Indeed, Gale argues, since it is impossible for an unsurpassably great necessary being to exist, the conclusion of the argument is necessarily false, and the argument unsound.[45]

However, the contention that the cosmological argument depends on the ontological argument is based on a confusion. The term *necessary being* can be understood in different ways. Kant, like some modern defenders of the ontological argument, understands "necessary being" as having to do with logically necessary existence – that is, with existence that is logically undeniable. But this is not the sense in which "necessary being" is understood in the cosmological argument. Necessity is understood in the sense of ontological or factual necessity. A necessary being is one that *if* it exists, it cannot not-exist; as self-sufficient and self-sustaining, its inability to not-exist flows from its nature. Since such a concept is not self-contradictory, the existence of a necessary being is not intrinsically impossible.

7 The Deductive Cosmological Argument from Coming into Existence

Whereas the previous rendition of the Cosmological Argument develops out of the notion of contingency, many who attempt to bridge the disciplines of religion and science focus on the need for an explanation of what comes to be in time. Craig terms this deceptively simple argument "the Kalam Cosmological Argument."

8 Whatever begins to exist must have a cause of its existence.
9 The universe began to exist.
10 Therefore, the universe has a cause of its existence.

We have already discussed and defended 8 (in first objection above), which is a version of the Causal Principle that underlies all cosmological arguments. The truth of 9 is supported by current cosmology, according to which somewhere around 15 billion years ago the universe suddenly exploded into existence in a violent event known as the "Big Bang." The theoretical model undergirding the Big Bang projected that if the universe had such an origin, heat radiation resulting from the event would still be observable. Confirmation of this occurred when in 1965 two scientists at Bell Laboratories, Arno Penzias and Robert Wilson, discovered the background radiation that is the remnant of this primeval, fiery explosion. Since the initial explosion, the universe has continued to expand, its galaxies speeding away from each other, as evidenced by the light from distant galaxies shifting to the red end of the color spectrum. The Hubble constant expresses the ratio of the velocity of the recession of objects to their distance from us. According to the Infinitely Expanding Universe model, the Big Bang occurred only once. Expanding from an initial singularity where the gravitational force and the

44 Immanuel Kant, *Critique of Pure Reason*, tr. Norman Kemp Smith (New York: St Martin's Press, 1929), p. A606.
45 Gale, *On the Nature and Existence of God*, pp. 282–4.

universe's density were infinite, where space-time and the laws of physics came into existence, the universe will continue to expand at an increasing rate, ending in an uncertain future once conceived of as a cold death (the Big Freeze).

7.1 First objection: the Oscillating Universe

Some suggest that although the infinitely expanding universe resulting from a singular event is consistent with the discovered data, so is the competing Oscillating Universe model, according to which the universe is eternal, undergoing repetitive cycles of expansion and contraction. Following each big explosion, the universe expands to a certain point, whereupon the gravitational force of its component matter slows and eventually ends its expansion, collapsing it until it reaches a point of almost infinite density (the Big Crunch), whereupon it explodes and expands outward again. This process repeats indefinitely, though not necessarily in the same way or invoking the same physical laws.

Determining whether the Big Crunch model can be correct depends, in part, upon calculating the total amount of matter in the universe. For contraction still to be possible, our universe must not have passed the critical threshold beyond which the gravitational force can no longer reverse its expansion. Some scientists hold that the density of matter is now insufficient to halt the expansion of the universe. The stars have only 1 percent of the matter necessary to collapse the universe. Having passed the critical gravitational threshold, the universe will continue to expand forever. Others maintain that a great quantity of currently undetected, invisible, or dark matter exists in the universe, scattered in dust clouds within and between the galaxies, so that we have not yet passed the critical threshold beyond which contraction of the universe is possible. Pictures from the Hubble telescope have confirmed the enormity of the galactic dust and gas clouds. Not-too-distant space probes using X-ray and infrared telescopes and the Microwave Anistropy Probe will look for invisible, superheated gas and massive, but faint, brown dwarf stars. However, determining that the universe has not passed the critical threshold will not establish the truth of the Oscillating Theory. At best, these observations can falsify but not confirm that theory.[46]

Very recent discoveries, however, appear to have mooted the argument that requires calculating the amount of matter in the universe. Focusing on supernovas, Saul Perlmutter and several other astronomers discovered that the universe is expanding not at a constant but at an accelerating rate. Some force in the universe not only counteracts gravity but pushes the universe apart ever faster. This discovery, confirming the infinite expansion hypothesis, makes a collapse most unlikely.[47]

7.2 Second objection: something can come from nothing

Some theoretical physicists, such as Stephen Hawking, contend that premise 8 is false, that on what is termed the "inflationary" theory of the origin of the universe, the uni-

46 For additional empirical evidence that we have passed the critical threshold, see Craig and Smith, *Theism, Atheism, and Big Bang Cosmology*, pp. 47–56.

47 James Glanz, "Cosmic Motion Revealed," *Science*, 282 (Dec. 18, 1998).

verse came into existence without a cause. The universe was originally a vacuum with no space-time dimensions. At this point quantum phenomena, which include the denial of the Causal Principle, came into play. This universe "found itself in an excited vacuum state," a "ferment of quantum activity, teeming with virtual particles and full of complex interactions,"[48] which, subject to a cosmic repulsive force, resulted in an immense increase in energy. Due to this repulsive force, the universe rapidly expanded in size. But what is the origin of this increase in energy, which eventually made possible the Big Bang? The response is that the law of conservation of energy, which now applies to our universe and holds that the total quantity of energy in the universe remains fixed despite transfer from one form to another, does not apply to the initial expansion. Cosmic repulsion caused the energy to increase from zero in the vacuum to a huge amount. This great explosion released energy, from which all matter emerged. In effect, contrary to the ancient Parmenidean Principle, out of nothing – a primeval vacuum – came everything.

But "even if the Big Bang is the result of a 'zero-point' fluctuation . . . it would be necessary to ask what caused this fluctuation."[49] We could abandon the Causal Principle, but then which appears to be more likely: that the Principle of Causation does not apply to this grand event (that the universe emerged from nothing) or that the universe resulted from the intentional act of a supernatural being? The second at the very least provides a plausible explanation of the universe's origin, something the first does not. But it is the provision of a reasonable explanation which is the very thing at stake in the cosmological argument to the best explanation.

The Kalam version of the cosmological argument combines deductive inference with inductive reasoning in an attempt to provide the best explanation for how the universe came to be. To the inductive argument we briefly turn.

8 The Inductive Theistic Arguments

The inductive cosmological argument is much weaker than the deductive argument in that it appeals to the inference to the best potential explanation. In brief, it contends that a divine being provides the simplest and best explanatory account for the Big Bang. "There is no ground for supposing that matter and energy existed before [the Big Bang] and was suddenly galvanized into action. . . . It is simpler to postulate creation *ex nihilo* – divine will constituted Nature from nothingness."[50]

Swinburne distinguishes between two varieties of inductive arguments: those that show that the conclusion is more probable than not (what he terms a "correct P-inductive argument") and those that further increase the probability of the conclusion (what he terms a "correct C-inductive argument"). The arguments he presents, he claims, fall into the category of C-inductive arguments, although others may want to construct a stronger case based on P-inductive arguments.

48 Davies, *Superforce*, pp. 191–2.

49 Betty, with Cordell, "God and Modern Science," p. 412.

50 Robert Jastrow, *God and the Astronomers* (New York: W. W. Norton and Co., 1978), pp. 111–12.

We do not have space to follow the reasoning of the inductive argument in detail, but two aspects deserve highlighting. First, the inference to the best explanation is best understood in comparative terms. First, one selects among the possible theories those to be considered, and from this select group ultimately judges which one provides the best explanation. In effect, such an inference involves "two filters, one that selects the plausible candidates (the live options) and a second that selects from among them."[51]

This leads to the second and more difficult problem: namely, determination of the criteria to be used to adjudicate between competing explanations when, as in the case of the cosmological argument, exact quantitative measures of probability are not only lacking but impossible to generate. Peter Lipton suggests two criteria: likeliness and loveliness. Likeliness has to do with the explanation that is the truest; loveliness has to do with which is most explanatory or provides the most understanding. As he notes, it would appear that the former criterion would be the one to select, since we are looking for the real cause of the phenomena in question. However, to use the criterion of the truest explanation when what we are searching for is the truest explanation appears to reason in a circular fashion. We need to develop a method by which we can generate potential causes and then use experimental methods to resolve which of these is most likely to result in the effect. Though this is a reasonable procedure where experimental methods can be used, when we deal with the origin of the universe, where not only is the event itself unique, but where the laws of physics as we know them probably do not apply in the initial stages (10^{-43} second), we are left to rely more heavily on the second criterion, loveliness.

Swinburne suggests four criteria for justifications which exemplify loveliness:

11 It leads us to expect (with accuracy) many and varied events which we observe.
12 What is proposed is simple. ("A theory is simple in so far as it postulates few mathematically simple laws holding between entities of an intelligible kind."[52])
13 It fits with our background knowledge.
14 We would not otherwise expect to find these events[53] – what he terms explanatory. ("A theory has explanatory power in so far as it entails or makes probable the occurrence of many diverse phenomena which are all observed to occur, and the occurrence of which is not otherwise to be expected."[54])

He suggests that criterion 13 does not apply in the case of the cause of the universe, for there are no "neighbouring fields of enquiry" where we investigate the cause of the universe. Indeed, he suggests that 13 reduces to criterion 12, which for him is the key to the inductive cosmological argument.

Swinburne argues that appeals to God's intentions and actions, although not leading to specific predictions about what the world will look like, better explain

51 Peter Lipton, *Inference to the Best Explanation* (London: Routledge, 1991), p. 61.
52 Swinburne, *Existence of God*, p. 52.
53 Richard Swinburne, *Is There a God?* (New York: Oxford University Press, 1996), p. 26.
54 Swinburne, *Existence of God*, pp. 52, 53.

specific phenomena than other accounts. Theism, he argues, has a probability close to neither 1 nor 0. It is not close to 1, because it lacks high predictive power. As an intentional free agent, God could have created many different worlds. God is not required to create any world, let alone the best possible one.[55] On the other hand, theism's probability is not close to 0 either, for it is consistent with the kind of phenomena that we experience in the world: the existence of an ordered universe capable of being known, the existence of intentional beings, and the theory's consonance with people's religious experience. Swinburne concludes: "Theism does not make [certain phenomena] very probable; but nothing else makes their occurrence in the least probable, and they cry out for explanation. *A priori*, theism is perhaps very unlikely, but it is far more likely than any rival supposition. Hence our phenomena are substantial evidence for the truth of theism."[56]

9 Why God Provides the Best Explanation

But why does God provide the best or ultimate explanation in the cases we have considered? Part of the answer is that God, or the necessary being, is a being who is not only uncaused but to whom the Principle of Causation is inapplicable. On the one hand, there can be no scientific explanation of God's existence, for there are no antecedent beings or scientific principles from which God's existence follows. On the other hand, the Principle of Causation applies only to contingent, and not to necessary, beings. Explanation is required only of those things that are contingent – that is, those things that if they do exist, could possibly not have existed. It is not that God's existence is logically necessary, but that if God exists, he cannot not-exist. God is both eternal and does not depend on anything for his existence. These, however, are not reasons for his existence, but his properties.

Another part of the answer is that explanation can be reasonably thought to have achieved finality when a personal explanation has been provided that appeals to the intentions of a conscious agent. One may, of course, attempt to provide a scientific account of why someone has the intentions that he or she has, but there is no requirement that such an account be supplied, let alone even be possible. We may not achieve any more explanatory value by trying to explain physically why persons intended to act as they did. However, when we claim that something happened because persons intended it and acted on their intentions, we can achieve a complete explanation of why that thing happened. [57]

55 For a defense of this, see Bruce R. Reichenbach, *Evil and a Good God* (New York: Fordham University Press, 1982), ch. 6.

56 Swinburne, *Existence of God*, p. 290.

57 Craig unpacks this in terms of the Islamic principle of determination. "When two different states of affairs are equally possible and one results, this realization of one rather than the other must be the result of the action of a personal agent who freely chooses one rather than the other.... For while a mechanically operating set of necessary and sufficient conditions would either produce the effect from eternity or not at all, a personal being may freely choose to create at any time wholly apart from any distinguishing conditions of one moment from another." This, he notes, results from the nature of the will (Craig, *Kalam Cosmological Argument*, pp. 150–1).

Third, appeal to God as an intentional agent leads us to have certain expectations about the universe: that it manifests order, that it is comprehensible, that it favors the existence of beings that can comprehend it.[58] The presence of these features helps to satisfy 11 above.

Swinburne and Haldane introduce a fourth feature: namely, the simplicity of God that, by its very nature, makes further explanation either impossible or makes theism the best explanation, thereby satisfying 12 above. But that leads to a whole other set of issues regarding God's properties and the nature of simplicity, a fit subject for another time and place.[59]

Much more can be said. In particular, it remains to be shown that the necessary being is the God of religion. This is not the task of the cosmological argument, but requires employment of the method of correlation, whereby the properties of the necessary being are correlated with those of the God of religion.[60] But enough has been presented to indicate that the deductive and inductive cosmological arguments provide part of a cumulative justification for theistic belief.

Why Traditional Cosmological Arguments Don't Work, and a Sketch of a New One that Does

Richard M. Gale

Bruce Reichenbach has done a masterful job of surveying traditional versions of the cosmological argument, as well as attempting to meet the standard objections to them. In addition, he has defended his own version of the argument. I will attempt to show that his argument, along with all other traditional cosmological arguments, don't work, and then go on to sketch a new one that does.

58 "I cannot believe that our existence in this universe is a mere quirk of fate, an accident of history, an incidental blip in the great cosmic drama. Our involvement is too intimate. The physical species *Homo* may count for nothing, but the existence of mind in some organism on some planet in the universe is surely a fact of fundamental significance. Through conscious beings the universe has generated self-awareness. This can be no trivial detail, no minor byproduct of mindless, purposeless forces. We are truly meant to be here" (Paul Davies, *The Mind of God* (New York: Simon & Schuster, 1992), p. 232).

59 At times it is unclear whether Swinburne is claiming the virtue of God's simplicity or that of theism. Swinburne entitles chapter 3 of *Is There a God?* "The Simplicity of God." But a subheading is "The Simplicity of Theism."

60 See Robin Attfield, "The God of Religion and the God of Philosophy," *Religious Studies*, 9 (1975), pp. 1–9.

1 Reichenbach's "Deductive Cosmological Argument from Contingency"

Reichenbach's argument has as its first premise that

1 A contingent being (a being which, if it exists, can not-exist) exists.

Because this premise can be known only via sense experience, it keeps his argument from being completely a priori. This is not a serious matter, since no one but a complete skeptic about the senses would doubt that there exists at least one contingent being, such as a chair or an apple. In the course of defending this argument, Reichenbach eventually makes this existent contingent being the aggregate of all existent contingent beings – that is, the universe.

The most controversial premise of the argument is

2 This contingent being [i.e., the universe] has a cause or explanation of its existence.

Herein appeal is made to a version of the Principle of Sufficient Reason (hereafter PSR) or Principle of Causation (hereafter PC), which holds that for every existent contingent being there is a cause or explanation of its existence. Once this principle is granted, the rest of the argument follows in due course.

3 The cause or explanation of its [the universe's] existence is something other than the contingent being itself.
4 What causes or explains the existence of this contingent being must either be solely other contingent beings or include a non-contingent (necessary) being.
5 Contingent beings alone cannot cause or explain the existence of a contingent being.
6 Therefore, what causes or explains the existence of this contingent being must include a non-contingent (necessary) being.
7 Therefore, a necessary being (a being which, if it exists, cannot not-exist) exists.

Premise 3 rests on the impossibility of something being a *causa sui*. This must be distinguished from an individual being a self-explainer in the sense that its existence is entailed by its essence, since there is a successful ontological argument for the existence of this individual, even if we aren't smart enough to give it. A self-explaining being satisfies PSR but not PC, since the explanation of its existence is not a causal one. Premise 4 follows from the application of the Law of Excluded Middle to premise 3. The truth of premise 5 becomes manifest once it is realized that the contingent being in question is the universe, and thereby includes every contingent existent. Were one of these contingent existents to causally explain the existence of the universe, it would have to causally explain, among other things, its own existence; but this is not possible, since no individual can be a *causa sui*. Premise 5 is an obvious consequence of 4, for the reason just given. Since the universe, being itself a contingent being, must have a cause, and this cause cannot be a contingent being, it must be, or include, a necessary being. This is because every being is either contingent, necessary, or impossible; and obviously, an impossible being cannot causally explain anything. The conclusion, 7, is an obvious logical consequence of 6.

1.1 Why Reichenbach's argument does not work

Three objections will be advanced against Reichenbach's argument: (1) the nontheist opponent of the argument is within her rights to reject its PSR or PC, especially since no positive support is given for PSR or PC by the cosmological arguer; (2) the argument violates the spirit and intent of PSR in countenancing a God who has a brute, unexplained existence; and (3) there is an unclosed gap between the necessary being that the argument allegedly proves to exist and the God of traditional Western theism.

1.1.1 Loch of support for PSR

This objection applies to all the traditional cosmological arguments surveyed by Reichenbach. What they have in common is that each employs a "strong version" of PSR, because it is required for every fact of a certain type that there actually is an explanation of it.[61] A "weak version," by contrast, requires only that for every fact of a certain type it is possible that there is an explanation of it. Within each of these two versions of PSR, distinctions can be made between weaker and stronger versions thereof. The strongest version of the strong version of PSR requires that for every fact or true proposition, without exception, there actually is an explanation of it. Reichenbach's version of the strong version of PSR is considerably weaker than this, for it requires only that for every proposition that reports the existence of a contingent being or the coming into existence of some being there actually is an explanation of it.[62] God, as conceived of by Reichenbach, falls outside the purview of this version of PSR, since he is neither a contingent being nor comes into existence. Rather, he is a necessary being, not in the absolute, unqualified sense of necessary, but in an existentially relative sense: namely, that if he exists, then he necessarily exists in the sense that it is impossible that he either come into or go out of existence.

Why should the nontheist opponent of Reichenbach's argument grant his version of PSR? Although it is not the strongest version, it is still quite strong, occupying a very exalted level in one's wish book, almost as high as that God exists. Reichenbach offers no direct argumentative support for his version of PSR, but instead implicitly

61 By "fact" is meant a true proposition, a proposition being an abstract entity that can serve as the bearer of truth-values and modalities, as well as the object of an intentional attitude, such as believing, and the meaning or sense of a sentence. For reasons that will not be gone into here, it is such abstract propositions that get filled in for the blank spaces in "—explains (or causes)—."

62 "What is contingent or what comes into being requires a sufficient reason for why it exists or comes into being."

shifts the onus onto his opponent to establish its falsity and, furthermore, attempts to shoot down only one effort to do so, Hume's.[63]

With what right does Reichenbach shift the onus? After all, it is he who is advancing an argument for the existence of God that crucially depends upon the acceptance of PSR, a principle that has been highly mooted throughout the history of philosophy. Thus, it would seem that the burden is on him to give positive argumentative support for it. I have not seen among the multitude of cosmological arguers, past and present, any positive argument for PSR. An example of what such an argument for PSR might look like was offered to me recently by Alexander Pruss, with a grin on his face. Nothing can exist without a sufficient reason for its existence; for then it would have no connection with existence and thus not exist. All that this argument shows is that if a being has no sufficient reason for its existence, it has no rational connection with existence, not that it has no connection at all. It still could be connected with existence in the sense of being a part of existence or instantiating the property of having existence.

The best that the cosmological arguer can do in support of PSR is to show that it is pragmatically rational for an inquirer to believe it, since by believing that everything has an explanation, the believer becomes a more ardent and dedicated inquirer, and thus is more apt to find explanations than if she did not believe this. This pragmatic sense of "rational" concerns the benefits that accrue to the believer of the PSR proposition, as contrasted with the cognitive or epistemic sense of "rational" that concerns reasons directed toward supporting the truth of the proposition believed. Since Reichenbach's argument attempts to establish the cognitive rationality of believing that God exists, it cannot employ a premise that concerns only the pragmatic rationality of believing that God exists, it cannot employ a premise that concerns only the pragmatic rationality of believing some proposition, such as PSR; for this would commit the fallacy of equivocation, since "rational" would be used in both the pragmatic and the cognitive sense. In essence, it would be arguing that it is cognitively rational to believe in a proposition p because it is pragmatically rational to believe some proposition q, from which p follows or which is needed for the deduction of p.

Not only does Reichenbach offer no positive argumentative support for PSR and PC, what little indirect support he gives is unconvincing. His indirect support consists only in an attempt to refute Hume's argument against PC. Simply put, Hume argued that we can conceive of an uncaused event; and, since whatever is conceivable is possible in reality, PC is false. Reichenbach's rebuttal holds that Hume "confuses epistemic with ontological conditions." To be sure, there is a distinction between what is conceivable and what could exist, the former concerning the epistemic, the latter the ontological order. Nevertheless, Reichenbach's rebuttal is far too facile, for it fails to face the fact that our only access to the ontological order is through the epistemic order. The only way that we humans can go about determining what has the possibility of existing is by appeal to what we can conceive to be possible. Such

63 Thus I was surprised to see Reichenbach subsequently write, "We have already discussed and defended 8, which is a version of the Causal Principle that underlies all cosmological arguments." This is quite misleading, since previously he gave only a weak, indirect defense of this principle.

modal intuitions concerning what is possible are fallible; they are only prima facie acceptable, since they are subject to defeat by subsequent ratiocination. They are discussion-beginners, not discussion-enders. What Reichenbach has failed to do is to give Hume any reason why he should not trust his prima facie modal intuition. And until such reasons are produced, Hume has a right to trust it. In philosophy we must go with what we can make intelligible to ourselves at the end of the day, after we have made our best philosophical efforts.

1.1.2 PSR and God's existence

This is a variant of Schopenhauer's objection to the cosmological argument, as being like a taxicab that we hire and then dismiss when we have reached our destination. We begin by demanding, on the basis of PSR, an explanation for a certain fact, but when we arrive at our desired destination, God, we dismiss PSR because we do not require an explanation for the fact that God exists. It is just this sort of argument that invites the response from the precocious child, "Yeah! And who created God?"

Reichenbach has a ready response to this taxicab objection that is based on an alleged crucial disanalogy between his version of the cosmological argument and those versions that are a suitable target for this objection. Whereas both arguments begin with a demand to explain the existence of some contingent being, his argument, unlike the objectionable versions, terminates with a non-contingent explainer. That its existence is a brute, unexplained fact is okay, since it is not possible that there be an explanation for its existence, this being due to its being neither a contingent being nor one that could begin or cease to exist. *Pace* Reichenbach, it will be argued here that it is possible for there to be an explanation for the existence of his God, and that even if this weren't the case, there would still be a violation of the spirit and intent of PSR.

In order to understand why, *pace* Reichenbach, it is possible for there to be an explanation for the existence of his God, thereby making the fact that his God exists fair game for any reasonable version of PSR, his notion of God's necessary existence must be made perspicuous. The sort of necessity that God has, we are told, must not be confused with logical or absolute necessity, terms that Reichenbach uses interchangeably, though the latter is preferable, since not all absolutely or metaphysically necessary truths can be proved by logic alone, such as that no object is larger than itself or red and green all over. At first glance, the difference between the two senses of "necessary" is that what is absolutely necessary is not relative to any world, whereas Reichenbach's sense of "necessary" is. If it is true in some possible world that a being X necessarily exists, then it is true in every possible world that X necessarily exists. By contrast, what is necessary for Reichenbach is relativized to the actual world, it being possible for some being, in particular his God, necessarily to exist in the actual world but not in every other possible world. This seems to be the implication of his claim in step 7 that a necessary being is "a being which, if it exists, cannot not-exist." His definition of a "contingent being" as "a being which, if it exists, can not-exist" also seems to relativize modalities to the actual world. Whereas absolute modalities are world-invariant, Reichenbach's are relativized to the actual world. As a consequence, his sense of necessity, unlike the absolute one, is not subject to system S5's basic axiom that if it is possible that it is necessary that p, then it is necessary that p. Although there is this important difference between absolute and Reichenbachian necessity, it does not adequately explain what the latter is. I believe that a perspicuous account of Reichenbachian modalities will show that, appearances to the contrary, they are analyzable in terms of absolute modalities.

Let us look first at his definition of a "contingent being" as "one which if it exists, can not-exist." The first thing to be noted is that this definition has the absurd consequence that every absolutely impossible being, such as the object that is larger than itself, is a contingent being, for it is true that if the building that is larger than itself exists, then it can not-exist. No doubt, Reichenbach would repair his definition by restricting it to absolutely possible beings. The question, then, is what his definition means by "can" of absolute possibility. Thus, his definition of a "contingent being" really says nothing more than that it is absolutely possible for such a being to exist as well as absolutely possible for it to not-exist. Reichenbach's God, it might be added, is a contingent being in this absolute sense of contingent, since it is absolutely possible that he exists and also absolutely possible that he does not exist.

It can be shown that Reichenbach's existentially relativized notion of necessity is also analyzable in terms of absolute modalities. What is meant by "cannot not-exist" in his definition of a "necessary being" as one which, "if it exists, cannot not-exist"? He explains this notion in terms of not having the possibility of beginning or ceasing to exist, in which case by "possibility" he would seem to mean "absolute possibility." Thus, the claim that God is a necessary being means that it is absolutely impossible that God begin or cease to exist. Again, it turns out that one of Reichenbach's existentially relativized modalities is reducible to absolute ones.

Having clarified what Reichenbach means by God's having necessary existence, it can be asked whether it is absolutely impossible that there be an explanation for the fact that Reichenbach's God exists. There is an explanation for God's not beginning or ceasing to exist based on it being a conceptual or metaphysical truth that God's nature precludes his doing so. But our question concerns whether there could be an explanation for the fact that he exists at all. Reichenbach so defines his God that the explanation cannot be in terms of God's nature, since he denies that his God necessarily exists in the absolute sense, thereby precluding the possibility of explaining his existence via an ontological argument. Although Reichenbach's God lacks such necessary existence, is it possible for some God-like being to have such necessary existence?[64] Reichenbach gives no argument against this possibility. If it is possible for there to be a such necessarily existent God – one that exists in every possible world – then it is possible that the existence of Reichenbach's God would be explained in terms of the causal efficacy of this necessarily existent God based on what this God wills. Thus, until Reichenbach produces a telling argument against the possibility of there being a necessarily existent God, he has no right to claim that it is not possible that there be an explanation for the fact that his God exists. And even if he could produce such an argument, it still would not follow that no explanation is possible for the existence of his God, since it is possible that there is an explanation for the

64 And, in what follows, I will argue that this is not only possible, but actually the case.

fact that his God exists in terms of the causal efficacy of some other equally contingent being. If Reichenbach's God is omni-temporally eternal, enduring throughout a beginningless and endless time, this second being could also be omni-temporally eternal and sustain Reichenbach's God throughout this infinite time. Thus, it could causally explain his existence without causing him to come into existence – that is, begin to exist in time, something that is conceptually precluded in virtue of his very nature. Because the causally explaining being does not have necessary existence, its existence is yet to be explained. But this shows only that the proffered explanation is not a final one, not that it is not a complete explanation. In conclusion, Reichenbach's claim that it is impossible for there to be an explanation for the fact that his God exists shows a lack of imagination.

Since his God is an absolutely contingent being, there should be at least the possibility of explaining his existence, just as there is for any other absolutely contingent being. That Reichenbach's version of PSR has the consequence that every contingent being other than his equally contingent God has an explanation makes his version of the cosmological argument a fit target for the taxicab objection. His version of PSR violates the underlying spirit and intent of the strong version of this principle, which, at a minimum, wants every absolutely contingent being to have an actual explanation for the fact that it exists. That Reichenbach's God has the wondrous property of lacking the possibility of beginning or ceasing to exist is not itself sufficient grounds for making it an exception to PSR's demand that every absolutely contingent being have an actual explanation.

1.1.3 The necessary being and the God of theism

The conclusion of Reichenbach's argument, it will be recalled, is:

7 Therefore, a necessary being (a being which, if it exists, cannot not-exist) exists.

Reichenbach rightfully claims that the necessary being in 7 does not provide a naturalistic explanation for the existence of the universe, but then dubiously adds that "What remains is a personal explanation in terms of the intentional acts of some supernatural being that is eternal and *a sei.*" This imputation of eternality, understood in the timeless sense, and aseity to this being appears to be a piece of prestidigitation of a similar ilk to St Thomas's terminating each of his Five Ways with the claim *et hic dicimus Deum* – "and this we call God." This papers over the gap problem of how we are to establish that his unmoved mover, first cause, etc. has all of the other required divine attributes, among which are omnipotence, benevolence, and omniscience. This problem infects every traditional cosmological argument. Reichenbach does nothing toward closing the gap between the necessary being in 7 and the God of traditional Western theism. Thus, he has no justification for ending his essay with the claim that his argument, along with other cosmological arguments, "provides a justification for theistic belief," if what is in question is traditional Western theistic belief. In fairness to the cosmological argument, it must be pointed out that even with an unresolved gap problem, it accomplishes something of great significance, if successful: namely, establishing the existence of a quite wondrous supernatural being who is the causal explainer of the existence of the universe. To close the gap, arguments are needed to show that the being who is the causal explainer of the existence of the universe has all of the other required divine perfections. Herein it will be necessary to make use of a variety of different inductive arguments based on the overall goodness of the universe, such as those from natural purpose and widespread law-like order and simplicity.

2 A Sketch of a Cosmological Argument that Works

The following is a new argument for the existence of a being who, if not the super-deluxe God of traditional Western theism, is at least a close cousin in that this God too is capable of playing the role in the lives of working theists of a being that is a suitable object of worship, adoration, love, respect, and obedience. Unlike the super-deluxe God, the God whose necessary existence is established by my argument need not essentially have the divine perfections of omnipotence, omniscience, and omnibenevolence. Furthermore, he need not even be contingently omnipotent and omniscient, just powerful and intelligent enough to be the supernatural designer-creator of the very complex and wondrous cosmos that in fact confronts us. Hopefully, his benevolence can be taken to be unlimited. My reasons for preferring to work with this more limited God is not just that I am able to prove his existence, but not that of the super-deluxe one. It also involves, as will emerge later, the ability of the concept of a finite God to get around certain difficulties that confront the traditional conception of God as an absolutely perfect being.

The new argument that I will now sketch is not just a cosmological argument, but a cosmological cum ontological cum teleological argument. The main argument is a watered-down version of the S5 modal version of the Ontological Argument, followed by a cosmological argument for its only controversial premise, and concluding with a collection of teleological arguments that attempt to close the gap between the absolutely necessary being whose existence is proved by the former arguments and the God of traditional Western theism.

2.1 The Main Argument

1 If it is possible that it is necessary that there exists a supernatural being who is a very powerful and intelligent designer-creator of the universe, then it is necessary that there exists a supernatural being who is a very powerful and intelligent designer-creator of the universe.
2 It is possible that it is necessary that there exists a supernatural being who is a very powerful and intelligent designer-creator of the universe.
3 It is necessary that there exists a supernatural being who is a very powerful and intelligent designer-creator of the universe. By *modus ponens* from 1 and 2.

Premise 1 is a substitution instance of the axiom of S5 that if it is possible that it is necessary that p, then it is necessary that p. This is a special case of the general principle that a proposition's modal status – its being necessary, possible, or impossible

– is world-invariant. A being has necessary existence if and only if it is necessary that it exists. Such a being exists in every possible world.

It might be wondered why I did not avail myself of the robust version of the S5 modal ontological argument, in which the first premise asserts that it is possible that it is necessary that there exists a being that is essentially omnipotent, omniscient, omni-benevolent, and so on for all the other essential divine perfections. Why did I not cast my Main Argument in terms of this absolutely perfect being rather than in terms of a finite God who does not have any of these omni-properties, possibly with the exception of omni-benevolence, no less have them essentially? It is not just that I am able to prove the existence of my less than absolutely perfect deity, but cannot do so for the super-deluxe model, but rather that the latter is an impossible being. The reason is that this being, since necessarily existent, exists in every possible world and is at its greatest greatness in every one of them, since it essentially has all of its omni-perfections. But this has the absurd consequence that certain things that are possible are not possible. For example, it is possible that there exists a completely gratuitous, unjustified evil – that is, an evil that is incompatible with the existence of God. But, since the super-deluxe God exists in every possible world, in no possible world will there be such an unjustified evil, and thus it is not possible that there exists a completely gratuitous, unjustified evil.[65] The danger of making God too perfect is that it makes him an impossible being, and thus not perfect after all. But the danger of making God finite, as my argument does, is that it might make him too finite, and thereby not a suitable object of worship, reverence, love, and obedience.

Since my main argument is a deductively valid *modus ponens* argument, the only way that it can fail is by having a false premise. Assuming that one is willing to grant the S5 axiom that underlies premise 1, the only possibly dubious premise is 2, and dubious it is indeed. For, whereas the biblical fool was happy to grant the possibility premise in St Anselm's ontological argument – that it is possible that there exists a being who essentially has all the divine perfections – he would have to be not just a fool but a complete schmuck to grant the possibility premise, 2, of the Main Argument. For he should not give a consent that is not an informed consent, and an informed consent to 2 requires knowing what is meant by its nested operators – it is possible that it is necessary that – namely, that it is subject to S5's axiom. But once the fool realizes this, he will withhold his consent, since he will rightly see premise 2 as begging the question against the nontheist opponent of the argument. Plainly, an argument is needed for 2, and it is the purpose of my Subsidiary Argument, which is a new version of the Cosmological Argument, to provide it.

2.2 The Subsidiary Argument

My argument will make use of some technical terms that need to be clarified at the outset. A possible world is a maximal, compossible set of propositions; maximal because for every proposition either it or its negation is a member of the set, and compossible because all of the propositions in the set could be true together. A contingent proposition or being is both possibly true or existent and possibly false or

65 This is argued for at length in chapter 5 of my book *On the Nature and Existence of God.*

nonexistent. Since my concern is with establishing that the proposition that God exists is a member of the actual world – that maximal, compossible set of propositions all of which are actually true – I will confine my attention to the actual world. There is a proper subset of the actual world consisting in all the contingent propositions in the actual world that do not report the action of a necessary being. Corresponding to this proper subset is the Big Conjunctive Fact that has as its conjuncts the members in this proper subset. In order to avoid the absurdity that the Big Conjunctive Fact is one of its own conjuncts, given that the Big Conjunctive Fact is itself a contingent proposition that does not report the action of a necessary being, it must be forbidden for the Big Conjunctive Fact to contain a conjunct that is truth-functionally equivalent to a simpler one, as for example the conjuncts p and (p and p), or p and (p or p). The universe or cosmos is comprised of all the contingent beings and the events in which they participate that are referred to and described by the propositions in the Big Conjunctive Fact. It is the universe that renders these propositions true, serving as their real-life verifiers.

The general strategy of my argument is to adopt the following weak version of PSR:

PSRw: For every true proposition, p, it is possible that there is an explanation for p,

and then show that the only possible explanation of the actual world's Big Conjunctive Fact is in terms of the creative actions of a necessary supernatural being who is possessed of very great power and intelligence. That it is possible that there is an explanation of the Big Conjunctive Fact in terms of the causal efficacy of such a necessary being entails that it is possible that it is necessary that there exists such a being, which is a stylistic variant of the proposition that is to be proved:

2 It is possible that it is necessary that there exists a supernatural being who is a very powerful and intelligent designer-creator of the universe.

By being able to make do with a weak version of PSR, my new cosmological argument has a distinct advantage over past cosmological arguments, in that it requires only the possibility, not the actuality, of an explanation for every fact.[66] Thus, it presents a less vulnerable target to its opponent, exacting a greater price for rejecting its version of PSR. The Principle of Minimal Ordinance enjoins us to make use of the weakest premises possible for establishing some conclusion, since thereby we render our premises less vulnerable to challenge.

There is, however, an ambiguity in PSRw between a weak and a strong version that must be faced and resolved at the outset. The ambiguity concerns whether a proposition that is a possible explainer of a proposition must be a member of the same world as it is. The weak version of PSRw holds that

66 The source of inspiration for my employment of the weak version of PSR is Duns Scotus, who used it in an ontological argument that went as follows. For every fact, it is possible that there is an explanation for it. Nothing can prevent God's existence. Therefore, it is not possible that there is an explanation for the fact that God does not exist. If God were not to exist, it would follow that it both is and is not possible that there is an explanation for this fact.

PSRww: For any possible world w and any proposition p, if p is a member of w, then it is possible that there is a world w_1 and a proposition q such that q is a member of w_1 and q explains p in w.

In which w need not be identical with w_1. The strong version holds that

PSRws: For any possible world w and any proposition p, if p is a member of w, then it is possible that there is a proposition q such that q is a member of w and q explains p in w.

It will turn out that my argument requires the adoption of PSRws. But the stronger version of the weak version of PSR is still considerably weaker than any strong version of PSR, thereby giving my cosmological argument an important advantage over all those cosmological arguments that require a strong version of PSR.

With these preliminaries out of the way, my argument can now be given. The actual world, which will be called *a*, is a set of propositions: namely, all the propositions that would be true were *a* to be actualized, which we are assuming actually to be the case. Let us give the name "p" to the Big Conjunctive Fact that has as a conjunct every contingent proposition in *a* that does not report the action of a necessary being. Thus, it is true *ex hypothesis* that

4 p is the Big Conjunctive Fact for *a*.

From 4 it follows, in accordance with PSRws, that

5 It is possible that there is a proposition q such that q is a member of *a* and q explains p in *a*.

Surprisingly, from 5 it can be deduced that

6 There is a proposition q such that it is possible that q is a member of *a* and q explains p in *a*.

I say surprisingly, because, in general, it is fallacious to reverse the order of 5's modal operators – that is, to deduce that there is an X such that it is possible that X is F from the proposition that it is possible that there exists an X who is F. For example, it could be possible that there is someone who flies to Venus without it being true that there exists someone who possibly flies to Venus, since the former proposition, unlike the latter, could be true even if there never exists such an individual. The reason why it is not fallacious to deduce 6 from 5 is because propositions, like other abstract entities such as properties and numbers, enjoy necessary existence, existing in every possible world. Thus, it is possible that proposition p exists (i.e., the proposition that p exists is a member of the actual world).

It might be objected that the possible proposition, q, that is the explainer of p in *a* need not be a member of *a*, as is allowed by PSRww; for, since q is possible, it is possible that q is a member of *a*, even if it isn't. This objection confounds

(a) The proposition that it is possible that q is a member of a.

with

(b) It is possible that proposition q is a member of a.

Proposition (a) is true in virtue of the fact that a proposition's modal status is world-invariant; thus, if p is possible in one world, it is possible in every world. Proposition (b), however, is not entailed by (a), since possibly p could be a member of a given world without it being possible that p is a member of that world. This is due to the fact that a possible world is a set of propositions, and that it is not possible that a set have different members than it in fact has. Its very identity is determined by its membership. Were it to have different members, it would be a different set. Therefore, unless q actually is a member of a, it is not possible that q is a member of a, even though the proposition that it is possible that q is a member of a. Furthermore, if it is possible that q is a member of a, then q is a member of a. Thus it follows from

7 There is a proposition q such that it is possible that q is a member of a and q explains p in a

that

8 There is a proposition q such that q is a member of a and it is possible that q explains p in a.

We are getting close to deriving premise 2 of the Main Argument, but, before this can be done, more must be said about what sort of proposition q is.

Recall that every contingent proposition in a that does not report the action of a necessary being is a conjunct in q. Since q is a member of a and possibly explains p in a, q cannot be a contingent proposition that does not report the action of a necessary being. Were q to be such a proposition, it would be a conjunct in p, and thus would have to explain, among other things, itself. But such an explanation, as Reichenbach has ably shown, would be viciously circular.

We need to know more about what sort of a proposition q is than just that it is not a contingent proposition that does not report the action of a necessary being. The open possibilities are that q is either a necessary proposition or a contingent proposition that reports the action of a necessary being. The former does not seem up to the task of explaining p, since the mere existence of a necessary being, even if it were God, could not explain why all of the contingent propositions in p are true together. In other words, it would not explain why there exists the universe that is reported by the members of p. It must be something that a necessary being does that explains p. This necessary being cannot be an entity without intelligence, power, and will, such as a number or a Platonic Form. The only type of explanation that we can imagine or conceive of for p, given that p cannot have an explanation whose explanans contains at least one contingent proposition that does not report the action of a necessary being, is a personal one in terms of the intentional actions of a necessary being. Of course, it is possible that there are forms of explanation that we are not capable of imagining or conceiving of, but, as has been argued already, in philosophy we must go with what we can conceive of after we have made our best effort. Given that, relative to our powers of conception, the explanation for *p* must be a personal one in terms of the intentional action of a necessary being, it is reasonable to assume that this action is a contingent one, and thus that *q* is itself a contingent proposition.

The conclusion that we must draw is that *q* is the proposition that there exists a necessary supernatural being who is the causal explainer of the universe: that is, *p*, the Big Conjunctive Fact. Given the wondrous complexity and the fine-tuning of the universe, this being must be a very powerful and intelligent designer-creator. Thus, *q* is identical with the proposition that there exists a necessary supernatural being who is a very powerful and intelligent designer-creator of the universe, and therefore the latter can be substituted for the former.

From step

8 There is a proposition *q* such that *q* is a member of *a*, and it is possible that *q* explains *p* in *a*

it can be deduced that

9 It is possible that there exists a necessary supernatural being who is a very powerful and intelligent designer-creator of the universe.

This is because of the following three facts: any proposition that is a member of the actual world, *a*, is true; we are licensed to substitute for *q* the proposition that there exists a necessary supernatural being who is a very powerful and intelligent designer-creator of the universe, since they are one and the same proposition; and the universe is what is reported by *p*, and thus whatever explains one explains the other. Given that if a being is necessary, then it is necessary that it exists, it can be deduced from 9, in accordance with S5's axiom, that

2 It is possible that it is necessary that there exists a supernatural being who is a very powerful and intelligent designer-creator of the universe. QED

I apologize for the looseness and sloppiness of this deduction of 2. For the sake of brevity, many crucial steps have had to be omitted. For a rigorous logistical deduction of 2 (containing 32 steps) I must refer the reader to my essay, "A New Argument for the Existence of God: One that Works, Well, Sort Of."[67]

2.3 Objections

I will now consider some objections, with the hope that this will help to deepen the reader's understanding of the significance of my argument, making clear just what it does and does not accomplish.

67 In Godehard Bruntrump (ed.), *The Rationality of Theism* (Dordrecht: Kluwer Academic Press, 1999).

2.3.1 *The explanation-is-agglomerative objection*

A crucial step in my argument was the claim that the Big Conjunctive Fact in a given world – the conjunction of all the contingent propositions in that world that do not report the action of a necessary being – is explainable only by a proposition that is not a member of the conjunction. It could be objected in the name of Hume that if the conjunction were infinite, with each conjunct being explained by another conjunct, the entire conjunction would thereby be internally explained. This assumes that explanation is agglomerative, meaning that it is closed under conjunctive introduction: if there is an explanation for *p* and another explanation for *q*, then there is an explanation for the conjunction (*p* and *q*). *Pace* the principle of the agglomerativity of explanation, it is possible that it is a mere coincidence that *p* and *q* are true together, even when each of them has some explanation. It is also possible that there is a common cause that explains their conjunction.[68]

2.3.2 *The taxicab objection*

A major virtue of my argument is that, unlike past cosmological arguments, including Reichenbach's, it escapes this objection, because my explanation for the Big Conjunctive Fact is in terms of a proposition that ends the regress of explanations. The proposition that there is a very powerful and intelligent necessary being that causes the existence of the cosmos in world *a* (or brings it about that the Big Conjunctive Fact for *a* is true) is a self-explaining proposition in spite of being a contingent proposition, provided it is added that it does so freely. The reason for this is that a necessary being is one whose existence can be explained by an ontological argument, even if we cannot give it, and that a being performs an action freely, such as causing world *a*'s cosmos to exist, stands in need of no further explanation, at least on the Libertarian Theory. Once it is said that the being does it freely, that explains his action. Thus, the proposition that some necessary being does action A freely is a regress-of-explanation ender.

But, it might be objected: Why assume that my necessary being freely causes the cosmos to exist? The reason is that it is hard to understand how a very powerful and intelligent supernatural being who is a cosmos-causer would not act freely. What could possibly coerce or compel him to act as he does, for he determines and controls every feature of the cosmos?

2.3.3 *The unintelligibility-of-theistic-explanations objection*

Some scientistically inclined philosophers find unintelligible the notion of a purely spiritual being freely causing there to exist a cosmos by his will, because there is not

68 This is argued for at length in chapter 6 of my *On the Nature and Existence of God*. Alexander Pruss, in his excellent article "The Hume-Edwards Principle and the Cosmological Argument," *International Journal for the Philosophy of Religion*, 33 (1998), gives additional arguments for why explanation is not agglomerative.

the required relation of statistical relevance between his free effort of will and its effect, the resultant cosmos. I cannot in this essay do justice to this objection, since a proper response to it would have to defend the coherence of theism against this and many similar types of objections, such as that the theistic explanation for the existence of the cosmos does not enable predictions to be made and thus is no explanation.

The general strategy for a response to the incoherence-of-theism objection is to charge it with employing a question-begging scientistic premise, which I will call "The Legislativeness of Scientific Contexts" principle. This principle holds that the features that inform the use of a concept in a scientific context are legislative for the use of this concept in every context, any use that does not incorporate them being unintelligible. Someone who finds, through analysis of the use of the concept of causation in scientific contexts, that it involves a relation of statistical relevance between a cause and its effect, thereby demands on the basis of the Principle of the Legislativeness of Scientific Contexts that every use of the concept of causation have this feature. Since theistic uses of the concept of causation do not have it, he charges them with being unintelligible. One has only to state this principle in order to defuse the unintelligibility-of-theistic-explanations objection that is based on it. For the principle is not one that is vouchsafed by science. Rather, it is a metaphysical thesis that fails to find adequate argumentative support and can rightly be charged by the theist with begging the question.

2.3.4 The nonpersonal-God objection

Phil Quinn, in correspondence, has questioned my claim that the only type of explanation that we can imagine or conceive of for the Big Conjunctive Fact, *p*, in the actual world, given that it cannot have an explanation whose explanans contains at least one contingent proposition that does not report the action of a necessary being, is a personal one in terms of the intentional actions of a necessary being.

He writes:

> I agree that the necessary being cannot be a number or Platonic form. Nor, I would add, can it be the Plotinian One, from which the cosmos emanates of necessity. I also agree that it cannot be without power. But I think it can be without intelligence or will. I can conceive of explaining *r* in the following way: There is an impersonal necessary being, rather like the Brahman of advaita Hinduism, that generates the cosmos by means of blind but indeterministic mechanical causation. So I am inclined to think that even if your Subsidiary Argument, as presented in the body of the paper, goes through, it will not yield the minor premise of your Main Argument.

There are several ways of attempting to meet this interesting objection. First, I could concede the objection and work with a more generic-brand deity who is a common denominator of the different cosmos-explaining necessary supernatural beings. My argument, then, would prove the existence of a necessary supernatural being of considerable power who is the cause, though not necessarily in a personal manner, of the cosmos. This is no mean feat; however, I don't think I have to concede

Quinn's objection. In the first place, the Brahman of the advaita is not a necessary being in the sense that is relevant to my argument: namely, a being the concept of which explains its existence. Furthermore, it is dubious that the purported explanation of the cosmos in terms of the blind, indeterministic activity of this impersonal force is any better explanation of the existence of the cosmos than that in terms of a mystical One out of which the actual cosmos emanates. This cosmos displays considerable law-like regularity and simplicity, as well as remarkable fine-tuning of its physical constants, all of which goes unexplained by an impersonal "explanation."

2.3.5 The my-argument-doesn't-do-enough objection

It was the aim of my argument to escape the closing of the gap problem that has infected past cosmological arguments, the unwarranted move from a conclusion that there exists a first mover (cause, etc.) to the claim that this being is God – that is, has all the divine perfections. But in avoiding the Scylla of the gap problem, I may have become wrecked on the Charybdis of proving the existence of a being who falls too short of the divine mark.

One aspect of the problem concerns whether my "God" is powerful and intelligent enough to be a suitable object of worship and adoration. Given the incredible complexity and wonderfulness of the actual cosmos, I am not too worried about this problem, since any being who is capable of designing and causing this cosmos is sufficiently awesome in his power and intelligence to be a suitable object of worship and adoration by the working theist. That this "God" need not be either omnipotent or omniscient, even less essentially so, will worry the great medieval theists, who were after bigger game, but it should not render him unserviceable to the needs of ordinary believers. Furthermore, having a finite God might make it a lot easier to construct plausible theodicies, such as were available to Plato in the *Timaeus*, but this is a direction that cannot be pursued here.

The most serious problem, however, concerns the moral attributes of my "very powerful and intelligent necessary being that causes the existence of the cosmos in the actual world." This issue concerns not the existence of this being, but rather whether it is a suitable object of worship, adoration, and obedience. If I cannot show that this being is at least a very good being, my argument may very well have created a Frankenstein.

To begin with, my creator God is not claimed to be essentially omni-benevolent, which, I take it, is a virtue of my argument. In the first place, it saves God's freedom, which was required to meet the taxicab objection. Most important, it results in God not being omni-benevolent in every world in which he exists. This is important for the reason given earlier: namely, that since he exists in every world, it would not be possible for there to be a morally unjustified evil in any world, assuming of course that he also is essentially omnipotent and omniscient. But plainly it is possible for there to be a purely gratuitous evil. What matters to the working theist is not whether it is logically possible that God do what is morally wrong, but whether he is capable of doing so in the actual world, in which "capable" is understood in terms of what a being has the capacity, knowledge, and opportunity to do. God could be said to be incapable in the actual world of doing wrong, in the sense that he could not get himself to do it, that he is above temptation, that we can place absolute confidence in him. What he does in other possible worlds is unimportant to the working theist.

But this still leaves it open whether we have good reason to think that my "very powerful and intelligent necessary being that causes the existence of the cosmos in the actual world, a," is benevolent in the actual world. It is here that my argument becomes quite vulnerable. To address this problem, I'll have to marshal all the extant theodicies for God's permitting all of the known evils of the world. My task is made easier because my God might be finite, and thus possibly could use the excuse of Plato's Demiurge. But this raises in turn the falsifiability problem. How finite is my God? I'll have to leave it to those more skilled in apologetics to take up the cause here. The best that I think can be done is to argue that the actual cosmos is overall a good one, in that it is better that it exist than that it not exist. And if there is an infinite regress of worlds in respect to goodness, as seems reasonable, God cannot be faulted for not actualizing the best possible world.

In conclusion, I believe that my argument goes quite some way to justifying theistic belief, maybe even making it more likely than not that my finite God exists. Although my argument justifies theistic belief, it does not make it rational for someone to believe in theism on its basis alone. The reason for this is that an essential requirement for it being rational to have a theistic belief is that the believer has had some experiential awareness of God or of God's presence in the cosmos. She need not have had a direct, nonsensory perception of God, much less a mystical experience of at least partial union with God, but at least she must have had experiences in which she perceived worldly items as being caused by God. William James and, following him, William Alston have been quite right to stress the central role that religious experience plays in religious belief. By driving a wedge between justification and rationality, it is shown how it is possible for someone to accept my argument and yet be an atheist. Recall in this connection Bertrand Russell's claim that at one time he accepted the ontological argument but still persisted in his agnosticism. If I am right, there is nothing absurd about this.[69]

Reply to Gale

Richard Gale uses a weak or limited version of the Principle of Sufficient Reason (PSR) to justify the claim that a finite God necessarily exists. One irony of his approach is that he uses a weaker version of PSR to prove a conclusion stronger than that found in traditional cosmological arguments: namely, that a logically necessary being exists.

69 In the discussion of my argument at a conference on "The Rationality of Theistic Belief" at the Munich School of Philosophy on May 27, 1998, Uwe Meixner raised a devastating objection to my argument; but, fortunately, Alvin Plantinga was in the audience and immediately showed me a way to avoid it. I am deeply indebted to both of them.

If we assume the truth of the axiom which Gale employs in premise 1, then the soundness of his version of the cosmological argument depends on the truth of premise 2. What makes premise 2 initially suspect is that in his hands the Weak Principle of Sufficient Reason yields results much like the stronger version about which he has qualms. Recognizing its suspect status, Gale proceeds to defend premise 2. But it is dubious that his defense succeeds. He correctly notes that proposition *q*, which affirms that the universe is created by the personal action of a necessary being, is a contingent proposition. But this contingent claim cannot be used to establish that necessarily there exists a supernatural being who created the universe. For if necessarily there exists a supernatural being who created the universe, the claim that the universe is created cannot be contingent; the claim would have to be true in all possible worlds.[70] Gale could modify premise 2, and consequently conclusion 3, simply to speak of a necessary being without attributing to it the property of being the creator of the universe, but then the support Gale intends to provide by his subsidiary argument for the truth of premise 2 would be irrelevant.

Suppose, however, that Gale's argument works. Why not, as Gale himself asks, avail oneself of a more robust God? Instead of a God with finite properties, why not plug into premise 2 a God who has the critical omnis – omnipotence, omniscience, omnibenevolence? Gale responds by raising the traditional problem of evil. Gratuitous evil is evil that does not lead to a greater good, and evil that fails to lead to a greater good is unjustified evil. Hence, if there is gratuitous evil, it is unjustified and conflicts with God's existence or his possession of the omnis.

Several replies to Gale are possible. Some theists grant this greater good analysis but then proceed to argue that one should not move from the appearance of gratuitous evil to its reality; it is possible that there is no gratuitous evil because, unknown to us, all evil leads to a greater good.[71]

Gale thinks this approach suspect, and possibly he is correct. But another account of gratuitous evil is more persuasive. Evil is unjustified, not when it fails to lead to a greater good, but when no morally sufficient reason exists for it. If there is a morally sufficient reason for gratuitous evil, then though the evil fails to lead to a greater good, it is justified. This is precisely what is argued in the free will theodicy, according to which a world with beings that can choose between good and evil and who choose a significant amount of good is better than a world without beings that can choose between good and evil. Freedom is a prerequisite for choosing meaningfully between good and evil. But where freedom exists, evil is possible. Hence, although the evil chosen does not itself produce a greater good, the evil is justified because the freedom that makes both good and evil possible is necessary for the greater good of there being moral agents. For God to eliminate gratuitous evil would remove the human freedom necessary for there to be moral agents.[72] Consequently, the existence

70 I owe this insight to William Hasker.

71 Stephen Wykstra, "The Humean Obstacle to Evidential Arguments from Suffering: On Avoiding the Evils of 'Appearance,'" *International Journal for Philosophy of Religion*, 16 (1984), pp. 73–94.

72 See my *Evil and a Good God*, pp. 10, 19, 39, 193. Others who have made this point in more sustained fashion are Michael Peterson, *God and Evil* (Boulder, Colo.: Westview Press, 1998), and William Hasker, "The Necessity of Gratuitous Evil," *Faith and Philosophy*, 9/1 (Jan. 1991), pp. 23–44.

of gratuitous evil is not incompatible with God's existence or goodness. God can have a morally sufficient reason for allowing gratuitous evil – for example, the greater good of there being moral agents. Accordingly, there are no grounds for rejecting a "super-deluxe" or traditional view of God as an instantiation in premise 2 of Gale's theistic argument. That is, if Gale's argument works for a finite God, it will likewise work for the God of traditional theism.

In short, either Gale's argument is suspect, or else it can be modified to suit the traditional theist. Either way, the "sort of" is ironically optimistic.

Reply to Reichenbach

Bruce Reichenbach has raised two excellent objections to my new cosmological argument. Each can be met, but to do so requires that the argument be given a more perspicuous reformulation. The first objection is that the conclusion of my argument – that it is necessary that there exists a supernatural being who created the universe – has the unwanted consequence that it is necessary that he created this universe, thereby negating the freedom with which he did so and, moreover, making this universe the only possible one, given that he exists in every possible world and determines which possible world, if any, gets actualized. Reichenbach parses my conclusions as

a. It is necessary that (there exists a supernatural being and he created the universe).

And given that necessity distributes over a conjunction, it follows that each conjunct is itself necessary.

But there is another way to parse my conclusion that does not have the consequence that it is necessary that he created the universe he did: namely,

b. It is necessary that (there exists a supernatural being and it is contingent that he created the universe).

Because necessity distributes over a conjunction, it follows from b that

c. It is necessary that it is contingent that he created the universe.

But because every proposition necessarily has the modal status it does, c entails that

d. It is contingent that he created the universe.

In order to escape Reichenbach's objection, I need to reformulate my Main Argument in terms of the b-type parsing of my conclusion.

1 If it is possible that it is necessary that (there exists a very powerful and intelligent supernatural being and it is contingent that he is the creator of the universe), then it is necessary that (there exists a very powerful and intelligent supernatural being and it is contingent that he is the creator of the universe).
2 It is possible that it is necessary that (there exists a very powerful and intelligent supernatural being and it is contingent that he is the creator of the universe).
3 It is necessary that (there exists a very powerful and intelligent supernatural being and it is contingent that he is the creator of the universe).

I thank Reichenbach for unearthing an ambiguity in my conclusion and trust that this way of disambiguating it escapes his objection.

Reichenbach's second objection is that if my argument works, it works equally well for a necessarily existent God who essentially has all of the omni-perfections. My reason for not wanting to apply my argument to this sort of absolutely perfect being is that it would have the unwanted consequence that it is impossible for there to be an unjustified evil. This is because this being exists and realizes his greatest greatness in every possible world, thereby precluding the existence of a morally unjustified evil in any possible world. I muddied the waters by carelessly using "gratuitous evil" as if it were interchangeable with "unjustified evil," but plainly, for the reason Reichenbach gave, there could be an evil that is both gratuitous and morally justified. My point must be restricted to unjustified evils. Again, I am indebted to Reichenbach for his helpful objection.

There is yet another confusion in my argument. The God whose necessary existence is proved by my argument, although not shown to be infinite in its perfections, need not be finite. It can be omnipotent, omniscient, and omnibenevolent. It just can't have these omni-perfections essentially, since this would entail, for the reason just given, that it is impossible for there to be a morally unjustified evil.

Finally, I want to address Reichenbach's remark that it is ironic that I can use a weaker version of the Principle of Sufficient Reason (PSR) than that used by traditional cosmological arguments to prove a stronger conclusion than they do: namely, that the designer-creator necessarily, rather than just contingently, exists. He does not claim that this ironic feature undermines my argument, but there is the suggestion that it should make us very suspicious of it. The irony disappears once it is seen that my weak version of PSR – that for every true proposition it is possible that there is an explanation for it – entails the strong version of PSR – that for every true proposition there is an explanation of it. I owe the following indirect proof of this to Alexander Pruss.

1 Proposition *p* is true and there is no explanation for *p*. Assumption for indirect proof
2 It is possible that there is an explanation for (*p* and there is no explanation for *p*). From 1 and the weak version of PSR

3 There is a possible world, w, such that in w there is a proposition, q, that explains (p and there is no explanation for p). From 2 by definition
4 In w, q explains p. From 3 because explanation distributes over a conjunction, and any proposition that has an explanation is true
5 In w, p has an explanation and p does not have an explanation. From 4 and 5 by conjunction.

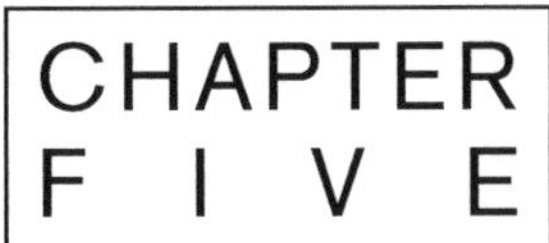

Does Religious Experience Justify Religious Belief?

In this exchange, William Alston argues that religious or mystical experiences can provide *prima facie* rational support for the beliefs about God that are based on them. This support can, however, be overridden by other considerations, as when the believer is given a reason to think that the religious beliefs based on an experience are false or that the experience is for some other reason untrustworthy. Evan Fales disagrees, arguing that if religious experiences are to justify religious belief, such experiences must be cross-checked and thereby shown to be genuinely from God. He argues, however, that most religious experiences cannot be appropriately cross-checked and that the ones which can – namely, experiences yielding prophetic beliefs – almost inevitably fail any attempt to authenticate them. Fales concludes that religious experience does not in fact justify religious belief.

Religious Experience Justifies Religious Belief

William P. Alston

1 Background

To answer the title question, the first job is to get straight about what *religious experience* is. In the widest sense, the term can be applied to any experiences one has in connection with one's religious life, including a sense of guilt or release, joys, longings, a sense of gratitude, etc. But here we are more specifically concerned with experiences taken by their possessor to be an awareness of God. As a way of focusing on this distinctive kind of "religious experience," I have called it *perception of God.*[1]

Two comments on this terminology. First, I use "perception" in a "phenomenological" sense. I will call anything a "perception of X" (a tree, God, or whatever) provided that is what it seems to the subject to be, provided the subject takes it to be a *presentation* of X to the subject's experience. It is then a further question whether X is really present to the subject, whether the subject *really* perceives X (in a stronger sense of "perceive"). When the supposed object of the perception is God, I will speak of *mystical perception.* Second, "God" may be used in a wider or narrower way. In the Judeo-Christian tradition and in Islam we think of God as a supreme personal being; but in Buddhism the object of worship is often taken to be some sort of impersonal reality. To maximize coverage, I will let "God" range over any *supreme reality*, however construed.

What kinds of beliefs about God might possibly be supported by religious experience? It is difficult to draw sharp boundaries here, but for purposes of this discussion I will restrict myself to beliefs about what God is doing vis-à-vis the subject – comforting, guiding, strengthening, communicating a message – and about divine characteristics one might conceivably experience God as having – being powerful, loving, merciful. Let's call these *M-beliefs* ("M" for "manifestation").

It will make the topic more concrete to consider a particular case of mystical perception. Here is one taken from William James.

> [A]ll at once I . . . felt the presence of God – I tell of the thing just as I was conscious of it – as if his goodness and his power were penetrating me altogether. . . . I thanked God that in the course of my life he had taught me to know him, that he sustained my life and took pity both on the insignificant creature and on the sinner that I was. I begged him ardently that my life might be consecrated to the doing of his will. I felt his reply, which was that I should do his will from day to day, in humility and poverty, leaving him, The Almighty God, to judge of whether I should some time be called to bear witness more conspicuously. Then, slowly, the ecstasy left my heart; that is, I felt that God had withdrawn the communion which he had granted . . . I asked myself if it were possible that Moses on Sinai could have had a more intimate communication with God. I think it well to add that in this ecstasy of mine God had neither form, color, odor, nor taste; moreover, that the feeling of his presence was accompanied by no determinate localization . . . But the more I seek words to express this intimate intercourse, the more I feel the impossibility of describing the thing by any of our usual images. At bottom the expression most apt to render what I felt is this: God was present, though invisible; he fell under no one of my senses, yet my consciousness perceived him.[2]

This report is typical in several respects.

(1) The awareness of God is *experiential*, as contrasted with *thinking* of God or *reasoning* about him. It seems to involve a *presentation* of God.

1 William P. Alston, *Perceiving God* (Ithaca, NY: Cornell University Press, 1991).

2 William James, *The Varieties of Religious Experience* (New York: Modern Library, 1902), pp. 67–8.

(2) The experience is *direct*. One seems to be *immediately* aware of God rather than through being aware of something else. It is like seeing another human being in front of you, rather than like seeing that person on television. But there are more indirect experiences of God.

> There was a mysterious presence in nature . . . which was my greatest delight, especially when as happened from time to time, *nature became lit up from inside* with something that came from beyond itself.[3]

(3) The experience is a *non-sensory* presentation of God. But there are also experiences of God with sensory content.

> I awoke and looking out of my window saw what I took to be a luminous star which gradually came nearer, and appeared as a soft slightly blurred white light. I was seized with violent trembling, but had no fear. I knew that what I felt was great awe. This was followed by a sense of overwhelming love coming to me, and going out from me, then of great compassion from this Outer Presence.[4]

(4) It is a *focal* experience, one in which the awareness of God is so intense as to blot out everything else. But there are also milder experiences that persist over long periods of time as a background to everyday experience.

> God surrounds me like the physical atmosphere. He is closer to me than my own breath. In him literally I live and move and have my being.[5]

This discussion will be limited to *direct, non-sensory, focal* experiences, since they give rise to the strongest claims to be genuinely aware of God.

2 The Case for Experiential Support

The reporter of our first case (a French-speaking Swiss whom I will call "Bonnet") obviously supposes that he has learned something about God from his experience. In particular he supposes that he has perceived God to be loving and powerful, and perceived him to be telling him, Bonnet, to do his will from day to day. And since the perception was completely convincing to him, he has no more inclination to doubt it than he would have to doubt the veracity of a normal visual perception of an oak tree. But, of course, this confidence of his does not guarantee that the experience is, in fact, veridical. Even with sense perception one can be deceived. At dusk one can suppose that what one sees in the distance is a car when actually it is a cow. With both sense perception and mystical perception contradictions between reports prevent us from taking all of them to be veridical. Think of the divergent reports that witnesses give of automobile accidents. As for mystical perception, some people think

3 Timothy Beardsworth, *A Sense of Presence* (Oxford: Religious Experience Research Unit, 1977), p. 19.
4 Ibid., p. 30.
5 James, *Varieties of Religious Experience*, p. 71.

they perceive God telling them to murder as many Communists, postal workers, or schoolteachers as possible, while other people perceive God as supremely loving. They can't all be right. Hence in both areas we need some way of separating the sheep from the goats.

But though neither mystical experience nor sense experience is infallible, there are solid reasons for taking beliefs formed on the basis of either kind of experience to be, as we might say, *prima facie* rationally acceptable, rationally acceptable in the absence of sufficient reasons to the contrary (*overriders*). (Swinburne calls this "The Principle of Credulity."[6]) In other words, being formed on the basis of experience gives a belief an *initial credibility*, a *presumption* of truth. It is innocent until proved guilty. It is rationally acceptable (justified, warranted) so long as no one has sufficient reasons for taking it to be false (*rebutters*) or for taking the particular situation to be such that the experience does not have its usual force (*underminers*). Thus overriders come in two versions; rebutters and underminers. For a simple example concerning sense perception, suppose I think I see an elephant in my front yard. My belief that there is an elephant there would be justified unless there are strong reasons for thinking that there is no elephant in the area (rebutter) or that my vision is not working properly (underminer).

The main reason for accepting the Principle of Credulity is that it is the only alternative to complete skepticism about experience. Consider how we would show sense perception to be a generally reliable source of belief if we did *not* accord every perceptual belief an initial credibility. A survey of the most promising attempts to construct such an argument reveals that any otherwise strong candidate suffers from "epistemic circularity."[7] This consists of relying on the belief source whose credentials we seek to establish to provide us with premises for that establishment. Arguments for the reliability of sense perception that are not disqualified on other grounds (and many that are) depend on premises for which our only basis is sense perception. As a simple example, consider the popular line of thought that sense perception proves itself by its fruits, particularly by the way in which it puts us in a position to predict and thereby to control to some extent the course of events. It provides us with data on the basis of which we establish law-like generalizations, which we can then use as the basis for prediction and control. In this way we learn that milk sours more slowly when cold than when warm. This puts us in a position to predict that a refrigerated bottle of milk will last longer than an unrefrigerated one, and we can use this knowledge to control the condition of our milk. This is the humblest of examples, and the predictive power is greatly increased in scope and precision as we move further into the higher reaches of science; but the general point is the same. If sense perception weren't usually giving us the straight story about what is happening around us, how could we have so much success in anticipating the future course of events?

That sounds right. But how do we know that we are often successful in prediction? By induction from particular cases of success, obviously. But how do we know that we are successful in particular cases? By using our senses to determine

6 Richard Swinburne, *The Existence of God* (Oxford: Clarendon Press, 1979).

7 See William P. Alston, *The Reliability of Sense Perception* (Ithaca, NY: Cornell University Press, 1993).

whether what was predicted actually occurred. It is not as if an angel tells us this, or as if rational intuition does the job. But then the argument is tainted with epistemic circularity. We have to rely on sense perception for some of our crucial premises. The argument establishes the reliability of sense perception only if sense perception is in fact reliable. And that leaves us wondering whether that condition is satisfied.

If, on the other hand, we begin by assuming that perceptual beliefs are justifiably taken as true in the absence of sufficient overriders, we can use our empirical knowledge to support the claim that sense perception is reliable. For there will be many perceptual reports that we have no sufficient reasons *against*, and these can be used with impunity to pile up empirical evidence for the reliability of sense perception.

But when the Principle of Credulity is applied to mystical perception, it will support the attribution of a significant degree of reliability only if there are no strong reasons for denying rational acceptability to all or most religious beliefs based on mystical experience. But many such reasons have been suggested. Most of these are based on dissimilarities – real or alleged – between sense perception and mystical perception. I will critically examine several of them in the next few sections.

3 Some Obvious Differences between Sense Experience and Mystical Experience

(1) Sense experience is a common possession of mankind, while mystical experience is not. To be sure, several recent surveys have shown that many more people than is commonly supposed, even in our "secular" society, take themselves to have been directly aware of the presence of God. And the incidence in many other cultures is much higher. But still, by no means all people enjoy mystical experience, whereas no human being is totally without sense experience. And most of us have a rich variety of the latter.

(2) Sense experience is continuously and unavoidably present during all our waking hours, while for most of those who are not wholly bereft of mystical experience, it is, at best, enjoyed only rarely. It is a very unusual person who, like Brother Lawrence of *The Practice of the Presence of God* fame, is blessed with a constant experiential awareness of God.

(3) Sense experience, especially visual experience, is vivid and richly detailed, while mystical experience is meager and obscure. Though Bonnet's experience of God was deeply meaningful to him, and though he took it to show him something about God, still it could not begin to compare in richness and complexity of detail with a single glance out my study window at my front yard, crammed as that latter experience is with details of trees, flowers, passing cars in the street, neighbors' houses, etc.

Obvious differences like these make it difficult for some people to believe that mystical perception involves a genuine experience of objective reality. But on careful reflection we can see that this reaction lacks any basis worthy of the name.

We can usefully treat differences (1) and (2) together: (1) degree of dispersal in the general population and (2) frequency in the life of a given subject. Both have to do with the proportion of some relevant totality. So what does the extent of distribution in the population or the frequency within one subject have to do with the question of whether the experience contains important information? Why suppose that what happens only rarely cannot have cognitive value? We wouldn't dream of applying this principle to scientific or philosophical insight. That comes only rarely, and only to few people, but it is not denigrated for that reason. Would any reasonable person suggest that the kind of insight that led Einstein to the development of his Special and General Theory of Relativity is inferior in cognitive value to everyday visual awareness of one's surroundings, on the grounds that the latter is more widely shared and occurs more frequently? We can safely neglect frequency as an index to informational content.

As for (3), richness and detail of content, I can't see that it fares any better. Within sense perception there are large differences of this sort between sense modalities. Vision is miles ahead of the others in that regard, with touch and hearing placing a rather distant second, followed at a more considerable distance by taste and smell. One glance at a scene before me gives a much greater variety of information that one sniff or one taste. And the latter are severely restricted as to the kinds of information they provide. One glance at a scene can tell me that I am looking across a verdant valley at a green hillside on which are beautiful meadows, forests, barns, white farmhouses, and cows. How much more I learn from this than from a sniff that informs me that there is hot tar nearby or from a taste that tells me that the substance tasted has an acrid and rather smoky flavor.[8] Yet this is no reason for denying that taste and smell can involve veridical perception of external realities and give us genuine information about them, albeit not as much. We cannot sensibly hold that less information is no information at all. That would be like maintaining that a simple folk melody, since it is much less complex than the Bach B Minor Mass, is not really music, or that since a crude map I draw for you of the route to my house gives much less geographical information than the Rand-McNally Atlas, it gives no information at all.

4 Attempted Naturalistic Explanations of Mystical Experience

A more serious argument for a general dismissal of epistemological claims for mystical perception is based on the general principle that one perceives an object X in having a certain experience only if X is among the causes of that experience, and only if X plays one causal role rather than others in the production of that experience. With vision, for example, one sees a dog only if light reflected from the dog produces the retinal stimulation that sets off the neural chain reaction that eventually leads to the excitations in the brain that are responsible for the visual experi-

8 These comparisons are asserted for the human case. With dogs, for example, smell provides a much greater richness of content.

ence in question. We get analogous stories for other modes of sense perception. Extrapolating this line of thought to mystical experience, such an experience can be a perception of God only if God plays a certain kind of causal role in the production of that experience. But it has frequently been claimed that mystical experience can be fully explained (its causes can be fully set out) in terms of processes within the natural world, without mentioning God at all. But if so, God does not figure anywhere among its causes and therefore has no claim to be perceived in a mystical experience. And if Bonnet was not perceiving God, as he supposed, then presumably the experience has nothing to tell him about God, at least directly.

Even if mystical experience can be adequately explained in terms of purely this-worldly factors (and I will have more to say about this below), it would be much too fast to conclude that God does not figure among the causes of mystical experience. Consider the point that though sense experience can be adequately explained by what goes on in the brain, we all take it that objects outside the brain are perceived in those experiences. How can this be? Obviously, it is because though brain processes are the *direct* cause of sensory experience, those processes themselves have causes, which in turn have causes . . . and if we trace that causal chain back far enough, we come to the external objects that are perceived. Analogously, even if the direct causes of mystical experience are all within nature, it is still possible that God figures further back in the causal chain that leads to that experience. And, indeed, that is the case, according to theism and theistic religions, which hold that God is responsible for the existence and functioning of the world of nature.

But, it may be contended, even if that were the case, it would not follow that God figures in the causal chain in such a way as to be the object of perception. Going back to visual perception, many items figure in the causal chain leading to visual experience – neural transmission to the brain from the eye, retinal excitation, light reflected from an object striking the retina, etc. Most of this is not visually perceived. So to figure as a perceived object, it is not enough that an item figure in some way among the causes of the experience. It must figure in a certain way, one that enables it to be perceived. And why should we suppose that God figures in *that* way in the causal chain leading to mystical experience?

When we think hard about this issue, we come to a startling result. Going back to sense perception, notice first that the way a perceived object figures in the causal chain differs for different sense modalities. In vision it is something like *reflecting or generating light that then reaches the retina without additional reflection*; for audition it is something like *generating or reflecting sound waves that strike the eardrum*; and so on. For mystical perception it will be something different, the exact nature of which is obscure to us. Further, note that the causal contribution required for objecthood in each case is something we can learn only from experience, including the experience involved in that case and similar cases. We must have a number of cases of genuine perception of X in that modality before we are in a position to discover inductively what kind of causal contribution is required for being perceived in that modality. There is no a priori way of determining this. But notice where this leaves us. Since we are in no position to say what kind of causal contribution is required for objecthood until we have some genuine cases of perception to work from, we can't even embark on the project of specifying the necessary causal contribution until we recognize that there are authentic cases of perception in that modality. Hence one who denies that people ever perceive God in mystical experience has no basis for any supposition as to how God would have to be involved in causing mystical experience for God to be genuinely perceived in such an experience. Hence the critic could have no basis for arguing that God does not satisfy the requirement. She could, of course, point out that the advocate of divine perception has no idea of what is required either. But that still doesn't give her an *objection* to her opponent's position.

So we are left with the conclusion that even if there is an adequate naturalistic account of the proximate causes of mystical experience, that does not rule out the possibility that God plays a role in eliciting such experience that renders him perceived therein. But there are also reasons for questioning the claim that there is any such account. If we consider the most prominent candidates (and this is not a popular research field for social and behavioral scientists), we must judge them to be highly speculative and, at best, sketchily supported by the evidence. Mystical experience poses severe problems for empirical research. In addition to the difficulties in determining when we have a case thereof, it is something that cannot be induced at the will of the researcher and so is not amenable to experiment. Attempts to get around this by substituting drug-induced analogues are of little value, since it is an open question whether findings concerning the latter can be extrapolated to spontaneous cases. Since the states are usually short-lived, the researcher must rely on autobiographical reports; we can't expect a researcher to hang around a person on the off chance that he might happen to have a mystical experience. Hence the data are subject to all the well-known problems that attach to first-person reports. Moreover, the most prominent theories in the field invoke causal mechanisms that themselves pose unsolved problems of identification and measurement: unconscious psychological processes like repression and mechanisms of defense, social influences on ideology and on belief and attitude formation. It is not surprising that theories like those of Freud, Marx, and Durkheim rest on a slender thread of evidential support and generalize irresponsibly from such evidence as they can muster.

5 Can Reports of Mystical Perception Be Checked?

It is not infrequently claimed by philosophers that the impossibility of effective public (intersubjective) tests of the accuracy of beliefs about God formed on the basis of mystical experience prevents that experience from being an awareness of any objective reality. Here are a couple of representative formulations.

> But why can't we have an argument based upon religious experiences for the existence of the apparent object of a given religious experience and its bearing the right sort of causal relation to the experience? There can be such an argument only if religious experiences count as cognitive. But they can count as cognitive only if they are subject to similar tests to those which sense experiences are.[9]

9 Richard Gale, *On the Nature and Existence of God* (New York: Cambridge University Press, 1991), p. 302. This quotation is set in an elaborate discussion that involves a list of 11 tests of the veridicality of sensory experiences.

But whereas questions about the existence of people can be answered by straightforward observational and other tests, not even those who claim to have enjoyed personal encounters with God would admit such tests to be appropriate here.[10]

The first thing to be said in reply is that there *are* tests for the accuracy of particular reports of mystical perception. Contemplative religious communities that, so to say, specialize in the perception of God, have compiled systematic manuals of such tests; and many of them are used more informally by the laity. These include such things as (1) conformity with what would be expected on the basis of doctrines concerning the nature of God, (2) "fruits" of the experience as a stable inner peace and growth in spirituality, (3) a content of the experience that the person would not have developed on their own. The satisfaction of such conditions counts in favor of the veridicality of the experience, and their absence counts against it. Obviously these tests do not conclusively establish veridicality or the reverse, but that does not render them without value. Tests of the accuracy of sense perceptions don't always settle the matter definitively either.

It is certainly true that sense-perceptual reports can be checked in ways that mystical-perceptual reports cannot. Let's look for a moment at some of these ways. The most obvious ones involve the experiences of other persons. Suppose I claim to have seen a Russian plane flying over my house at a certain time. If we can find other people who were in the area at that time and looking up into the sky, we can determine whether they saw a Russian plane overhead. To be sure, if one or a few such people failed to notice a Russian plane, that would not decisively disconfirm my report. Perhaps they were inattentive, blinded by the sun, or preoccupied with other matters. But if a large number of people were in the area, were not especially preoccupied, were disposed to look up to determine the source of any loud noise, and none of them saw any such plane, my report would have been decisively disconfirmed. The general principle involved here is that if a visible object were present at a certain place and time, then any competent observer who was at that place and time and was looking in the right direction would (at least most probably) have seen it. If a large number of such observers did not see any such thing, we must conclude that the object wasn't there at that time. If, on the other hand, all or most such observers take themselves to have seen it, that confirms the original report. Thus sense-perceptual reports are often subject to a decisive test on the basis of the perceptions of other persons.

There are other kinds of public tests as well. The credentials of the reporter could be examined. Is his visual apparatus in order? Does he know how to distinguish a Russian plane from other kinds? Was he in a drugged or intoxicated condition? Did he have his wits about him at the time? And so on. To change the example, suppose the report is that baking soda is sprinkled over my serving of rice. In addition to taste tests by others, the substance can be subjected to chemical analysis.

There is nothing comparable to this with mystical perception. God is always present everywhere, if present anywhere, and so the whereabouts of a subject has no bearing. If a mystical report were to be given a test by other observers in the sense-perceptual way, we would have to say that S really perceived God at time *t* only if

10 Antony Flew, *God and Philosophy* (London: Hutchinson, 1966), pp. 138–9.

every competent subject perceives God all the time. But no one would take this to be an appropriate test. "Why should we expect God to be perceivable by everyone all the time even if he is present everywhere all the time?" one might ask. To put the point more generally, there is no set of conditions such that if God is present to me at time *t*, then any other person satisfying those conditions would also perceive God at *t*. To be sure, we can say something about what is conducive to perceiving God. One must be sufficiently "receptive," sufficiently "spiritually attuned." It is only if one who possesses those characteristics fails to perceive God that this counts against the original report. But how can we tell whether a given subject qualifies? Again, something can be said. Those who address such matters typically lay down such characteristics as the possession of certain virtues (humility, compassion) and a loving, obedient attitude toward God as productive of openness to the presence of God. "Blessed are the pure in heart, for they shall see God" (Matt. 5:8, KJV). But there are two reasons why we still lack the kind of test we have for sense-perceptual reports. First, we are far from having reliable intersubjective tests for humility and a loving attitude toward God. And second, it can't seriously be claimed that any set of conditions we can list is such that one will perceive God *if and only if* those conditions are satisfied. The situation with respect to mystical perception is much more obscure and mysterious, much less tight than this. And so we are still a long way from being able to carry out the kind of *other observers* tests we have for sense perception. As for the other kinds of tests I mentioned above, what I have just said implies that we have no effective *state of observer* test to rely on here. And obviously nothing like chemical analysis is relevant.

But what epistemic relevance does this difference have? Why should we suppose that it prevents mystical reports from enjoying prima facie justification? Those who take this line make an unjustifiable assumption that reports of perception of God are properly treated by the same standards as reports of sense perception, so that if the former cannot be tested in the same way as the latter, they cannot provide a cognitive access to objective reality. But this assumption is no more than a kind of epistemic *imperialism*, subjecting the outputs of one belief-forming practice to the requirements of another. It can easily be seen that not all our standard belief-forming practices work like sense perception. Consider introspection. If I report feeling excited, there are no conditions under which my report is correct *if and only if* someone who satisfies those conditions also feels excited. Introspective reports can be publicly checked to a certain extent, but not in that way. Again, the fact that we can't use perceptual checks on mathematical reports has no tendency to show that rational intuition cannot yield objective truths. Different belief-forming practices work differently.

Thinkers like Gale and Flew will undoubtedly respond to this last example by saying that the availability of tests like those for sense perception are at least required for the epistemic efficacy of *experiential* sources of belief. But that no more goes beyond a mere prejudice than the more unqualified claim for belief sources generally. What basis do we have for the claim that the features of sense perception constitute *necessary* conditions for any effective experiential cognitive access to objective reality? I take it as uncontroversial that sense perception is *a* way of acquiring reliable beliefs of certain sorts about the world. Sense perception satisfies sufficient conditions for epistemic efficacy. But why suppose that this is the only set of sufficient conditions?

Experience amply attests that, in cognitive as well as in other matters, sharply different maneuvers can achieve a certain goal. Excellent dishes can be prepared by meticulously following well-tested recipes or, with experienced cooks, by inspired improvisation. Mathematical problems can be solved, in some cases, by following established algorithms, or, in some cases, by flashes of intuition. The picture of an ancient civilization can be built up from archeological remains or from extant documents or from some combination thereof. And so it goes. It would be the reverse of surprising if the purchase on objective reality attained by sense perception were only one of many experiential ways of achieving such a result. And the fact that the aspects of reality that mystical perception claims to put us in contact with are very different from those that are explored by sense perception reinforces the rejection of the idea that only what conforms to the latter can reveal anything about reality.

Do Mystics See God?

Evan Fales

> *And [the Lord] said, Thou canst not see my face* [panim]*: for there shall no man see my face and live*
>
> – Exod. 33:20

> *And Jacob called the name of the place Peniel: for I have seen God face* [panim] *to face, and my life is preserved*
>
> – Gen. 32:30

> *There's more than one way to skin a cat.*

1 A Cautionary Tale

Theistic philosophers have perennially cited mystical experiences – experiences of God – as evidence for God's existence and for other truths about God. In recent years, the attractiveness of this line of thought has been reflected in its use by a significant number of philosophers.[11] But both philosophers and mystics agree that not all mys-

11 e.g., Alston, *Perceiving God*; William Wainwright, *Mysticism* (Madison: University of Wisconsin Press, 1981); Keith Yandell, *The Epistemology of Religious Experience* (New York: Cambridge University Press, 1993); Swinburne, *Existence of God*, rev. edn; Jerome I. Gellman, *Experience of God and the Rationality of Theistic Belief* (Ithaca, NY: Cornell University Press, 1997); Alvin Plantinga, "Reason and Belief in God," in Alvin Plantinga and Nicholas Wolterstorff (eds), *Faith and Rationality: Reason and Belief in God* (Notre Dame, Ind.: Univerity of Notre Dame Press, 1983); Steven Payne, *John of the Cross and the Cognitive Value of Mysticism: An Analysis of Sanjuanist Teaching and its Philosophical Implications for Contemporary Discussions of Mystical Experience*, Synthese Historical Library (Dordrecht: Kluwer Academic Publishers, 1990); and Carolyn Franks-Davis, *The Evidential Force of Religious Experience* (Oxford: Clarendon Press, 1989).

tical experiences can be relied upon; many are the stuff of delusion.[12] So they have somehow to be checked out, their bona fides revealed. But can they be? I will be arguing that (a) they must indeed be cross-checked to serve as good evidence; and that (b) they can't be – or not nearly well enough to permit pressing them into service as serious support for theism. The need for cross-checking, necessary in any case, is made acute by two facts: the extreme variability of mystical experiences and the doctrines they are recruited to support, and the fact that, especially in the face of this variability, mystical experiences are much more effectively explained naturalistically. Furthermore, our ability adequately to cross-check mystical experiences (hereafter, MEs), in a way that would reveal the hand of God, is crippled by the fact that theists offer no hypothesis concerning the causal mechanism by means of which God shows himself to mystics.

Let's begin with my third epigraph. This insightful, if grisly, bit of folk wisdom tells much of our story. Permit me to spell out the dolorous tale. I am greeted by the sight of poor Sylvester, a heap of flayed flesh upon the lawn. I set out to reconstruct the crime. With but the denuded corpse as evidence, the possibilities are multiple. So I must locate other clues. A bloodied knife nearby might have secrets to reveal: suppose the hemoglobin tests out feline. Even better, perhaps I can find an eyewitness or two, discovering through further investigation that they are both sober and honest. I might find fingerprints on the knife. And so on.

In all this, I rely upon my senses to convey evidence of the deed. How is this managed? Why, through some causal sequence, a continuation of some of those sequences that converged upon the destruction of poor Sylvester, and that then diverged from there. Light waves bearing news of cat skin and flesh make their way from the *corpus delicti* to my "sensory surfaces," there to be processed in those still and possibly forever mysterious ways into cat-corpse-consciousness. Mysterious or not, what we do know is that cat and conscious episode are related as (partial) cause to (partial) effect. But for there being some suitable causal link between cat and experience, that experience, no matter its intrinsic characteristics, is not a perception of that cat.[13]

But if the intrinsic content of my experience can be caused in multiple ways (the presence of an actual cat-corpse being but one of these), then how shall I ascertain

12 Contrary to what is sometimes claimed, mystical beliefs are surely not self-certifying, no matter how much certainty mystical experience may generate in the mystic. On this point most philosophers – and mystics themselves – are agreed. The reason why testing is needed is, as I shall show, that mystical claims, when they are about an extra-subjective reality, aren't of the right *sort* to be self-certifying. It doesn't help the mystic's case, of course, if her mystical beliefs are contradicted by those of another mystic who displays equal certitude.

13 There are direct realists who deny that "*S* perceives *C*" entails any causal claim about *C*. That is not something that someone who rejects the direct realist's theory of perception need be concerned to deny. Nor, for present purposes, need I deny the view that, when I really do perceive a cat, I do so "directly," that is, not "in virtue of" perceiving something else more directly. So I shall here concede both these points. It suffices for my present purpose that we do not allow, where *C* is an "external" entity or state of affairs, that *S* perceives *C* unless *C* in *fact* plays a causal role in the production of *S*'s experience. I should say more: for external *C*, it is a metaphysical necessity that *C* be so involved in the production of *S*'s experience. The notion of externality can be sufficiently captured by saying that *C* is external to *S*'s experience just in case *C*'s existence doesn't entail the existence of *S*.

that my senses do not deceive? The short answer to this importunate and persistent problem, the problem of perception, is: I must cross-check. But we cannot explore the substance of this remark without making two antecedent observations. First, no amount of cross-checking can produce evidence that will satisfy the radical skeptic. I can decide to pinch myself to check that I'm not just dreaming of cats; but of course I might just be dreaming that I've pinched myself. Second, because of this, and because our project is to examine whether putative experiences of God must be cross-checked to carry evidential weight, not to respond to radical skepticism, we shall have to frame our discussion with some care. One could, of course, accept a counsel of despair: neither ordinary sense experience nor mystical experience can form the basis of justified beliefs about external matters. In that event, mystical theistic beliefs are in no worse shape, epistemically speaking, than ordinary perceptual beliefs. But that would be because neither set of beliefs could be in any worse shape, so far as justification goes. That sort of "pox on both your houses" skepticism is, however, not a very interesting position from the perspective of traditional debates about the warrant for theism. The interesting question is: If we suppose ordinary perceptual beliefs (and we may throw in scientific theory for good measure) to be warrantable by appeal to sense experience, then why shouldn't theistic beliefs be similarly warrantable by appeal to perceptual experience, whether sensory or mystical?

Here, in a nutshell, is what I shall argue. The problem of perception derives largely from the general truth that any effect – hence a perceptual experience – can be caused in more ways than one. Our strategy for removing this ambiguity is cross-checking. Ultimately, cross-checking involves just collecting more data, which are subject to the same ambiguity. Our implicit reasoning is that the total amount of ambiguity can nevertheless be progressively reduced in this way. The means by which science draws a bead on postulated "unobservable" entities (like electrons) is not in principle or in practice different in kind; it is just more systematic and careful than the humdrum of everyday perceptual judgments. In everyday contexts, cross-checking is informal, and it is so automatic, continuous, and pervasive that, except under duress (e.g., as we try to catch out a magician), it is scarcely noticed. I propose to show how cross-checking works; to argue that it is a mandatory feature of any recruitment of perceptual experience to epistemic ends; and that, therefore, it is a requirement that must be met in theistic appeals to mystical experience as evidence for theism. Finally, I shall argue that this requirement has not, and probably cannot, be met. So, I shall conclude, mystical experience provides hardly any useful support for theism.

2 Cross-Checking Explained

So, what is cross-checking? Why is it needed? And how does it work? Let "cross-checking" denote all those procedures and strategies we use to settle questions about the causes of something. These include, in particular, (1) using Mill's methods to pick out causally relevant antecedent conditions; (2) exploiting the fact that events have multiple effects, to "triangulate" the event in question, on the principle that qualitatively different causes will have *some* differences in their (potential) effects;[14] and (3) confirming the existence of causal mechanisms allegedly connecting a cause to its effects (when it is not a proximate cause). These strategies depend upon putting forward hypotheses and testing them by means of diagnostic experiments. I shall discuss mainly tests of type (3), but invoke strategy (2) when considering prophetic revelations as a test of MEs.

There are various ways in which cross-checking principles can be formally stated. One way to approach type-3 cross-checks is to consider the problem posed by Duhem's thesis. We have a hypothesis H (e.g., that the cat was skinned with a knife), on the basis of which we can, with the assistance of auxiliary hypothesis A, infer some observable effect E_0. In general, the occurrence of E_0 should confirm H, and its nonoccurrence disconfirm H. How that goes depends upon how strongly H & A probabilifies E_0 (or its negation), and how strongly it or its negation is probabilified by competing hypotheses-cum-auxiliaries.

But, as we know, even when E_0 fails to materialize and H & A is thereby disconfirmed, the opprobrium need not fall on H: the falsehood of A may be to blame. Here is where type-3 cross-checking comes in. It comes in two varieties. First, we can run further tests on H, pitting it against its rivals either in repeat performances of the first experiment or, often more tellingly, in different experiments which call upon different auxiliaries and predict different observations. Second, we can check A, now employing *it* as a hypothesis to be tested.[15] Thus, a defender of H in the face of *not*-E_0 might insist that the relevant auxiliary is not A, but A^*, where H & A^* entails *not*-E_0. Now A and A^* are competitors, and we can require an independent "crucial experiment"[16] in which they make conflicting predictions, E_1 and E_1^*. But of course, those predictions cannot be made without invoking further auxiliaries – call them A_1 and A_1^*. Clearly, if the experimental outcome is E_1, the defender of A^* (and hence H) can protect A^* by insisting upon modifying his A_1^*. And then we can play another round. Can this testing game go on forever, or will the regress eventually run the quarry (the truth-value of H) to ground? One way to capture the radical skeptic's intuition is by arguing that the cycle of modifications to save the appearances can go on forever. (This is one form of the so-called underdetermination of theory by data.) The other side of the coin is that this way of formulating the problem of skepticism helps us see what sorts of minimal assumptions might head off an infinite regress, thereby making the evidential issue an interesting one. And this is just what we need to see when the observations in question are the mystic's experiences, and the hypothesis is theism.

I do not regard it as a settled question whether adjustment of auxiliaries in the face of recalcitrant data can go on forever. But even if after-the-fact revising can proceed indefinitely, there is a strong intuition that a system of beliefs which must constantly be revised as new evidence comes in loses plausibility in relation to one

14 See Evan Fales, *Causation and Universals* (London: Routledge, 1990), ch. 8.

15 In practice, A will be a long conjunction of hypotheses which describe the antecedent conditions and the laws governing the causal mechanisms upon which the making of any measurement or observation depends. In the case of perception, H will articulate the causal pathways which mediate the transmission of sensory information. The component hypotheses of A will typically be independently (of each other) testable. For simplicity, I shall treat A as if it were a single hypothesis.

16 That is, one that does not make use of H.

that does not. Let us make this anti-skeptical assumption. Evidence, in the face of which a hypothesis can be rescued only by revision of auxiliary assumptions, works to the disadvantage of that hypothesis – though perhaps not decisively so – in comparison with competitors which accommodate that evidence without revisions.[17]

An obvious objection to all this will be that, plausible as it may be as a rational reconstruction of scientific reasoning, it does not at all capture the process by which we acquire warranted perceptual beliefs. Perceptual knowledge seems much more direct than this, even to those who concede the obvious fact that it is causally mediated. So I now want to argue that this is an illusion, that in fact warrant accrues to perceptual beliefs only insofar as, rationally reconstructed, their acquisition, too, requires inference to the best explanation.

3 The Pervasive Need for Cross-Checking

What, then, is it about cross-checking that establishes its essential and fundamental place as an epistemic method, even in the case of sense perception? This standing is a consequence of the fact that we are physical beings, situated within a spatiotemporal world in an environment with which we communicate via physical – that is, causal – processes. But the centrality of cross-checking is still more fundamental than this. It is demanded for knowledge of *any* causal process, in which causes are known *via* their effects. In particular, it is demanded in connection with any claim to have perceptual access to an extra-mental reality. It would be demanded, for example, if we were bodiless minds claiming perceptual contact with disembodied demons, evil or benign, with angels, or with a god. That is because the contact is perceptual, and because of the principle

P: If *S* perceives (has a perceptual experience of) *X*, then *X* is a suitable cause of *S*'s experience.

First, three comments about P; and then, more on the connection between (P) and cross-checking:

1 When I say that *X* is *a* cause of *S*'s experience, I mean just that it plays a role as one of the causal antecedents of *S*'s experience.
2 Strictly speaking, it is events or states of affairs that are causes. If *X* is a particular, then it is not *X per se*, but *X*'s having some property or undergoing some change which constitutes the cause in question.
3 When I say that this is a *suitable* cause of *S*'s experience, I mean that it must cause the experience in the right sort of way for the experience to count as per-

17 Our goal is to vindicate the inverse-probability reasoning we use to infer causes from their effects as the best explanations of those effects. If we employ Bayes' theorem (or some qualitative analogue) for this purpose, we shall also need to assume some rough way to assign credences to competing hypotheses, antecedently to considering any of the empirical data. Let us assume this can be done. For present purposes, these anti-skeptical assumptions are enough to be getting on with.

ception *of X*. Obviously, not all of the causal conditions of my now perceiving this pen are conditions I now perceive (those conditions include my eyes and brain working properly, the pen being illuminated, and even God, if God caused the pen to exist and sustains me in existence). We cannot say *in general* what criteria distinguish the "right" sort of causal ancestry from the wrong sorts; but cross-checking has everything to do with how we justifiably identify the right items in particular cases.

Knowing what we are perceiving is a matter of knowing what is causing our experience in the right sort of way. But that is a matter of narrowing down the candidate causes of an experience so that – ideally – just one cause, situated in the right way, can explain our data. It is precisely here that cross-checking plays the crucial role, by enabling us to eliminate possible causes and to form a sufficiently precise conception of our environment and the causal processes that occur in it to "zero in" on the (or a) "suitable" cause.[18]

William Alston misses the mark when he insists that a demand for similar cross-checking of the claims of mystics amounts to a kind of epistemic imperialism.[19] He insists that each epistemic practice, including mystical practice, gets to dictate its own standards and cross-checking criteria. But, as we shall see, those invoked by mystics are characteristically vacuous. Obviously, the sorts of evidence relevant to checking a perceptual claim will depend upon its modality and content. But determining what makes something *count* as evidence and justification is dictated by the causal structure of perception and cannot be commandeered by epistemic practices, so-called.

Many philosophers will reject this conception of perception and perceptual knowledge. They do so partly for dialectical reasons – that is, because they believe that the road so paved leads straight to skeptical perdition. They do so, further, for broadly phenomenological reasons – that is, because we do not ordinarily make perceptual knowledge claims on the basis of anything more than having the right sort of experience. We don't indulge in any cross-checking or inference in judging, for example, that there is someone in the seat next to us.

But these objections are, in the present context, misdirected. The phenomenological objection ignores what we might call "subliminal information processing," both past and occurrent, and the vital role that cross-checking plays in this processing.[20] What sort of perceptual seemings a given environment can produce in one is a function not only of recent sensory stimulation, but of much else: of attention and motivational factors, of past experience and concepts thereby acquired, of expectations for which an inductive rationale could be supplied if required (but which ordinarily

18 There is often more than one. Even though I could not, ordinarily, be said to observe an image on my retina, I could be said, when watching a presidential press conference, alternatively to see either the TV or George W. Bush. An elementary particle physicist could rightly say both that she is observing tracks in a bubble chamber and that she is observing electrons.

19 See Alston, *Perceiving God*, pp. 209–22.

20 It also ignores the difference between our just perceptually *taking* there to be someone in the adjoining seat, perhaps in part because of the operation of hard-wired belief-forming mechanisms that operate "automatically," and our being *justified* in that belief.

does not – and need not – enter into perceptual engagement with the world). We can look and just "see" that the refrigerator in the kitchen is white, in part because we have acquired an understanding of what refrigerators are and what they look like, readily expect such items to appear in kitchens, and know that white things look a certain way under the apparent conditions of illumination. An ability to "just see" directly that this refrigerator is white is a hard-won skill. Learning endows us with unconscious cognitive mechanisms that operate to apply concepts in forming a percept as if on the basis of various inductions.

Moreover, past learning and also the present cognitive processing incorporate cross-checking in fundamental ways. What our cognitive systems have learned is how "automatically" to make judgments that, were we rationally to reconstruct them, would involve *causal* reasoning to the best explanation for the multitude of sensory inputs with which we are provided. For example, the supposition that light travels in more or less straight lines, together with the hypotheses that there is a bulky, stationary, solid white object before us, and that we are in motion in a certain way relative to it, can help explain the sequence of our visual/tactile inputs. But any such reasoning (or unconscious surrogate for it) must invoke, implicitly, cross-checking. It is as if, for example, the various visual and tactile inputs serve to corroborate the judgment that there is a refrigerator, by eliminating alternative possibilities.

This kind of implicit cross-checking is absolutely pervasive; it comes to permeate all our perceptual "takings" as we mature and piece together our world.[21] This feature of sense-perceptual processes explains a fundamental phenomenological feature of perceptual judgments: namely, how we can directly take ourselves to be *en rapport* with our physical surroundings, even though no single bit of sensory information could form an adequate basis for such a judgment (or even, I would add, for the formation of the *concepts* required to envision a three-dimensional space inhabited by physical continuants). It explains how it is that we do this without seeming to engage in any processes of inference from representations – of inference from effects to causes. That is why direct realist theories of perception can seem so plausible, even though in a *causal* sense, we are obviously *not* in direct contact with our physical surroundings.

4 Skepticism Bracketed

I have dwelt upon this point because I take it to be crucial to an assessment of the epistemic status of mystical experience, interpreted as perceptual contact with supernatural realities. But it also permits a response to the objection that conceding perception to involve an "indirect" (causal) contact with extra-mental reality, and perceptual judgment to require reasoning from effects to causes (or surrogates for that), gives the skeptic all he needs to undermine claims to have knowledge or justification.

21 In young infants these cognitive processes are observably in the process of formation.

Alston is particularly forceful and insightful in making this case with respect to sense perception (but of course it applies to mystical perception equally).[22] He argues that any attempt to justify a perceptual practice must fail on grounds of either unsoundness or circularity. Though Alston's argument is complex, we have seen why this result is to be expected and, consequently, can specify the way in which I believe the issue concerning mystical perception ought to be framed.

So as not to beg any questions, I shall adopt Alston's view that there are distinguishable belief-forming practices, including different perceptual practices.[23] Two such practices take as their inputs sense perception and mystical perception. If the possibility of mystical evidence for God is not automatically to be ruled out, we must find some way of deflecting skeptical objections as they apply to perceptual judgments generally. Seeing how this goes for sense perception will enable us to generalize to other perceptual practices, for the relevant similarities between them are more important than the differences. Alston, in spite of his insistence that each perceptual practice is beholden only to its own epistemic standards, recognizes this when he invokes, for all perceptual practices, what amounts to a kind of Principle of Credulity.[24] Alston takes it that, provided a perceptual practice meets certain conditions,[25] perceptual judgments formed in the normal ways provided for in that practice are prima facie justified. (They are only prima facie justified: every such practice must include what Alston calls an "overrider" system, and so a judgment can be overridden. Indeed, Alston's overrider systems reflect the importance of cross-checking, without properly recognizing its fundamentality.)

Any appeal to prima facie warrant – warrant occurring in the absence of even implicit or preconscious processes that could be rationally reconstructed in terms of inductive inference and cross-checking – is just the *wrong* way to bracket (radical) skepticism and frame our question. It is wrong because it short-circuits precisely the crucial justificatory procedures (or at least a crucial stage in their application), thereby begging, or at least certainly obscuring the bearing of, critical questions that the mystical theist must confront. They include the question whether cross-checking procedures must be, but are not, appropriately "built into," and cannot retrospectively be applied to, mystical experiences and the judgments they deliver. I shall argue that they are not, and that this flaw is fatal to mystical justifications of theism.

Cross-checking and cross-checkability must be integral parts of any perceptual epistemic practice because what a perceiver takes to be present on the basis of her experiences might not be what is in fact causally responsible for those experiences.

22 See Alston, *Perceiving God*, ch. 3, and *idem, Reliability of Sense Perception.*

23 For details, see Alston, *Perceiving God*, ch. 4.

24. The term, and the principle itself, are due to Swinburne, though the idea can be traced back at least to Reid.

25 These conditions include being socially established, incorporating an overrider system, and being free of massive contradiction from within and from beliefs generated by other doxastic practices (see Alston, *Perceiving God*, ch. 4).

Cross-checking "pins down" stages of the causal process, thereby eliminating alternative hypotheses as to how the input is produced.[26]

What goes for sense perception goes for mystical experience as well. Theists who invoke such experiences as evidence may help themselves to the same inductive principles that our sensory practices evidently presuppose – in particular, those that vindicate cross-checking. However, if, granting those principles, mystical experiences fail to supply significant evidence for theism, an appeal to them will be of little help to theists.

I have been insisting that what we need to frame the debate productively is *not* some principle of credulity, but more general and fundamental inductive principles that will not short-circuit the issues. But even if I were to *grant* some form of credulity principle,[27] it would avail the theist little. For the warrant it confers is only prima facie warrant, and, as it happens, there are good reasons to question that warrant in the mystical case. Since that is so, cross-checking can't be avoided, and its demands are made acute in proportion to the cogency of the cognitive challenges that mystical practices (MPs) confront.

5 Christian Mysticism: Challenges and Checks

There are a number of such challenges, in the form of alternative explanations for mystical experiences (MEs). One of these, which I shall not pursue, comes from within many MPs. It is the possibility that an ME is demonically caused.[28] There are also naturalistic explanations. Here I shall mention two which complement one another and are jointly strong enough to outdistance any theistic explanation.[29] Fortunately (and *pace* Alston[30]), patterns of mystical encounter are so predictable and overtly manifested, in religious traditions ranging from Pentecostal worship to the ritual seances of Dinka and Tungus shamans, that it has been possible for anthro-

26 The trouble with this story is, as we saw, twofold. First, the only means we have for "pinning down" the facts about a given causal process are perceptual means; and if there is a skeptical question to be raised about the *original* process – the one generating the perceptual experience upon which a perceptual judgment is based – then entirely similar doubts will apply to the perceptual processes upon which cross-checking procedures depend. Second, our problem arises in the first place – and hence in the second place – because effects underdetermine their causes. (This is just a special case – undoubtedly the most central case – of the problem that theory is underdetermined by data: any given data can be explained by any number of incompatible theories.) It is to evade the skeptic here that we invoke the anti-skeptical principles.

27 Whether it be that adopted by Swinburne, *Existence of God*, Alston, *Perceiving God*, or Gellman, *Experience of God*.

28 I shall also largely ignore the major challenge which derives from the enormous variety and conflicting content of MEs worldwide. That is a severe problem in its own right.

29 So I argue with respect to Lewis's theory in Fales, "Scientific Explanations of Mystical Experience, Part I: The Case of St. Teresa," and "Scientific Explanations of Mystical Experience, Part II: The Challenge to Theism," *Religious Studies*, 32 (1996), pp. 143–63 and 297–313 respectively. This can now be supplemented with the neurophysiological findings.

30 Alston, *Perceiving God*, pp. 240–1.

pologists and psychologists to study the phenomenon in great detail in its natural settings.[31]

The first naturalistic explanation is due to the anthropologist I. M. Lewis, and derives from worldwide comparative studies which reveal certain general patterns among MPs.[32] In brief, Lewis shows that, at least where mystics "go public" and appeal to their experiences in the social arena, mysticism serves mundane interests either of the mystic him or herself, or of some group with which he or she identifies. Lewis discerns two types of mystics: socially marginalized mystics whose mysticism is a weapon in the struggle to achieve social justice for themselves and their group, and upwardly mobile mystics who use their mystical experiences as credentials to legitimate their claim on positions of social leadership. Lewis shows how the *descriptions* that mystics give of their experiences and the *behaviors* they exhibit prior to, during, and after mystical episodes serve these social ends in quite precise and predictable ways.

One of the great strengths of Lewis's theory is that it cuts across the entire spectrum of MPs, providing a unity of explanation that the theist cannot hope to match.[33] Lewis's theory has, however, a significant lacuna. It says little about how the occurrence of favorable social circumstances gets translated into the incidence of mystical phenomenology. Moreover, Lewis gives no very adequate explanation for the apparent frequency of MEs which remain private. Many people, it seems, have occasional mystical experiences, but almost never disclose them.

But it looks now as if these gaps can be closed by the second naturalistic approach, which has begun to indicate the details of the neurophysiological mechanisms by means of which mystical experience is mediated. Such experiences, it turns out, are associated with micro-seizures of the temporal lobes of the brain. When these seizures are severe, they result in temporal lobe epilepsy. But mild seizures, which can even be artificially induced during brain surgery, can result in powerful mystical experiences.[34] A substantial portion of the general population has a disposition to such mild seizures, and there is some circumstantial evidence that they can be provoked by techniques traditionally used to induce mystical trance states.[35]

A theist may wish to reply here that God may well have a hand in these mechanisms, indeed employ them as his means for appearing to his worshippers.[36] But this is implausible on a number of counts. For one thing, it is extraordinarily hard to

31 I have the report (private communication) of a Christian mystic trained in neurophysiology who has been able to record her own brain waves, and those of a colleague, during trance, who confirms the temporal lobe finding (see below). For a more detailed summary of the evidence and references, see Fales, "Scientific Explanations," Parts I and II, and *idem*, "Can Science Explain Mysticism?" *Religious Studies*, 35 (1999), pp. 213–27.

32 I. M. Lewis, *Ecstatic Religion*, 2nd edn (London: Routledge, 1989).

33 See Fales, "Scientific Explanations of Mystical Experience, Part II."

34 The literature is substantial and growing. For a good bibliography, see Susan Blackmore, *Dying to Live: Near-Death Experiences* (Buffalo, NY: Prometheus Books, 1993), especially the citations for ch. 10.

35 See William Sargant, *The Mind Possessed: A Physiology of Possession, Mysticism, and Faith Healing* (Philadelphia: J. E. Lippincott, 1974).

36 Alston has suggested this possibility on a number of occasions – e.g., in "Psychoanalytic Theory and Theistic Belief," in John Hick (ed.), *Faith and the Philosophers* (New York: St Martin's Press, 1964), and in *Perceiving God*, pp. 230–3.

explain why God would appear through the figure of Jesus to a Christian, as Allah to a Muslim, Brahman to a Hindu, the god Flesh to a Dinka, and as a variety of *loa* spirits to voodoo practitioners. And if a purely naturalistic explanation can be given for the nontheistic experiences, then why not also for the theistic ones?[37]

There are other problems. Suppose we take a naturalistic explanation of MEs and tack on the hypothesis that God is involved in some way. This is a God-of-the-gaps strategy. Given the lacunae in our understanding of even simple physical processes – to say nothing of the neurophysiology of the brain – this strategy is one a theist can deploy with some ease.

Indeed, it incurs the danger of being too easy. A theist could invoke divine intervention to explain why the radiator of my car cracked overnight. Our natural explanation is full of holes: we may not know exactly how cold the engine got last night, nor exactly how strong the walls of the radiator were at the rupture point, nor how to apply the known laws of nature to such a complex system. So, in principle, all the theist need do is find some gap in the posited causal etiology, and tack on the hypothesis that here the finger of God helped the process along – no doubt, to punish my sins.

Why do we (most of us!) not credit such an "explanation"? First, of course, because a long history of experience teaches us that such gaps are often eventually filled by natural causes. But second, because the theistic explanation comes too cheaply: there are no constraints on when, how, and where God is likely to act, no attendant procedures for cross-checking or ferreting out the precise mode and locus of divine intervention, no positive suggestions about how the theistic account of theophysical interaction might be investigated, fleshed out, ramified – and virtually no concomitant predictive power. This theoretical poverty cripples cross-checking for divine influence.

Still, the presence of naturalistic competitors makes it imperative that we examine what sorts of cross-checking MP admits, and how successful such cross-checks have been. We run here into a number of obvious difficulties. Most prominent among them is the fact that mystical experiences are not public.[38] Moreover, the sorts of checks typically invoked, by Christian mystics at least, are either epistemically irrelevant or question begging, absent quite strong auxiliary assumptions.

37 This argument is fleshed out in Fales, "Scientific Explanations of Mysticism, Part II." It is, moreover, very unclear just how, in principle, God would be able to communicate with human beings. If this is to occur via divine influence upon a person's brain states, and those states are macroscopic physical states, then any divine intervention will involve local violations of the highly confirmed laws of conservation of momentum and energy. If, one the other hand, we suppose that God intervenes at the quantum level, acting as a kind of "hidden variable" in determining the outcomes of indeterministic processes, as Nancey Murphy has recently proposed, then we can avoid the violation of physical laws, but only at the price of making in principle unknowable (since hidden by quantum uncertainties) the presence of divine intervention. On these issues see the articles by Murphy and Tracy in Robert J. Russell, Nancey Murphy, and Arthur R. Peacocke (eds), *Chaos and Complexity: Scientific Perspectives on Divine Action* (Vatican City: Vatican Observatory Publications, 1995).

38 There are occasional reports of *sense*-perceptual supernatural apparitions witnessed by many – e.g., at Fatima and Zeitoun. Also, some mystics do report perceiving God via several sensory modalities – e.g., vision, hearing, and smell. I cannot pursue these matters here; and in any case, many theists – e.g., Alston and Wainwright – de-emphasize this sort of experience.

It is not that mystics are unconcerned about the veridicality of MEs. On the contrary, they often display a lively concern with this and offer multiple tests. But let us look at some of these tests, using Teresa of Avila as a guide. Teresa exhibits a strong interest in the question of how veridical experiences are to be distinguished from those produced by what she calls "melancholy" and by Satan. (This interest is hardly surprising, given the regularity with which the Inquisition accused mystics – especially women – of nefarious motives, fraud, or demonic possession.) Teresa's list of tests includes: (1) the fruits of an experience – both in the actions and personality of the mystic and as producing an inner peace rather than a troubled state of mind, (2) the vividness of the memory of the experience, (3) conformity to Scripture, and (4) validation by the mystic's confessor.

It is not hard to see how these criteria might be designed to secure for the mystic immunity from Inquisitional prosecution, but not easy to see what epistemic force they could have.[39] Test 3 looks straightforwardly question begging, inasmuch as the authority of Scripture rests largely on the supposed authority of the revelations upon which it is based.[40] Tests 1, 2, and 4 have no epistemic force except on the assumption that only God, and neither Satan's best deceptive efforts nor natural causes, can produce experiences that are memorable, convincing to confessors, or have good fruits. But what independent evidence is there for that? What cross-checks for these claims can theists supply? On this, Teresa is silent.

The final – and in principle the best – hope for cross-checking MEs lies with successful prophecy. Perhaps a theistic account *does* after all yield checkable predictions in a way that bears directly upon the evidential force of MEs. For, often enough, one of the fruits of a mystical encounter with God has been the revelation of a prophecy. Not only that, but prophecy has figured as a central component of Christian mystical practice (CMP) and many other MPs, and of the apologetical strategies associated with them. This is because prophecies permit, when certain conditions are satisfied, type-2 cross-checks of a fairly powerful and peculiarly direct sort. When the *content* of a ME contains some message, putatively from God or some supernatural source assumed to be in the know, concerning future events, the claim of genuineness can in principle be checked; ordinarily, the prophesied events will be of such a sort that it is within the purview of ordinary sense perception to determine their occurrence or nonoccurrence.

Yet, Alston tries to downplay the prophetic dimensions of MP.[41] Why? After all, the plain fact is that prophecy is a major and central feature of the MPs of many reli-

39 Indeed, most such tests aim at social acceptance within the religious community. These, and all the other tests of which I know, are such that passing them is largely under the control of the mystic or of her religious community. Thus, unlike proper cross-checks, they do not risk invalidation of the tested hypothesis by an uncooperative tester-independent world.

40 It is all too likely that the content of Teresa's experiences, as she describes them, is conditioned by her (and her superiors') prior acceptance of Scripture. And she gives no independent evidence that Scripture is authoritative. That authority could be independently confirmed by miracles and successful prophecy, however. Concerning the latter, see below.

41 See Alston, *Perceiving God*, pp. 222–5. Alston is there concerned with the general predictive power of CMP and does not mention religious prophecy specifically at all. On p. 291, he mentions in passing fulfillment of prophecy as a test, not of MEs, but of divine inspiration not associated with MEs. Yet on p. 298, he expresses skepticism concerning the record of Christian miracles generally.

gious traditions; moreover, putatively successful prophecy is regularly appealed to precisely by way of confirming the genuineness of the prophet, the veridicality of his or her ecstatic visions, and the uniquely truth-connected status of the tradition that claims him or her as its own. Ecstatics who develop prophetic practice into a vocation are familiar figures in religious traditions – witness the oracle at Delphi, the Hebrew prophets, John on Patmos, and Jesus of Nazareth. Nor is this an aspect only of ancient MPs, long since superseded (within Jewish and Christian MPs). Far from it, as anyone who considers the claims of contemporary televangelists can confirm.

Prophecy, therefore, is a feature intrinsic to CMP, a feature by means of which the truth-claims produced by that practice can be quite directly checked. However, no such check will be very informative unless certain conditions are satisfied. Briefly, these include:

1 The prophecy must be of some event not intrinsically likely (not, e.g., "wars and rumors of wars" – Mark 24:6).
2 The prophecy must not be self-fulfilling, or of events the prophet or his or her followers can themselves bring about.
3 The prophecy must demonstrably have been made prior to the events which count as its fulfillment.
4 The prophecy must be sufficiently specific and unambiguous to preclude *ex post facto* reinterpretation to fit any of a wide range of possible "fulfillments."
5 The fulfillment of the prophecy must be verified independently of the say-so of the prophet or his or her partisans or tradition.[42]

Here we have, at last, a cross-check which really *does* offer a test of mystical experience. The reasoning is straightforward: given 1–5, only the mystic's having received a message from a superhumanly prescient being (or, improbably, wild luck) can explain his or her prophetic success. (There are, to be sure, some added complications: for example, we must be careful to avoid the Jean Dixon fallacy. A clever prophet can issue hundreds of risky prophecies, in the hope of scoring a few memorable "hits," calculating that the "misses" will be forgotten. Our reasoning to the best explanation must take into account the prophet's entire track record.)

Now, just what is the record of Jewish and Christian MPs on this score? Rather than pursue this question at length, let me observe that I know of no recorded prophecy, either within the Jewish/Christian canon or outside it, that clearly satisfies

42 It might be protested that this last condition reflects an improperly imperialistic imposition on CMP of criteria indigenous to SP. But to excuse CMP from this requirement on such grounds is to abandon good sense. First, the fulfilling events are typically ones which would be observed by ordinary sense perception; and second, as Hume correctly observed, the temptation to prevarication is too great here to rely upon the say-so of those whose interests are directly at stake. We have ample demonstration of the perennial creative reconstruction of the historical record by those who have a religious agenda; and the New Testament is certainly no exception.

criteria 1–5. (There are, however, a number of demonstrably *false* prophecies. Of these, perhaps the most decisive and poignant occurs at Matt. 16:27.[43])

Conclusion: Like any perceptual practice, CMP requires an elaborate system of cross-checks and cross-checking procedures. But, because of its theoretical poverty with respect to the causes of mystical experiences, no such system has been, or is likely to be, forthcoming. With respect to the one relatively strong cross-checking strategy that CMP has available (and has purported to use), its record is one of failure. Until these defects are remedied, mystical experience cannot hope to provide significant evidential support for theism.

Reply to Fales

Fales has two main reasons for denying that mystical experience provides support for theism. (1) It can do so only if it (sometimes) constitutes a genuine perception of God, and this is possible only if it can be successfully "cross-checked," which itself is not possible (so far as we can tell). (2) Mystical experience can be adequately explained naturalistically, which cuts the ground out from any supposition that it is a genuine perception of God. I shall devote most of my remarks to (1).

It is not clear from Fales's exposition just what cross-checking (CC) is and how it works. He introduces it by saying that it denotes "all those procedures and strategies we use to settle questions about the causes of something." If "we" is given the widest possible extension so as to include, *inter alia*, me, this can't be his position. For I hold that in the perceptual case, one is justified in supposing that *S* sees *X*, provided that *S* has an experience that involves an (at least apparent) visual presentation of *X*, and there are no sufficient overriders for the claim that *S* does perceive *X*. And since, as Fales and I both hold, one sees *X* only if *X* causally contributes to the production of the visual experience in question *in the right sort of way*, this would be a way of detecting a certain causal relation. But Fales opposes this approach to the matter, in his discussion of the Principle of Credulity (PC), and *contrasts* that with a CC approach. Thus he must be presupposing some more restricted conception of CC. But his presentation contains no specification of just what that might be. He does mention three types of CC, but with no suggestion that they exhaust the genus. Lacking any alternative, I will take them as an indication of the sorts of procedures of which Fales approves, and glean whatever general conception of CC I can from that.

Fales claims that one has adequately justified a claim to have perceived *X* only if one has successfully "cross-checked" that claim, and that this cannot be done with

43 Others occur at Josh. 4:7, Ezek. 26:14–21, and Isa. 60:1–62:12, esp. 62:8. Augustin Poulain, *The Graces of Interior Prayer: A Treatise on Mystical Theology*, 6th edn, tr. Leonora York Smith (Westminster, Vt.: Celtic Cross Books, 1978), ch. 21, reports with considerable embarrassment the false prophetic utterances of a number of mystics canonized by the Roman Catholic Church. As regards Matt. 16:27, see parallels at Mark 8:38–9:1 and Luke 9:26–7. John, writing later, discreetly omits this prophecy; see John 6 and 12:25, which in other respects parallel the Synoptic pericopes. It is clear that the parousia and final judgment are intended: cf. Matt. 25:31f and Rev. 20:11–21.

claims to have perceived God in mystical experience (ME). It's not clear whether he takes the stronger position that some kind of CC condition is required for its being the case that *S* perceives *X*. He does argue that the "subliminal information processing" that gives rise to conscious perceptual experience always involves CC, which would imply that all veridical perception (and nonveridical as well!) involves CC. But what he claims not to be available for ME, though it is for sense experience (SE), is fully conscious and deliberate deployment of CC. And he could hardly suppose that one genuinely perceives X only where such procedures have in fact been carried out. But exploiting the hint given by his statement that "cross-checking and cross-checkability must be integral parts of any perceptual epistemic practice," we may take it that he holds that S genuinely perceives X only if that could be validated by a successful CC procedure.

Being unable to tell exactly what it takes for something to count as CC, I am hardly in a maximally favorable position to criticize this position. But we need merely to appeal to Fales's apparent stipulation that CC covers only ways of determining what is causally related to what in order to call into question his supposition that "cross-checking plays the crucial role" in zeroing in on the contribution a cause has to make to an experience in order to be what is perceived in that experience. For the most that CC can do here is to determine what factors causally influenced the occurrence of a certain perceptual experience. But, as both Fales and I note, there are many causal contributors to an SE, most of which are not perceived in having that experience. Hence, if we take a casual route to determining what, if anything, is genuinely perceived in a certain experience, it is crucial to determine what kind of contribution a cause has to make to earn that status. But since CC is limited to procedures for detecting causal relationships, it will, at most, serve to identify the various causal contributors to an experience; it will do nothing to pick out that contributor among those that one is perceiving in having that experience. Thus Fales is quite wrong in saying that "cross-checking has everything to do with how we justifiably identify the right items in particular cases." As for that task, Fales has not provided a viable alternative to the use of PC to identify some cases of genuine object perception, so as to give us a basis for determining, for a given modality, what kind of causal contribution to the experience qualifies a cause for the status of what is perceived therein.

This throws us back to my position that PC is more fundamental to the epistemology of perception than CC. Even if we could use the latter without reliance on the former to determine the causal antecedents of an experience (and I will shortly argue that even this is not possible), it would not enable us to pick out what is perceived in that experience, and hence pick out what it is about which the experience provides us with usable information. In opposition to my position, Fales suggests that PC is useless for providing us with initial cases of genuine object perception because it provides only prima facie justification for perceptual beliefs, and this may be overridden.[44] But the mere possibility of being overridden should not frighten us. So long

44 I will not have time to go into the way Fales ignores the very important distinction between whether a given object, X, is genuinely perceived by S, and whether one or another perceptual belief S thereby forms about X is justified.

as a prima facie justification is not in fact overridden, it will count as unqualified justification.

There is another respect in which PC counts as more fundamental epistemologically than CC. As I have argued before,[45] we cannot show the general reliability of all of our most basic belief-forming practices without running into "epistemic circularity," taking some of our premises from the very practice for the reliability of which we are arguing. We must assume the reliability of some such practices in order to get started on any inquiry whatever. Even if by making such an assumption for one practice – for example, sense perception – we could then proceed to establish the reliability of the others, we would still have taken sense perception to be reliable without a noncircular argument for this. And, in any event, this procedure is not viable. How would we establish the reliability of induction or rational intuition just on the basis of particular pieces of perceptual information? Thus we are left with no real alternative to taking "on faith" the reliability of our basic, socially established belief-forming practices. This is my version of the more individually slanted PC which, in my essay, I was using for the sake of concision. Since the use of CC clearly depends on assuming the reliability of sense perception, and since its investigation of causal relations involves using observation to determine whether something occurs that would occur if a certain causal relation obtains, it cannot be carried out without considerable reliance on PC (or a social practice version thereof). Hence this is a more general way in which PC is epistemologically more fundamental than CC.

Fales takes note of this line of argument and my use of it to argue for the prima facie justifiability of beliefs based on mystical experience, but his discussion distorts the matter in two ways. First, he supposes that my epistemic circularity argument is a skeptical argument. But it need not be taken that way. I use it not to support skepticism, or even to exhibit a reason for skepticism, but rather to point out a basic feature of the human cognitive condition. Second, thinking of the matter in connection with skepticism, he seeks to ignore it by simply setting radical skeptical doubts aside. But what he calls "the interesting question" is one that results from an arbitrary partiality to sense perception in the setting aside of skepticism. It consists of taking perceptual beliefs to be warrantable by appeal to SE, but declining to make a like concession to beliefs based on ME. If this is to escape the charge of arbitrariness, an adequate reason will have to be given for the double standard. Fales's reason seems to be that sense-perceptual beliefs can be "cross-checked," while beliefs based on mystical experience cannot. But, on his own showing, the use of CC involves reliance on the deliverances of SE. And when he finds mystics seeking to validate the deliverances of ME by appealing to other such deliverances, he accuses them of "begging the question." In contrast to this blatantly ungrounded double standard, PC (or my social practice version thereof) takes the output of all firmly socially established "doxastic" (belief-forming) practices to be thereby prima facie justified, with the final verdict on them awaiting further investigation into whether they are disqualified by one or another "overrider."

Even if Fales were to accept all that, he would still have another card to play: namely, the claim that prima facie justification is always overridden for mystical

45 Alston, *Reliability of Sense Perception.*

beliefs, but not for sense-perceptual beliefs. I have considered various alleged over-riders for ME in my essay and in much more detail elsewhere.[46]

One alleged overrider that Fales discusses in some detail is that ME can be better explained naturalistically. In my essay I cast some doubt on the thesis that even a complete naturalistic account of the proximate causes of ME would be incompatible with God's causing the experience in a way that would qualify him as an object of the experience. But this issue arises only if it is plausible to suppose that there is, or could be, such a complete naturalistic explanation. On this point I must plead guilty to handling the problem in much too sketchy a fashion in my essay and even in my earlier book on the subject.[47] In particular, in neither place do I discuss recent attempts. Although I don't have the space here to remedy this lack properly, I will say this. The suggestions which Fales draws from the work of I. M. Lewis and from studies of micro-seizures of the temporal lobes of the brain seem to me to have little promise of making a major contribution to the dreamed-of complete naturalistic explanation. The most obvious lacuna is this. Before studies of particular sorts of alleged MEs can provide substantial promise of a general naturalistic explanation, much more preliminary taxonomy is required. How do we draw boundaries around the territory being investigated? What does it take for a particular experience to be an ME? What are the species of this genus? Studies in the field all bear marks of neglecting these crucial conceptual issues. I. M. Lewis, whom Fales cites,[48] concentrates on "possession cults," which can hardly be taken as encompassing all the experiences that are taken by their subjects to be direct experiences of an object of worship or an alleged ultimate reality. I am dubious about the prospects of justifying Fales's claim that Lewis's theory "cuts across the entire spectrum of MPs." In any event, it is far from being justified at present. As for evidence that micro-seizures of the temporal lobes of the brain "can be provoked by techniques traditionally used to induce mystical trance states," the apparent fact that putative direct experiences of God are by no means limited to "trance states" raises serious questions as to how general this explanation is.

Reply to Alston

Between Alston's position and mine there are three main areas of dispute. The first concerns the nature of perceptual warrant – specifically, the employment of a Principle of Credulity and the significance of cross-checks. Second, we disagree about whether there are checks that significantly confirm theistic mystical experiences (MEs). Third, Alston stoutly maintains that serious difficulties hobble scientific investigation and naturalistic explanation of MEs. Let me take these in order.

I have argued that cross-checking is fundamental to establishing the veridicality of perception, whereas Alston mentions checking mainly to argue that MP needn't in

46 Alston, *Perceiving God.*

47 Ibid.

48 For move detail, see Fales, "Scientific Explanations," Parts I and II.

this regard approach the standards of sense perception. I have argued that a Principle of Credulity (PC) obscures the essential sources of warrant and should be dispensed with (but that cross-checks are indispensable even given the PC, because of independent doubts concerning MEs).

Alston argues that it is an *empirical* question what causal processes connect an object X to the perceiver's consciousness in the right way to count as a perceiving of X. Determining that for a perceptual modality, he claims, presupposes that we can identify *bona fide* examples of veridical perception in that modality. Otherwise, we won't even know what sorts of causal processes cross-checking is to identify.[49] This suggests a difficulty in my claims for cross-checking that Alston doesn't himself raise; for if he's right, then, arguably, cross-checking *presupposes* the PC.

For we may surmise that Alston would invoke the PC to underwrite the credentials of the perceptual episodes which are to serve as standard cases of veridical perception. The PC would thus be more fundamental than cross-checking. But (a) the principle is too weak for this purpose, and (b) it is unneeded. It is too weak because a prima facie warrant doesn't tell us which experiences in a given modality are veridical – only cross-checking may reveal some overriders – and does not even entail that *most* of them are. It is also unneeded, though the reasons are unavoidably complex and cannot be spelled out here.[50]

I do not in any case think it would be hard to judge, given a knowledge of precisely what causal role(s) God plays in the production of MEs, whether to count them as cases of perceiving God. The necessary conditions include (1) that the experience seem to the perceiver to be one of God's being present, (2) that it would not have occurred were it not for some divine influence upon the perceptual capacities of the perceiver, and (3) that this influence be such as to convey correct information to the perceiver concerning some of God's properties – that is, some of God's properties must cause it to be the case that the perceiver's perceptual processes are so stimulated as to make it seem to him or her that God has those very properties. These three conditions may not be jointly sufficient, but I am content, for the purposes of the present dispute, to accept them as being so. The trouble is that theists have characteristically said nothing *at all* (that is independently testable) about how God acts here.

49 So Alston argues that the atheist would have no basis for specifying where God must enter the causal etiology of an ME in order for it to qualify as a perception of him – and hence no basis for denying that God plays the requisite role. But the shoe is on the other foot. Let the theist who takes certain MEs as veridical use them to formulate criteria for how God must enter the picture. Then we can consider how to design tests to determine, in any given case, whether he does so. Theists have done nothing of this kind.

50 The solution requires an a priori component, a conceptual component grounded in immediate experience, and the empirical evidence germane to understanding how particular sense modalities function. The a priori component includes two principles: namely, (1) that qualitatively different causes differ somewhere in the sorts of effects they produce, and (2) that the sort of object intended in an act of perceptual awareness is an object such that it, or objects of the same sort, have figured as the sole element common to the causal chains culminating in a certain reference class of perceptual experiences, and to no others. The conceptual component includes the principles of causal inference, which are grounded in our perceptual acquaintance with causal relations – and, in particular, our comprehension of the way in which causes can combine to produce an effect and which an event can causally contribute to multiple effects. Details are spelled out in Fales, *Causation and Universals*, chs 1, 8, and 12. I should emphasize that Alston does not lay claim to the argument to which I am responding.

A fourth condition that is plausible would require that the causal process employ some mechanism (in the brain?) whose natural function, the function it evolved to serve, is to detect God. Is there such a perceptual center that detects God? If so, how would we discover it? As we saw, there is a candidate for such a "God module," as it has been dubbed: the temporal lobes of the brain. However, (a) there is no hint that God figures in the production of micro-seizures; and (b) the content of the experiences generated by micro-seizures is clearly conditioned by social/cultural factors. Thus, even *if* God were somehow to contribute to the production of mystical experiences, it would hardly be possible to characterize the divine causal role as being of such a kind that perceiving God was the "normal" or naturally evolved function of the "God module." In short, the extreme variety of content of MEs rules out *in principle* a divine causal role in virtue of which an ME could be characterized in these terms as a perception of God.

I have argued, secondly, that such cross-checks as have been performed on MEs do not confirm them. Those cross-checking procedures that are internal to mystical practices are (with one exception) not of a sort that *could* genuinely confirm MEs, because they either have no apparent evidential bearing at all, or because they can be brought to bear only by making ancillary theological assumptions that are themselves not subject to independent tests, or because they confirm at least equally well some naturalistic hypothesis. The exception – prophecy – has a striking, and telling, record of failure. Nor are there cross-checking procedures external to mystical practice that support it. Indeed, until theists formulate serious, testable hypotheses concerning the manner in which God provides theophanies, there is not much that can be done along these lines.

Although Alston recognizes that the use of various procedures I have included under the heading of cross-checking is desirable, he seems not to think it is as essential for MEs as it is for more ordinary experience-based claims. Thus he minimizes the demand *within* mystical practices for criteria that discriminate the genuine from the bogus, and suggests that weaker controls are all right because the elusive nature of the object of MEs (God) precludes stronger checking. But that is like saying that, where the nature of a crime makes it hard to establish guilt, we should just lower the standards of evidence required for conviction. On the contrary: we should just admit ignorance. Alston calls the demand for independent cross-checks imperialism. I call it common sense.

A third focus of disagreement is Alston's insistence that MEs can't be controlled, or predicted; nor are there causal mechanisms accessible; thus they resist adequate scientific investigation. He is mistaken on all three counts, though certainly *some* MEs are more elusive than others. The literature on these matters – ethnographic, sociological, psychological, and neurophysiological – has moved well beyond the work of the figures whom Alston cites, who wrote nearly a century ago. Interested readers are invited to familiarize themselves with this literature and draw their own conclusions.

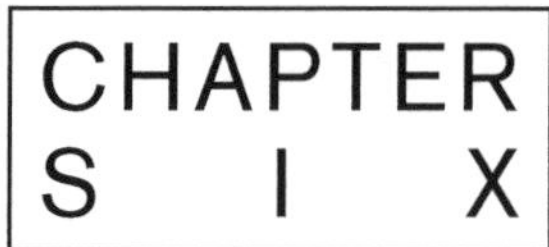

Is It Rational for Christians to Believe in the Resurrection?

The belief that Jesus rose from the dead is central to the Christian faith. If it were irrational to believe in the Resurrection, this would seriously call into question the rationality of Christian belief. Stephen T. Davis argues that it is indeed rational for Christians to believe that the Resurrection occurred. Michael Martin opposes this position, contending that it is not rational for anyone to believe that it took place.

It Is Rational to Believe in the Resurrection

Stephen T. Davis

1 Introduction

The question that Michael Martin and I are discussing – whether it is rational for Christians to believe that Jesus was raised from the dead – is in one sense odd. According to the vast majority of Christians, past and present, belief in the resurrection of Jesus is a defining belief of Christianity; you cannot be a Christian without having the belief. True, there are *avant-garde* theologians who argue against the Resurrection. But a few super-sophisticates and controversialists do not speak for the Christian community. The vast majority of Christians of all denominations and groups would deny that Christianity makes any sense apart from the resurrection of Jesus.

Still, let us waive that point and discuss the issue before us: Is it rational for Christians to believe that God raised Jesus from the dead?

2 The Meaning of the Christian Resurrection Claim

The claim, then, is that *God raised Jesus from the dead.* For the sake of convenience, let's refer from now on to what we will call claim *R*:

> *R*: Jesus died, and some time after his death God raised Jesus from the dead.

First we must clarify what *R* means. Two points: (1) the phrase "God raised Jesus from the dead" is to be understood in a robust sense. Jesus was truly dead, and was genuinely brought back to life by God; after his resurrection, he again existed as a living person. The words "God raised Jesus from the dead" do not constitute a symbol or code talk for something else (like, say, Jesus' influence living on). (2) *R* does not report an episode of *resuscitation* – the kind of thing that occasionally occurs in hospitals these days, where someone shows some of the signs of clinical death, would indeed die without heroic medical intervention, and is brought back to life by such intervention. No, *R* reports not resuscitation but *resurrection.* That is, Jesus was truly dead and was brought back to life, never to die again.

Obviously, then, *R* claims that a highly unusual event occurred. It isn't like claiming that Jesus *died*, which everyone will grant. After all, we are used to the idea that people die; but not to the idea that truly dead people live again. Something like that would be so unusual as to constitute a miracle. Even people who believe in God have a sensible bias against claims of this sort. Unless the evidence in its favor were powerful indeed, they would and should reject it.

How should a person go about deciding whether to believe *R*? I think it would depend, to a great extent, on one's view as to what sort of world we live in. Let's define three terms. *Naturalism*, we'll say, is the doctrine which says: (1) nature alone exists (where "nature" is the sum total of physical reality); (2) nature is everlasting and uncreated; (3) nature is uniform, regular, and continuous; there are no nonnatural events; and (4) every event is in principle explainable in naturalistic terms. *Supernaturalism*, we'll say, is the doctrine which says: (1) something else besides nature exists: namely, God; (2) nature depends for its existence upon God; (3) the regularity of nature can be, and sometimes is, interrupted by God; and (4) such divine interruptions are in natural terms quite unpredictable and inexplicable. *Deism*, we'll say, is a doctrine that shares with supernaturalism the claim that God created the world and set its natural laws in motion, and shares with naturalism the claim that nature is uniform and uninterrupted. Naturalists and deists agree that God never intervenes in the regular flow of events; there are no divinely caused voices, dreams, prophecies, visions, epiphanies, miracles, or incarnations.

If you are a committed naturalist or deist, it virtually will not matter how strong a case can be made in favor of *R*; you will almost certainly reject it. You are metaphysically unprepared to accept the idea that God intervened in human history and brought Jesus back to life. If you are a supernaturalist, this does not mean that you must accept *R*. Many supernaturalists (e.g., the vast majority of Jews and Muslims) deny *R*. So I am not claiming that *R* is rationally obligatory for all supernaturalists. But if you are a supernaturalist, at least you are metaphysically prepared to believe that God might have raised Jesus.

It is at least possible for a naturalist or a deist to study the evidence in favor of the Resurrection and become so convinced by it as to undergo something like a paradigm shift toward supernaturalism. Similarly, it is also possible for a supernaturalist to become a naturalist or a deist. But normally one's presuppositions prevent things like that. They exercise a powerful control over how we approach issues such as the truth of *R*. So in this essay I claim to demonstrate the rationality of belief in *R* not to all people but to Christian supernaturalists.

3 Probability and the Christian Expectation of Resurrection

One way to approach our question is to ask: What is the probability that *R* is true? Probability is simply a measure of the probable truth of a statement or claim whose truth-value we do not know. The probability of a statement is normally a function of two things: (1) its prior probability (i.e., its probability based on our general background knowledge); and (2) its fit with specific evidence that is relevant to its truth and falsity (things like memories, witness testimony, and physical evidence). Those who believe that *R* is probable do so in part because they think the evidence that we find in its favor is exactly what we would expect to find if *R* were true.

Suppose that one is a Christian supernaturalist who wonders about the truth of *R* – that is, a person who believes most of what Christians believe but is unsure about *R*. For such a person, the prior probability of the Resurrection will not be low, despite our normally quite sensible aversion to claims of miracle S. As Richard Swinburne correctly points out, Christians expect that God will want to redeem human beings, and one aspect of redemption is redemption from the power of death.[1] And part of the Christian theological inheritance is the Old Testament, in parts of which the promise of eternal life is held up (e.g., Daniel 12:1–3). So, given Christian supernaturalism, resurrection of some sort is to be expected.

4 What Caused the Initial Christian Belief in the Resurrection?

It is commonplace among scholars who write about the resurrection of Jesus, whether they believe it or not, that the earliest Christians were truly convinced of *R*. Mary Magdalene, Peter, and the rest were not pretending. They truly believed that God had raised Jesus from the dead.

1 See Richard Swinburne, *Responsibility and Atonement* (Oxford: Clarendon Press, 1989), pp. 148–62; *idem, Revelation* (Oxford: Clarendon Press, 1992), pp. 71–2; *idem, The Christian God* (Oxford: Clarendon Press, 1994), pp. 216–23.

But *why* did they do so? What caused them to believe *R*? Let me mention several possibilities:

1 There was a hoax; someone or some group fooled the earliest Christians into believing *R*.
2 One or more of the earliest disciples had visions or hallucinations of the risen Jesus, started believing *R*, and convinced others to believe *R*.
3 The earliest believers, who were all Jews, borrowed the Jewish concept of resurrection, applied it to their beloved but dead leader, and convinced themselves of the truth of *R*.
4 The earliest believers, influenced by Greek ideas of immortality and pagan ideas of dying and rising gods, applied such notions to their beloved but dead leader, and convinced themselves of the truth of *R*.
5 *R* is true.

There are other hypotheses besides (1)–(4) that deny *R*, but this schema will have to suffice.

My own view, as a believer in the resurrection of Jesus, is that, given the assumption of Christian supernaturalism, (5) is by far the best explanation. And of course evidence renders (5) improbable only if it renders probable the disjunction of the alternatives: namely (1)–(4). And if none of them has any strong probability, that strengthens the case for *R*.[2] In this brief essay, I do not have space to establish this point, but (1), (2), (3), and (4) (and all the other proposed alternative hypotheses) look like feeble explanations. Fortunately, I believe this point has been established by other writers.[3] In fact, one strong argument in favor of *R* is that critics have never been able to agree on a sensible skeptical explanation of what happened in the days after the crucifixion. This is a major embarrassment for them.

Any acceptable explanation of the evidence surrounding the resurrection of Jesus that is an alternative to *R* will have to do two things: (1) explain accepted facts like "Jesus was truly dead" and "The earliest Christians truly believed Jesus was raised by God"; (2) explain why false testimony (that Jesus was seen risen, etc.) was given; and (3) explain the absence of any evidence in its favor (e.g., evidence that Jesus' body was hidden or disposed of). The evidence in favor of the alternative explanations of the Resurrection that I have seen is on all counts very weak. The old nineteenth-century rationalistic explanations (hallucination, swoon theory, stolen body, wrong tomb, etc.) all seem to collapse under their own weight once they are spelled out. And no strong new theory has emerged – despite the exertions of such contemporary resurrection skeptics as Hugh Schoenfield, Thomas Sheehan, John Dominic Crossan, John Spong, and the Jesus Seminar – as the consensus of scholars who deny *R*. It is perhaps for this reason that some critics of *R* do not even attempt to offer an alternative expla-

2 See Richard Swinburne, "Evidence for the Resurrection," in Stephen T. Davis, Daniel Kendall, SJ, and Gerald O'Collins, SJ, (eds), *The Resurrection* (Oxford: Oxford University Press, 1997), pp. 191–212.

3 See, e.g., George E. Ladd, *I Believe in the Resurrection of Jesus* (Grand Rapids, Mich.: Eerdmans, 1975); Gerald O'Collins, SJ, *Jesus Risen* (New York: Paulist Press, 1987); William L. Craig, *Assessing the New Testament Evidence for the Historicity of the Resurrection of Jesus* (Lewiston, NY: Edwin Mellen Press, 1989). See also my own *Risen Indeed: Making Sense of the Resurrection* (Grand Rapids, Mich.: Eerdmans, 1993).

nation. And surely this is odd. If *R* is false, it is puzzling that no consensus skeptical explanation of what happened has emerged.

Indeed, it seems to me that the evidence in favor of *R* and against the disjunction of (1) – (4) is so strong that for Christian supernaturalists, belief in *R* is rendered rational.

5 Evidence for the Resurrection of Jesus

Aside from the weakness of the alternative explanations, what else can be said in favor of *R*? Let me now discuss – far too briefly[4] – two crucial items of evidence.

5.1 The empty tomb

The evidence strongly supports the claim, found in all four gospels, that the tomb in which Jesus was buried was found empty on Easter morning. Indeed, this is doubtless the reason that a strong majority of contemporary New Testament scholars who write about the empty tomb accept it.[5] Let me now discuss three robust arguments in favor of the empty tomb, arguments which I believe have never been refuted.

First, the believability of the burial tradition supports the empty tomb tradition.[6] The basic gospel story of the death and burial of Jesus is accepted as fundamentally historically reliable by a majority of New Testament scholars who write about it. And if the central claims of this story are accepted, the further claim that Jesus' tomb was found empty is not far away. The site of the burial would have been known (Luke 23:55), and the presence of the body in the tomb would have made early Christian preaching of the Resurrection impossible.

How do we know that the burial story is reliable? (a) It is simple and factual and lacks the theological and apologetic coloring we would expect if it were late. (b) Most Markan scholars hold that the burial story was part of Mark's source material – that is, it came from a pre-Markan Passion story. (c) In 1 Corinthians 15, written in the 50s, Paul makes reference to a tradition that had been passed on to him and that included the claim, "he was buried." Most scholars hold that that tradition goes back to the earliest Christian community.

Moreover, it is clear that the empty tomb tradition is not a late or apologetic development. Far from being presented as an irrefutable argument for the resurrection of Jesus, the empty tomb is seen in all the gospels as an ambiguous fact, a puzzle that needs explanation (cf. Luke 24:22–3). The empty tomb plays almost no apologetic role

4 They are discussed in much more detail in the works listed in n. 3, as well as in Gary R. Habermas, *The Resurrection of Jesus: An Apologetic* (Grand Rapids, Mich.: Baker Book House, 1980); and Gerald O'Collins, *The Resurrection of Jesus Christ* (Valley Forge, Pa.: Judson Press, 1973).

5 William L. Craig, who has exhaustively studied the recent literature on the empty tomb, lists 28 scholars who accept its historicity. See Craig, *Assessing the New Testament Evidence*, p. 373. Of course, truth is not decided by majority vote; still, it is important to note this consensus.

6 This point is well argued in Craig, "Did Jesus Rise from the Dead?," in Michael J. Wilkins and J. P. Moreland (eds), *Jesus under Fire* (Grand Rapids, Mich.: Zondervan Publishing House, 1995), pp. 146–9.

in the New Testament – much less than it would have done were it an invented apologetic device. Almost nobody in the New Testament comes to believe *R* on the basis of the empty tomb.

Note also that Jewish criticism of the Christian proclamation of the Resurrection never disputed the empty tomb. Matthew's telling of the often-maligned account of the guards at the tomb (Matt. 28:1–10) makes no sense without agreement between all parties that the tomb was empty. Note also that as apologetics, the empty tomb story is weak. The account is made crucially to hang on the testimony of women, whose evidence was inadmissible in Jewish courts. In Mark's version, the earliest account, the empty tomb leads only to fear, silence, and flight on the part of the women. And it is openly admitted that the women were suspiciously in the vicinity of the tomb on Easter morning.

Second, the tradition of the empty tomb enjoys wide support in the New Testament. It is in all four gospels, with possible indirect references to it in Acts 2:29–32 and I Corinthians 15:4. And the admitted discrepancies between the accounts argue against the claim that the empty tomb was an agreed-upon, invented "story" in the early church or else a claim that the other evangelists accepted only under the influence of Mark. What we have in the New Testament is a variety of interpretations of the empty tomb, at many points quite independent of each other. Critics of the empty tomb have not succeeded in locating a period, let alone a document, in which Christians believed in the resurrection of Jesus but not the empty tomb.

Of the discrepancies between the empty tomb stories, most (not quite all) can be harmonized fairly easily. Note that the evangelists all agree on what we might call the main elements: *Early on the first day of the week certain women, among them Mary Magdalene, went to the tomb; they found it empty; they met an angel or angels; and they were either told or else discovered that Jesus was alive.* In addition, there is striking agreement between John and at least one of the Synoptics on each of these points: *The women informed Peter and/or other disciples of their discovery; Peter went to the tomb and found it empty; the risen Jesus appeared to the women; and he gave them instructions for the disciples.*

Third, early Christian proclamation of the resurrection of Jesus would have been psychologically and apologetically impossible without safe evidence of an empty tomb. How could the earliest Christians have believed in and preached the resurrection of Jesus had they had to contend with the presence of the corpse? How could they have defended their claim against skeptical critics, and convinced people to believe in the resurrection of Jesus (as they did with great success), had the tomb not been empty?

Accordingly, the empty tomb tradition is reliable. It clearly amounts to powerful support for the truth of *R*.

5.2 The appearances of the risen Jesus

There is also an ancient tradition that the risen Jesus appeared to various persons and groups of persons. Jesus is said to have appeared in various settings, to various individuals and groups, at various times of day, for various lengths of time, doing such things as walking, talking, distributing food, performing signs, and allowing himself to be touched.

It is often said that there were no eyewitnesses to the resurrection event itself, and except for Jesus himself (who presumably witnessed that part of the event that occurred after his revivification), that is almost certainly true. But since many people saw Jesus die and be buried, and then later saw him alive, we nevertheless have powerful evidence of his resurrection. What counts is not the number of eyewitnesses but the accuracy of the testimony. But there is at least one eyewitness report in the New Testament to seeing the risen Jesus – that of Paul in 1 Corinthians 15:8. The apostle also supplies a list of individuals and groups to whom the risen Jesus appeared, many of whom were still alive at the time Paul wrote (in the 50s, about 25 years after the event).

The two most common skeptical responses to the appearances is that they were either legends or visions.

First, they could not have been legends. (1) There was not enough time for legends to develop. Not only does Paul list the appearances in 1 Corinthians only some 25 years after the events, but the way he introduces the material ("what I have in turn received" – using, as exegetes note, the technical Greek terms for the passing on of tradition) shows that the list of appearances antedated Paul by years. Most scholars hold that the list goes back to less than five years after the events. And Greek and Roman historian A. N. Sherwin-White, arguing from what we can learn from Herodotus and other ancient historians, claims that not even two generations are enough for legendary accumulations to replace memories of what had actually occurred.[7] (2) The earliest Christians, all Jews, would have passed on and guarded the integrity of the appearance stories with the reverence for tradition that was characteristic of that culture. (3) The presence of living eyewitnesses and of apostolic control of the traditions would and, I believe, did act as a brake on legendary elements creeping into the tradition. There is no evidence whatsoever of any controversy in the pre-Pauline church about whether Jesus was raised by God and appeared to people.

Second, the appearances could not have been hallucinations. (1) Hallucinations are essentially private, and Jesus appeared to groups of people (in various settings and at various times of day), and even to unbelievers like James and Saul.[8] (2) The resurrection appearances involved too much physical detail – not just seeing the risen Jesus but conversing with him, walking with him, feeling his wounds, etc. (3) Hallucination cannot account for the disciples' belief in the Resurrection and their subsequent steely determination to preach the message of their risen Lord. The disciples were not expecting a resurrection; after the crucifixion they were scattered, discouraged, and despondent. And it is hard to imagine them being motivated, as they obviously were, by mere hallucinations.

7 See A. N. Sherwin-White, *Roman Society and Roman Law in the New Testament* (Oxford: Clarendon Press, 1963), pp. 188–91.

8 See the discussion by Gary Habermas in "The Resurrection Appearances of Jesus," in R. Douglas Geivett and Gary Habermas (eds), *In Defense of Miracles* (Downers Grove, Ill.: InterVarsity Press, 1997), pp. 262–75, 313–19.

6 Answering Objections

Michael Martin has criticized my own defense of *R* in previous of my writings. His main point is that the probability of the truth of *R* is far too low to be worth believing.[9] He stresses the claim that *R* is initially improbable. And it is certainly true that belief in *R* is intellectually difficult; resurrections (if they happen at all) are rare, and that God would raise someone from the dead is surprising indeed. But does it follow from this that the Resurrection is improbable based on our general background knowledge? Well, the question, *Is the resurrection initially improbable?*, is too ambiguous to admit of a clear answer. The answer will depend on who is asking. If the one who is asking is a naturalist, then *R* will be judged to have a low initial probability – so low that the evidence in favor of it will probably never raise the probability of *R* to anywhere near 0.5.

Whose background knowledge is allowed to count in determining the initial probability of *R*? Critics usually presuppose that the only generally shared beliefs count, beliefs accepted by believers and nonbelievers alike. Those will presumably be beliefs like *grass is green*; *San Francisco is north of Los Angeles*; *7 + 5 = 12*; and *the earth revolves around the sun*. But if those are the only sorts of beliefs that Martin wants to count in determining the initial probability of *R*, then believers will simply reject his argument as a piece of intellectual imperialism.

What about beliefs like *God exists*; *God wants to redeem human beings*; *Daniel 12:1–3 is part of inspired Scripture*; and *God occasionally performs interventionist miracles*? These are beliefs that I hold and Martin doesn't. But I consider these beliefs rational and see no reason why they cannot count in figuring the initial probability of *R*. Indeed, I think anybody who does not count them will miss crucial evidence and emerge with skewed results.

The initial probability of *R* is not nearly so low as Martin imagines, once we look at it from what believers regard as a correct set of assumptions: namely, those of Christian supernaturalism. And here is where the point mentioned earlier – the failure of those who deny *R* to come up with a plausible alternative account of what happened – emerges in all its importance. Evidence can only fail to make a given hypothesis probable if it renders probable instead the disjunction of all the competing hypotheses. But suppose none of them is any good. Perhaps this will be because they all seem historically implausible. Perhaps it will be because they cannot explain why there is so little historical evidence in their favor. Perhaps it will be because they are unable to account for known facts. Then the first hypothesis retains its overall probability.[10]

How should we try to assess the probability of the truth of testimony to extraordinary events? Martin thinks we should consider (a) the probability of the event in question and (b) the probability that the witnesses are telling the truth. But that can't be the whole story. For then we would have to disbelieve somebody who tells the truth 99 percent of the time who reports that the number 893420 was the winning

9 See Michael Martin, "Why the Resurrection Is Initially Improbable," *Philo*, 1 (1998), pp. 63–74.

10 See Swinburne, "Evidence for the Resurrection," p. 200.

number in yesterday's lottery! So the probability must also be determined in the light of (c) the probability of the witnesses reporting as they did had the event not taken place.[11] In the case of the Resurrection, this means that we must assess the alternative hypotheses: for example, fraud, myth, hallucination, wrong tomb, swoon, conspiracy, etc. Thus, even if the initial probability of the Resurrection is not high, the probability of the testimony to it being true may be high enough to make it rational to believe it.

Martin uses Bayes' theorem, an important theorem in probability theory. One central insight of the theorem is that a given hypothesis is probable if the evidence that we encounter is what we would expect to encounter if it were true. Let R = the resurrection hypothesis, K = our background knowledge, EH = relevant historical evidence, and AT = alternative hypothesis to R (myth, conspiracy, etc.). Bayes' theorem says:

$$\text{Prob}\,(R/K \,\&\, EH) = \frac{\text{Prob}\,(R/K)\times\text{Prob}\,(EH/K \,\&\, R)}{\text{Prob}\,(R/K)\times\text{Prob}\,(EH/K \,\&\, R)+\text{Prob}\,(AT/K)\times\text{Prob}\,(EH/K \,\&\, AT)}$$

The first term, Prob (R/K & EH), is the overall epistemic probability of the Resurrection, and is what we are trying to establish. Prob (R/K) is the inherent plausibility of the Resurrection hypothesis. Prob (EH/K & R) is the explanatory power of the resurrection hypothesis. Prob (AT/K) is the inherent plausibility of the alternative hypothesis. And Prob (EH/K & AT) is the explanatory power of the explanatory hypothesis. So what the theorem says is that the overall probability of R is equal to the inherent plausibility of R times the explanatory power of R divided by those same two terms plus the inherent plausibility and explanatory power of the alternative hypothesis.

What Martin wants to establish is that the inherent plausibility of R is very low, so it will not matter whether any of the alternative hypotheses are any good; it will still turn out that Prob (R/K & EH) will be so low that it will be irrational to believe R. But what I say is: (a) the inherent plausibility of R may be low, but when looked at from the perspective of Christian supernaturalism (which is surely acceptable in this context, since we are debating whether *Christians* are rational in believing R) is not nearly so low as Martin imagines. And (b) given that fact, Bayes' theorem clearly implies that R will have a high epistemic probability (i.e., Prob (R/K & EH) > 0.5) just in case it has a greater balance of inherent probability and explanatory power than any of its alternatives (i.e., Prob (R/K) × Prob (EH/K & R) > Prob (AT/K) × Prob (EH/K & AT)), which it surely has.

And, as I have claimed, the alternative theories that have been proposed are far weaker than R at explaining the available historical evidence. That is, there is a patch of first-century history that makes sense from a Christian perspective but not from a naturalist's perspective. Those who push the alternative theories normally do so, in my opinion, because they are metaphysical naturalists or deists.

11 See S. L. Zabell, "The Probabilistic Analysis of Testimony," *Journal of Statistical Planning and Inference*, 20 (1988), pp. 327–54.

Notice also that the resurrection hypothesis involves the free choice of an agent: namely, God. This is why the rarity of resurrections – which everybody will grant – cannot be equated with improbability. Suppose I want to buy a car at a lot where there are 1,000 cars for sale, only one of which is red. Now what is the probability that I buy the red one? Clearly, that probability is not just a function of the infrequency of red cars in the lot. This is obviously because my selection of a car might not be entirely random as to color. Indeed, I might freely choose to buy the red one precisely because of its uniqueness. So if God had wanted to vindicate Jesus after his death, God might well have chosen to raise him from the dead in part precisely because resurrections are so rare and striking. Thus the very infrequency of resurrections may actually *increase* the probability of the resurrection of Jesus.

Bayes' theorem is a useful tool in probability logic, but it is a blunt instrument when used in discussions of the resurrection of Jesus. The main problem is the assumption that you can read probabilities from frequencies (miracles occur infrequently; *ergo*, miracles are improbable). But as John Earman has pointed out, the attempt to argue in that way is almost universally recognized in the philosophy of science as unsuccessful.[12] An observed frequency may be flatly zero (cf. an event of proton decay, never before observed, but which scientists are spending huge amounts of money and effort to detect), but it would be simple-minded accordingly to set the probability at zero.

So Martin's argument based on Bayes' theorem fails to undermine the rationality of Christian affirmation of *R*.

7 Conclusion

What, then, *did* cause early Christian belief in the resurrection of Jesus? Although there is much more that I would like to have said but did not have the space to explore, it seems clear that by far the best explanation of early Christian belief in the Resurrection, given Christian supernaturalism, is that God really did, as claimed, raise Jesus from the dead.

Again, suppose you are a Christian supernaturalist who is unsure about whether to believe *R*. As a supernaturalist, you are prepared to believe that God might well bring about miraculous events on occasion. You know that *R* is a crucial belief of all Christian communities, past and present. You accept the idea that God desires to redeem human beings and allow them to live eternally after death. You are aware that the alternatives to *R* that have been proposed are weak. You are also aware that the standard objections to belief in *R* can be answered. If all this were the case, it would follow, I believe, that you would be fully rational in embracing *R*.

The proper conclusion is that Christians are rational in believing that God raised Jesus from the dead.

12 John Earman, "Bayes, Hume, and Miracles," *Faith and Philosophy*, 10 (1993), pp. 293–310.

It Is Not Rational to Believe in the Resurrection

Michael Martin

1 Introduction

On my view it is not rational for either a naturalist or a supernaturalist to believe that Jesus was resurrected from the dead.[13] In contrast to my position and that of most traditional Christian apologists, Stephen T. Davis believes that it is rational for some supernaturalists to believe in the Resurrection *and* for naturalists not to believe in the Resurrection.[14] Professor Davis calls his position "soft apologetics," to distinguish it from the hard apologetics of traditional Christianity, which maintains that it is irrational for naturalists to reject the Resurrection. In this debate I accept Davis's definition of supernaturalism as the view that something besides nature exists, namely, God; that nature depends on God; that the regularities of nature are occasionally interrupted by God; and that such divine actions are humanly unpredictable and inexplicable (p. 18). My burden in this debate will be to show that the soft apologetic position of Davis is mistaken, and that it is irrational for *any* supernaturalists to believe in the Resurrection.

Davis and I are in close agreement on what the Resurrection means. He and I both understand the resurrection of Jesus to be a historical event which should be interpreted literally rather than symbolically or metaphorically. We both understand it to involve more than simply the resuscitation of Jesus' corpse. It involves the transformation of Jesus' corpse into a live body with supernatural properties such as being able to walk through walls.

Davis and I are also in agreement that even for a supernaturalist the resurrection of Jesus is initially very unlikely, and that to overcome this initial skepticism extremely good evidence is needed.[15] Davis says, "Christians need to recover a sense of the shocking absurdity of the resurrection" (p. 168). The difference between us, as I see it, turns on whether a good enough case has been made to overcome this initial absurdity. I will show that Davis's case for the occurrence of the Resurrection is not nearly as good as it needs to be to overcome supernaturalists' justified initial skepticism.

However, I think it worth noting that even if the initial probability of the Resurrection were unknown, this would not obviously affect my ultimate conclusion: belief in the Resurrection is not rational. For if the initial probability for the Resurrection were unknown, then one would presumably have to base one's belief on the historical

13 I will understand someone's belief in the Resurrection to be rational if and only if there is no competing belief that is more probable in the light of the historical evidence and background knowledge. Cf. Davis, *Risen Indeed*, pp. 3–6.

14 Ibid., p. 19, n. 21. Subsequent references to this book will be placed in parentheses in the body of the text.

15 See Martin, "Why the Resurrection Is Initially Improbable."

evidence alone. However, this evidence is not good and does not support belief in the Resurrection as much as the competing belief that the Resurrection did not occur.[16]

2 Overcoming Initial Improbabilities

The probability of the hypothesis that Jesus was resurrected possessing a body with the supernatural properties specified above is a function of the initial likelihood of the Resurrection relative to the relevant background theories assumed (which for purposes of this debate include supernaturalism as defined above), and the likelihood of the Resurrection in terms of the particular historical evidence that is available. Since Davis admits that the initial probability is extremely low – so low he calls the Resurrection "shockingly absurd" – it would seem to follow that the probability of the Resurrection on the basis of the historical evidence alone would have to be *overwhelmingly* strong in order to overcome this initial improbability. The evidence would have to have more than basic reliability (p. 19, n. 21); it would have to have such *prodigious* force that a rational Christian knowing this evidence would affirm that the Resurrection occurred despite its initial absurdity.

Bayes' theorem of the probability calculus is helpful in estimating the requisite strength of the historical case.[17] Let us take Davis's idea that the Resurrection is initially shockingly absurd and assume conservatively that the initial probability of the Resurrection is very low – for example, 0.0001 probable – on a supernatural world view. Let us also assume for the sake of argument that the probability of the historical evidence is 1 relative to the truth of the Resurrection and a supernatural world view. On this very generous assumption, in order for the probability of the Resurrection to be believable at all on the basis of the historical evidence and a supernatural world view – that is, to have a probability above 0.5 – it would be necessary to show that the available historical evidence is *less* than 0.0001 probable on the basis of a supernatural world view and the falsehood of the Resurrection. In a nutshell, for the probability of the Resurrection to be high enough for rational belief relative to the historical evidence and supernaturalism, the probability of the historical evidence relative to the falsehood of the Resurrection and the truth of supernaturalism would be even lower than the initial probability of the Resurrection.

Another indirect way to approach our problem is to consider some paradigmatic historical statements that are extremely well supported, so well supported that it would be irrational to doubt them, and then see how the Resurrection measures up. Consider the following historical statements:

1 George Washington was the first president of the United States.
2 Julius Caesar was a dictator of the Roman Empire.
3 Abraham Lincoln was assassinated at the Ford Theater in 1865.

16 I owe this point to Jeff Lowder.

17 Let R = the Resurrection, HE = historical evidence, and S = supernatural background theory. Then:

$$\text{Prob}\,(R/HE\ \&\ S) = \frac{\text{Prob}\,(R/S) \times \text{Prob}\,(EH/R\ \&\ S)}{[\text{Prob}\,(R/S) \times \text{Prob}\,(EH/R\ \&\ S)] + [\text{Prob}(\sim R/S) \times \text{Prob}\,(EH/\sim R\ \&\ S)]}$$

The historical evidence for these statements is overwhelming. Evidence of approximately this strength is needed to overcome the initial absurdity of the Resurrection. The question is, of course, whether the evidence for the Resurrection measures up to this.

Notice that the evidence cannot just be good. Consider two other historical examples:

4 Harvey Lee Oswald acting alone shot and killed President Kennedy in Dallas in 1963.
5 William Shakespeare wrote *Hamlet.*

Most scholars judge (4) and (5) to be rather well established, but in neither instance is the historical case overwhelming. Indeed, critics maintain that there are good grounds for being skeptical of the truth of (4) and (5). The question is whether the probability of

6 Jesus was resurrected

based on just the historical evidence – that is, exclusive of its initial probability – resembles the probabilities of (1), (2), and (3) or of (4) and (5). In fact, I believe that my arguments indicate that the probability of (6) is considerably less than that of (4) and (5). Indeed, the probability of (6) is closer to probability of

7 The Book of Mormon was revealed to Joseph Smith by the Angel Moroni.
8 An alien spacecraft crashed near Roswell, New Mexico, in 1947.

However, it is strictly speaking only necessary that I show that the probability of (6) is no higher than that of (4) or (5).

3 Problems with the Historical Evidence

The preceding lines of argument indicate that the historical case for the Resurrection must be overwhelmingly strong to defeat its initial improbability. Davis apparently thinks that it is this strong, although, oddly enough, he is keenly aware of at least of some of the problems with the evidence. For example, he admits that biblical testimony is unreliable: "It was written years after the event by unsophisticated, myth-prone people who were more interested in formulating statements of faith and in furthering Christian ends than writing accurate history. Furthermore, the evidence they present is contradictory."[18] Much more than this can be said about the weakness of the evidential case, however.

(1) There were no eyewitnesses to the Resurrection. (2) Other than Paul, there were no contemporary eyewitnesses to the post-resurrection appearances of Jesus. In all

18 Stephen T. Davis, "Is It Possible to Know that Jesus Was Raised from the Dead?" *Faith and Philosophy*, 1 (1984), p. 153.

the other cases of post-resurrection appearances we have at best second- or perhaps third-hand reports of what eyewitnesses claimed to see, recorded decades after the crucifixion. Paul's account does not contain a detailed description of the resurrected Jesus. (3) Besides being inconsistent, the empty tomb stories are at best second- or perhaps third-hand reports of what eyewitnesses claimed to have seen recorded several decades after the crucifixion. (4) New Testament scholars disagree about when the stories of the empty tomb entered the Christian tradition.[19] Yet this is surely relevant to their evidential value, for the later they entered the tradition, the less evidential import they have. (5) There is no reason to suppose that the alleged eyewitnesses to the post-resurrection appearances of Jesus or to the empty tomb were reliable and trustworthy. Indeed, it is well known that eyewitness testimony is very often unreliable. Eyewitness testimony is influenced by what psychologists call "post-event" and "pre-event" information. In the case of Christianity, for post-event information we can read "early Christian beliefs," and for pre-event information we can read "prior messianic expectation."[20] Furthermore, even if the eyewitnesses were reliable, we have no good reason to suppose that the people who reported the eyewitness accounts were reliable and trustworthy; nor do we have good reason to suppose that those who wrote down the stories were reliable and trustworthy.

(6) Given all these uncertainties, we need independent confirmation of the Resurrection.[21] Yet this is what is lacking. First, the genuine Pauline letters *and* the earlier non-Pauline letters provide no details of Jesus' life or death, and thus lend no independent support for the empty tomb stories.[22] Paul's belief that Jesus was crucified and arose from the dead does not entail that he thought that Jesus was buried in a tomb. In fact, it seems highly unlikely that if Paul and other early letter-writers knew about this detail of Jesus' life and death, they would not have mentioned it.[23] In fact, some scholars have argued that Jesus' post-resurrection appearance to Paul is prima facie inconsistent with the accounts of Jesus' appearances in the gospels.[24] Second, the Resurrection is not independently confirmed by Jewish or pagan sources.[25]

One would think that these problems would be sufficient to show that the historical case for the Resurrection is not overwhelming; that its strength is closer to that

19 See Michael, Martin, *The Case Against Christianity* (Philadelphia: Temple, University Press, 1993), p. 82. Davis (pp. 70–1) attempts to answer scholars who argue that the empty tomb is a late tradition. Whether he is successful or not is unclear. But the controversial nature of the issue cannot be denied, and surely this weakens the probability of his case.

20 Robert M. Price, *Beyond Born Again* (San Bernidino, Calif.: Bongo Press, 1995), ch. 5 (http://www.infidels.org/library/modern/robert_price/beyond_born_again/). See E. F. Loftus, *Eyewitness Testimony* (Cambridge, Mass.: Harvard University Press, 1979).

21 See Martin, *Case Against Christianity*, ch. 3.

22 See, e.g., Uta Ranke-Heinemann, *Putting Away Childish Things* (San Francisco: Harper, 1994), ch. 9.

23 Davis (pp. 76–7) attempts to answer the objection that Paul did not know about the empty tomb. However, his arguments fail to convince, since he fails to come to grips with the fact that Paul's silence about the empty tomb is part of a larger problem. He does not explain why Paul *and* other earlier letter-writers were also silent about *other* aspects of Jesus' life and death that it would have been to their advantage to refer to. See Martin, *Case Against Christianity*, pp. 52–8.

24 See Robert Price, "By This Time He Stinketh," (http://www.infidels.org/library/modern/robert_price/stinketh.html); Ranke-Heinemann, *Putting Away Childish Things*.

25 For details see Martin, *Case Against Christianity*, pp. 84–7.

of the case for Oswald being the only assassin of Kennedy than for Washington being the first president of the United States. Indeed, just as scholars debate whether Oswald was the only assassin, they debate the question of whether Jesus arose from the dead. Moreover, this debate is not just between naturalists and supernaturalists; it occurs among supernaturalists and even among Christians. It seems to me that the existence of such intra-supernaturalist and intra-Christian debates creates a strong presumption that the historical case for the Resurrection is not overwhelming. In order to suppose otherwise, one would have to suppose that New Testament scholars of the caliber of John Dominic Crossan, who are working *within* the Christian tradition, are being that irrational in denying the Resurrection occurred.[26]

4 Need We Know What Happened?

Why does Davis suppose that, despite the problems with the historical case for the Resurrection and despite the existence of rational debate among Christian New Testament scholars, the case for the Resurrection is so overwhelming that the evidence swamps the initial absurdity on a supernaturalistic world view? I conjecture that his reasoning runs as follows: Critics of the Resurrection story who deny Jesus' resurrection have never been able to give a likely account of historical evidence such as the empty tomb, the growth of Christianity, the inability of critics to produce Jesus' body. However, given the supposition that the Resurrection occurred, apologists are able to give an excellent account of this evidence. The failure of critics to give a good account of the facts and the ability of Christians to do so is enough to overcome the initial improbability of the Resurrection and the faults with the historical evidence for Resurrection.

But this reasoning is invalid. It is not necessary for Christians to give a likely alternative to maintain that the Resurrection is beyond the pale of rationality. Bayes' theorem indicates why.[27] What is important are the *relative* probabilities. Even if the historical evidence is improbable relative to the falsehood of the Resurrection and the truth of the supernatural, so long as the probability of the Resurrection relative to supernaturalism is still lower, rational belief in the Resurrection relative to historical evidence and supernaturalism is impossible.

Let us consider Davis's arguments and see if he really shows that, relative to alternative hypotheses, the historical evidence has a probability lower than the initially extremely low probability of the Resurrection.

26 See, e.g., John Dominic Crossan, *Who Killed Jesus?* (San Francisco: Harper, 1995), p. 214.

27 If the initial probability of hypothesis H is extremely low on the basis of background assumptions A, then the evidence E does not have to be very probable on the basis of the falsehood of H and the truth of A to indicate that the probability of H is below 0.5 on the basis of E and A. Thus, the historical evidence need not be probable on alternative hypotheses to show that the probability of the Resurrection is below 0.5. Indeed, the probability of E could be quite low.

5 Davis's Case for the Resurrection

5.1 Evidence of the empty tomb

(a) Davis says that the empty tomb story appears in all four gospels. Yes, but what historical accuracy do these stories have? Well-known New Testament scholars such as Crossan[28] and Gerd Lüdemann[29] argue that the traditional biblical account is unlikely. Given Roman crucifixion customs, Jesus was probably not buried at all; even if Jewish customs were followed, Jesus was probably buried ignominiously in an unmarked grave by his enemies. The traditional story of Jesus' burial, according to Crossan, was likely inspired by the hope of a decent burial rather than by historical truth. Lüdemann points out that Jesus' disciples did not know where he was buried, for "given the significance of tombs of saints in the time of Jesus, it can be presupposed that had Jesus' tomb been known, the early Christians would have venerated it and traditions about it would have been preserved."[30] Many other New Testament scholars agree.[31]

Although Davis tries to meet the objection that Jesus was either not buried or was buried in an unknown grave, his defense is unconvincing (pp. 81–2). He says that, although such scenarios are possible, they are highly improbable. For example, he maintains that the claims about the empty tomb would not have had much apologetic value if they had been made years after the event since opponents could have objected that the tomb was lost. However, for all we know, this is precisely what critics did maintain. As I argue below, zealous disciples are often not persuaded by arguments or strong negative evidence.

(b) Davis argues that the empty tomb could not have been invented by later Christians, since the tomb was discovered by women "whose value as legal witness in the culture of the day was virtually negligible" (p. 182). However, in Jewish society, women *were* qualified to give testimony if no male witness was available.[32] Moreover, the care and anointing of bodies was women's work at this time, so it is to be expected that a writer of fiction would depict women as the ones who go to seek Jesus' body.[33]

28 Crossan, *Who Killed Jesus?*, ch. 6.

29 Gerd Lüdemann, *What Really Happened to Jesus?* (Louisville, Ky.: Westminister John Knox Press, 1995), pp. 22–4.

30 Ibid., p. 24.

31 For example, over 70 percent of the members of the Jesus Seminar, a group of non-fundamentalist New Testament scholars devoted to the historical study of Jesus, have maintained that the gravesite of Jesus was unknown and that the empty tomb stories are a creation of Mark. See "The Jesus Seminar Voting Record," *Forum*, New Series 1/1 (Spring 1998), pp. 231–2.

32 John Wenham, *Easter Enigma: Are the Resurrection Accounts in Conflict?*, 2nd edn (Grand Rapids, Mich.: Eerdmans, 1992), pp. 150–1. I owe this point to Jeff Lowder. Moreover, Davis's argument assumes that if later Christians had invented the story, they would have used only epistemic criteria. But this is not necessarily so. Crossan suggests an entirely different explanation: see Crossan, *Who Killed Jesus?*, pp. 181–8. See Kathleen E. Corley, "Women and the Crucifixion and Burial of Jesus," *Forum*, New Series 1/1 (Spring 1998), pp. 163–80; G. A. Wells, *The Jesus Legend* (La Salle, Ill.: Open Court, 1996), pp. 60–1.

33 I owe this point to Keith Parsons.

(c) Davis maintains that Christians could not have falsely claimed that the tomb was empty, for their enemies could have produced Jesus' body. However, this assumes that Jesus was buried, and that the place of burial was known. Moreover, as Robert Price has pointed out, "the only estimate the New Testament gives as to how long after Jesus' death the disciples went public with their preaching is a full fifty days later on Pentecost! After seven weeks, I submit, it would have been moot to produce the remains of Jesus."[34] In this period of time, Jesus' corpse would have decayed sufficiently to have made identification impossible. In addition, the estimate of 50 days might be wrong; for all we know, the empty tomb stories may have emerged many months after Jesus' death. In addition, it assumes an interest in Christianity which first-century non-Christians did not have. There is reason to believe that the early Christian community was unobtrusive and as good as unnoticed by the Jewish community at large. Consequently, Christian claims about the empty tomb could have gone unnoticed.[35]

5.2 The evidence of the conduct of the disciples

(a) Davis attempts to refute the deliberate fraud theory of the Resurrection by arguing that the behavior of the early Christians indicates that they sincerely believed the Resurrection was true. However, there are not just two alternatives: either the Resurrection was a deliberate fraud or it was true. People down through the ages have sincerely believed strange and irrational things despite the evidence. Their beliefs have been based on self-delusion and wishful thinking in which legends grow, feed on themselves, and are mistaken for reality. One illuminating example of the growth of a religious legend is the movement associated with Sabbatai Sevi, a seventeenth-century Jewish messianic pretender who eventually converted to Islam. Because of his conversion, the movement associated with Sevi suffered a setback, but surprisingly it did not die away. Indeed, within weeks of his public appearance, a surge of miracle legends appeared.[36] In this case and in many others, religious disciples were not deliberately perpetrating a fraud and yet their beliefs were completely out of touch with reality.

(b) Davis says that if the Resurrection story was invented within the lifetime of eyewitnesses to the events, they could have easily refuted the false claims. But, as Price points out, such a view of the apostles is anachronistic, since it assumes them "to be a sort of squad of ethnographer-detectives, ranging over Palestine, sniffing out legends and clamping the lid on any they discover."[37] In any case, Davis apparently thinks such a refutation was not accomplished, for if it had been, Christianity would not have prospered. But Davis's assumption that religious believers would give up

34 Price, "By This Time He Stinketh."
35 I owe this point to Jeff Lowder.
36 See Gershom Scholem, *Sabbatai Sevi: The Mystic Messiah* (Princeton: Princeton University Press, 1973), pp. 252, 265; cited by Price, *Beyond Born Again*, ch. 5.
37 Price, *Beyond Born Again*, ch. 5.

their beliefs in the light of negative evidence is mistaken. Consider what happened to religious movements such as the Seventh-Day Adventists, Jehovah's Witnesses, and Sabbatainism where negative evidence had no effect on the zeal of the followers. In the case of Sevi, the efforts of the chief apostle, Nathan of Gaza, could do nothing to stop true believers from producing a legend complete with stories of miracles.[38] In any case, as I have already mentioned, the detailed story of the Resurrection seemed to be unknown to Paul *and* other early Christian letter-writers, and the gospel stories with all their details appeared generations after Jesus' death, when many eyewitnesses were either dead or very old.

5.3 The evidence of agreement between the gospels

Davis says that despite many discrepancies in the New Testament accounts, there is agreement on many of the details concerning the death and resurrection of Jesus, and there is no resurrection text that questions these. He also suggests that even the discrepancies themselves "testify in a left-handed way to the accuracy of the essential story: if the resurrection of Jesus were a story invented by the later Christian Church, or by certain members of it, no discrepancies would be allowed" (p. 181).

To doubt the reality of the Resurrection is not necessarily to assume that the story was deliberately invented by the Christian Church. The story might be in large part legendary, and legends, although not true, are not intentionally created. Various versions of the same legends might well agree on the main points but vary widely in detail. Their discrepancies do not testify in a left-handed way to their historical accuracy concerning the points on which they agree, but rather to the piecemeal and fragmentary way in which legends grow.

5.4 Evidence that the resurrection appearances were not hallucinations

Davis claims that many factors indicate that the Resurrection appearances of Jesus were not hallucinations: the disciples were not expecting the Resurrection; the idea of the resurrection of one individual before the end of the world is not found in the Jewish tradition; the resurrected Jesus was not immediately recognized; some who saw him doubted; many different people saw the risen Jesus at different times and in different circumstances; and there were none of the usual causes such as drugs, lack of food, water, or sleep, and so on. He also seems to reject the idea that one person's hallucination could start a chain reaction among other members of the group (p. 183, n. 30).

However, the historical reality of the Resurrection is not the only alternative to the hallucination theory. Stories about Jesus' appearances in the Gospels may be legends that cannot be completely traced to hallucinations. Recall that the detailed stories of Jesus' appearances do not appear in Paul and other earlier letter-writers. This is

38 Ibid.

surprising on the theory that the appearances are historically accurate, but not on the legend theory, according to which details are developed over time.

In fact, resurrection stories were common in Jesus' era and before.[39] Ancient heroes such as Romulus and Hercules were rewarded by being taken up into heaven and made divine beings. Romulus's ascent was seen by "eyewitnesses." In other cases the hero's ascent was shown by the lack of bodily remains. Sometimes the hero might return to earth and appear to his friends. Similar legends have been associated with more recent or contemporary personages, such as Apollonius of Tyana, the prophet Peregrinus, and the Emperor Augustus.[40]

According to Davis, doubters and skeptics of the Resurrection in the gospel stories themselves testify to the truth of the stories. But this is questionable. In some of the legends, the skepticism of characters is used as a literary device to stress the reality of miracles performed by the hero.[41] Given this background, it is not surprising that the Resurrection story would develop complete with skeptical characters. It hardly seems to matter, as Davis thinks, that the Christian story might have some elements not found in the Jewish tradition. There are other traditions not mentioned by Davis, including Egyptian, Zoroastrian, and Greek, which might have influenced Christian legends. However, suppose that it is shown that Christianity has elements not found in any other tradition. Legend making is to some extent creative. Nothing follows from this fact that a story contains elements that cannot be traced to older myths and legends as to whether these elements reflect historical reality.

Moreover, it is not clear that the hallucination theory can be so easily dismissed. Hallucinations plus legends can explain more than either phenomenon taken in isolation. Despite what Davis suggests, collective hallucinations are well-known phenomena, and there is every reason to suppose that they can occur without Davis's "usual causes" being present. Further, we know that one hallucination can trigger other hallucinations. The history of witchcraft indicates that people who were thought to be bewitched had hallucinations that caused those around them to also have hallucinations.[42] In the case of Sevi, the visions of his followers were infectious, one person's vision triggering hundreds of others.[43] In a series of visions of the Virgin Mary in Dordogne, France, in 1889, one child's vision triggered similar visions in other children and then in a large number of peasants.[44] In these cases, there is no reason to suppose that Davis's usual causes were present.

39 For example, the Sumerian goddess Innana and the Thracian god Zalmoxis. See also resurrection stories from ancient mythology concerning Demeter, Dionysos, Persephone, Castor and Pollux, Isis and Osiris, and Cybele and Attis. (I owe these references to Richard Carrier, personal correspondence.) There are also the Old Testament stories of Enoch and Elijah, who were taken up to be with God and left no traces. (See Price, *Beyond Born Again*, ch. 6.)

40 Price, *Beyond Born Again*, ch. 6.

41 Ibid.

42 Martin, *Case Against Christianity*, pp. 93–5.

43 Scholem, *Sabbatai Sevi*, pp. 417, 446; cited by Price, *Beyond Born Again*, ch. 6.

44 George Barton Cutten, *The Psychological Phenomena of Christianity* (New York: Scribner's Sons, 1908), pp. 65–6; cited by Price, *Beyond Born Again*, ch. 6.

Davis argues that hallucinations are ruled out by the fact that neither Jesus nor his disciples were expecting the Resurrection, Jesus was not immediately recognized, and different people in different times and circumstances saw him. With respect to the first point we know from the gospels that people did believe in the resurrections of individuals before the general resurrection at the end of time. The public appearance of Jesus was interpreted as the resurrection of John (Mark 6:14) and some suspected that John was the Messiah (Luke 3:15).[45] Furthermore, Davis's argument assumes that the historical account is accurate. What if part of the story is legendary? Legends of the time and earlier suggest that heroes are resurrected, ascend to heaven, and sometimes return to earth. So was it really true that the disciples could not expect some sort of resurrection? These legends also indicate that skepticism is used as a literary device to authenticate miracles. The stories of the initial failure to recognize Jesus surely could function in a similar way.[46] Moreover, the evidence cited above show that collective hallucinations do not always appear in a particular place or in one group of people.

5.5 Evidence of the rise of Christianity

Davis argues that only the historical reality of the Resurrection can explain why or how the Christian Church came into existence proclaiming the Resurrection. Without the reality of the Resurrection, Davis says, there would not have been a Christian movement, or at least it would have taken a different form. The faith of the disciples was new, not traceable to Jewish sources, and not explicable by Jesus' life or teaching. The real Resurrection provides an explanation of the Easter faith: namely, that "the disciples saw the risen Lord, . . . and interpreted their experience in a theologically novel way . . . " (pp. 184–5).

However, why is the reality of the Resurrection the only explanation of the rise of Christianity? Surely, there is at least one other: that early Christians believed deeply, but falsely, that the Resurrection occurred. They *thought* that the disciples saw the risen Jesus and interpreted their beliefs theologically at least partly in terms of the myths and legends of their times. We have no more need to appeal to the reality of the Resurrection to explain the rise of Christianity than to appeal to the reality of the revelation of the Book of Mormon to Joseph Smith by the Angel Moroni to explain the rise of Mormonism.[47]

Moreover, there is a plausible naturalistic explanation for why some groups in the early Christian Church advocated a physical resurrection. As Elaine Pagels has argued, a physical interpretation of the Resurrection gave "orthodox" Christians political advantages over Gnostic Christians who stressed subjective spiritual experience.[48]

45 Price, *Beyond Born Again*, ch. 6

46 Ibid.

47 This example was used by Jeff Lowder in personal correspondence.

48 I owe this point to Jeff Lowder. See Elaine Pagels, *The Gnostic Gospels* (New York: Random House, 1979).

6 Conclusion

My position is based on two basic theses. First, the initial probability of the Resurrection is extremely low, regardless of one's metaphysical orientation. Davis agrees with this, but does not fully appreciate what it means. It means that the historical case he makes in order to overcome this initial improbability must be overwhelmingly strong such that no rational Christian could doubt it. Second, the historical case for the Resurrection is not overwhelming, and rational Christians can and have doubted it. Davis's case for the Resurrection can be objected to at practically every point; it is not even a good case, let alone an overwhelmingly strong one. These objections lower its probability significantly and make the historical evidence on the alternative accounts, if not more probable than not, at least more probable than the initial probability of the Resurrection. This is all that is needed to show that the probability of the Resurrection is not worthy of rational belief by Christians.[49]

Reply to Martin

For lack of space, I cannot answer all Michael Martin's arguments (several are addressed in my main essay). And I must be brief about the points I do answer. Let me concentrate on (1) seven of his arguments concerning the historical evidence; and (2) his assessment of the overall epistemic situation.

1 The Historical Evidence

(a) Martin misconstrues a quotation from my *Faith and Philosophy* article on the Resurrection (see note 18). In these words I was not speaking in my own voice; I was citing an argument of nonbelievers in *R*. Although there are discrepancies in the biblical accounts of the Resurrection, I do not consider them contradictory, and certainly not on essential points.

(b) True, Paul is probably the only eyewitness to the risen Jesus whose direct testimony we have. But we know Paul's character well from the book of Acts and his own writings; I find him highly "reliable and trustworthy." Moreover, while Martin is correct that eyewitness testimony can be unreliable, it is usually trustworthy on central points. Our legal system depends on that fact. If a robbery occurs in front of ten people, they may later differ on things like what color shirt the robber was wearing. But they won't normally differ on whether the thief was an elephant as opposed to a human or whether it was a robbery as opposed to a baptism. Moreover, there was

49 I would like to thank Jeff Lowder for reading an earlier draft and making suggestions.

no first-century Jewish expectation of a dead-and-risen messiah, and thus no such "pre-event information" produced belief in *R* in the eyewitnesses.

(c) Martin cites John Dominic Crossan to prove that supernaturalist Christians doubt the Resurrection. Doubtless some do. But this example supports my case rather than Martin's. Crossan is no supernaturalist; he is something like a deist. His views rule out miracles.[50]

(d) Martin may be correct that first-century Jewish women could serve as legal witnesses in the absence of male witnesses. But that only underscores my point: if the empty tomb tradition is an apologetic legend, reliable men would certainly have discovered the tomb and encountered Jesus.

(e) In order to hold, as Martin does, that earliest Christianity went unnoticed in the larger Jewish society, you must virtually ignore Acts 1–9, which no sensible scholar does. Lüdemann's argument that the disciples did not know the burial site is feeble, since it simply assumes the falsity of *R*. The reason early Christians did not venerate the tomb was precisely because of their conviction that Jesus was no longer there.

(f) Martin considers anachronistic my argument (which I do not recognize in the parody from Robert Price) that the apostles and eyewitnesses exercised control over resurrection accounts. The fact that there was no inner-circle controversy over *R* proves my point. If *R* were false, very probably *some* Jesus-follower would have blown the whistle and said so. But nobody did.

(g) Martin's claim that the appearance stories were late and unknown to Paul is an argument from silence. What if Paul knew the appearance traditions but simply chose not to describe them for the Corinthians? Since Paul did *list* appearances (I Cor. 15:5–8), each was surely embedded in a narrative of some sort that had been explained to him.

2 The Epistemic Situation

Is it rational for Christians to believe *R*? Again, Christians believe that God will redeem us, and that includes redemption from death. So, despite the surprising nature of claim *R*, Christians can rationally expect resurrection. Accordingly, *for Christian supernaturalists*, the prior probability of *R* is not low, and is nowhere near the absurdly low 0.0001 that Martin assigns it. Is the evidence in favor of *R* strong enough to overcome our rational suspicion of miracle claims? For Christians, definitely.

Would Martin's overall argument still stand *even if the prior probability of* R *were unknown*? Of course not: if there were no prior probability, and thus no "appropriate skepticism" toward *R*, it would be rational on the evidence for *everyone* (and not just Christians) to believe it. Believing *R* would be about like believing that Jesus died, which few bother to doubt.

Martin is mistaken that critics of *R* have no rational obligation to explain what they think *did* happen after the crucifixion. And, aside from vague talk about legends and hallucinations (which notions have been refuted by defenders of *R*), Martin offers

50 See Crossan, *Who Killed Jesus?*, pp. 94–5: "[an event like resurrection] never did or could happen."

no alternative explanation. Who started the legend? Why? Who had the first hallucination? Why did the story spread?

Evidence makes a given hypothesis H improbable only if it renders probable the disjunction of H's competing hypotheses. If none seems plausible – as surely is the case here – that strengthens H. Martin's argument would be far stronger if he could plausibly explain what happened after the crucifixion. But, like every critic, he cannot.

The evidence is much as Christians would expect it to be if *R* were true, and not at all as anyone would expect it to be if *R* were false. Given Christian supernaturalism, the probability of *R* on the historical evidence is far greater than the probability of the historical evidence being as it is if *R* were false. It is rational for Christians to believe in the resurrection.

Reply to Davis

Stephen Davis's essay contains a number of errors, misunderstandings, omissions, and confusions.

(1) Davis thinks that the rationality of belief in the Resurrection is a defining property of Christianity. Consequently, he finds it odd that we are debating whether it is rational for Christians to believe in the Resurrection. However, many Christians hold their belief in the Resurrection on faith.

(2) In his book Davis writes, "Christians need to recover a sense of the shocking absurdity of the resurrection."[51] This striking claim is inexplicably omitted from his essay in this volume, and we instead find Davis denying that the Resurrection is initially improbable for supernaturalists. How can this inconsistency be explained except on the assumption that in the light of my arguments he has now realized that his original claim was indefensible?

(3) In his book Davis understood Jesus' resurrected body to possess supernatural properties such as the ability to walk through walls. This amazing claim has also inexplicably dropped out of his essay. This omission is hardly surprising, for none of Davis's arguments, even if free from other problems, shows that this claim is true.

(4) Davis's critique of my arguments (see note 15) for the initial improbability of the Resurrection on a supernatural world view fails. Of course, if one is a supernaturalist, one is "metaphysically prepared" to believe that God might have performed miracles, and even to believe that it is probable that God would redeem humanity through some miracle or other. But even for supernaturalists, miracles are rare events. God's redeeming miracles could take countless forms and occur at any one of a number of different times and places; consequently, supernaturalists should believe that the initial probability of *the* Resurrection – an event occurring at a *particular* time and place – is very low. Davis's car lot example is based on a confusion. Consider the probability of Davis's free choice of the only red car in the lot of non-red

51 Davis, *Risen Indeed*, p. 168.

cars from the point of view of onlookers who do not know his preference for red cars. The initial probability of choosing this car from a lot of a thousand cars is very low. By analogy, God's choice to enact some redeeming miracle or other is a free individual act. But, as far as supernaturalists are concerned, God has numerous options, and any *particular* one such as the Resurrection is initially improbable.

(5) Davis's lottery example rests on a misunderstanding too. I do not claim that the probability of a witness's testimony is based simply on the probability of a witness telling the truth and the initial probability of the event in question. It is also based on many background factors, including whether it is confirmed by other independent witnesses and sources. This independent confirmation is lacking in the case of the Resurrection.

(6) Davis says that assessing alternative theories to the Resurrection is essential to judging the probability of witnesses' testimony. Yes, but only in this sense: the probability of the historical evidence (*E*) relative to the disjunction of these alternatives theories (*A*) must be more probable than the initial probability of the Resurrection itself (*R*) in order to show that *R* is not worthy of rational belief. But since the initial probability of *R* is low, *A* need not be very high. I have shown in my essay that Davis's objection to many alternative theories is not nearly as powerful as he supposes. The reader is referred to my essay for rebuttals to Davis's objections to these alternatives.

(7) Davis says at one point that the initial probability of the Resurrection is "not nearly as low as Martin imagines." But how low is that? I really do not need to imagine it as low as he thinks. For example, using Davis's own notation, if Prob (R/K) is as high as 30 percent (an extremely generous assumption), then in order to have the Resurrection rationally unbelievable, Prob $(EH/K \;\&\; AT)$ could be 0.5. However, given Davis's assumption that there are four alternative disjoint explanations, *EH* could be as little as 12.5 percent probable given *K* and each of these alternatives. The reader of Davis's essay must ask whether there are any reasons to suppose that this is true.

(8) One issue that I did not explicitly consider in my essay is Davis's claim that the Resurrection cannot be a legend, since there was not enough time for a legend to grow. In fact, there are many historical cases where legends have developed quickly including, for example, the movement associated with Sabbatai Sevi mentioned in my essay.[52] It is significant that Davis ignores these examples.

52 See Price, *Beyond Born Again*, ch. 5, for more examples.

PART III

ISSUES WITHIN RELIGION

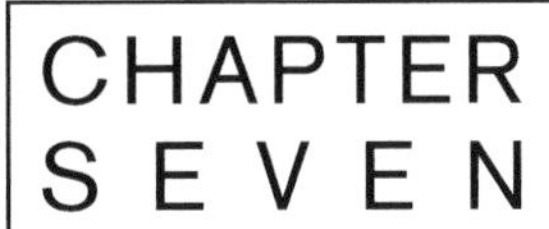

Can Only One Religion Be True?

Keith Yandell and Peter Byrne agree that it is *possible* that only one religion is true, but there agreement ends. Yandell believes that one religion is true, and he argues that the view known as "religious pluralism" – which rejects that belief – is fraught with contradiction and slyly sets up its own exclusivist religion which claims all others to be false. On the other side, Byrne argues that, given the plurality of world religions, it is most reasonable to suppose that there is some divine reality to which each is responding, but that each religion is strictly false in its exclusivist claims, or at any rate that none has anything like a complete picture of this reality.

How to Sink in Cognitive Quicksand: Nuancing Religious Pluralism

Keith E. Yandell

The answer as to whether just one religion can be true is "Yes." A religion proposes a diagnosis of a deep, crippling spiritual disease universal to non-divine sentience and offers a cure. A particular religion is true if its diagnosis is correct and its cure is efficacious. The diagnosis and cure occur in the setting of an account of what there is – an account whose truth is assumed by the content of the diagnosis and cure. Some religions at least do not assert logically incompatible propositions.

So it is possible that at least one religion be true – that its account of what exists is correct.[1]

One variety of monotheism can be true, and another be false. It is possible that, given the actual religious traditions there are, each monotheism contains some proposition that is false, but that (say) God exists, so that *insofar as they are monotheistic*, religious traditions are true but (say) *insofar as they contain some false proposition not entailed by monotheism*, they are all false. *Mutatis mutandis*, the same holds for other types of traditions.

It would be impossible that a religion be true only if all religions contained as an essential element some necessary falsehood or if no religion contains any assertion at all. Neither of these things is true. So the answer to our question is "Yes." Since it is "Yes," there is always the danger that some religion actually be true. A typical religious believer will think that is the case. There are some who seem to think that the idea that some religion actually is true is a dangerous idea. Insofar as this idea is politically motivated – its basis is the fear that if someone believes her religion is true, she will kill people – this is the case only for religions that require that their devotees kill people. Most don't. In any case, the cause of this strange fear, which seems largely to live in the academy, is not centrally political. It goes by the name of "Religious Pluralism."

1 The Nature of Religious Pluralism: A Thumbnail Sketch

Religious pluralism, put in the most general terms, is committed to two fundamental, if general, themes. The first is that no religion is true. The second is that everyone will do very well in the long run. Universal pessimism about getting anything religious right and universal optimism about everyone's ultimate fate join hands and march from the academy into the world at large. Put this way, it is a wonder the view is not more popular than it is. *Believe what you like and all will be well* has great potential as the Ungospel of the Future.

2 Nuancing the Sketch

Advocates of religious pluralism (hereafter, RP) will be unpersuaded that this general description is accurate or fair. I grant that it needs to be nuanced. For one thing,

1 Elsewhere, I've cited chapter and verse regarding background to, and the details of, religious pluralism, and discussed topics relevant to it, as follows. **Ineffability**: "On Windowless Experiences," *Christian Scholar's Review*, 4/4 (1975), pp. 311–18; "Some Varieties of Ineffability," *International Journal for Philosophy of Religion*, 6/3 (Fall 1975), pp. 167–79; "The Ineffability Theme," *International Journal for Philosophy of Religion*, 10/4 (1979), pp. 209–31; *The Epistemology of Religious Experience* (Cambridge: Cambridge University Press, 1993), chs 3–5. **Irreducible religious plurality**: "On the Alleged Unity of All Religions," *Christian Scholar's Review*, 6/2 and 3 (1976), pp. 140–55; *Epistemology of Religious Experience*, ch. 1; *Philosophy of Religion* (London: Routledge, 1999), chs 3–5. **John Hick's religious pluralism**: "Some Varieties of Religious Pluralism," in James Kellenberger (ed.), *Inter-Religious Models and Criteria* (New York: St Martin's Press, 1993), pp. 187–211; *Philosophy of Religion*, ch. 6; "Revisiting Religious Pluralism," *Christian Scholar's Review* (forthcoming). Here, I discuss a more generic religious pluralism.

sometimes its advocates put the first theme, not by saying that no religion is true but by way of more modestly saying that, if one is, we cannot tell which it is. We can take account of this by distinguishing between two claims. There is the RP metaphysical claim: *No religion is true.* There is the RP epistemological claim: *If any religion is true, we cannot tell which it is.* We can call these the *no religious truth* and the *can't religiously tell* claims. An RP advocate, let us say, must accept at least one of these claims.

It is worth reflecting on the different implications of these claims. The *no religious truth* claim is, bluntly put, to the effect that *All religions are false.* While RP presents itself as a religion-favoring position, and sometimes as good news to religious believers, it isn't. RP brings the news that, relative to each religion, there isn't the disease it diagnoses, and its cure isn't needed. Since something seems to be terribly wrong, the news is to the effect that the religious believer doesn't know yet what it is and hasn't come to terms with it. Condolences seem more in order than do congratulations. The *no religious truth* claim is just what the varieties of secularism have always claimed, and RP looks a lot like secularism with incense.

Put in concrete terms, to the Jew, the news is that God does not exist and did not choose the Jews. To the Christian, the news is that Jesus was not God Incarnate and did not die for our sins or rise from the dead for our justification. To the Muslim, the news is that no Allah gave any revelation to Mahomet and there is no Koran in Heaven or Heaven for the Koran to be in. To the Buddhist, the news is that there is no Buddha-nature and no Nirvana. To the Jain, the news is that Kevala, or enlightenment, is an illusion. And so on through the various religions. If this is good news to the religions, what would bad news be?

The *can't religiously tell* claim entails that, even if some religious believers have gotten things right, they do not know that they have done so. No one can tell. Every believer who thinks she knows her tradition has gotten things right, religiously speaking, is wrong about that. There is, then, the *no religious truth* claim and the *can't religiously tell* claim, and either can serve as a way of expressing the first general RP theme.

For another thing, RP qualifies the *everyone will be well* theme by requiring that those for whom all will be well meet certain basic moral standards. Only the morally decent are all right. Perhaps everyone sooner or later will become morally decent; at any rate, only the decent will flourish.

3 Some Prices of the Nuancing

The qualifications, however, come with a high price. The first qualification comes with the price of showing that all religions are epistemically tied – that the truth-favoring considerations on behalf of any two religions R1 and R2, whichever two you happen to select, are even; so are the considerations against the truth of R1 and R2, whichever religions these may be. Showing anything like that would take a tremendous amount of work, and there seems to be nothing even vaguely resembling a set of massive volumes in which any such thing is argued for. So RP, to be frank, simply asserts it. This may take more faith than any religion ever requires.

The second qualification also comes with a high price. The RP advocate has to hold that some ways of living are better than others, some actions are right and some are wrong, some sorts of moral character are good and some are evil, and the like. RP requires that there is an objective, discernible distinction between right and wrong, virtue and vice, good and evil, and the like, to provide content to its notion of moral decency. It adds that those who dwell in the neighborhood of the right, the good, and the virtuous will find that all is well in the long run, and that those who dwell in the neighborhood of the wrong, the vicious, the evil – well, either things won't be well for them in the long run, or (more in accord with RP optimism) they won't until they eventually see the moral light.

But then how are these matters to be understood? After all, it is not impossible to find intelligent people who hold theses analogous to those an RP advocate favors concerning religion. There is Anti-RP Moral Relativism: *No ethical theory or morality is true.* There is Anti-RP Moral Skepticism: *If any ethical theory or morality is true, we cannot tell which it is.* We can call these the *no moral truth* and the *can't morally tell* claims. An RP advocate apparently must deny these claims.

There are, of course, various questions about RP as so far stated. Why believe the *no religious truth* or the *can't religiously tell* claims, and why reject the *no moral truth* and the *can't morally tell* claims? Why suppose that rational assessment of religious claims is impossible and that rational assessment of moral principles is possible? One would think that RP advocates would attempt to provide powerful arguments for these assumptions. Yet they do not do so. In any case, we now have a more nuanced account of RP.

4 Initial Deep Problems

RP faces some deep problems already. One is this: Why are we to think that all will be well for everybody, or everybody who is decent? One philosopher expressed his view of the afterlife succinctly, if crudely: first we die, then we rot. What reasons are there for thinking that there is an afterlife? In the light of RP's pessimism or skepticism about religious claims generally, why believe this one? Even if one believes that we will survive the death of our bodies, why suppose that people who accept and live by the values of which RP approves will end up well?

The basic point can be put like this. American Protestant modernists or liberals held that God is in heaven and smiles on those who are morally decent. Moral decency is the ticket to heaven because God runs the railroad. RP advocates cannot seriously appeal to God. RP, viewed from one angle, is American Protestant modernism minus monotheism. But, minus monotheism, why think that moral decency is a ticket to anywhere? (I don't suggest that monotheism entails Protestant modernism.) If it is a ticket to somewhere, why not to hell? RP's optimism is groundless.

Another problem is this. The only real consideration that is typically offered by RP advocates that there is an evidential tie among religious traditions is that there continues to be disagreement concerning how the traditions should be rationally assessed.

Some think that rational assessment and religious tradition can't even date, let alone wed. Some think that religious traditions have been rationally assessed, and the result is that they are one and all false. Some think that religious traditions have been rationally assessed and one, or at least one type, of religious tradition comes out far better than the others. Some presumably believe that the result of rational assessment is a tie. *This* disagreement is utterly unimpressive to RP advocates; they simply ignore it.

They are, however, impressed by this: the fact that the apologists for various religious traditions, and the philosophers who offer rational assessments of religious traditions, don't agree on the results. In this respect, RP is like the standard argument for moral relativism. That argument, stated with more rigor than usual, goes like this. A moral rule tells you that some sort of action is right or wrong without telling you why. A moral principle tells you what makes an action right or wrong without telling you which ones are right or wrong. For example, *Lying is wrong* is a moral rule, and *Persons ought to be respected* is a moral principle; *being disrespectful to persons* makes an action wrong, and lying to someone is typically disrespectful to her. (These examples come from a broadly Kantian perspective; other examples would do as well.) Cultural relativism claims that cultures disagree about moral principles; culture A accepts a moral principle P, and culture B accepts moral principle Q. From this, moral relativism is inferred; it is concluded that no moral principle is true. This is the *no moral truth* view noted above.

The argument won't bear examination. Suppose that cultures A and B do have deep moral disagreement; A accepts P, and B embraces Q. Then either Q is identical to not-P, or P and Q are contraries (both can be false, but they cannot both be true). Either P or not-P is true; of an exhaustive set of contraries, one is true. Either way, if A and B disagree as required, there is some true moral principle. What follows from cultural relativism is that moral relativism is *false*.

One might instead argue from cultural relativism to moral skepticism – the *can't morally tell* view. The argument from disagreement to skepticism here is exactly analogous to the RP move from religious diversity to the *can't religiously tell* view, as the inference from moral diversity to the *no moral truth* view is exactly analogous to the inference from religious diversity to the *no religious truth* view. It is curious that RP advocates seem enthusiastic about one inference and not about the other. Of course, neither moral nor religious skepticism follows from moral or religious diversity. Further, in both cases, the issue is whether there are ways of rationally deciding between the relevant alternatives – ways of rationally appraising competing moral principles and incompatible religious claims. Even in the presence of disagreement, there seem to be such ways. What RP requires is that there be such ways in ethics but not in the philosophy of religion. At the least, it requires the presence of discernible moral truth and a lack of discernible religious truth, except for the claim that those who are morally decent are religiously well.

Once one sees this, two further, perhaps unintended, features of RP come into view. One is that there must be a little religious truth after all; *the morally decent are religiously well* (or something in this neighborhood) is a religious truth that RP claims to know. The other is that RP itself is in conflict with those religious traditions that deny that moral decency is sufficient for religious flourishing. So one would think that, in all consistency, religious pluralism would renounce this optimism about the fate of the morally decent. It offers no reason to accept it, and cannot offer any such reason consistent with its *no religious truth* or its *can't religiously tell* theses. Its pronouncements about what matters religiously differs from those of various religions. So in all consistency it should apply a *no truth* or a *can't tell* doctrine here and stop advocating RP. Unwilling to do so, RP advocates arbitrarily pick and choose which disagreements to promote to doctrines that don't follow from them, and which to simply ignore. In so doing, while they appeal to religious diversity as a reason for accepting RP's theses, they must ignore the fact that RP's own claim that moral decency is sufficient for religious well-being is part of that religious diversity, and so can't be true and/or can't be known on its own RP terms.

In fact, RP itself looks remarkably like a religion. It, in effect, tells us that our problem arises if we lack moral decency and that a happy fate of some sort awaits those who achieve it. RP is either a second-order religion that supposedly trumps, or perhaps serves as an acceptance filter for, all first-order religions, or RP is just a first-order religion itself.

If it is surreptitiously a first-order religion, if it is true, it is either false or unknowable. Of course, if it is false, it is false and unknowable. So, on its own terms, each of its varieties is unknowable, and its *no religious truth* version is false.

Perhaps, then, it is a second-order religion – an apparently serious religious proposal about first-order religions. But then we need good reasons for accepting its claim about the first-order religions. It is uncommonly shy about offering any such reasons, not atypically admitting it altogether lacks any. To the obvious question of why anyone should think it true, there seems to be but a single answer: it explains religious diversity.

That, by itself, is not much of a reason. There are purely secularist explanations of religious diversity. These share the feature of appealing to things to explain those beliefs and experiences whose existence provides no obvious confirmation of religious beliefs or of the reliability of religious experiences. If it is asserted that the secularist explanations are the whole story concerning religious traditions, the inference is made that the *no truth* line is correct. The conclusion drawn from that is that the best that can be said for religion is that it is a crutch for the weak to lean on in a hostile world; religion is at best non-chemical Prozac.

There are religious explanations of religious diversity, among them the following. Human sin blinds us so that without divine revelation we can't see the truth, and even if we see it, we need further grace to embrace and live by it. Revelation can be ignored or misinterpreted, and grace can be rejected. Satan is more than willing to provide illusory salvations and enlightenments to mislead.

There are more neutral explanations of religious diversity. People have offered different accounts of a basic religious disease and of a corresponding cure, generally being smart enough to propose a cure appropriate to the disease diagnosed. These efforts reflect different personalities, feelings, perceptions, beliefs, and so on. One may go on to say that they can be rationally assessed after all.

But RP has its own claim about the religious traditions. All religious traditions are responses to the same Something or Other. Amidst this diversity of explanations of religious traditions, RP again avoids appeal to *no truth* or *can't tell* strategies. Such strategies would get in its way here; they are used only when they are RP-favorable.

5 Some More Nuancing

The RP term for the Something or Other is "the Real," the idea being that each religious tradition will fill in the blank for which "the Real" stands in its own way. Since "the Real" does misleadingly tempt one to thinking of its alleged referent as having some properties, I will adopt a less loaded term: namely, "X." RP advocates hold that this alleged being exists and can be referred to. Beyond that, none of our concepts apply to it. This would seem to render RP incapable of saying that X is that to which any religious tradition or experience is a response. To say that a religious tradition or experience is a response to X is to say that there is something X did to elicit the response. If all that can be said regarding X is that it exists and somehow can be referred to, X can't be said to do anything to which anything might be a response. It cannot even be said that it is passive and we somehow respond to it. Reference to X cannot, consistently with RP constraints, be an explanation of anything.

It is hard to see how something as thin as X allegedly is can be referred to at all. The idea is that X exists, but that for any property Q other than such indeterminates as *having properties, having consistent properties,* and *being a possible object of reference* X lacks Q. X isn't one item or many; even number concepts fail to fit it. Is it really possible to use the term "X" – defined as "that which exists, can be referred to, has some highly indeterminate properties, and for any other property Q, X lacks it" – referentially?

There are two questions here. The term "unicorn" means something like "equine creature, silver in color, one-horned, and magical." The sentence "There are unicorns" is false; the term "unicorn" has reference according to this doctrine: term T has reference if and only if, should there be something corresponding to T, *There is a T* is true, and, should there not be anything corresponding to T, *There is a* T is false. *Having reference* is then a matter of *having referential success or having referential failure,* where *T has referential failure* entails *There might have been a T, but there isn't.* One question regarding "X," understood in terms of RP, is whether X has *either referential success or failure.* Both "round square" (being contradictory) and "bliftic bostrocity" (being meaningless) lack both referential success and referential failure, at least on the account thereof just provided. Is "X," like "round square" and "bliftic bostrocity," without referential success or failure, or, like "unicorn," possessed of *either referential success or failure*? If "X" lacks even this feature, it can't have referential success.

RP can hypothesize that X's essence is utterly unknown to us except that it is incompatible with that essence that X have any determinate property known to us. Whether this notion is logically consistent or not is harder to say. If it is, then "X" could have *either referential success or referential failure.* What reference to X cannot do is *explain* anything. Any explanation-relevant property that we can ascribe to X has been ruled out in principle.

Another question regarding "X," understood in terms of RP, is whether "X" has referential success; is there an X? The only reason to think so is granted to be that such appeal explains religious diversity. But for reasons by now familiar, it can't explain religious diversity, and so does not. Such notions such as *causes, elicits, grounds,* and even *explains itself* go well beyond the allowable concepts attachable to X.

This point is worth examining more fully. Consider the concept C, *being circular*, and an actual circle named "Sam." The concept C, let's say, *fits* Sam. Concept C *fits* item A if and only if C *is true of A as is circular* is true of Sam. The concept *being circular* also *applies to* Sam. Concept C *applies* to item A if and only if C *is either true or false* of A. So *being a prime number* and *being a groundhog* apply to Sam though they don't fit Sam, since they are false of Sam. The fits/applies distinction is relevant to RP's view of X.

Consider the concept *being a property*. This is a highly, perhaps maximally, indeterminate concept. Under it, and more determinate than it is, are the concepts *being a color property* and *being a shade of blue*. These, in turn, while more determinate than *being a property*, are less determinate than *being navy blue*, which presumably is as determinate as concepts get. Concepts fall into a hierarchy of determinacy (or, going in the other direction as it were, of indeterminacy).

The RP metaphysics of X, then, goes something like this. For any property concept C that we have that fits X, C is indeterminate. For any determinate property Q that X has, we have no determinate concept of Q. For any determinate concept C that we have, X lacks the property of which C is a concept.

It is clearer what this denies than what it affirms. X is not loving, not a creator, not providential, does not know that any of us exists, does not have thoughts or beliefs, does not act, has no will, does not in the least care whether any of us exists, cannot be attained or achieved, is not blissful or calm, is not benign, and so on. We have these concepts, but none of them fit X. So X has no property expressed by any such concept.

The metaphysics of X obviously relies heavily on reference to us and our concepts. If there is any actual doctrine of *being X* buried here, it is extremely thin. One could try either of two views here as follows.

> *The no-fit view*: for any at all determinate concept that we have, it does not fit X, but it does apply to X.

> *The no-application view*: for any at all determinate concept that we have, it does not apply to X.

The former view is self-contradictory. Consider the determinate concept *is navy blue*. On the *no-fit* view, it is both the case that *X is navy blue* is false and *X is not navy blue* is false. But one must be true.

One might reply to the claim that the *no-fit* view is contradictory in either of two ways. On *no-fit* doctrine, X is such that neither *X is omnipotent* nor *X is not omnipotent* is true of it. On one account, this can be the case if X does not exist. On one account, if "X" lacks referential success (if there is no X), sentences of the form *X has Q* as well as sentences of the form *X does not have Q* are neither true nor false. But RP holds that X does exist, so this won't help. On another account, if an item X is the sort of thing that cannot have Q – its essential properties are incompatible with Q-possession – then both *X has Q* and *X does not have Q* lack truth-value. But since, for RP, we haven't any idea what X's essence, if any, is, we aren't in a position to claim that X's essence precludes its being anything. So this line won't do either.

The *no-application view* says of X that it is neither colored nor not-colored, neither temporal nor not-temporal, neither spatial nor nonspatial, neither identical to Socrates nor not identical to Socrates, and so on through all the at all determinate concepts we have. Again, how could we know this, given that we cannot know what concepts do apply to it? Correspondingly, it is not as if we know it cannot have the property of being colored because it has some other quality Q such that *being colored and having Q* is impossible; that would require more information about X (namely, that it has Q, which is a property incompatible with having the property of being colored) than RP allows.

It is tempting simply to argue that, necessarily, for any item Y and property Q, either Y has Q or Y lacks Q, so the *no-application* view is also self-contradictory. But I waive that argument here.

RP, on the present construal, does not claim that X has no properties at all or has no determinate properties that ground its indeterminate properties. It holds, in effect, that determinate properties come in two (presumably epistemic) kinds: those we have concepts of and those we don't have concepts of. Call these *captured* and *uncaptured* properties. Captured properties correspond to possessed concepts. In these terms, X has only uncaptured properties, and only unpossessed concepts apply to, or else fit, it (presumably with the exceptions of *exists* and *can be referred to*).

It isn't clear what one's reaction should be to something that allegedly has only uncaptured properties. One thing that is clear is that no such thing can properly be said to be what religious experiences or traditions respond to; for description uses possessed concepts and refers to captured properties.

Perhaps one should see RP as holding:

> *The no-positive-fit view*: for any at all determinate concept that we have, it applies to X but does not fit X.

Then, if some proposition P says of X that some at all determinate concept fits (is true) of X, then P is false. Then it is, on RP's terms, false that the concept *explains religious plurality* applies to X; *X* (*or X's activity, or response to X, etc.*) *explains religious diversity, religious traditions, or religious experiences* is false on RP doctrine. So we have less than one reason to think that X exists.

That we have no somewhat determinate concepts that fit X and that X lacks any captured properties presumably is not accidental. It is not part of RP's perspective that tomorrow, if we are lucky, we will come to have concepts of determinate properties that fit X. RP would be true only so long as our colossal bad luck concerning X and our concepts continued. Presumably the idea is that X is altogether beyond our conceptual grasp no matter what we do. Thus the fact that reference to X and X itself cannot – consistent with RP – be said to explain anything is an incurable state of affairs according to RP.

6 Still Further Nuancing

There are other themes to which RP appeals for support. One is metaphysical: one can find in some religious traditions, usually as a minor theme of altogether dubious consistency with the rest of the tradition, an appeal to what we might call Absolutist metaphysics. Advaita Vedanta Hinduism, one variety of Mahayana Buddhism, various passages in the writings of some mystics, and the like suggest that the goal or object of religion is a propertyless being. If such a being is even possible, it is utterly unclear of what religious (or other) interest it might be. If we assume for the sake of the argument that such a thing is possible, and add for some reason that (so to speak) this is what all RP-approved religions are about, then all those religions will be false except those that teach that what exists is the qualityless Absolute – in Advaita, a qualityless being; in Mahayana, a qualityless state, though of course what *that* difference amounts to, if anything, is not clear. On this account, what RP is really saying is that all religions that think that God (Brahman with qualities) exist are false. If full-blown Absolutism is affirmed, then there is only the qualityless Absolute, and any religious tradition that thinks that there is either at least one thing with qualities, or that there are at least two things that exist, is false. But then the *no religious truth* line is false, and if RP thinks it has any good reason to accept Absolutism, the *can't tell religiously* theme is rejected by RP. On this line, RP sides with Advaita and Mahayana and holds that some religious traditions are true after all. It chooses the least plausible of all possible religious traditions and speaks in their favor, thereby abandoning an essential tenet of RP itself. Taking sides within religious diversity thus provides no help for RP. Moreover, if Absolutism is true, religious diversity, and RP advocates themselves, only appear to exist.

A different line concerns the nature of language in general and religious language in particular. There are again many ways of developing the claim, but the basic idea is that language evolved to deal with simple things – basically, middle-sized physical objects and our interaction with them and other people – and in religion is stretched to the breaking point. It is aided by the popular nonsense that all language is non-literal, which of course is a counterexample to itself. In its more formal modes, the theme in question results in such theories of meaning as Hume's empiricist theory and Logical Positivism's verification principle. The more clearly the expression of the theme, the more clearly false it is; thus the theme is often left vague. Were it true, it would not be possible to state it in its various manifestations, offer competing theories, develop and assess the various relevant arguments, and so on, as these things occur in the philosophy of language. Nor would RP itself be so much as stateable. After all, it deals with quite a variety of abstruse matters hardly limited to our concourse with middle-sized items, and purports to provide the literal truth about these matters. The generally strongly empiricist theory of language that RP advocates tend to favor because it lends support to their claim that religious language is not to be understood literally is not something they typically defend, and it is not successfully defensible. But if it were, it would make RP's own claims non-literal.

7 Conclusion

RP is right that religious plurality is an interesting and important fact. It is worthwhile to attempt to explain it. The sooner we realize that RP, rather than providing such an explanation, is a tissue of inconsistencies, the better placed we will be to offer a possibly true account of religious plurality.

It Is Not Reasonable to Believe that Only One Religion Is True

Peter Byrne

1 Introduction

There is a great variety of religions in the world. They differ one from another in doctrine, ethics, spirituality, institutional structure, historical claims, and so on. Could one of them be true? Yes of course: there is no incoherence in the thought that one of these traditions is true in its main doctrinal and historical claims and that all the others are false in their doctrines and historical beliefs where these conflict with the true religion. The real question is whether it is reasonable to suppose that this possibility is exemplified.

But the real question needs a great deal of refinement if we are to take it any further. First we must note that the idea of one "religion" being true rests upon an artificiality. The artificiality lies in the supposition that there are a number of discrete religions in the world, each united internally and separated externally from each other by a set of essential doctrines, ethical beliefs, and the like. In reality, entities such as "Christianity," "Buddhism," and "Hinduism" are semi-fictional.[2] What correspond to the labels are historical complexes found in many different cultures and exhibiting variety in belief, institution, and practice. In the case of Hinduism and Buddhism we must accept that the very idea that there are discrete religions with these labels is a creation of Western scholarship.[3] "Christianity," "Buddhism," and the rest denote useful fictions. Any attempt to find an essence (say in the form of essential doctrines) amongst these semi-fictional entities is bound to result in legislation, with the scholar in effect deciding what he or she thinks is the "true" heart of the religion in question. This is transparently true in the instance of Buddhism, but holds even for Christianity, where the religion gave itself some definition in the form of conciliar documents. The conciliar statements of the Christian Church have been subject to markedly different interpretations in its later history. Things calling themselves branches of the Christian Church have added to, and in some instances departed from, conciliar pronouncements – usually in the name of recovering the "true" message of the founder.

What correspond to our labels are more or less loosely structured families of belief, action, and institution (how tight knit they are varies from case to case). It thus

2 See P. J. Griffiths, *An Apology for Apologetics* (Maryknoll, NY: Orbis, 1991), p. 4.

3 See P. Almond, *The British Invention of Buddhism* (Cambridge: Cambridge University Press, 1988).

behooves us to note that our labels do not pick out watertight entities impervious to influence from other families. The religions have not been afraid of borrowing from each other.[4]

2 Philosophy and Religious Diversity

It looks as though our simple idea of one religion being true really is a question of whether one particular brand of, or strand within, one of the religions may be true. Is it reasonable to suppose that this is the case? How we proceed to answer the question depends on who we are. We may be dogmaticians of a particular religion or branch thereof. Presumably, we would then answer the question dogmatically. Given the governing aim of seeking to articulate and to remain faithful to the world view of a particular brand of religion, it would be unreasonable not to deem that one's own particular faith was indeed true and other forms of faith false where they contradicted it. We may, on the other hand, be philosophers of religion when we answer the question. As such, I take it that we are not governed in our answer by the requirement to remain faithful to a particular brand of religion. We may end up arguing that some such brand provides the basis for the best answer to the question but will have to argue for that conclusion philosophically.

We can see why the question "Can any one religion be true?" is of interest to the philosophy of religion. The question highlights the fact that different brands of religion claim cognitive successes and achievements of various kinds. They claim to have a true account of the nature of sacred, transcendent reality. They claim to give a true analysis of the ills of the human condition and of what is required to achieve liberation or salvation from those ills. They claim that their spiritual, mystical traditions enable and record genuine encounters with the sacred, transcendent reality. They claim that their ethical principles and rules capture the right way for human beings to live. Prima facie, if the cognitive successes of one brand of religion in these regards are genuine, then some, perhaps many, of the achievements of other brands of religion are illusory. Philosophy likes to get involved in intellectual disputes and arguments which throw up interesting puzzles and arguments, and there seems to be no end of such puzzles and arguments provoked by these disagreements.

In addition, philosophy of religion has an interest in developing theories of the religious: theoretical accounts of the meaning and place of religion in human life and culture. Such theorizing impacts upon and is influenced by our interpretation of religious diversity. Consider a wholly naturalistic, secular interpretation of the religious such as we find in Feuerbach's *The Essence of Christianity* and *The Lectures on the Essence of Religion*.[5] On Feuerbach's account, those things we call "religions" are nothing other than the product of human nature (in the form of the structure of self-consciousness and of the character of human wishes) in its various historical and cultural settings. On this naturalistic interpretation, the religious life of the human

4 See W. C. Smith, *Towards a World Theology* (London and Basingstoke: Macmillan, 1981).

5 L. Feuerbach, *The Essence of Christianity*, tr. M. A. Evans (New York: Harper and Row, 1957), and *idem*, *Lectures on the Essence of Religion*, tr. R. Mannheim (New York: Harper and Row, 1967).

race does not arise out of any kind of contact between humanity and a divine or transcendent reality. It is the work of the imagination and what influences it. Naturalism in the interpretation of religion is given prima facie support by the picture of religious diversity and cognitive conflict we have alluded to. The picture seems to show that the human race has no reliable way of deciding which brands of religion attain cognitive success and which fall flat on their faces. More generally, the picture of the ebb and flow of religious movements and sects and of the constant elaboration of the human religious scene seems to point to the fact that humanity has not here embarked upon an enterprise in which sure knowledge of reality has been achieved, knowledge which accumulates and which can be built upon from generation to generation. It all looks like the lush product of the human imagination. Compare the question "Can any one scientific theory be true?" Noting the way in which science appears to accumulate reliable beliefs about the world and continues to lay down a deposit of such belief from one generation of investigators to the next, we might feel much happier answering that question with a "Yes."

3 Theories of Religious Diversity

Naturalism in the theory of religion contrasts with "confessionalism." This is the label I give to any view which states that one religion is indeed true and that we must view other religions in the light of that fact. It finds cognitive success in religion but confines it solely or primarily to one brand of religion. Confessionalism then divides into exclusivism and inclusivism. The confessional exclusivist thinks that the doctrines, ethics, salvific scheme, and spiritual paths of one religion have truth/success to the exclusion of those of other brands of religion. The confessional inclusivist modifies this divisive picture of the human religious scene. One brand of religion is true/successful and the measure of truth and success in religion as a whole. But other brands of religion are deemed to partake of this success. For example, it is a long-established view in Jewish theology that, while Judaism provides the true picture of God and his plans for human creatures, many people in other religions and cultures are on the path to salvation, to right relation with the God of Judaism. They are on this path if these cultures and religions teach and respect the Noahhide laws. These are a fundamental series of socio-ethical norms which are deemed not to be exclusive to Judaism at all. In short, this brand of Jewish, confessional inclusivism can find success in non-Jewish cultures and religions because it places great stress on the social and the ethical as the means of relating to God and allows ethical truth to be present even where people's theological theories are haywire (by the standards of Jewish orthodoxy). In a manner which might irritate some philosophers, it simply refuses to let successful relation with the divine depend overmuch on having the right theory of the divine.[6]

Note that the two forms of confessionalism agree on one fundamental point: one religion is sufficiently certain in its dogmatic formulations to be the means of interpreting the whole that is human religion. We can be assured that one brand of reli-

6 N. Solomon, "Is the Plurality of Faiths Problematic?," in A. Sharma (ed.), *God, Truth and Reality* (London and Basingstoke: Macmillan, 1993), pp. 189–99.

gion has the details of the nature of the divine sufficiently correct in order for it to be the means of judging the other brands.

To the question "Can any one religion be true?" the naturalist answers that we know enough to know that they are all false. The confessionalist answers "Yes; and we know that *this* one is in fact true." A third answer to the question is given by a pluralist theory of religion. Pluralism borrows from, yet differs from, both naturalism and confessionalism. The pluralist must ascribe cognitive success to a great many of the brands of human religion. (Neither the pluralist nor the confessionalist must attribute success to everything that has counted as a religious tradition in human history.) The pluralist must assert of each of the forms of religion covered by the theory that it provides people with real contact with a sacred, transcendent focus. Pluralism is not committed to asserting that no judgments of superiority of any kind can be made about religions; all that need be asserted is that there is the key cognitive equality mentioned.[7]

The affirmation of this cognitive success and equality does not distinguish pluralism from confessional inclusivism. To a minimal definition of pluralism we must add the element of skepticism or agnosticism with regard to the detailed dogmatic structure of a particular brand of religion. The pluralist must, on reasoned grounds, doubt whether the detailed dogmatics of any particular religion can be known with sufficient certainty to enable such a form of religion to be the means of interpreting the whole that is human religion. There is not the certainty in any particular form of religion to enable its world-view to be the basis for a viable interpretation of religion. In this way pluralism can agree that one brand of religion could conceivably be true while claiming that it is not reasonable for the philosophy of religion to judge of any one particular brand that it is true.

4 The Character of Pluralism

Pluralism as a theoretical response to religious diversity can now be summarily defined by three propositions.[8] (1) All major forms of religion are equal in respect of making common reference to a single, transcendent sacred reality. (2) All major forms of religion are likewise equal in respect of offering some means or other to human salvation. (3) All religious traditions are to be seen as containing revisable, limited accounts of the nature of the sacred: none is certain enough in its particular dogmatic formulations to provide the norm for interpreting the others.

Now we can see how pluralism borrows from both the naturalist and the confessionalist responses to religious diversity and intellectual conflict and thus represents a compromise between them (whether it is a good compromise is another matter). Like the naturalist, the pluralist is impressed by the way in which the very fact of diversity argues against confessionalism. Diversity brings disagreement both in regard to

7 Some pluralists do appear to go for all-out equality. See J. Hick, "On Grading Religions," *Religious Studies*, 17 (1981), pp. 451–67, and *idem*, "On Conflicting Religious Truth Claims," *Religious Studies*, 19 (1983), pp. 485–91.

8 See P. Byrne, *Prolegomena to Religious Pluralism* (London and Basingstoke: Macmillan, 1995), p. 12.

dogmas and in regard to the means for deciding which dogmas are true (different forms of religion have different, competing authority sources). Perceived lack of the means of adjudicating amongst these disagreements provokes a skeptical response. Take an example: Judaism, Christianity, and Islam overlap considerably in dogma and much else. An issue that divides Christianity from the other two is the status of Jesus of Nazareth in the continuing work of divine providence. The disagreement is many centuries old, and it remains unresolved. Both naturalist and pluralist infer that it is not resolvable. Moreover, diversity and disagreement suggest the following interpretation of it: religious diversity is explained by the setting of religious life in the concretely different forms of human culture. It has a natural, ready anthropological explanation: the influence of cultural forms and contingencies on the religious imagination. In this respect, both naturalist and pluralist favor a certain deconstruction of religious traditions. These traditions are, in at least some very large measure, the product of the same anthropological forces which shape other facets of culture. There is no need to think that their symbols or beliefs derive from knowledge of a divine being outside human life. This is a perspective which some argue is strongly suggested by the development of the empirical sciences of religion.[9]

If a partial commitment to a deconstructive anthropological perspective on religion is something which pluralism shares with naturalism, let it be noted that confessionalism is going to partake of this perspective in some measure as well. The exclusivist regards one particular strand within religion as cognitively successful and sees multiple error in all the other strands. Exclusivism must therefore conclude, surely, that while the adherents of these other strands of religion consider themselves to be in touch with a sacred, transcendent reality through their devotions, their thought and behavior have a thoroughly human explanation. These other strands of religion are indeed no more than expressions of the human imagination in its various historical and cultural settings. Inclusivism must likewise explain how, for all that many strands in human religious life are in touch with religious reality, forms of religion outside the favored one come to arrive at the erroneous conceptions they have of the nature of religious reality. Once again, appeal must be made to the culture-bound way in which these strands of religion have been formed.

The above points show that *all* of the general perspectives on human religion listed involve interpretations of the religions which depart from the "insider's" viewpoint. In the case of forms of naturalism, all brands of religion are interpreted through the categories of illusion. The pluralist regards all religions through the lens of some error theory, though that error theory is not so radical as the naturalist's. Confessionalists are in this same boat. They will take one particular brand of religion on the terms which its adherents take for granted. But they will radically reinterpret other brands of religion in the very act of explaining them from the viewpoint of the favored brand of religion. How Christianity has seen Jewish faith has not been how Jews have seen it.

Some might be tempted to view the fact that interpretations of religion involve going beyond the self-understandings of religious believers as problematic. However, this need not be tantamount to reductionism. We must distinguish between descrip-

9 See J. Hick, *An Interpretation of Religion* (London and Basingstoke: Macmillan, 1989), pp. 1–2.

tive and explanatory reduction.[10] In *describing* what believers say and do, we must acknowledge that they consider themselves to be making absolute claims. In *explaining* those claims, we have to consider them in the light of the phenomenon of religious diversity. Diversity and conflict amongst those claims tell us that they cannot all be true. The different theoretical options in explaining the diverse religious scene then present themselves. And all turn out to imply that, at the very least, the vast majority of these different sets of absolute claims cannot be accepted. An *explanatory* theory of religion must invoke error and the anthropological perspective.

Pluralism departs from naturalism and joins company with confessionalism in a basic realist commitment. The pluralist thinks that the religious traditions covered by the pluralist thesis are alike in making a successful reference to a sacred, transcendent reality. This is a judgment that the confessionalist will likewise make about one favored form of religion (exlusivism) or about very many traditions (inclusivism). Thus the pluralist goes only so far in the deconstructionist, anthropological reading of religious traditions favored by naturalism. Two questions about this realism immediately arise: "Is it at all coherent?" and "Are there any grounds on which it might rest?"

The doubt about the coherence of the realist postulate takes the following form. On the pluralist interpretation of the religions, specific forms of religion are theoretical failures. That is to say, the detailed theories they have about the focus of religion, the religious ultimate, cannot be judged to be true (in the present state of our knowledge, at least). Furthermore, the pluralist acknowledges that different forms of religion contain accounts of the nature of the sacred transcendent which are incompatible to some significant degree or other. How, given this failure and incompatibility, can they nonetheless be said to be successful in reference and to make the same reference? There is a ready response to this twofold problem which the pluralist can draw upon: in recent philosophy of language and philosophy of science the notion that reference can succeed in the presence of descriptive failure and that co-reference is possible between competing theories has been explored and defended. There is a broadly analogous problem in the philosophy of science. Interpreters of science may, for good reason, want to say of earlier scientific theories that they genuinely refer to things and stuffs that our present theories commit us to (for example, viruses, atoms, genes) even though these theories disagree with current definitions of these entities and thus are largely mistaken in their characterization of them (when judged by the norm of present theories). The answer to the conundrum from recent semantic theories is that reference is for the most part not a function of descriptive success, but of causality and context. (Readers can explore these ideas in the writings collected by Schwartz, in the works of Harré, and in Alston and Byrne.[11])

Let us swallow hard and suppose for the sake of argument that the pluralist can make use of these non-descriptive ideas of reference to get over the objections to the

10 See W. Proudfoot, *Religious Experience* (Berkeley and Los Angeles: University of California Press, 1985).

11 See S. P. Schwartz (ed.), *Naming and Necessity* (Ithaca, NY: Cornell University Press, 1977); R. Harré, *The Varieties of Realism* (Oxford: Blackwell, 1986), *passim*; W. P. Alston, "Referring to God," in Alston, *Divine Nature and Human Language* (Ithaca, NY: Cornell University Press, 1991), pp. 103–17; Byrne, *Prolegomena to Religious Pluralism*, pp. 39ff.

coherence of pluralism so far considered. On what might pluralism rest its interpretation of religion?

Pluralism is like confessionalism in endorsing a realist commitment within the various strands of religion to the existence of some sacred, transcendent absolute. It is like naturalism, but unlike confessionalism, in trying to offer a non-divisive picture of human religious life. So, to argue for pluralism is to argue for a non-divisive picture of religion which preserves a realist thrust to it.

Pluralists can argue for the non-divisive element in their portrait of religion by pressing the point that there is no brand of religion which stands out as an exception to the general perception created by the modern sciences of religion to the effect that all strands of human religion are integrally related to elements of human culture and history. From confessionalism's viewpoint there will be significant discontinuity in human history and culture – with one brand of religion being an exception to the rule that forms of religiosity have a socio-historico-anthropological explanation. Pluralists will have to contend that this confessionalist picture is implausible a priori and even more so empirically.

Confessionalists must defend a kind of "exceptionalism": one strand in human religion resists the categories of explanation and interpretation found suitable for the other strands. The reasonableness of exceptionalism (and thus of pluralism, which is one form its denial may take) crucially depends on our estimation of the prospects of interreligious apologetics.[12] If exceptionalism is true, then one brand of religion can be picked out from the herd by means of both positive and negative apologetics. Its specific dogmatic claims can be shown to be true, or very probably true, by reference to positive arguments in their favor. Similar positive apologetic arguments are not available for the other brands of religion. The favored brand will likewise have negative apologetic arguments against the truth of rival brands and will be able to defeat the negative apologetic arguments directed against its own dogmas.

The pluralist is likely to be someone who is impressed by the fact that the great religions of the world are all systems of great antiquity and are associated with long histories of literate and developed religious argument and exegesis. As such, they all abound in positive apologetic arguments, have developed responses to negative apologetics, and have worked out negative apologetics against perceived rivals in their home cultures. Pluralists interpret this age-old dialectic as producing a mutual destruction of arguments.

5 For and Against Pluralism

We have here reached a Big Point in the argument about the interpretation of religious diversity. If we think that interreligious apologetics is fruitful and that it points to one strand of religion as true, showing that other strands are false insofar as they depart from this strand, then we have a case for confessionalism. If we return a negative verdict on the course of, and prospects for, interreligious apologetics, then plu-

12 Much of what follows is indebted to the analysis in Griffiths, *Apology for Apologetics*, though his view and my view of prospects for success differ.

ralism or naturalism beckons. Now, some might hold that philosophy of religion must, as a subject, be committed to the viability of interreligious apologetics. The "must" derives from the fact that philosophy is of its nature an argumentative, dialectical subject. Even if none of the brands of human religion have come up with successful positive and negative apologetic strategies to date, it is the job of the philosopher to find the arguments which will show one brand of religion to be true over and against the others.

The pluralist will resist this. It is the first task of the philosopher surveying religious diversity to make a considered estimate of the limits of human reason. It may be perfectly respectable for the philosopher to conclude that reason does not extend so far as to proving one strand in religion to be true over and against the others.

A considered estimate of this kind can rest on a number of considerations. First, it is possible to perform an induction on the results of interreligious apologetics down the centuries and across many cultures. Whether we survey debates between the Indian philosophical-cum-religious traditions or reflect, as above, on the arguments between the Abrahamic faiths, we find the fruitlessness of attempts to establish conclusions about the cognitive superiority of one religion over others on the basis of publicly agreed criteria. Second, we can note that the disagreements between different brands of religion are in some areas particularly resistant to anything like proof and disproof. Many of the disagreements are on matters of history, matters indeed of ancient history when judged from our standpoint. In the nature of the case, we are not going to find evidence which we can use now to settle what took place thousands of years ago. Many of the disagreements are on metaphysical matters. It is hard, to say the least, to prove or disprove metaphysical assertions. What seems metaphysically plausible to us is liable to depend on our prior metaphysical commitments.

By way of illustrating the final point above, consider Yandell's disproof of the metaphysics of the Indian monist religious system Advaita Vedanta. The Advaitins claim that the ultimate religious reality is an impersonal and absolutely simple substance – Nirguna Brahman. As absolutely simple, Brahman is without qualities. Yandell writes:

> It looks as if Advaita wants to hold all of a set of logically inconsistent theses. In particular, it begins with the claim that something exists but altogether lacks properties, and that something that altogether lacks properties can be identical to a variety of things that have properties and are distinct from one another . . . if we have no idea what properties Brahman has, and can form no concept of them, how could we possibly know that Brahman is qualityless or with what Brahman was or was not identical?
>
> Ramanuja, for example, held that it was contradictory to hold that There is an X such that for any property P, X lacks P . . . Thus to claim that Brahman, or anything else, is qualityless is to claim that it exists and deny an entailment of that very claim. Hence Advaita Vedanta metaphysics is not even possibly true. Ramanuja's critique seems decisive, and there is no point lingering over logical impossibilities.[13]

13 Yandell, *Philosophy of Religion*, p. 242.

The Advaitin system entails a contradiction only *on the assumption that all that is must have qualities.* It is therefore only expressive of logical falsehood if that assumption is necessarily true. Yandell gives no argument in the passage to show that the assumption is necessarily true. The assumption is in fact a substantive metaphysical principle which many, many thinkers, East and West, have denied. There is a strand of Western metaphysical reflection which holds that for the compounded, contingent things of the empirical world to exist, they must depend on a metaphysical substratum which is absolutely simple and therefore without properties. Thus things with qualities are only derived, contingent things; they are real only because something exists which is without properties. This line of reflection goes back at least to Plotinus and can be found in *theistic* thinkers such as Maimonides and Aquinas. There are defenses of it in contemporary English-speaking philosophy from the likes of Kretzmann and Miller.[14] For this tradition of thought the postulation of a qualityless metaphysical/religious ultimate, far from being the expression of the logically impossible, has to be true for us to make final sense of the world. The natural theological arguments hinted at in Plotinus and explored by the likes of Aquinas indicate, for those persuaded by them, that something defined negatively and relationally as the absolutely simple thing on which all things depend can be introduced into religious discourse in a meaningful way. Such systems can give a sense in which this qualityless thing is nonetheless identical with all things: it is Being, or the power of being, and thus present in all things at each and every moment of their existence.

One person's metaphysical profundities are notoriously another person's examples of pretentious nonsense. The pluralist has a well-founded skepticism about the degree to which we can sort out rival metaphysico-religious systems on the score of the obvious coherence of one and the obvious incoherence of another. What the pluralist can note is that many of the so-called higher religions in human history have been united in a quest to seek out an ultimate reality, a reality which is presumed to be ultimate ontologically (it is the ground of all being), ultimate rationally (it provides the reason why all things are what they are), and ultimate evaluatively (it is the norm and source of all value).[15] In the nature of the case, anything which serves this role will be radically unlike ordinary, contingent things. It will be radically transcendent. It may be picked out negatively and relationally, as, for example, Aquinas did when he wrote that the prime intent of those who use the word "God" is to pick out that whatever it is that is above all things (that is, of transcending value), is the source of all things (that is, sustains all things continually in their being and properties), and is removed from all things [that is, is utterly unlike the things it sustains in its nature or mode of being].[16] This prime intent then leads to the postulation of something

14 See L. P. Gerson's account of Plotinus in *Plotinus* (London: Routledge, 1994), pp. 12–22; and N. Kretzmann's account of Aquinas in *The Metaphysics of Theism: Aquinas' Natural Theology* (Oxford: Clarendon Press, 1997), ch. 4; B. Miller, *A Most Unlikely God* (Notre Dame, Ind.: University of Notre Dame Press, 1996), ch. 8.

15 See D. Pailin, *The Anthropological Character of Theology* (Cambridge: Cambridge University Press, 1990), p. 9.

16 Aquinas, *Summa Theologiae*, Ia, 13, 8 ad 2; translation by the Fathers of the English Dominican Province (Westminster: Christian Classics, 1981).

which is radically unknowable so far as its positive characterization is concerned, a point echoed in a number of religious traditions.[17]

I have tried to show how the agnosticism about the detailed dogmatics of brands of religion on which pluralism depends has some warrant. But pluralism is also characterized by its realist commitment. It wants to have its skeptical cake and eat it too. It is clear enough in a very broad way how it is going to attempt this: behind the many, apparently irresolvable disagreements between the religions are areas of overlap and commonality. These are significant enough and sufficiently supported by areas of human experience to support the claim that human religions are humanly rooted responses to a transcendent reality defined negatively and relationally in the manner introduced above.

Unfortunately, space allows me only the briefest sketch of how this generic religious apologetic might go. It can appeal to the broad thrust of religious experience. Many human beings at many times and places record encounters with God or some sacred, transcendent reality. The power of these experiential reports to warrant the metaphysical claims of particular brands of religion is weakened by the fact that different and incompatible claims are made on the basis of them. However, they can be presented, at a higher level of reflection and generality, to support some generic, syncretistic claims. Readers are directed to the studies by Franks Davis and Gellman to see how this may be accomplished.[18] The pluralist in effect tries to use the many facets of religious experience as grounds for thinking that an anthropological interpretation and explanation of human religious life is not sufficient.

Another area from which a global, positive religious apologetic can draw sustenance is the moral and spiritual fruits of the great religious traditions. This is a prominent theme in the writings of John Hick.[19] The Hick claim is that many religious traditions are alike in being morally and spiritually fruitful, and that their moral and spiritual fruits are very similar. These facts give grounds for supposing that the various strands of religion are in touch with an ultimate reality described negatively and relationally, as above. It is easy to sneer at this argument, as when it is said that it transforms the word "true" when used of religious traditions into "effective in producing nice people."[20] But this is too easy. What the pluralist means by "true" can be old-fashioned correspondence truth. The pluralist takes some generic religious claim introducing the postulate of a religious ultimate, defined negatively and relationally, to be true. One ground of this alleged truth, and therefore against a naturalistic interpretation of religion, is the moral and spiritual fruits of the manifold strands of religion. The grounds are pragmatic insofar as they cite a facet of human praxis. But there is then an argument to a truth: certain fruits of religion are best explained by invoking contact with a moral and spiritual reality which transcends human powers. Religious truth is not converted into "what works."

17 A point explored by D. Burrell, *Knowing the Unknowable God* (Notre Dame, Ind.: Notre Dame University Press, 1986).

18 See C. Franks Davis, *The Evidential Force of Religious Experience* (Oxford: Clarendon Press, 1989), and J. Gellman, *Experience of God and the Rationality of Theistic Belief* (Ithaca, NY: Cornell University Press, 1997).

19 See Hick, *An Interpretation of Religion*, chs 19 and 20.

20 Yandell, *Philosophy of Religion*, p. 68.

Reply to Byrne

The RP that Byrne clearly presents seems subject to the critique already offered. Here is a supplement.

1 The Appeal to Anthropology

Byrne appeals to anthropological explanations of religions. He takes these to be a source of support for naturalism. They are not. The same sort of anthropological explanation that RP applies to religions can also be applied to naturalism, to RP itself, and to anthropological explanations themselves – to the cultural context in which they arose, the way people came to accept them, and the way they came to be thought of as debunkers. If the former debunk religions, the latter debunk naturalism, RP, and anthropology. If the latter do not debunk naturalism, RP, and anthropology, the former don't debunk religious traditions. So much for the alleged support.

Further, RP must hold that all religious traditions are anthropologically explicable in a sense and to a degree that this explicability rules out there being good reason to think any of them true, and that the corresponding explicability of naturalism, RP, and anthropology does not rule out there being good reason to think naturalism, RP, and anthropology true.[21] I have yet to read the massive works in which this has been proved. In fact, this is another case in which RP is arbitrarily selective in what it takes seriously and what it dismisses, as well as another case in which RP's argument is self-defeating.

There is no incompatibility between *being anthropologically explicable* and *being discernibly true*.[22] Only if we have some reason to think that what is anthropologically explained is also false are we justified in adding that the anthropological explanation is sufficient in the sense of telling the whole cognitive and causal story regarding what is explained.

One might object that the discussion here is unfair, in that RP appeals to both anthropological explicability and nonagreement regarding rational assessment of the religious traditions, not to the former alone. But note that lack of agreement (i) does not entail that there are no discernibly correct assessments, (ii) is compatible with agreement that *some* religious traditions are false, (iii) leaves each religious tradition in as justified a position as is RP itself, (iv) and exists regarding both RP and skepticism concerning the rational assessment of religious traditions.[23] In sum, RP itself

21 The fact, if fact it be, that anthropological explanations of naturalism, RP, and anthropology lag behind that of religious traditions is an accident of history, irrelevant to our argument.

22 This is argued in some detail in my *Epistemology of Religious Experience*.

23 Counting noses here is of course irrelevant. If someone mistakenly thought it wasn't, that would not help either. Suppose for simplicity that there are four basic types of religious traditions, R1–R4, and there is RP. Suppose each tradition's members typically suppose that rational assessment shows their tradition to be correct. Then, as to whether (say) rational assessment favors R1, there are four noses against and only one – R1 – for. But if we switch to the question as to whether rational assessment of religious traditions is viable, there will be a four noses (R1–R4) in favor, and one nose – RP – against. Nothing of philosophical significance follows from this.

is anthropologically explicable and something academicians disagree about. Thus on its own argumentative terms, it is at best an object of skepticism and at worst something to be explained away.

2 "A Western Metaphysic" and More Disagreement

Byrne's apologetic for RP is welcome. Nonetheless, it is dubious in its interpretive claims and self-defeating.

First, it appeals to some "Western metaphysical reflection," exhibited by Maimonides and Aquinas, as another example of Advaita Vedantic thinking. This is not the place to consider the matter in detail, but we can note some relevant points. Maimonides and Aquinas do not deny that God has properties, whereas, according to Sankara, Brahman is propertyless. They do not hold that God alone exists, whereas Sankara holds that only propertyless Brahman exists. Aquinas is explicit that some assertions concerning God are literally true, saying (*contra* Advaita and RP), "not all names (= terms) are applied to God in a metaphorical sense, but there are some which are said of Him in their literal sense. . . . the words *being*, *good*, *living*, and the like . . . can be literally applied to God."[24] Arguably, Maimonides and Aquinas accept a constituent ontology whose roots are in Plato through Plotinus. Whether that ontology is itself logically consistent, and if so, whether it is logically consistent with Jewish or Christian theology, is an interesting, difficult issue. But it remains clear that Maimonides and Aquinas hold that the creation is distinct from the Creator, and that Aquinas at least holds that we can say substantial things that are literally true about God. I know of no reason to think that it is constitutive ontology that provides any alleged rationale for Sankara's view. The "Western metaphysic" that Byrne cites lacks the features he claims it has. It seems quite distinct from any reasons Sankara thought he had for holding that Brahman is propertyless. The constituent ontologist does not argue that God has no properties. She argues that the relationship between God and God's properties is to be understood in a constituent ontologist manner.

Related to all this is the fact that, while Byrne cites only my *Philosophy of Religion*, there is an entire chapter in *The Epistemology of Religious Experience* arguing against Advaita Vedanta. Byrne ignores the argument in the one passage he does quote to the effect that a propertyless Brahman is not identical to the things we have good reason to think do exist and have properties. Further, even John Hick does not think that his "Real" has no qualities; he thinks it has qualities but that we don't know of any of them.

Suppose Byrne actually does think that the notion of something existing and lacking properties altogether is just fine – that there can be a bare particular that not only lacks any essential properties but never has any nonessential property either, thus always existing in propertyless splendor. In my sad ignorance, I find this logically impossible. So we disagree. No doubt our disagreement is anthropologically explicable. So my view, and his as well, is to be dismissed. Further, it is a metaphysical disagreement, and Byrne is a skeptic about such matters to the degree that he can't

24 Aquinas, *Summa Theologica*, Ia, 13, 3.

know he is right or more likely right than not. As a metaphysical skeptic, he has no good reason to think himself right about this matter. But his brand of RP needs either a sort of cosmic bare particular or a Hickian "Real" (a view also subject to anthropological explicability and metaphysical skepticism). So all these views are to be dismissed. So there goes RP. For that reason, the Byrnean defense of RP is self-defeating. And we have still another case where RP arbitrarily makes itself an exception to the method by which it allegedly was able to downgrade its competitors.

3 RP Exclusivism

There is a feature of religious traditions that some philosophers find irritating. Here are some examples, the first from Advaita Vedantin Sankara:

> From whatever new points of view the Bauddha [Buddhist] system is tested with reference to its probability, it gives way on all sides, like the walls of a well dug in sandy soil ... Buddha by propounding the three mutually contradictory systems, teaching respectively the reality of the external world, the reality of ideas only, and general nothingness, has himself made it clear either that he was a man given to make incoherent assertions, or else that hatred of all beings induced him to propound absurd doctrines by accepting which they would become thoroughly confused. So that ... Buddha's doctrine has to be entirely disregarded by all those who have a regard for their own happiness.[25]

Vsistadvaitin Ramanuja, concerning views which proclaim the desirability of an enlightenment in which what used to be Ramanuja sort of survives as something else, comments:

> If he [one seeking enlightenment] ... were to realize that the result of such activity would be the loss of personal existence he would surely turn away as soon as somebody began to tell him about "release." ... Nor must you maintain against this that even in the state of release there persists pure consciousness ... No sensible person exerts himself under the influence of the idea that after he himself has perished there will remain some entity termed "pure light."[26]

A text from the *Jaina Sutras* bluntly tells us that:

> Those who do not know all things by *kevala* (knowledge), but who being ignorant teach a law (of their own), are lost themselves, and work the ruin of others in this dreadful,

25 S. Radhakrishnan and C. Moore (eds), *A Sourcebook of Indian Philosophy* (Princeton: Princeton University Press, 1957), pp. 534–5. He also says: "It has, in fact, no foundation whatever to rest upon, and hence the attempts to use it as a guide in the practical concerns of life are mere folly." Sankara can be accused of being unfair in that the three Buddhist views cited express alternative if incompatible Buddhist traditions, each of them being ascribed to the Buddha's own teaching. Further, it is dicey for an Advaita Vedantin, who holds to the single existence of a propertyless Absolute described as a substance, to chide Mahayana absolutism, which holds to the single existence of a propertyless Absolute, described as a state. But none of this makes any difference to the point being made here.
26 Ibid., p. 547.

> boundless Circle of Births. Those who know all things by the full Kevala knowledge, and who are practicing meditation and teach the whole law, are themselves saved and save others.[27]

A Buddhist text speaks plainly to this effect:

> If one does not proceed in this manner [to "proceed in this manner" is to "develop the understanding which results from the study of the (Buddhist) teachings"], inasmuch as meditation on some erroneous idea cannot even clear away doubt, recognition of reality will not arise and consequently meditation will be profitless like that of the Tirthikas [i.e., non-Buddhists, especially Jains].[28]

The theme of these passages is clear enough. To put them in one jargon: there is a heaven to gain and a hell to shun; there is one way to gain heaven and shun hell, and there are plenty of ways to shun heaven and gain hell.

RP entails that Sankara, Ramanuja, the Jain author, and the Buddhist author are all wrong. The diagnoses and cures that their traditions present are mistaken. It is the generic diagnosis and cure of RP that is correct. Any appearance of religious neutrality, of standing on the sidelines neutrally observing the diversity of religions while approving all and rejecting none, goes by the board once this is recognized. In this respect, RP itself is to be found amidst the religious diversity it seeks to explain. Further, it is itself exclusivist. As Byrne so correctly explains, his version of RP claims to make a true claim: "certain fruits of religion are best explained by invoking contact with a moral and spiritual reality which transcends human powers" to such an extent that the descriptions of it that the various religious traditions typically offer are false of it.[29] The religious traditions don't think that this is the best explanation. Their core doctrinal content has entailments regarding the matter, which is one reason why RP must deny that that content is true. The actual religious traditions, as opposed to pale secularized versions as they appear in much of the academy, don't think that the RP diagnosis and cure – and RP does offer a diagnosis and cure, though it does not say it does – are correct. So RP is in fact exclusivist regarding religious explanation (in a way that is inconsistent with the truth of various religious traditions) and regarding the correct diagnosis and cure. RP offers its own brand of exclusivism while often criticizing others for being exclusivist in RP-unapproved ways. Byrne is delightfully free of this hypocritical criticism, but his version of RP is nonetheless exclusivist in the senses noted.

27 I have not been able to locate the reference.

28 Geshe Sopa and Elving Jones, "A Light to the Svatantrika-Madhyanika" (privately circulated MS), p. 62.

29 I don't see that there is much by way of an *argument* for this claim – just a presentation and explanation of it and its historical and anthropologically explicable context.

Reply to Yandell

Theories of religion are as old as the philosophy of religion itself. Many are offered by authors unconvinced of the truth of any of the dogmatic systems of the world's great religions. Some such theories are pluralist. They speculate on the epistemology, ethics, metaphysics, and anthropology of human religion in the light of religious diversity. They do not respond to this diversity with out right skepticism. They hold that the world's religions do provide good reason to suppose that humanity is in touch with a sacred, transcendent reality, even while no particular stream of human experience has exclusive contact with that entity or a definitive, reliable account of it. Forms of religious pluralism are not religions (at any level). They are not systems of faith and worship. They cannot be practiced. They are philosophical theories about actual systems of religious practice.

Readers may find no particular member of this family of theories of religion convincing. All members face internal and external difficulties. But it beggars belief that all members of the family entail self-contradictions. Yandell states in the final sentence of his essay that religious pluralism is "a tissue of inconsistencies." Yet his conclusion and the critique which precedes it are hardly definitive. Readers will note that he does not cite or discuss the works of any religious pluralist, but makes reference only to his own writings. His strategy is to ignore what has been written on this subject in favor of what religious pluralists *must* say. But this approach then fails to consider *actual* reasons that pluralists offer for their views. What a waste of time. Readers with any interest in exploring religious but non-confessional interpretations of religion are strongly urged to look at what pluralists themselves say by way of setting out and supporting their ideas. My *Prolegomena to Religious Pluralism* provides a critical but sympathetic survey of these theories.

Pluralist theories of religion have a partly critical, skeptical attitude to the dogmas of the major world religions, while seeking some minimalist, irenic affirmations about the divine and about salvation/liberation arising from comparative reflection upon them. Some allege that there must be incoherence here: pluralists can know only that the dogmatic, detailed accounts of the transcendent are false/uncertain and the minimalist account reliable, because they have an access to the true nature of religious reality arbitrarily denied to the confessionalist.

Not so. Consider the following analogy. I am sitting in my office. Six people come in with different accounts of an incident they have seen take place on the Strand. Their differences mean that I cannot be sure that anyone of them has the whole, detailed truth, but I may be able to be sure that they did collectively see something, and I may be able to construct a minimal account of what happened, surrounded by much agnosticism, from their witness. I do not need to claim a vision they lack.

The above example gives the essential form of pluralism. The conclusion reached from noting both disagreement and overlap is defeasible, in the way noted in my essay. Note that the analogy shows that the pluralist need not hold that there is no religious truth or that we can make no religious judgments. From the different reports coming to me in my office I can deduce some things about the incident and that some irenic account of what happened is plausible.

Yandell thinks there is gross incoherence in taking religious disagreement to count towards religious pluralism but in not taking moral disagreement to count toward moral skepticism. Not so. The pluralist can reason *as many confessionalist theologians do* that agreement on basic moral principles and rules exists alongside religious diversity. It is clearly the view of many Jewish thinkers (see note 6) that awareness of the Noahhide laws extends to the nations. Roman Catholic theologians speak in similar terms of the natural law (citing Christian Scripture: Romans 1:19–21). Moreover, it is obvious (though not to Yandell) that it is one thing to be agnostic about the precise details of the higher management of the universe, but another to be agnostic about a moral rule like "Murder is wrong."

The great religions seem to have a shared vision of the final good: it will consist in eternal union with or contemplation of a superhuman, supersensual spiritual source. Yandell ridicules the pluralist's reliance on a facile optimism about the human future and our ability to get to this supreme goal by being moral and then believing whatever we like. But we must note that many have argued from *within the religious traditions* that the supreme good will not be barred from those who have struggled for good and against evil, and that a large part of the transformation needed to gain union with the spiritual source is indeed moral. Confessionalist theorists of religious diversity have been troubled by the following problem, which they see as a deeply serious: if the transcendent source of all is supremely good and just, how could it make entry into right relationship with it dependent on having the right beliefs about higher management when access to these beliefs is so much a matter of the accidents of one's birth in this or that time or region? Confessional inclusivists have used this as an argument against exclusivism and for universalism in soteriology. It is grist for the pluralist mill. A commitment to the fundamental justice of the world is at the heart of many faiths and thus something that pluralists can pick up on in constructing their irenic accounts of soteriology.

Pluralists see common witness to the existence of a superhuman, supernatural, spiritual source in all the major faiths. Their account of it must be minimalist, by definition. If it were not, pluralism would slide into some form of confessional inclusivism. In his section "Some More Nuancing," Yandell asserts, without the slightest attempt at argument, that this irenic account must be cast in terms of a propertyless X. Later we're told that not even concepts such as *causes*, *elicits*, *grounds*, and *explains* apply to it. But, though something like this view can be found in the writings of John Hick, religious pluralists are not as such bound to accept it.[30] A demonstration of its incoherence is thus no demonstration of the incoherence of pluralism. A serious attempt to refute Hick on the ineffability of the Real would in any event have to take account of Hick's responses to this type of critique. Of course, this is simply an example of why I criticized Yandell's *a priori* approach.

In the next section Yandell's ignorance shows itself in his assertion that we find a version of the Absolute-has-no-properties view in only a few places in the religions. As my contribution makes clear, such a view is central to the metaphysics of many theologians in the Jewish, Christian, and Islamic traditions.[31] They argue that a reli-

30 See Byrne, *Prolegomena to Religious Pluralism*, ch. 6.

31 For further documentation of this tradition, see Burrell, *Knowing the Unknowable God*.

giously and philosophically adequate divine principle must have an utterly different mode of being from the human and the finite. Such a being must be metaphysically uncompound and thus must have no properties, where that means no properties distinct from each other, from its essence, or from its being. It follows that human descriptions of it as *good*, *wise*, *powerful*, etc. are attenuated at best. We can know what it is not, not what it is. We know it from its operations. We cannot know its essence. It is radically transcendent and unknowable. *Contra* Yandell, no crude positivist theories of meaning are at work here. But these doctrines indicate that religious agnosticism can be drawn from the religions.

Yet more grist for the pluralist mill.

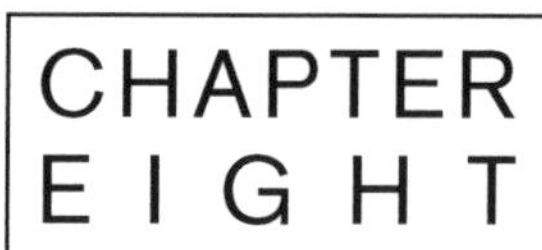

Does God Take Risks in Governing the World?

In this debate, William Hasker and Paul Helm both assume that if human beings have genuine libertarian freedom, freedom to do other than what they in fact do, then God leaves himself open to the possibility of surprise as well as disappointment. In other words, if God has given human beings libertarian freedom, then God is a risk-taker. But Hasker and Helm disagree on whether human beings have libertarian freedom. Hasker argues that we do have it, and thus that God takes risks. He contends that his view fits better with both the biblical portrayal of God and a commonsense understanding of what kind of creatures God would want to create. Helm, on the other hand, argues that God does not take risks. God exerts strong providential control over his creation, but does so without at the same time being morally culpable for the evil that arises within it.

God Takes Risks

William Hasker

Is God a risk-taker? In governing the world, does he act in ways that expose him to the possibility of disappointment and failure? Or are all such possibilities excluded from divine providential governance? This is one of the deepest questions concerning God's action in the world, and as we shall see, it is closely connected with other important questions. It is my hope that this discussion, together with that of my counterpart Paul Helm, may help to illuminate these issues.

These questions, of course, are intended as questions about the God of the Bible, the God who is the object of Christian worship. As philosophers, however, our concern is not primarily with biblical interpretation. Rather, we shall focus primarily on clarifying the meanings of the respective positions, and on determining their logical implications. At a later stage, however, we will need to consider briefly which view is more in accord with the biblical texts through which God is believed to have revealed himself.

1 Freedom and Risk

But what exactly would it mean for God to take risks? Let me put it like this: *God takes risks if he makes decisions that depend for their outcomes on the responses of free creatures in which the decisions themselves are not informed by knowledge of the outcomes.*[1] For if he does this, the creatures' decisions may be contrary to God's wishes, and in this case God's intentions in making those decisions may be at least partly frustrated. If, on the other hand, God's decisions are always guided by full knowledge of how creatures will respond, he takes no risks, even though some of the creaturely responses may be unfavorable. The unfavorable responses, in this case, are simply part of the "cost of doing business"; in incurring these costs, God was not taking any risks, but was merely accepting what he knew in advance would be the mixed results from his decision.

But if this is what it means for God to take risks, what is it that determines whether God's actions are risky or risk-free? There is a surprisingly simple answer to this question, one on which Helm and I are agreed: *God is a risk-taker if he endows his creatures with libertarian freedom; otherwise not.*[2] By "libertarian freedom" is meant freedom such that the agent who makes a choice is really able, under exactly the same circumstances, to choose something different from the thing that is in fact chosen. The choices in question, then, are not causally determined to occur as they do; libertarian freedom is inherently indeterministic. This means that there is *nothing whatever* that predetermines which choice will be made, until the creature is actually placed in the situation and makes the decision. God may know in advance how the creature will *probably* decide, but he cannot make his own decision in the light of the creature's *actual* decision.

It needs to be said, however, that this rather simple answer suffices only if another possible theory, that of divine middle knowledge, is excluded. According to the theory of middle knowledge, there is a vast array of propositions that are known to God, generally termed "counterfactuals of freedom." These propositions state, with

1 This formulation is adapted from my *God, Time, and Knowledge* (Ithaca, NY: Cornell University Press, 1989), p. 197. I note that Paul Helm quotes this formulation of the issue, with apparent approval, in his *The Providence of God* (Downers Grove, Ill.: InterVarsity Press, 1994), p. 41. (Page references in parentheses throughout this essay are to Helm's book, unless otherwise noted.)

2 A minor qualification is needed here. Even without libertarian freedom, providence could be somewhat risky if the world includes genuinely uncaused events such as are postulated in the usual interpretation of quantum mechanics. Advocates of a risk-free providence will hold that such physically undetermined events, if they exist, are directly controlled by God.

regard to each actual or possible free creature, what that creature would freely (in the libertarian sense) decide to do, in any possible situation of free choice with which that creature might be confronted. And given this knowledge, God is able to make his decisions in full knowledge of exactly how the creatures will respond, even though the creaturely decision is free in the libertarian sense and thus not causally determined. Once again, the element of risk is completely eliminated.

Paul Helm and I are agreed, however, that the theory of middle knowledge cannot be true, because the truths God is alleged to know – the "counterfactuals of freedom" – simply do not exist to be known. As Helm says, "the circumstances [of a libertarian free choice] never ensure one determinate freely-chosen outcome; they provide only the conditions for the free choice of one of several outcomes. Hence God cannot . . . use his knowledge of what a free creature would do under certain circumstances to achieve a desired end" (p. 59). The reason why God cannot do this is that there simply is no such truth to be known; insofar as an agent is genuinely free, there *are* no true counterfactuals stating what the agent would definitely (as opposed to probably) do under various possible circumstances.

Having said this much, let me acknowledge that the subject of middle knowledge is complex and difficult, and a full treatment of it would need to be much more extensive than can be attempted here.[3] But since Helm and I are agreed in rejecting middle knowledge as impossible, I will say no more about it in this essay. And this returns us to the position previously stated: God is a risk-taker if he endows his creatures with libertarian freedom; otherwise not. This connection, furthermore, suggests a pair of useful labels for the positions under discussion: the view that affirms divine risk-taking may be termed *free-will theism*, whereas the contrary view can be described as *theological determinism*.

2 God's Freedom, Power, and Knowledge

Thus far we have been discussing freedom for human beings, but what about the freedom of God? Are God's decisions free in the libertarian sense? One might expect that a view bearing the label, "free-will theism," would attribute libertarian freedom to God as well as to creatures, and this expectation is not disappointed. But what of theological determinism? Does this theory, also, consider God as being free in the libertarian sense? This is not always so clear; theological determinists like to speak of the "freedom of God," but it may not be immediately evident what sort of freedom they have in mind. A little reflection, however, suggests that theological determinists too must attribute libertarian freedom to God – at least, they must do so if they wish to be orthodox Christians. For if God is not free in this sense, then the divine act of creation must be somehow necessitated by the nature of God; the creation will then

3 Middle knowledge is discussed in Hasker, *God, Time, and Knowledge*, ch. 2; see also my "Middle Knowledge: A Refutation Revisited," *Faith and Philosophy*, 12/2 (April 1995), pp. 223–36. By far the best recent defense of middle knowledge is Thomas Flint, *Divine Providence: The Molinist Account* (Ithaca, NY: Cornell University Press, 1998).

be *necessary for God*, and not a free and gracious act as the Christian tradition has affirmed it to be.[4]

So free-will theism and theological determinism do not differ with regard to the freedom of God. Freedom is, of course, only one divine attribute among many, and the two views will indeed differ with regard to some divine attributes. But these differences are less than many suppose. For example, the *power* of God, the essential divine attribute of omnipotence, will not be different for the two views: in either case, it can truly be said that God is able to do anything that is neither self-contradictory nor in conflict with God's perfect nature.[5] To be sure, the *extent of the exercise* of divine power may in a sense be somewhat greater for the deterministic view, in that on this view there are fewer kinds of events that God does not actively control.[6] But this difference does not concern God's essential omnipotence, but rather the sort of universe God has freely decided to create in which to exercise his omnipotence. A universe containing genuinely free creatures is one in which God has generously decided that there shall be certain events that are *not* positively controlled by him: namely, the free choices of the creatures.

Some readers may be surprised to learn that free-will theism and theological determinism do not differ with regard to the *essential omniscience* of God. The reason why this is especially surprising is that free-will theism, when held consistently, entails that God does not have comprehensive foreknowledge of future free actions.[7] Yet this does not imply any difference in God's essential nature from that which is posited by theological determinism. To see this, consider once again God's situation as he contemplates whether or not to create a universe, and if he does create, what sort of universe to create. Among God's choices, both views will concede, is the choice whether or not to endow his creatures with libertarian free will.[8] Both views, furthermore, will recognize the following truth: If God creates persons with libertarian freedom, he will not have exhaustive knowledge of the future, whereas if he creates no such persons, he will have exhaustive knowledge of the future.[9] Both possibilities are consistent with God's perfect nature, and therefore with his essential omniscience, which is no different for free-will theism than for theological determinism. As in the case of omnipotence, the difference does not concern the essential divine attribute but rather the sort of universe God has freely chosen to create.

4 Consider in this regard Helm's criticism of panentheism, because on that view "the universe does not depend for its existence on the free choice of God, but is an inevitable emanation of his goodness" (p. 73).

5 This is the point that is overlooked (or sometimes, one fears, deliberately suppressed) by those who equate free-will theism with process theism.

6 It should be noted, however, that theological determinism also recognizes acts not directly controlled by God: namely, morally evil actions.

7 For argument, see Hasker, *God, Time, and Knowledge*, chs 4–7.

8 Some theological determinists would dispute this, holding that "free will" as understood by libertarians is an incoherent notion. Helm does not take this line (see p. 55), and it is difficult to see how such a view could be sustained, given the need to attribute libertarian freedom to God.

9 This point rests on the assumption, which I accept, that God, God's knowledge, and God's actions are temporal. If God is timelessly eternal, then he will have timeless knowledge even of the future actions of free creatures. But this makes no difference to the question whether providence is risky or risk-free. (See Hasker, *God, Time, and Knowledge*, pp. 176–7.)

3 What Kind of Universe Is This?

But what sort of universe *has* God created? Or rather, what sort of universe is it reasonable for us to think that he has created? One important bit of evidence here concerns our *experience* of being free agents. According to John Searle,

> [I]f there is any fact of experience that we are all familiar with, it's the simple fact that our own choices, decisions, reasonings, and cogitations seem to make a difference to our actual behaviour. There are all sorts of experiences that we have in life where it seems just a fact of our experience that though we did one thing, we feel we know perfectly well that we could have done something else. We know we could have done something else, because we chose one thing for certain reasons. But we were aware that there were also reasons for choosing something else, and indeed, we might have acted on those reasons and chosen that something else.[10]

A striking fact about this quotation is that Searle himself is a determinist, one who feels that this experience of freedom must ultimately be illusory! Nevertheless, he testifies that this is indeed how we experience our lives to be. Now it must be admitted that Searle, and other determinists, are right in holding that our "experience of freedom" does not *prove* that we are free, because there could be determining causes of our actions of which we are unaware. But unless there are compelling reasons to think this experience is illusory, we must acknowledge that it gives us a strong *reason*, though not absolute proof, to think that we really do possess free will just as libertarians say we do.

But here we are raising the question of free will primarily from the perspective of God's decision about what sort of world to create. As a start on answering the question, I am going to ask my readers to join me in a thought experiment. Imagine yourself, then, as a prospective parent shortly before the birth of your first child. And suppose that someone has offered you the following choice. On the one hand, the child will be one that, without any effort on your part, will always and automatically do and be exactly what you want it to do and be, no more and no less. The child will have no feeling of being constrained or controlled; nevertheless, it will spontaneously carry out your wishes on any and every occasion. Or, on the other hand, you can choose to have a child in the normal fashion, a child that is fully capable of having a will of its own and of resisting your wishes for it, and even of acting against its own best interests. You will have to invest a great deal of effort in the child's education, with good hopes to be sure, but without any advance guarantee of success. And there is the risk, indeed the near-certainty, that the child will inflict on you considerable pain and suffering, as you strive to help the child become all that he or she can be and ought to be. Which do you choose?

Such a choice is admittedly deeply subjective, and it may well be that some readers will choose the first alternative, to have a child that is always and automatically in compliance with their wishes for it. (And if you have chosen that way, I probably have little hope of persuading you to accept the view of God as a risk-taker.) It is my

10 John Searle, *Minds, Brains, and Science* (Cambridge, Mass.: Harvard University Press, 1984), pp. 87–8.

hope, however, that many readers – perhaps even a strong majority – will agree with me in saying that it is far better to accept the challenge of parenting a child with a will of its own, even at the price of pain and possible heartbreak, than to opt for an arrangement in which the child's choices will all really be my choices made for it, its life a pale reflection of mine lived through the child.

The friends of a risk-free providence may charge me with excessive anthropomorphism in this analogy. It *is* anthropomorphic, but so is the Bible in its portrayal of God as a loving Father – for instance, in the parable of the Prodigal Son. And it is difficult to see the point of such portrayals, unless one is permitted to make some inferences from the character and conduct of good human parents to that of the divine Parent. In any case, Helm has opened the door to such analogies by arguing (in favor of the no-risk view) that genuine personal relationships are compatible with a certain amount of constraint, manipulation, and pressure, and that close relationships typically involve a high degree of predictability by each other of the partners' behavior (see pp. 150–3). I agree with all of this, but with the following proviso: the better the relationship is, the more mature the partners become in their dealings with each other, the less need there is for either pressure or manipulation. After nearly 40 years of marriage, my wife and I know each other reasonably well. We seldom attempt to pressure or manipulate each other, and while we can often anticipate each other's responses, we are still quite capable of surprising each other – and thank God for that! The notion that one partner to a relationship could exercise complete, unilateral control over the other, and yet the relationship remain a genuinely personal one, strikes me as unconvincing in the extreme.

4 Evil in the World

Our considerations to this point have been in a sense a priori, in that we have paid little or no attention to the actual character of the world God has created. As we turn to consider the way the world is, we cannot help but be struck by the troubling prevalence of sin, evil, and suffering. A theory of providence must reckon with these facts, and they create formidable problems for any such theory. It seems, however, that the difficulties for the no-risk view are especially severe.

One such difficulty concerns the issue of responsibility for sin and moral evil. Given the assumptions of the no-risk view, are human sinners truly responsible for their evil actions? And how does God escape being responsible for moral evil – from being, as some have said, the "author of sin"? In responding to this, theological determinists stress the obscure and mysterious nature of the relationship between human and divine willing. As Helm says, "The basic question . . . has to do with the very nature of the division and connection between divine and human reality" (p. 162). That this relation is obscure and mysterious (whatever one's theory of providence), no one should deny. This obscurity should not, however, lead us to neglect or overlook what is clearly implied about the relationship by the no-risk theory. Here is one such implication: *God himself is the sufficient cause of all events, including sinful human actions, in that he deliberately and without constraint establishes the causal conditions that of necessity lead to these events and actions.*

That God is in this sense the "cause of sin" simply cannot be denied by theological determinists.

There are, to be sure, certain explanations and clarifications that need to be made here. God is not, on this view, the *sole* cause of all worldly events, as has sometimes been claimed. The creatures serve as "secondary causes," and their causality, though needing to be sustained by God in his conserving activity, is genuine and distinct from that of God himself. Furthermore, God's causal involvement in worldly events is different for different classes of events. In particular, God's relation to morally evil actions is not the same as his relation to good actions (see pp. 168–71, 190–1). It is often said in this connection that God "permits" evil actions to occur, but does not cause them to occur. But this language of permission can easily become evasive and misleading. No doubt, on this view, God "permits" evil actions without actively assisting them in the way that he assists good actions through his gracious influence. Nevertheless, *the evil actions are the necessary consequence of causes that were deliberately created by God with full knowledge of what their results would be.* God's involvement may be less direct than in the case of good actions, but it is no less decisive. In the end, it is simply incoherent for the no-risk view to deny that God is the cause of sin. As Helm states, his view "does not, in the final analysis, attribute certain evils to the human will and certain others to natural causes; rather, all are finally attributed to the divine reason and will" (p. 198).

How, then, is the human responsibility for sin and evil to be preserved? At this point Helm embraces "divine compatibilism," a view that agrees with the "compatibilist" account of free will which holds that free and responsible actions need not be causally undetermined, so long as they are not the result of compulsion. This view is a fairly common one in contemporary philosophy, and it has been developed with considerable sophistication. Helm's "divine compatibilism" adds to this secular view the claim that "if compatibilism is true, the fact that it is God who ordains those factors which determine human agency, and that the factors are not determined in a purely natural or secular way, is not an *additional* difficulty for compatibilism" (p. 174).

For some of us, the suggestion that theological determinism suffers "only" from the same difficulties that afflict compatibilism in a secular setting is a weak recommendation at best. Nevertheless, it is true that compatibilism is a widely held philosophical view, and the fact that theological determinism can avail itself of this support is of some benefit to the latter. But is it really the case that supposing God to be the ultimate cause of all human actions creates no additional difficulty?[11] When we think of responsibility in a secular context, we will be thinking primarily of responsibility *to society,* whether this is expressed through the law or through more informal means. Now whatever the natural causes of human behavior are thought to be, it is clear that society exerts at best very limited control over them. On the other hand, it is unavoidable that some sort of sanctions will be applied to those who act destructively, since

11 Helm replies to an argument by Antony Flew, himself a compatibilist, to the effect that the assignment of responsibility to the human agent breaks down if God is the ultimate cause (see pp. 175–6). In what follows, I attempt to sharpen and reinforce Flew's argument.

without this the maintenance of social order would be impossible. So in this context the assignment of responsibility to causally determined actions makes some sense, even if the conceptual situation remains murky.

In the theistic context, however, things are much different. God is not the unfortunate onlooker forced to put up with behavior determined by forces over which he has little control. On the contrary, it is God himself who has ordained those very forces with full knowledge of their consequences. Nor is God faced with the need to impose penalties as the only means by which he can maintain order; instead, he could simply have refrained from setting up the causal chains that led to the behavior in the first place. The picture we have, then, is of God, with full knowledge and deliberation, intentionally creating a situation in which human beings act in morally abhorrent ways and then punishing those humans for that behavior, while remaining all the while beyond reproach himself. Is this picture credible?

Let me reinforce this reasoning by formulating a principle which seems to be applicable to the situation; we may term it the *transfer-of-responsibility principle*:

> TR: If agent A deliberately and knowingly places agent B in a situation where B unavoidably performs some morally wrong act, the moral responsibility for that act is transferred from B to A, *provided that* the morally wrong act results exclusively from A's actions and is not the result of an evil disposition in B which preceded A's actions.

The qualifying phrase is needed in order to account for this sort of situation: an undercover policeman offers to buy narcotics from a known drug-dealer, in order to obtain evidence to convict the dealer. The drug-dealer is still responsible, even though the sale resulted from the policeman's offer, because there was already on the dealer's part the disposition and intention to participate in such transactions. (If the policeman induced comparable behavior from a person with no prior intention to commit such an offense, this would be entrapment, and the person would not be held guilty.) I believe that the principle as stated is quite compelling, and I am confident that most compatibilists would agree with it. But when we apply the principle to God, using the assumptions of theological determinism, the consequences are grim. For on that view *all* human sinners have been placed by God in situations where they unavoidably (even though "freely" in the compatibilist sense) perform morally wrong actions. And while there may indeed be an "evil disposition" prior to a specific sin that is committed, *this evil disposition is itself the product of the divinely ordained causality and does not precede it.* So the consequence of TR is that God is morally responsible for human sin and human sinners are not responsible – a consequence which is fatal for theological determinism.

Theological determinists, then, must reject TR and affirm instead the following *no-transfer-of-responsibility principle*:

> NTR: If God deliberately and knowingly places a human agent in a situation where that agent unavoidably performs some morally wrong act, the moral responsibility for that act is *not* transferred from the agent to God but remains solely with the human agent, even though the morally wrong act results exclusively from God's actions and

is not the result of an evil disposition in the human agent which preceded God's actions.

Here, then, we have a principle concerning responsibility which theological determinists can affirm – indeed, which they *must* affirm if they are to save their position from collapse. But is there any morally credible reason why NTR should be accepted? Does it not have every appearance of being a desperate expedient – an arbitrary exception to an apparently compelling principle, adopted only because its denial is fatal to theological determinism?

On the view of God as a risk-taker, things become vastly simpler. To quote Helm once again, "the circumstances [of a libertarian free choice] never ensure one determinate freely-chosen outcome; they provide only the conditions for the free choice of one of several outcomes." And since this is the case, it is clearly the human agent and not God who bears responsibility if the choice made is a morally bad one. There are, admittedly, difficult questions still remaining concerning the relationship between God and evil. Why does God permit such vast amounts of evil when he has the power to prevent it? Why doesn't he intervene (or do so more frequently) to stop especially horrendous evils from happening? But free-will theism is completely free from the special problems about responsibility that are incurred by a no-risk view of providence.

5 God's Relation to the World

Let us now place on one side the issue of responsibility and ask instead a more general question. What shall we take God's attitude to be towards the world he has created and the sin and evil it contains? On the no-risk view of providence, we obtain the following answer: *God is entirely pleased with the world exactly as it is; there is no single fact he would wish to alter in any respect.* This may, on first glance, seem somewhat surprising, but the reasoning leading to this conclusion is quite compelling. For consider, on the no-risk view, the situation of God prior to creation, as he is deciding what sort of world to bring into existence.[12] God holds before his mind every possible scenario for world history – all the different "possible worlds," as philosophers say – and selects the very one that he finds most satisfying and most in tune with his creative purposes. Then he proceeds to put that scenario into effect, and of course there is no possibility whatever that the actual result will differ in any respect from that envisioned prior to creation. Since God in his wisdom has selected the "best of all possible worlds" (or one of the best, in case there are several tied for that distinction), he cannot fail to be entirely delighted with the course actually taken by his creation.

There is, to be sure, a small qualification that is needed at this point. We need not suppose that, on the no-risk view, every single fact in the universe is exactly as God would prefer it to be, *if he were to consider that fact in isolation from its context in*

12 Here and elsewhere the temporal language in describing God's decisions as viewed by the no-risk view is a concession to ease of understanding; on this view, God's creative decisions are taken outside the time sequence.

creation as a whole. So it may be that, for instance, some episode of sexual child abuse is not the thing God would most prefer, considered simply as an isolated fact. But of course, God's evaluation of events is *not* as isolated facts, but precisely in the broader context of which they form a part. And considered in the broadest possible context, not only that instance of child abuse but every other crime and atrocity *is exactly what God desires for it to be*.

And this brings us to one of the divine attributes on which the risk-taking and no-risk views differ. The no-risk view is committed to the traditional doctrine of *divine impassibility*, which holds that God is, of necessity, completely free from negative emotions, but lives his life in a continual state of bliss and serenity. Sometimes metaphysical reasons are given for this doctrine, but we are now able to see a rather direct connection between divine impassibility and the basic assumptions of the no-risk theory. Since God has selected exactly the world history he desires, and obtains precisely what he has selected, it would be simply unintelligible to suppose that God experiences aversion, anger, or disappointment over the actual course of events. He has chosen the best, and the best is what happens, so how could he be less than supremely happy with the result?

Nevertheless, the implications of impassibility in this context are deeply troubling. *How can* God be so delighted with the actual course of events, we may ask, in view of the enormity of the evils that continually occur? And what becomes of the biblical teaching that God hates sin, that he is angry with oppressors, and feels compassion for innocent sufferers? "As a father pities his children, so the LORD pities those who fear him" (Ps. 103:13) – are we to understand that this is not, after all, a truthful account of God's mind and heart? Helm recognizes that the Bible presents God's emotional life – the "divine pathos," as it has been termed by Abraham Heschel[13] – in a far different light. If we were to take various biblical statements at face value, he acknowledges, "we should be committed to maintaining that God has a rich, ever-changing emotional life" (p. 51). He takes it for granted that we would not want to maintain this – but the implications of the contrary doctrine of divine impassibility are soul-chilling. Consider, above all, the biblical teaching that the Lord is "not wishing that any should perish, but that all should reach repentance" (2 Peter 3:9). How can this be, when what the Lord truly desires is precisely what actually happens – including the fact that, as Scripture attests, some persons do indeed fail to repent and thus perish everlastingly? The no-risk view has an answer for this, but it is a very troubling answer. The no-risk view distinguishes two different senses of the will of God, sometimes termed the "revealed will" (the will of God as declared in Scripture) and the "will of God's good pleasure" which is the will that determines what actually takes place (see p. 131). So what God actually desires to happen is that some do indeed perish eternally, never reaching the repentance that would open them

13 Heschel writes, "God does not simply command and expect obedience; He is also moved and affected by what happens in the world and he reacts accordingly. Events and human actions arouse in Him joy or sorrow, pleasure or wrath. He is not conceived as judging facts, so to speak, "objectively," in detached impassibility. He reacts in an intimate and subjective manner, and thus determines the value of events" (Abraham J. Heschel, *Between God and Man: An Interpretation of Judaism*, ed. Fritz A. Rothschild (New York: Free Press, 1959), p. 116).

to God's love and forgiveness. But for some reason his revealed will, as portrayed in the Bible, is quite the opposite of this.[14] Readers must decide for themselves whether this is an acceptable answer, one that presents to us the loving God who disclosed himself to us in Jesus.

The view that sees God as a risk-taker rejects the doctrine of impassibility as one that lacks biblical warrant and has no very impressive support from any other quarter. And thereby it is enabled to take seriously the biblical representation of God's emotional involvement with the world he has created. God is described as alternately comforting, indignant, triumphal, furious, grief-stricken, tender, threatening – the range of emotive responses is very wide. We need not deny that there is in these descriptions a measure of anthropomorphism; nevertheless, free-will theism takes them as an essentially truthful rendition of the inner life of God. The acknowledgment of negative emotions in God goes hand in hand with the view of God as a risk-taker. This view is able to take with full seriousness the anger of God against sin and also the ecstatic joy that God experiences when, as in the parable of the Prodigal Son, one of his lost children returns to the fold. In escaping from the dark paradoxes of theological determinism, and freeing us to take seriously the pervasive biblical witness to God's emotional involvement with us, his creatures, the view of God as a risk-taker stakes out a strong claim to being the best and most attractive version of Christian theism.[15]

God Does Not Take Risks

Paul Helm

1 Some Assumptions

The question of whether God takes risks might be understood in at least two ways. It might be taken to be asking whether God chooses to take risks in governing the universe, or whether God of necessity takes risks. I shall answer "No" to both questions, arguing that there is no compelling reason to think that he does, in either sense.

I take it that the risk in question has to do not with mere ignorance, the sort of risk that is involved in guessing the date on the coin in one's pocket, but what might be called "real" risk: namely, that there is a real possibility that the universe might not turn out, or might not be turning out, in the way that God, in governing it, wished

14 Helm points out that the risk-taking view must also distinguish multiple senses of God's will, for evil actions are at least *permitted* by God, and therefore are in some sense willed by him (p. 132). This may be so (though the slide from "permits" to "wills" could be questioned), but it hardly raises the troubling questions that arise from the two-wills doctrine described in the text.

15 For a readily accessible discussion of the view that God is a risk-taker, see Clark Pinnock et al., *The Openness of God: A Biblical Challenge to the Traditional Understanding of God* (Downers Grove, Ill.: InterVarsity Press, 1994). The most extensive presentation to date is John Sanders, *The God Who Risks: A Theology of Divine Providence* (Downers Grove, Ill.: InterVarsity Press, 1998).

or wanted or intended. So the risk in question has an ontological or metaphysical dimension. And further, while it is not strictly implied by the question that God *actually* risks and loses, I shall assume that the question does have that implication.[16] (It is perfectly possible to suppose that God might take risks in making such-and-such an arrangement, but that nothing in that arrangement turns out other than as he wants it to turn out; as when I take a risk in crossing a busy street, but nevertheless cross it safely). And I shall further assume that the governing in question is purposive, means–end governing; a carburetor governs the mixture of air and fuel in an engine, but it does not have any further end in doing so, though carburetors are installed by engineers to achieve such further ends.

So the divine governing in question is purposive, and is also for the most part what I shall call "positive government." Positive government is government in which the governor brings about whatever he governs. Finally, I assume that the risks in question have a certain significance or importance.[17]

A person might govern a situation simply by frustrating any event that he does not want to occur, like a bouncer outside a night-club. On this model, God would certainly be said to govern the universe, to be "in control," if he adopted such a strategy with respect to all events as they unfold. Let us call such modes of government – no doubt there are many sub-varieties – "negative government."[18]

Even given a strong, libertarian sense of freedom, many have argued that perfect divine foreknowledge, divine omniscience as it relates to what is future, eliminates risk, because God knows beforehand what will occur. Such foreknowledge would be sufficient to eliminate mere epistemic risk, of course, but the universe might nevertheless turn out in important respects other than God intended, and so have been risky to create – risky, but without surprise for God. But I will not argue thus here. Instead I shall agree with my interlocutor William Hasker that divine foreknowledge is incompatible with human freedom.[19] Further, I shall agree with Hasker that even if God did possess simple foreknowledge, foreknowledge that embraces all actual free choices, this by itself has no bearing on our understanding of divine providence.[20]

16 This, of course, assumes that God is passible, but I shall not discuss that issue here any more than I shall discuss the implications of the divine upholding of the universe for the "risk" view.

17 It would be difficult, if not presumptuous, to say what is or is not significant or important to God. But if, say, the exact arrangement of molecules in some lump of coal is not significant or important for him, and if there are structures and mechanisms which, independently of anything else that is important for God, determine the arrangement of molecules in that lump of coal, then the working of those structures and mechanisms need not be subject to the positive government of God.

18 For a further exploration of some of these issues, see Nelson Pike, "Overpower and God's Responsibility for Sin," in Alfred J. Freddoso (ed.), *The Existence and Nature of God* (Notre Dame, Ind.: University of Notre Dame Press, 1983).

19 Though in fact I have doubts about the incompatibility of divine foreknowledge and indeterministic freedom, I will not pursue them here. For Hasker's position see Pinnock, et al., *Openness of God*, p. 147. His view is given at greater length in Hasker, *God, Time, and Knowledge*.

20 Pinnock et al., *Openness of God*, p. 149, and Hasker, *God, Time and Knowledge*, ch. 3. See also John Sanders, "Why Simple Foreknowledge Offers No More Providential Control than the Openness of God," *Faith and Philosophy*, 14/1 (January 1997), pp. 26–40. Hasker says that simple foreknowledge is "useless." This is so if such foreknowledge embraces all free actions (Hasker, *God, Time, and Knowledge*, p. 55). If it includes only some free actions, then it is far from useless, for in the light of this information God could bring about certain other events.

Some have argued that a no-risk sense of divine governing can be held consistently with libertarian free will by appealing to God's middle knowledge, but as I further agree with Hasker that middle knowledge faces difficulties that render it implausible, I shall not rehearse these points here either.[21]

So in what follows I explore the idea of the divine governing of the universe, assuming that these mediating positions, the claim that the foreknowledge of God is compatible with human indeterministic freedom and middle knowledge, are not available, and accepting the uselessness of simple foreknowledge.

It is of course very difficult, if not impossible, to argue convincingly for any philosophical thesis *ab initio*. Furthermore, in the space of a short essay it is not possible to offer plausible versions of the entire assemblage of convictions, observations, and arguments that might support a negative answer to the question. I shall be satisfied – I shall have to be satisfied – if a negative answer to the question can be made plausible, and I shall try to do this in a number of ways: first, by claiming that there is an initial presumption in its favor; then by attempting to clarify the position against misunderstanding and to rebut a number of objections to it, one central objection in particular; and finally by raising a difficulty for the opposing view.

2 The Presumption of Omnipotence and Omniscience

My positive philosophical argument for the presumption that God does not take risks in governing the universe derives from the ideas of divine omnipotence and omniscience. We may distinguish between the connotation and denotation (or between the sense and reference) of expressions such as "an omniscient being" or "an omnipotent being." For ease, and because it figures more centrally in the issue of divine control than does omniscience, let us chiefly consider omnipotence, while not ignoring omniscience altogether. And let us assume, fairly uncontroversially in present circumstances, that the denotation of "an omnipotent being" is God alone.

The connotation of omnipotence, "having unlimited or very great power, force or influence" (*Shorter Oxford Dictionary*), may also seem uncontroversial. If God is omnipotent, then he has such unlimited or very great power. But (as is well known) matters become more difficult when we inquire more precisely into the connotation of omnipotence. What exactly are the limits which omnipotence does not have, and what are the very great powers that an omnipotent being possesses? For example, is what God can do "limited" by the laws of logic, or by the character of moral principles or laws, or even by his own nature? Can God make it, by an act of his power, that 2 + 2 = 5, or that adultery is morally permissible? Two people may each agree that God alone is omnipotent, but disagree on the connotation of the term. Thus while Thomas Aquinas believed that the power of God was subject to the laws of logic, René Descartes thought otherwise. So there is philosophical disagreement among major philosophers about the connotation of "omnipotence" as this applies to God. Similarly with omniscience. Omniscience might be defined as the

21 Pinnock et al., *Openness of God*, pp. 143f, and Hasker, *God, Time, and Knowledge*, ch. 2.

knowledge of all truths, but omniscience is limited by what it is possible for God to know, and some have argued that it is not possible for God to know the future, since there is no future to know (though God could, presumably, have *beliefs* about the future), and that it is not possible for him to know what it is like to be a bat, or what I am doing now.

So there is scope for disagreement about the precise connotation of "omnipotence" and "omniscience." However, it seems a reasonable principle, in reflecting upon the concept of God in philosophical fashion, that *the connotation of "omni" terms, terms such as "omnipotent" and "omniscient," should, when applied to God, be as wide in their connotation as possible* (Principle A). Thus the term "omnipotent" is more appropriately applied to God when it connotes power over more types of actions and events. Further, the term is more appropriately applied to God when it connotes the power over more tokens of each type of action over which power is exercised than power over fewer such tokens. And similarly with the scope of omniscience. After all, the rationale for employing such "omni" terms of God is to convey the idea of maximality, and so it must be reasonable not to limit their application unnecessarily; otherwise the danger is that such terms when applied to God come to possess only rhetorical or hyperbolical value. The presumption must be, therefore, with respect to any type of event and to any token of that type, that an omnipotent being has power over them in the sense that he positively governs them, and that an omniscient being knows the truths that are the correct descriptions of all such actions or is directly acquainted with the relevant states of affairs. Of course, omnipotence and omniscience may be said to extend further than power and knowledge over what is the case; they extend to possibilities, though in rather different senses. An omniscient being knows not only all actualities but the contents of all possible worlds, while an omnipotent being has power over possibilities, power to prevent or to actualize them, though whether he can actualize just any possible world is also controversial.

So I am claiming that wherever possible one should interpret the terms "omniscience" and "omnipotence," when applied to God, as generously as possible, pushing their connotation as far as one can, unless there are overriding reasons not to do so. It seems clear that there is such an overriding reason in the case of the laws of logic, for such laws mark the bounds of the possible, and one simply misunderstands the scope of divine power rather than pays respect to it if one says that God can do the logically impossible, though it is very difficult to argue for this position decisively, and obviously Descartes would not agree. Matters are less clear in the case of God"s power over moral principles, as the popularity of the divine command theory of ethics shows. There is controversy over whether one can integrate the idea of divine command ethics with our intuitions about the necessity or overridingness of certain moral principles. And parallel problems arise over whether God has power over the past.

In the case of God's government of the universe, we are clearly concerned primarily with an aspect of his omnipotence: namely, with the question of the extent of God's positive government. Given Principle A, it is a priori desirable that divine positive government should extend to as many facets of the universe as possible, and undesirable that God merely negatively govern the universe he has created. For an omnipotent being who positively governs the universe is exercising greater power than an "omnipotent" being who chooses to govern aspects of it negatively, who in turn exercises greater power than an "omnipotent" being who for many event types and many event tokens provides only necessary conditions for their occurrence.

Let us call the understanding of omnipotence which thinks of its connotation as positively governing as many events, including human acts, as possible, the *strong* sense of this term; anything less than this, the *weak* sense(s). And let us similarly understand strong omniscience as that degree of knowledge which encompasses all events, past, present, and future. Strong omnipotence entails strong omniscience, and indeed requires it, but not vice versa. My argument is that the ascription to God of strong omnipotence and omniscience, as part of ascribing perfection to God's nature, creates a presumption in favor of the no-risk view of divine government; but no more than a presumption.[22]

If God is essentially strongly omnipotent – if strong omnipotence is a part of his nature – then the presumption must be that of necessity he takes no risks. And *a fortiori* that he cannot choose to take risks.

But are not essential strong omnipotence and essential strong omniscience inconsistent with other essential features of God's character: notably, his goodness as expressed in his perfectly righteous and holy moral character? If God positively governs as many events that occur as possible, if he enjoys large degrees of positive government together with much negative government of the universe, then surely he is implicated in the fact of evil, and his essential goodness or righteousness is compromised?

Many argue that it is possible to preserve the divine righteousness by postulating a class of actions which God cannot possibly positively govern: namely, indeterministically free actions. The occurrence of such actions is compatible with strong essential omnipotence, but it follows that there are many types of human action which engender risk for God (assuming, as stated, that middle knowledge is not an option). These actions entail risk for God in the sense that, as a result of the exercise of such freedom, the world might not be as God intended it to be and so (maintaining our assumption of the incompatibility of divine omniscience and human freedom) entail surprise for God. But I wish to argue that such a move is not necessary for this purpose, since the divine righteousness can be preserved in another way.

Let us suppose (what is not too difficult) that some human acts are evil. Could such evil actions as these be positively governed by an essentially righteous God? My answer is that I do not believe that they could be. Here is another point at which it is necessary to safeguard the idea of omnipotence against misunderstanding. God is omnipotent, essentially strongly omnipotent (as I have argued), but this does not mean that he is the author of evil. The occurrence of evil is, nevertheless, compatible with essential strong omnipotence, because, thus understood, God *could not* positively govern evil acts. So God is essentially strongly omnipotent in the sense that he posi-

22 As I shall endeavor to discuss the issue of whether or not God's control of his creation may be risk-free without discussing the issue of human freedom directly, I shall not avail myself of Hasker's own understanding of risk. According to him, a decision is risky for God when it is one that depends for its outcome on the response of free creatures in which the decision is not informed by knowledge of the outcome (*God, Time, and Knowledge*, p. 197).

tively governs all events except those the positive government of which is inconsistent with his essential righteousness.

3 Willing Permission

But does this mean that a deity who cannot positively govern evil takes risks? I do not think so. For there is at least one way of safeguarding the risk-free-less control in the case of God's government of human actions which are morally evil: namely, the idea of God *willingly permitting* particular evil actions. Such permission is not compatible with positive government as I have characterized it, but it is consistent with risklessness. God does not and cannot will such evil actions, but he may nevertheless be willing for them to occur. But is not anyone who is willing for an evil action to occur the cause of that action, or at least an accessory, and so himself evil? I wish to present two alternative arguments for thinking not. But first, before we look at these arguments, it is necessary to get clearer about the meaning of willing permission.

God positively governs acts which are not evil. How exactly he does this raises other questions which we cannot address in detail, though some brief comments follow later; he governs all other acts, evil acts, by permitting them, since he cannot positively govern them. However, if such permission is to be consistent with the absence of risk, then it has to be a particular kind of permission of particular actions; the willing permission governs particular action tokens.[23]

Such an idea of permission may appear to be an exception to essential strong omnipotence as I have defined it, for the idea of permission introduces an element of conditionality. But since God must permit evil if there is evil, such permission cannot in fact be an exception. So a God who is essentially strongly omnipotent positively governs all acts which occur except those which are evil, and he negatively governs evil acts by willingly permitting them.

So one may make sense of the idea of divine permission in a way that is compatible with risk-free-ness if one is prepared to maintain that there are types of actions which God can prevent but which he nevertheless cannot cause, even though he may be willing for them to occur. Then God can only control an evil action by willingly permitting it, by deciding not to prevent it; and the evil action occurs because it is caused by the natures and circumstances of those who perpetrate it, but not by God (because God cannot cause it), though willingly permitted by God (because though he cannot cause it, he can willingly permit it, and does so (we might presume) as a necessary component part of some broader overall will). One is still left with the questions of exactly why God willingly permitted evil and of exactly *how* evil comes about in a world created by an all-good God. But these questions, surely among the most fundamental of all theological questions, have to be faced by other accounts of God's relation to evil.

23 There are problems about the individuation of actions, and the relation of an action's description to its identity is important. I shall assume that these difficulties can be overcome and that it is possible for an act to have more than one individuating description.

So God may willingly permit an evil act; indeed, since God cannot perform an evil act, if an evil act occurs, he must have willingly permitted it, and only permitted it, and if his government of that action is risk-free, necessarily willingly permitted it.[24] The nature of such permission is well expressed by Augustine:

> In a way unspeakably strange and wonderful, even what is done in opposition to His will does not defeat His will. For it would not be done did he not permit it (and of course His permission is not unwilling but willing); nor would a Good Being permit evil to be done only that in his omnipotence He can turn evil into good.[25]

So for X willingly to permit an action A is at least this: for A to be the action of someone other than X, for X to foreknow the occurrence of A and to have been able to prevent A, and for A not to be against X's plan. So on this conception God foreknows everything, and unconditionally governs everything, but does not causally determine everything in the sense that he is the efficient cause of everything. Nevertheless, nothing happens that God is unwilling should happen.

But it may still be insisted – somewhat implausibly, it seems to me – that if God willingly permits X, then God is the cause of X. So let us now consider a number of arguments against the claim that if God willingly permits the occurrence of an action, then he is the cause of that action.[26]

4 Objections

First, the claim that an appeal to divine willing in the sense defined is a case of divine determinism. It is tempting, but I believe crude and misleading, to assimilate the working of such permission to intramundane models of causation, and particularly to general physical determinism. Such willing permission has this in common with determinism: that what is physically determined and what is willingly permitted will each, in virtue of the determinism and the occurrence of what is willingly permitted, come to pass. However, willingly to permit an action is not to cause that action; it is to provide a necessary, but not sufficient, causal condition for the action. Whereas physical determinism has a strong tendency to be reductionist and has difficulty in finding a place for a range of objects having their own causal powers, the divine willing permission is most certainly not reductionist in this sense.

So it is a serious mistake to suppose that classical Christian theism claims that God monopolizes power.[27] "As He is the Creator of all natures, so is He of all powers: but not the giver of all wills; for wicked wills are not of Him, being against that nature which is of Him."[28]

24 It may be said that God suffers loss in the case of any action that is evil – for example, he suffers the loss of being disobeyed – but he does not suffer loss as a result of only taking a risk.

25 Augustine, *Enchiridion*, tr. J. F. Shaw (Chicago: Henry Regnery, 1961), p. 117. See also pp. 33 and 110.

26 God is, of course, an accessory to the evil. But as God is an accessory to evil in many other accounts of God's relation to evil – for example, the Free-Will Defense – and as being an accessory is (in any case) a legal term of art, this hardly amounts to a serious objection.

27 Pinnock et al., *Openness of God*, p. 113.

28 Augustine, *City of God*, tr. John Healey, book V, ch. 9 (London: Dent, 1945).

God is the source of all creaturely power, but the powers of creatures, even when efficaciously empowered by God, are really theirs, and so are distinct from his. If God efficaciously empowers me to type this essay, still the typing of this paper is my action, not God's. The wicked men who crucified Jesus were the cause of his death, even though he was crucified by the determinate counsel and foreknowledge of God (Acts 2:23).

One way of expressing this difference might be as follows. While it seems clear that intramundane causation is transitive, that if (where A, B, and C are events) A causes B, and B causes C, then A causes C, there is no necessary transitivity in the case of any causal aspects or features of the divine willing permission, if there are any.[29] It is not necessarily the case that if God governs by willingly permitting some event B, and B causes C, then God causes C; rather, God may will by permitting that B causes C and so willingly permit C. God's willing permission is thus not a straightforward case of causation, and those who seek to assimilate God's willing permission of evil to the actions of someone manipulating a puppet, or to hypnotism, or to brainwashing or programming, have not recognized the true character of such permission.

Alternatively, one may allow that while God is the primary cause of all events that occur, even of all evil acts, he is not, and cannot be, the secondary cause of any evil act, because he is not the secondary cause of any act. But this requirement as it stands is almost certainly too strong; it seems to have the deistic consequence that God cannot directly act in the world that he has created. It may be modified to allow that God is the secondary cause of some acts. This is consistent with his being the secondary cause of morally indifferent acts and of morally good acts. The exact scope of what God causes and what he permits does not matter here, provided that we are clear that he cannot cause evil.

So those who hold that God governs whatever comes to pass may nevertheless make a distinction, within that overall government, between what God causes and what he permits. William Hasker says that the central idea of Calvinism is quite simple: "everything that happens, with no exceptions, is efficaciously determined by God in accordance with his eternal decrees."[30] This is not the place to comment on whether Hasker is accurate in what he says about Calvinism, but we have seen, I hope, that there is reason to doubt that it need be, as Hasker says, the central idea of Calvinism without surrendering risk-free government. To say that everything is risk-freely governed by God is not to say that everything is efficaciously determined by God.

So there are ways of preserving the integrity of divine righteousness in the case of human acts which are morally evil: namely, the idea of God willingly permitting particular evil actions, in the sense understood.

So it is possible that God risk-freely governs whatever comes to pass, and plausible (if God is omnipotent and omniscient) to suppose that he does so. If, for any event E, E occurs, then God risk-freely governs E either by bringing it about or being

29 There are presumably some causal features if wicked people are upheld and conserved in being by God.

30 Pinnock et al., *Openness of God*, p. 141.

willing for it to occur. Whatever occurs, occurs because God risk-freely governs it in this sense; whatever is true in virtue of what occurs is true because God so governs it. So to say that all events are risk-freely governed by God, while it entails that all events are *intended* by God, is not equivalent to asserting that, for any event E, if E occurs, then God has *caused* it.

Just as many argue, in developing a free-will defense, that not even God can ensure that a free agent does only what is morally right, so I argue that there is no possible world in which the righteous God can be the author of evil. He may, however, willingly permit evil – that is, actualize that possible world in which he foreknows that Jones will do a particular evil act.[31] This is an instance of *particular* permission; God permits particular acts, as distinct from giving *general* permission, as when a teacher permits a class to write an essay on any topic they choose. And God may do so willingly, not because he is willing for the evil act to occur *per se*, but because he ordains some wider good of which that act is a necessary part. The willing permission of evil may in many cases be like the willingness of a parent to allow one of her children to undergo some extremely painful, but necessary, course of treatment (say the removal of a vital organ) to ensure the survival of another of her children by transplanting the removed organ into that child. And God may willingly permit such a particular action, for some further good, though of course without any of the feelings of psychological pressure or tension that accompany such human permittings.

So does it follow from such willing permission of evil that the universe is in every detail as God intends it to be?[32] This is an interesting question, but unclear as it stands. There is no reason to think that God intends the details of the universe separately; there is one divine will, which encompasses all events. It would be fallacious to suppose that the divine attitude is the same with respect to every detail; for one thing, as we have already seen, God is the efficacious cause of some events and willingly permits others.

As Aquinas put it, "God, and nature, and indeed every causal agent, does what is best overall, but not what is best in every part, except when the part is regarded in its relationship to the whole."[33] Those events which God permits he does so in furtherance of some wider consideration with respect to which they are a logically necessary condition. And likewise, some of those things which he causes are means to some further end. It is a fallacy to think that because some arrangement is wise, every detail of that arrangement considered in isolation is wise. It does not follow that every thread of my tartan tie is tartan.

A second objection is that this view is a species of fatalism. But it is certainly not logical fatalism, since the universe is the outcome not of some principle of logic alone, but of the divine creative and providential will which, we may assume, is logically contingent.

31 Such foreknowledge cannot be a case of middle knowledge, since I have earlier gone along with Hasker in rejecting middle knowledge. This fact may, of course, be thought to have implications for the sort of freedom that Jones may have in choosing to do evil.

32 This issue is raised by Keith Ward, *Religion and Creation* (Oxford: Clarendon Press, 1996), p. 219.

33 Aquinas, *Summa Theologiae*, I, 48, 2, reply 3.

A third objection is that on such a view God cannot be responsive to what occurs in the universe, and hence the position entails some version of deism.

Among the aspects of the one creative and providential will of God it is possible to distinguish those aspects that are unconditional or unilateral from those that are conditional and bilateral. Unconditional aspects are of the form "Let X be," whereas conditional aspects are of the form "Given W, let X be" (where W is brought about by someone other than the utterer of the statement). An example of the first might be "Let the planet Earth be"; an example of the second, "If A sins, let him be forgiven." However, we must interpret these conditional expressions in the light of the place of conditions in the overall will of God.

There are two logically separable aspects: God foreknows what will happen in certain circumstances unless he prevents it happening, and in the case of some evil he wills that it should be permitted to happen. There is, nevertheless, an element of necessary conditionality about God's willing permission of such evil, since necessarily he is not the author of it. Nonetheless, as Creator he upholds the perpetrator of evil and willingly permits the occurrence of the evil. So the way to understand such conditional aspects of God's overall willing is not as God's response to what he has merely foreseen will happen, but as his response to what he has both foreseen and been willing to permit – say, that A will sin. That is, God wills to permit the evil and wills the consequence. He wills evil by willing to permit it, willing it in such a way that he is not himself the author of evil, which he could not be, while he may will what is not evil by being the author of it, by bringing it about. There is a crucial distinction between a willing of conditionals and a conditional will. God may know all truths infallibly, including all conditional truths, as well as know what his response to the antecedents of some of these conditional truths is. But it does not follow from this that his knowledge is conditional knowledge in a temporal sense. God's knowledge that C will happen if A does B does not depend upon him first knowing the conditional "If A does B, then C will happen" and then deciding that because A does B, he will bring about C.

5 An Obstacle to the Risk View

In bringing this discussion to a close, I wish briefly to turn attention to the risk view, and to attempt to strengthen my case by considering one weakness of riskiness. The risk view at first glance appears to offer gain in our understanding of petitionary prayer and prophecy. For God takes risks by permitting autonomous human actions, including the autonomous actions of those who pray and prophesy. He cannot know what a person will pray for, and may adjust his purposes in the light of her prayers; for is not this precisely what an account of petitionary prayer requires, that God may change his mind?

But the central place that the risk view gives to human autonomy in its account of prayer comes back to haunt this view. God's will may be changed by prayer, but what God can in turn change in answer to prayer is limited. It would seem that God cannot answer, say, a prayer for the conversion of another person by bringing about her conversion, because to do so would be to compromise the freedom of that person; in fact, according to this view, God will never, or only rarely, answer any prayer that will trespass on the freedom of his creatures.[34]

Prophecy is in the same position. God cannot foretell anything that requires him to change a human will in order for what he foretells to certainly come about. However, the risk view takes the greatest risk if it seeks to combine such a view of prophecy with a high view of divine revelation. For any revelation involving people is (presumably) the result of the agency of those people. How can a Christian believer be sure that the Scriptures that we possess accurately express the will of God? How can we be sure that autonomous human agency has complied with what God wishes to reveal? Perhaps God has made several attempts to convey his will accurately, only to be frustrated by the perversities of human freedom, and what we possess is only the latest and best such attempt; or perhaps it is worse than some earlier attempt. Perhaps the dunes and caves of the Middle East are littered with earlier versions. How, then, could we ever be sure, on the risk view, that we have the word of God?

Reply to Helm

I agree with Paul Helm that divine omnipotence should not be limited in such a way that it possesses "only rhetorical or hyperbolical value." But this is hardly a forceful objection to the view of God as a risk-taker, because *the risk and no-risk views can endorse precisely the same conception of divine omnipotence.* I showed this in my essay with regard to my favored definition of omnipotence, and Helm has done the same with regard to his own conception, that of "essential strong omnipotence." According to essential strong omnipotence, God's essential nature is such that he "positively governs as many events, including human acts, as possible." Helm rightly asserts that this is compatible with the risk-taking view, because indeterministically free actions cannot possibly be "positively governed" by God.[35]

Somewhat surprisingly, then, there *is no difference* between the risk and no-risk views in their conception of divine omnipotence. Where the difference arises is over how God has chosen to *use* his omnipotence. Has he created a world in which God alone unilaterally determines everything that comes to pass, or one in which there are genuinely free creatures that make their own contribution to the course of events?

34 As David Basinger puts the point, "A key assumption in the open model (viz. the risk model) is that God so values the inherent integrity of significant human freedom – the ability of individuals to maintain control over significant aspects of their lives – that he will not as a general rule force his created moral agents to perform actions that they do not freely desire to perform or manipulate the natural environment in such a way that their freedom of choice is destroyed" (in Pinnock et al., *Openness of God*, pp. 160–1). The use of the word 'force' here betrays misunderstanding of the no-risk position.

35 I should state here that I am not at this point prepared to fully endorse essential strong omnipotence, or to adopt it as my own conception of omnipotence. But what is important at this juncture is that this conception is, as Helm recognizes, compatible with the risk-taking view of God.

I've said a good deal about this in my essay, and in view of space limitations I will now refer the reader to those earlier remarks.

What really surprises me about Helm's essay is his reluctance to admit that, on his view, God is the cause of sinful human actions. I agree, of course, that on this view God is not the *direct and immediate* cause of sinful acts, and I acknowledged as much in my essay. It is also true that, in general, *permitting* an event to occur is not the same as *causing* that event. But I have to say that this talk of "permission" is somewhat evasive, in that it ignores a crucial aspect of the situation. As I stated in my essay, on the no-risk view, *God himself is the sufficient cause of all events, including sinful human actions, in that he deliberately and without constraint establishes the causal conditions that of necessity lead to these events and actions.* How can Helm deny this? He clearly rejects the indeterministic, or libertarian, view of human free will that would interrupt the causal chain between God's actions and human sinning. Possibly he accepts that there are physically undetermined events on the micro-level, as posited by modern physics. But if these "chance events" make a significant difference in the outcomes, God will have to control them; otherwise they bring with them the very risk that Helm is anxious to avoid. And if they don't make a significant difference, then for all practical purposes we are back to a straightforward theological determinism. Helm doesn't like that term, and I would agree that "divine determinism" is not the same thing as physical determinism. The problem, however, lies not in the terminology but in the doctrine itself, which does have the unavoidable implication that God is the ultimate cause of sinful actions.[36]

In closing, I will address one aspect of the "obstacle to the risk view" with which Helm concludes his paper. He asks, "How, then, could we ever be sure, on the risk view, that we have the word of God?" Part of what Helm is implying here is correct. It is quite true that a revelation given through human beings will involve the minds and wills of those human beings. And we do not suppose that God "takes over" the prophets in such a way that their own personalities are negated or suspended. But does this mean that God is unable to insure that his message is communicated adequately? I think not. Let me suggest an analogy. A recovering alcoholic prays to God for help, and as a result of divine assistance he abstains from taking a drink under circumstances in which, given only his own natural desires and dispositions, he would have succumbed. Has God trampled under foot the free will of this man? Assuredly not, for in praying for assistance, the man has invited God to intervene, overcoming if necessary the man's own desire for drink in order to enable him to live a better life. But now consider the prophet Isaiah, who in accepting God's call, said "Here I am, send me" (Isaiah 6:8). In saying this, he surely expressed a willingness to go where God wanted him to go, and to say what God wanted him to say, even if doing so would "go against the grain" of Isaiah's own natural desires in certain situations. And having been thus invited, God in no way violates Isaiah's freedom or integrity if he works in Isaiah's mind and heart in such a way as to insure that his message is truthfully conveyed.

36 Here I would remind readers of Helm's own assertion that his view "does not, in the final analysis, attribute certain evils to the human will and certain others to natural causes; rather, all are finally attributed to the divine reason and will" (*Providence of God*, p. 198).

There is a larger message we can take from this: God, who has granted to his creatures the priceless gift of freedom, is by no means resourceless in dealing with the problems that such freedom presents. We can trust God to take risks; he is able to handle them.

Reply to Hasker

Hasker's arguments against the no-risk position seem to me to raise an important question about our language about God, or rather to presuppose one definite answer to that question.

In talking about God, and particularly about God's relation to the world, we are talking about a situation which is unparalleled. We have no direct experience of such a relation, but only of relations between created things. Our language about God's causal powers must be qualified, therefore. Thus it is misleading to assimilate the working of the divine decree as understood by a no-risk position to ordinary instances of causation. We need always to bear in mind the words of Nicolas Malebranche, "God is a mind, or spirit, He thinks, He wills; but let us not humanise Him – He does not think or will as we do."[37]

This is not an appeal to semantic fuzz, as I show by the remarks on causal transitivity in my essay. To underline the point further, both Hasker and I have taken it for granted that divine foreknowledge is incompatible with indeterministic human freedom. It follows from this that if God infallibly knows the future, then no free act is indeterministic. But it does not follow from this, without further argument, that such a divine foreknowledge is the *cause* of the action foreknown. Failing a convincing argument of this kind, we might say that foreknowledge ensures the occurrence of the action in question without causing it. And this is similar to what I am claiming on behalf of the no-risk view, that God ensures that every event occurs without causing (in the ordinary sense) every event.

So words like "cause" or "decree" or "permit," when used of God the uncreated cause, are used in rather different ways, with rather different logical implications, from those in which our ordinary notions of cause are used. By contrast, Hasker is happy to use as arguments thought experiments in which a strong parallel is drawn between human and divine causation. Behind these arguments lies a commitment to a fairly literalist understanding of biblical language about God. Because the exchange between Hasker and myself is primarily philosophical, it does not seem appropriate to attempt to show here that such biblical data are consistent with a no-risk view, but there is some reason to think that this can be done,[38] and that plausible alternative interpretations of these and other scriptural data can be offered.

37 Nicolas Malebranche, *The Search after Truth*, 3. 2. 9, tr. T. M. Lennon and P. J. Olscamp (Columbus: Ohio State University Press, 1980), p. 251.

38 See, e.g., Paul Helm, "God in Dialogue," in. A. N. S. Lane (ed.), *Interpreting the Bible* (Leicester: Apollos, 1997), pp. 223–40.

It needs to be emphasized that to suppose that divine causation must be analogically related to ordinary causation between events is a perfectly general point about divine causation, and is not a case of special pleading on behalf of a no-risk position. For all theists, including Hasker, are faced with the problem of characterizing in a philosophically adequate manner the unparalleled causal feats of God's creation of the universe *ex nihilo*, and of his conserving his creation in existence by upholding what he has created. It is hard to see that these are cases of ordinary causation, even supposing that we understand what ordinary causation is.

On the question of the transfer of responsibility, if it is plausible (as Hasker argues) to suppose a transfer of responsibility on the no-risk view (and it can hardly be denied that on this view God bears some responsibility for evil[39]), it is equally plausible to suppose such a transfer on the risk view, in accordance with the following principle, RTR: if an agent A deliberately and knowingly supports agent B in a situation in which B avoidably performs some morally wrong act which A could have prevented, then some of the moral responsibility for that act is transferred from B to A.

I turn finally to make a brief comment on one particular criticism of Hasker's, his strictures on the idea of God having two wills: a will whereby he commands certain things and forbids others and the will of his decree. Hasker is troubled by this, but his own view seems to be committed to something very similar. For if God's upholding of the creation from moment to moment is a case of his willing that the creation continues to exist (as seems plausible), then on the risk view God wills that evil people continue their evil while at the same time commanding them not to do so.

39 Incidentally, such a possibility is explicitly envisaged in Helm, *Providence of God*, p. 177; so the no-risk view is not necessarily committed to Hasker's NTR principle.

Does God Respond to Petitionary Prayer?

It is clear that petitionary prayer can have many benefits – it can impact on the one praying and on the person prayed for, if she is aware of it. But does prayer have an effect on what God does? The common religious view is that it does. Prayer can prompt God to perform actions that God would not otherwise have performed. In the following debate, Michael Murray defends the common view by arguing that there are goods that God can attain only by acting in response to prayer. David Basinger rejects the common view, arguing that God would not give what is bad for us even if we ask for it, and that God would not make our petitioning a necessary condition for giving us what we actually need.

God Responds to Prayer

Michael J. Murray

The belief that God responds to prayer is widespread. According to a recent *Newsweek* survey, 87 percent of Americans said that they believe that God answers prayers. In fact, they believe so heartily in the efficacy of prayer that nearly one-third of those polled said that they prayed to God more than once a day. What is even more interesting about this belief among ordinary Americans is that it has been denied by so many theologians. One might think such denials would be found only among contemporary liberal theologians who deny that miracles are possible or that God would deign to interfere in human affairs. But in fact, such denials can be found in the writings of the founding fathers of many religious traditions. Of course, these theologians do not thereby deny that prayer is important or meaningful. Instead, they argue that it is meaningful because it brings about certain internal, psychological benefits for the petitioner.

But why, one might wonder, would these traditional theologians deny the popularly held belief that petitionary prayer is efficacious, not only in the sense that it affects the heart of the petitioner, but also in the sense that it moves God to act? The reason is, in fact, quite straightforward. If God were perfectly good, he would want to provide us with any good that would improve our true well-being and, further, would deny us anything that would detract from our well-being. Thus, if one prays for something that it would be truly good to have, a perfectly good God would have already intended to give that good thing, whether it was prayed for or not. Likewise, if the thing prayed for is not good for us, God would not give it to us regardless.

However, this argument stands in tension not only with overwhelming popular opinion, but with the claims of central texts of the major Western religious traditions – texts which resoundingly affirm the efficacy of prayer.

The argument offered in short fashion above against the efficacy of prayer is a powerful one, and unless we can find some way to circumvent it, the traditional teaching that God does answer prayer seems to run the risk of making traditional religious belief incoherent. So, our question is, can it be circumvented? I will argue that it can. In order to show this, I will begin, in section 1, by tracing out the argument against the claim that God responds to prayer with greater care. In section 2, I will look at what must be shown in order to defeat the argument. In sections 3–5, I will offer a number of reasons for thinking that the argument is in fact defeated. And finally, in section 6 I will look at some global objections that can and have been raised against the reasons offered in sections 3–5.

1 The Argument against the Claim that God Responds to Prayer

The argument goes like this:

1 A perfectly good being will seek to maximize the true goods of each individual to the extent that (a) doing so is possible for such a being, and (b) doing so does not preclude the provision of equal or greater goods to others. (definition)
2 God can be said to respond to petitionary prayer if and only if God provides the petitioner with what is asked for and would not have done so otherwise. (definition)
3 If what is requested would be good for the petitioner, then God, being perfectly good, would provide what is asked for even without being asked, if it is logically possible for him to do so, and if doing so does not preclude provision of equal or greater goods to others. (from 1)
4 If what is requested is not good for the petitioner, then a perfectly good being would not give it, even though it has been asked for. (from 1)

5 It is never the case that God provides the petitioner with something which was asked for and which would not have been provided without the petition. (from 3 and 4)

6 Thus, God does not respond to petitionary prayer. (from 2 and 5)

2 Strategies for Defeating the Argument

There are some troubles with the argument in section 1. The first is that it is invalid, since (5) does not follow from (3) and (4). The reason is clear once we take a closer look at (4). The words "not good" in (4) either mean "bad" or "either bad or indifferent." If the former, then (5) does not follow, since it could be that some things petitioned for are, in the end, simply indifferent for the one making the petition. Such things, we might suppose, are the sorts of things that God might be willing to provide if asked, but not otherwise. Since they are "discretionary," there is nothing in God's goodness that requires that he give such a thing. And since they are not bad either, there is nothing in his goodness that prevents them being given. If, however, "not good" means "either bad or indifferent," then (4) is simply false, because there is no reason to think that God would be obliged to provide indifferent things if not asked.

But while this is a problem, it is a minor one. Religious people believe that prayer is important not just when it comes to the insignificant "little extras." In fact, many believe that prayers for trifling things are the very prayers God does not answer (as evidenced by the fact that a majority of respondents in the *Newsweek* poll do not believe that God answers prayers regarding the winning of sporting events!). Rather, religious believers usually hold that prayer is most important when it comes to the most serious events we face in life, even matters of life and death. Surely it cannot be true that such things are always indifferent for us. That is, religious people seem to believe that prayer is efficacious not just for the discretionary things, but that it is efficacious for the "big things" as well. And this argument, one might think, at least shows that this is false.

Thus, we might reformulate the argument so that it provides a less stunning, but still troubling, conclusion by changing (5) and (6) to read as follows:

5* It is never the case that God provides the petitioner with something which (a) was asked for, (b) is either good for the petitioner to have or bad for the petitioner to have, and (c) which would not have been provided even without the petition. (from 3 and 4)

6* Thus, if God responds to petitionary prayer, it is only in cases that concern provisions which are neither good nor bad for the petitioner. (from 2 and 5*)

However, this revised argument faces further problems. Premise 3 is supposed to follow from (1). While (1) is controversial in a number of respects, the problem I would like to note here is that (3) simply does not follow from (1). To see why, consider a certain good: say, relief from physical pain. Imagine that during her workout, Olympic athlete Gail Devers has a mild cramp in her leg. The coach knows that if she were to stop practicing immediately, the pain would go away. But he also knows that she needs to complete this regimen in order to be in good enough shape to compete at the time trials. According to (3), if the coach is good, he is required to stop the practice, since doing so will yield a good for Ms Devers: namely, relieving the mild pain she is experiencing.

Clearly nothing about the notion of perfect goodness requires the coach to do that. In fact, we might imagine Ms Devers being quite angry at his order to stop practicing, recognizing that relieving this bit of suffering now will likely deprive her of a very great good she wants even more than she wants relief from this momentary pain.

Premise 3 as it stands is false, then, since it requires that a good being will bring about goods even if doing so will preclude the possibility of outweighing goods in the future; and this claim is clearly false. Thus, the argument needs a replacement for (3) that is true and follows from (1). I suggest:

3* If what is requested would be good for the petitioner, then God, being perfectly good, would provide what is asked for even without being asked, if (a) it is logically possible for him to do so, and (b) doing so does not preclude provision of equal or greater goods to others, *and, (c) doing so does not preclude God's securing future outweighing goods for the petitioner.* (from 1)

Of course, once we replace (3) with (3*), the argument is again invalid, since (5*) does not follow from (3*) and (4). What does follow from (3*) and (4) is this:

5** It is never the case that God provides the petitioner with something which (a) was asked for, (b) is either good for the petitioner to have or bad for the petitioner to have, and (c) would not have been provided even without the petition, unless doing so would preclude the possibility of outweighing goods in the future.

The reader who is following along up until now might wonder just what this line of response to the argument in section 1 means for petitionary prayer. The answer is this: (5**) is consistent with God's sometimes making the provision of certain goods depend on petition being made for them, in order to secure certain outweighing goods that could not have been secured if they had been provided unconditionally. Thus, the defender of the claim that God responds to prayer might hold that there are certain goods God wants to secure, goods he can only secure by making the provision of certain other goods depend on them being petitioned for. If this is right, then it would also be right to say that, in those cases, if no petition is made, it would be better for God to withhold the good in order that the outweighing good might be obtained (the outweighing good, that is, which comes from making the provision dependent on the petition).

3 Are there such Outweighing Goods?

One way to defeat the argument of section 2, then, is to show that there are outweighing goods that God can secure by making provision of certain other (lesser) goods depend on petitions, outweighing goods which (a) in fact outweigh the good of providing the thing asked for unconditionally, and (b) could not have been secured in a way that entails less evil.

I think that there are such goods, and that there are different goods to be secured from the different types of prayers that religious believers are requested to offer. In this essay I will look at the two most common types: prayer for goods for oneself and prayers on behalf of others. (I will call these "self-directed" and "other-directed prayers," respectively.)

3.1 Outweighing goods arising from self-directed prayer

In this section I will examine three outweighing goods that arise from self-directed petitionary prayer: preservation from idolatry, coming to a greater understanding of the divine nature and purposes, and the promotion of friendship between God and the creature.

3.2 Preservation from idolatry

In *Making Sense of It All*, Thomas Morris argues that atheism is an urban phenomenon.[1] As we have become progressively distanced from our natural sources of sustenance, we have come to view ourselves as largely self-sufficient. When the rural, eighteenth-century farmer considered his situation, it was easy for him to recognize that his continued existence was due, in large measure, to forces beyond his control. Would a late frost take the potato crop? Would a drought dry up the corn? Would a flood wash out the seed? These questions led the farmer to rely on the only Being to whom he could appeal for help in these matters. It was evident to him that he was directly dependent on the Superintendent of nature for his "daily bread." For the urbanite, whose water and gas come from a pipe, whose waste exits likewise, whose food comes from the grocer, shelter from the contractor, light from the bulb, etc., it can come to seem that we are largely self-sufficient and are dependent only on other people and the products of their hands. As a result, when things go wrong (or right), we tend to look for human agents to blame (or praise). And conversely, when we are in need, we tend to look to the appropriate human benefactors for their provision. In doing so, however, we tend to put creatures in the position reserved for God as the giver of "every good, and perfect gift" (James 1:17), as he is described in the Christian Scriptures; thus we are at risk of committing idolatry.

Petitionary prayer can short-circuit this tendency by forcing the believer to realize that the goods she receives have their source beyond human agency. While her food might still come from the grocer's hand and her drink from a tap, it is still God who brings the rain, provides the chemist with the intellect required to thwart white-fly infestations, and gives the physical strength to the assembly-line worker who constructs the tractors which harvest the wheat. With each petition, the believer is made aware that she is directly dependent on God for her provisions in life.

1 Thomas Morris, *Making Sense of It All* (Grand Rapids, Mich.: Eerdmans, 1992).

One might object at this point that while this is surely a good that might result from the practice of petitionary prayer, it is just another internal psychological benefit, one that can be secured whether prayer is ever efficacious or not. What seems to be important in this case is just that we come to recognize God as the ultimate source of all the goods that we enjoy, and in coming to recognize it, we see him and ourselves in our rightful place in the universe. None of this presupposes that prayer is actually efficacious.

The point of this section, however, is that making provision of certain goods truly dependent on petitioning is what allows many, and maybe all, to "recognize God as the ultimate source of all the goods that we enjoy" in the first place. My son, who likes to play with action figures, provides a helpful example. If I were simply to shower him with new figures regularly and indiscriminately, I can imagine him becoming spoiled and presumptuous. Thus, I often do not give him any new figures until he asks for them. And even then I might sometimes refuse for other reasons. Still, by making his having the figures dependent on his asking for them, and, further, by making the granting of the request something less than automatic, he not only has a genuine appreciation for the opportunity to play with them, he has a genuine appreciation of the fact that *I provided it for him.* While it could happen that he would have such an appreciation even if he were to receive the toy without asking, it is common for such appreciation to wear thin and become downright hollow unless the economy of provision is of the sort I have described.

As a result, it seems reasonable to suppose that God might likewise make the provision of at least some goods depend directly upon our making petition for them. Not only does doing this preserve us from idolatry by forcing us to recognize that God is the ultimate source of all the goods we enjoy, it further, as the example of my son illustrates, fosters in us a genuine appreciation for the provisions that are made.

3.3 Promotion of divine friendship

Eleonore Stump has described a second sort of good that is secured by making provision sometimes depend on petition.[2] In general, she argues that petitionary prayer is a hedge against the dangers of a "bad friendship" between God and his creatures. Throughout Christian Scriptures there are passages that describe the type of loving relationship that ideally exists between God and humans. Images of bride and groom, parent and child, friend, and so on are regularly employed to emphasize different facets of this relationship. Stump's contention is that in any relationship or friendship between two persons, one of whom is perfect and powerful and the other of whom is neither, there are certain dangers which can preclude friendship. She highlights two. The first is the danger of God "overwhelming" the creature. When the balance of power and abilities is so vastly uneven, the weaker member of the pair has a marked tendency to become a pale shadow of the stronger member, losing all sense of individual personality and personal strength. Stump argues that efficacious petitionary prayer guards against this potential to overwhelm because it precludes God from providing for needs that are not understood or even felt. If God refrains

2 Eleonore Stump, "Petitionary Prayer," *American Philosophical Quarterly*, 16 (April 1979), pp. 81–91.

from making provision except in response to prayer, it allows him, in turn, to refrain from imposing his potentially unwanted designs upon his creatures.

As an example, Stump describes a teacher who notices one of her students procrastinating on a term paper and thereby "storing up trouble for himself."[3] If the teacher were to call the student at home and present him with the scheduling help he needs, Stump believes that his justified response might be, "Who asked you?" or "Mind your own business." However, if the student were to ask for help, the teacher could provide the student with needed instruction without the danger of overwhelming him. Similarly, if humans were led to docile acceptance of God's unrequested provision, it would infringe on their autonomy. Only if believers ask for those things they are given can the necessary conditions for true friendship between God and his human creatures be met.

Stump describes the second potential harm to the divine–human relationship as that of becoming "spoiled." The advantages of a friendship with a perfect Being, she argues, are likely to cause the weaker member to become willful and indulgent. Prayer helps safeguard against spoiling in that the petitioner is forced to acknowledge her need, and to further acknowledge a dependence on God for fulfillment of that need. In addition, if that prayer is answered, the petitioner must in turn be grateful to God for his grace. This helps avoid the kinds of human pride and indulgence that might occur if God were to make provisions for us without petitionary prayer.[4]

In a similar vein, Vincent Brümmer notes that if God did not, at least in some cases, make provision for our needs dependent on our requests, the relationship would become "depersonalized." He argues that if God provided for all of our needs automatically, we would be akin to the potted plant on the kitchen window sill which is watered when and only when its caretakers decide to water it. But just as we cannot have a personal relationship with an entity of this sort, God would be cut off from a personal relationship with his creatures without efficacious petitionary prayer.[5]

3.4 Understanding the divine nature and purposes

The Hebrew Scriptures contain a widely-known story in which the prophet Elijah faces off against the prophets of the Canaanite deity Baal on Mt Carmel (1 Kings 18:16–39). Both Elijah and the prophets of Baal were to prepare sacrifices and call upon their respective deities to consume the sacrifice. The prophets of Baal spent hours engaging in a variety of religious rituals attempting to cajole Baal into intervening. When they had finished, to no avail, Elijah stepped up, prayed that God make his power evident to those who were there, and God immediately sent fire from the heavens to consume the sacrifice.

This, of course, is not the ordinary mode of discourse one finds in the relationship between God and his creatures. But it points to a centrally important good that can arise from efficacious petitionary prayer. One result of God's miraculous display on

3 Ibid., p. 87.

4 This part of Stump's argument points to a good which is quite similar to the good that we think occurs when idolatry is avoided. In both cases, the petitioner is reminded that his needs are ultimately fulfilled through God, and not himself.

5 Vincent Brümmer, *What Are We Doing When We Pray?* (London: SCM Press Ltd., 1984), p. 47.

Mt Carmel is that those who witnessed it immediately acknowledged "Jehovah" as the true God. And it was not, of course, simply the miraculous display that brought about their change of heart, it was the fact that the display came in response to Elijah's petition. Seeing God respond affirmatively to Elijah's petition was, one might say, instructive.

We can generalize from this example, and see that God can teach us a number of things about his own good nature and purposes in the world by responding one way or another to our petitions. In doing so, God can teach his creatures in much the way that parents teach children when they honor or fail to honor their requests. When my children ask for chocolate bars for breakfast and I deny the request, I hope to teach them something about eating well and maintaining their health. When I deny my children's requests to forgo doing their homework, I hope to show them something about the importance of learning and meeting their obligations. And so on.

Of course, there are some serious obstacles to be overcome in trying to apply this analogy to the relationship between God and his creatures. When I pray for rain for my vegetable garden and no rain is forthcoming, should I conclude that God wants me to cut back on vegetables in my diet, or that I am spending too much time in my garden? Maybe God didn't send the rain because, were he to do so, some tragic result would occur which I am completely unaware of. It seems that this ambiguity is going to infect and thus undermine any opportunity I might have to learn something about God's nature and purposes on the basis of his responses to petitionary prayers.

There are surely limits to the sorts of things that God can teach his creatures through responses to petitionary prayers alone. Few would deny that those on Mt Carmel drew the correct conclusion. Of course, it is rare that a request and a response are given in circumstances that lead to such unambiguous conclusions.

Yet, many religious believers are quite convinced that they do learn about God's nature and purposes from seeing God respond to prayer. In most cases where this is so, however, the believer usually claims that God made it clear that the provision or the lack thereof was indicative of some important truth about God's nature or purposes. We see a representative case of this in St Paul's Second Letter to the church in Corinth. In the letter Paul tells the church that he petitioned God three times to take away a particular infirmity. God revealed to Paul that he refused to grant the request in order to make it clear to others that his success was not due to Paul's efforts and abilities alone.

Of course, many religious believers claim that God similarly teaches them in such circumstances, though often by means less overt than booming audible voices. Instead, they claim, God enlightens the mind of the petitioner to make certain features of the world salient (features related to the provision or failure thereof), and to see the reasons for the provision or its failure.

As in the "idolatry" account given above, one could argue that the relevant benefit here could be secured without efficacious petitionary prayer. If God can "enlighten" the mind to teach a person why a prayer was granted or not, God can simply enlighten the person's mind to teach them the relevant truth about God's nature or purposes alone. Of course, God could simply insert occurrent beliefs in our minds, but it is no surprise that truths learned by experience are more vivid, effective, and deeply rooted for us. There are some lessons that simply cannot be taught in an enduring way by sanitized didacticism. Instead it takes, for example, getting or failing to get something we desperately wanted for such truths to take hold. And so, while a similar outcome might be secured without making provisions dependent on petitions, a much greater good can be secured by God allowing such a dependence relation to obtain.

4 The Problem of Other-Directed Prayer

Up until now, our focus has been on self-directed petitions. But the major Western theistic traditions are united by the fact that they advocate other-directed prayer as well. The Christian Scriptures repeatedly state that this is just what is required of believers. In Paul's letters, for example, we find him not only giving explicit teaching about the efficacy of corporate prayer, but also requesting the prayers of his audience. To the Colossians he writes, "at the same time pray for us as well that God will open to us a door for the word, that we may declare the mystery of Christ" (Colossians 4:3), and to the church at Corinth: "On him we have set our hope that he will continue to deliver us, as you help us by your prayers" (2 Corinthians 1:10–11). The implication of the practice is, of course, that more people petitioning for a particular outcome makes it more likely that it will be granted.

If self-directed prayer seems initially baffling, the practice described here is all the more so. Why, one might wonder, would God choose to grant a request to provide a petitioner or petitioners with some good because more people pray for it? Such a practice seems to treat God as a cosmic vending machine, dispensing goods as long as the right combination of prayers is inserted.

Without reformulating the argument of section 1 into an argument against other-directed prayer, one can still see what must be done to make sense of this second practice. As before, we must look for some good which arises out of the practice of other-directed prayer which outweighs both the good of God simply providing that which is requested and the good of provision by way of mere self-directed prayer.[6]

5 Outweighing Goods Secured Through Other-Directed Prayer

5.1 Cultivation of community and interdependence

One reason for God to make provision of certain goods contingent upon corporate requests is that allowing his creatures to assist one another in this manner generates an interdependence among believers – one that fosters the sort of unity that God demands of the Church. In Scripture, the Church is often portrayed as a body. The picture is of many parts that, while all individually useful and important, depend on one another for their effectiveness. In his First Letter to the Corinthians (12:24–6) Paul

6 Of course, in some cases, petitions might be made on behalf of someone who is not praying on their own behalf. In such cases, the second disjunct here is irrelevant.

writes, "But God has combined the members of the body . . . so that there should be no division in [it], but that its parts should have equal concern for each other. If one part suffers, every part suffers with it; if one part is honored, every part rejoices with it." Paul explains that spiritual gifts are distributed among members of the Church so that they may realize God's purpose for the Church on earth. But they are also distributed in such a way that the members of the body must rely on one another to perform their own function effectively, in the way that the parts of our bodies do.

Thus one of God's purposes for the Church is that its members recognize their interdependence and, through this, cultivate healthy mutual relationships within the community. Other-directed prayer can serve this end by leading believers to humbly share their needs and shortcomings with each other so that others might pray for them. But more than this, other-directed prayer forces believers' interdependence, since God has, to some extent, made the granting of petitions contingent upon them recruiting others to pray for their needs. Unity among the members of the Church is a good significant enough for God to make many of his provisions to individuals contingent upon their securing the other-directed prayers of different members of the Church.

By way of analogy, we might imagine a parent telling her children that in order for them to receive certain goods, they must not only ask for them themselves but must also enjoin their siblings to ask for the goods on their behalf. No doubt, this would be an odd practice for earthly parents to adopt. But consider what would likely result. Since the siblings would recognize the importance of making requests on each others' behalf, they would, first, be moved to share their deepest needs and hopes with one another. Since the children do not know which goods depend on multiple petitions, they would be moved to share things that are most important to them. Second, since aiding a sibling requires actively making a request on their behalf, good will is generated between the siblings. Seeing that my brother was willing to help me out by asking on my behalf deepens my gratitude towards him and thus deepens our relationship. Finally, such an act deepens my brother's love for me, since by acting on my behalf he thereby involves himself in the promotion of my interests.

From this analogy we can come to have a sense of how similar benefits might arise for the Church when God has made provision of some goods truly dependent on other-directed petitions being made for them.

5.2 Meeting the needs of one another

But other-directed prayer serves not only to achieve the indirect benefit of fostering unity among members of the Church. In addition, it serves the more direct purpose of making the community of believers aware of each others' needs so that they themselves can meet them. In this way, other-directed prayer helps believers to avoid the pitfall, described in the Epistle of James, of deserting the cold and the hungry with the mere salutation, "be warmed and be filled" (James 2:16). When petitioners are confronted with the needs of others directly, they are moved not only to intercede for them but to provide for them themselves. Thus, praying for one another develops a pathos among the members of the community that again disposes them towards interdependence and away from independent self-reliance.[7]

Of course, this too might be seen as a benefit which can be secured even if prayer is not efficacious. This is true insofar as believers would willingly agree to share their deepest needs with one another even if prayer were not efficacious. But such an arrangement might not be effective, since those in the community of believers might be much more reluctant to share their needs with one another. By making the efficaciousness of prayer depend, at least in some cases, on other-directed petition being made, the believer has a powerful and immediate incentive to share those needs with others in the community.

6 Some Further Problems for Petitionary Prayer

While sections 3–5 have, I think, successfully undermined the central argument against petitionary prayer outlined in section 1, there are some lingering objections against the view of petitionary prayer I have developed here that must be addressed. We can put the first objection as follows:

> The view of petitionary prayer you offer here suggests that God makes provision of certain goods directly dependent on our petitioning for them. Of course, there are plenty of people out there who never petition God for anything since, among other things, they don't even believe God exists! If provision of some goods is a necessary condition for their being provided, we should expect those who pray to receive certain goods that those who do not pray never do. But such an expectation is clearly not met. The unbeliever and the believer alike receive their "daily bread" without regard to whether they pray or not. Thus, while the claim that petitionary prayer is efficacious might be philosophically defensible, the empirical evidence proves that it is false.

This sort of criticism rests on a number of mistakes. First, it assumes that provision of every instance of some type of good requires petition for that type of good. That is, it assumes that some good such as "daily bread" – that is, nourishment – is provided only to those who pray. And, the objection continues, since this is false, provision of nourishment does not depend on prayer.

Nothing in the view developed above, however, requires that prayer is a necessary condition for receiving every instance of a given type of good. God does not need to make provision of every good or even of every instance of a type of good rest on petition to secure the goods mentioned above. All we can infer from the model I have offered is that there are some times when God makes provision dependent on petition, and in those particular cases, those who fail to pray will fail to receive what is dependent on petition. Nothing in the empirical evidence could show us that this never happens.

In addition, even if prayer were a necessary condition for receiving certain types of good, it might be that those who do not pray receive the good in question by pig-

7 A similar idea is advanced by George A. Buttrick in his book *Prayer* (New York: Abington-Cokesbury Press, 1942), and also by Brümmer, *What Are We Doing When We Pray?*, pp. 57–8.

gybacking on the provision for those who do. When the rain falls on the faithful farmer's field, it falls on his infidel neighbor's as well. But this provides no evidence against the efficaciousness of petitionary prayer.

There is, however, another response that one might make to this objection. The outweighing goods described above are largely goods aimed at those who are already believers in God. Prevention of idolatry, promotion of friendship with God, securing unity within the community of believers, etc. are all goods aimed at those already in the believing community. As a result, one might hold that petitionary prayer is a condition for provision of goods only for believers, since it is only in their case that having this dependence relationship will even possibly bring about the desired outweighing goods. If this view is right, then we might expect that religious believers would have even less in the way of goods, since only they stand to lose out on some goods for failure to pray. The empirical evidence provided by the fat pagan would then, far from undercutting the support for efficacious petitionary prayer, actually support it!

There is a second objection, however, that has troubled critics of petitionary prayer. We can put the objection this way:

> We can think of the goods God might provide for us as falling into two categories: (a) basic goods which are required to ensure that our long-term quality of life is not significantly diminished and (b) discretionary goods which serve simply to enhance an already acceptable quality of life. While it seems reasonable to suppose that God might sometimes withhold discretionary goods to secure the outweighing goods mentioned above, it also seems reasonable that he could *never do so when* it comes to basic goods. The problem, of course, is that religions that believe in petitionary prayer usually highlight the fact that one ought to pray (even especially) for basic goods. Thus, while the account given above makes sense of some types of petitionary prayer, it does not make sense of the sort advocated by most major theistic traditions.[8]

Notice, first, that the objection raised here only gets worse if we assume that God sometimes withholds basic goods from those who are not religious believers because of their failure to pray. For, in that case, not only are they unable to have the outweighing goods mentioned above that come from making provision depend on petition, but they lose out on the good petitioned for as well – a very serious matter in the case of basic goods. As a result, let's suppose for the remainder of the essay that provision hangs on petition only for believers.

The objector here assumes that the good secured from allowing provision to depend on petition is never sufficient to outweigh the basic goods that could be lost were the person to fail to pray. Is this true? One philosopher has argued that we can see that it is true when we reflect on the analogous situation between parent and child. A parent, it is argued, would never be justified in withholding basic goods simply because they are not requested. And there is no reason to think that what is transparently true in the parent–child case does not apply equally to the case of God and his creature.[9]

8 David Basinger raises a criticism very much like this one in his "Petitionary Prayer: A Response to Murray and Meyers," *Religious Studies*, 31 (1995), pp. 481–4.
9 See ibid., p. 483.

There are, however, a number of problems with the parent–child analogy. First, it is a caricature to say that basic goods are withheld because the creature "fails to pray." While it is true that this is the proximate reason, the ultimate reason is that the person "failed to pray in a situation in which there was an outweighing good that could be secured only if the provision was made in response to a petition." Thus, the failure to receive the basic good would be due to the fact that an outweighing good would be secured by not making the provision.

Second, is it clear that a parent is never justified in withholding basic goods under such circumstances? Maybe it is true that the parent is never justified in withholding every instance of a type of basic good – for example, every instance of nourishment – but it is not at all clear that the same is true for some instances of a basic good – for example, one meal. And since, as we argued above, the view I develop here does not require God to make every instance of a type of good dependent on provision, the criticism seems to fail.

Some, however, might not be satisfied with these responses. There is something about this view, the critic might persist, that seems to make God into a utilitarian accountant, weighing up the goods of provision and the outweighing goods to be had from not providing. And while this may be acceptable in some contexts, it just seems that anyone who would withhold basic goods as defined here just does not love the person needing the basic goods.

I think this objector has not appreciated the force of the above replies. As a result, let me add one more. There are two disanalogies in the parent–child relationship that make it clear why it is not a fitting analogue for the relationship between God and his creature in this case. The first disanalogy is that parents who choose to make provision depend on petition do not know whether they will be petitioned or not. But God, if he has middle knowledge, as I suppose he does, can know prior to creating any world whether or not a policy of making provision (of even basic goods) hang on petition will have significantly bad consequences. If God foresees that such a policy will result in some being denied basic provision to a severe extent, he might find creating such a world morally unacceptable. Alternatively, God might simply choose, in such a world, not to make that sort of basic provision dependent on petition.

The second disanalogy is that parents, unlike God, do not know whether or not the outweighing goods that one seeks by making provision depend on petition will actually be realized or not if such a policy is established. Thus, a parent might institute such a policy in vain, since it might turn out that, in her case, setting up such a dependence relationship yields only bitterness in the child. God, on the other hand, who can know perfectly just what results will arise from such a policy, can make provision depend on petition selectively, and thereby ensure that the outweighing goods are largely (if not completely) secured by such a policy. Thus, if the parents had perfect middle knowledge, and knew perfectly if and when the child would refuse to request provision, and further knew just what outweighing goods would be secured by establishing such a policy, it is clear that the parent would be justified in setting up such a dependence between provision and petition.

7 Conclusion

The practice of petitionary prayer and the belief in its efficacy are deeply rooted in the major Western theistic traditions. A number of philosophical arguments have been raised against such a practice, the most powerful of which I have discussed here. While it may seem that there are no reasons why God would make provision depend on petition, we have seen that in fact there are a number of outweighing goods that can be secured through God's establishing such a dependence. Further, we have seen that the most serious potential problems that can arise from establishing such a dependence can be mitigated if we assume that God has middle knowledge.

God Does Not Necessarily Respond to Prayer

David Basinger

1 Introduction

No one denies that petitionary prayer – prayer in which God is asked to do something – remains a very important and popular theistic activity. Moreover, no one denies that such prayer can in some ways be efficacious – can in some ways change things. For instance, the act of petitioning itself clearly has the potential to affect the petitioner in many ways. It might motivate her to act beneficially, or at least cause her to be more open to ways in which she might influence the outcome of that for which she is praying. And clearly petitionary prayer can directly affect an individual who discovers that prayers are being offered on his behalf. He may well be motivated to act in ways that he otherwise would not have acted, or he may at least hold the petitioner in higher esteem.

Within most religious traditions, however, the *primary* reason why individuals continue to petition God is the belief that such prayer can influence God to act in ways he would not have acted if he had not been requested to do so. For most theists, it is important to note, this does not mean that prayer can bring about that which is logically impossible – for example, can change the past. Nor does it mean that prayer can "force" God to do that which he does not desire to do – for example, give an indolent student the answers to an exam. Rather, what theists normally mean when they claim that prayer influences divine activity is that whether God actually does unilaterally bring about certain states of affairs that he *can* and *would like* to bring about in our lives, or the lives of others, depends in part on whether *we* choose to request that he intervene.

The purpose of this essay is to challenge the claim that God actually responds to prayer – that prayer actually "changes things" – in this important sense.

2 Basic Problems

It is first important to note that proponents of two influential theistic perspectives – process theism and theological determinism – are required by the tenets of their system to agree with me. Process theists believe that all aspects of reality – even in what we normally identify as the natural realm – always possess some power of self-determination (some freedom of choice). Hence, they must (and in fact readily do) deny that God could ever unilaterally ensure any earthly outcome, whether petitioned to do so or not.[10] Moreover, process theists believe that God displays his concern for our world by presenting to every entity at every moment the best option available and then attempting to persuade each entity to act in accordance with it. Thus, they can never claim that petitionary prayer brings it about that God becomes more involved than he would otherwise have been. God is already involved in earthly affairs to the extent that any petitioner could request that he be.[11]

Theological determinists believe that God has total control over everything in the sense that all and only that which God wants to occur will occur. Specifically, they deny that human decision making can in any way limit God's providential activity in our world. Accordingly, for such theists, it can never be the case that God is prevented from bringing about that which he can and would like to bring about because we have not requested that he do so. That is, it can never be the case that whether God brings about some state of affairs in our world is dependent on whether we petition his assistance.[12] Rather, as Thomas Aquinas, John Calvin, and Martin Luther all clearly understood, if the God of theological determinism has decided to bring about some state of affairs in response to a prayer offered freely, he can *always* ensure that this prayer will be offered freely and thus that the desired state of affairs will come about.[13]

However, there are a significant number of theists – hereafter referred to as free-will theists – who view the relationship between God and the world quite differently from both process theists and theological determinists. Unlike theological determinists, free-will theists do *not* believe that God can unilaterally ensure that all and only that which he desires to come about in our world will in fact occur. They maintain, rather, that since God has chosen to create a world in which we possess the freedom to make significant moral choices, and since we can be significantly free in this sense only if God does not unilaterally control how this freedom is utilized, God voluntarily forfeits total control over earthly affairs in those cases where he allows us to exercise meaningful moral freedom.

10 The most accessible introduction to basic process thought remains John B. Cobb, Jr, and David Ray Griffin, *Process Theology: An Introductory Exposition* (Philadelphia: Westminster Press, 1976).

11 See Marjorie Suchocki, "A Process Theology of Prayer," *American Journal of Theology and Philosophy*, 2 (May 1981), pp. 33–45.

12 See, e.g., Gordon H. Clark, *Religion, Reason and Revelation* (Philadelphia: Presbyterian & Reformed Press, 1961), pp. 221–41, and G. C. Berkouwer, *The Providence of God* (Grand Rapids, Mich.: Eerdmans, 1972), chs 4 and 6.

13 See Aquinas, *Summa Theologiae*, Ia, 19, 8 ad 2. See also John Calvin, *Institutes of the Christian Religion*, tr. Henry Beveridge, II (Grand Rapids, Mich.: Eerdmans, 1979), p. 147, and Martin Luther, *Martin Luther: Selections from his Writings*, ed. John Dillenberger (Garden City, NY: Anchor Books, 1961), p. 217.

However, unlike proponents of process theism, these theists maintain that God does retain the power to intervene unilaterally in earthly affairs. Specifically, they believe that God retains the power to suspend freedom of choice and/or modify the natural order.[14]

Consequently, free-will theists are not required by their theological perspective – by the relationship they perceive between God and the world – to deny that our prayers *could* influence divine activity. Since proponents of free-will theism deny that God can unilaterally control human decision making that is truly voluntary but affirm that God can unilaterally intervene in earthly affairs, it becomes *conceptually possible* for free-will theists to maintain that petitionary prayer is at times efficacious in the sense in question – that is, to maintain that God could *upon occasion*[15] intervene in earthly affairs at least in part because his assistance was requested.[16]

But is it reasonable for free-will theists to maintain that prayer *actually* is efficacious in this sense? Can free-will theists justifiably maintain that God sometimes acts primarily because requested to do so? Here free-will theists face a significant "moral" challenge, a challenge that serves as the focus for the remainder of this essay.

All free-will theists believe that God is more knowledgeable about any situation, including the actual needs of those involved, than are we. And it is normally held that God, to a greater extent than any human parent or friend, is *always* concerned with the welfare of each of his "children" – always desires that the true needs of each person be met. However, if God knows better than any of us exactly what every person really needs and he always desires that these needs be met, then why would he, even occasionally, refrain from giving that which he *can* and *would like* to give until requested to do so? That is, if God knows better than we do exactly what every person really needs and he always desires that these actual needs be met, why would he ever make *our* petitioning a necessary condition for such assistance?

3 Responses

A number of responses to this prima facie challenge have been offered. Michael Murray and Kurt Meyers have suggested that God sometimes withholds provisions until asked so as to help the believer learn more about, and thus become more like, God. Human parents, they point out, sometimes use the opportunity to respond to their children's petitions to "teach their children what is right and important and what is not." And the same basic principle, they maintain, may also hold for the believer and his or her heavenly Parent:

14 For a more thorough discussion of free-will theism, see my book *The Case for Freewill Theism* (Downers Grove, Ill.: InterVarsity Press, 1996).

15 This qualifier is necessary and significant. Since free-will theists believe that God's decision to create a world in which individuals exercise meaningful freedom does in fact significantly limit his ability to intervene in earthly affairs, it seems quite probable that there would be many prayers for assistance that the God of free-will theism would like to answer affirmatively but simply cannot.

16 This characterization of the potential efficacy of petitionary prayer for the three perspectives in question is a modified, abridged version of what first appeared in my contribution to *Pinnock et al., Openness of God*, pp. 156–62.

> The believer is not merely enjoined to pray for perceived needs, but to do so with the sort of humility that permits her to say "Thy will be done." If the request is granted, she not only has a need fulfilled, she has continued the process of learning what sorts of things are in accordance with God's will. Likewise, if the believer prays and her request is not granted, she learns that her desires are not in accordance with God's will.

And by learning in this fashion about God's will, Murray and Meyers conclude, "the believer may in turn learn to become more righteous, and thus better conformed to the image of God."[17]

Another set of responses centers on what might occur if God were "automatically" to grant all that he wants us to have and can supply. Murray and Meyers also suggest, for instance, that at times God refrains from granting petitions because this helps the believer recognize her dependence on God. When what a believer desires comes to her as the result of her own human efforts, they point out, it is easy for her to believe that she is master of her own fate. But if God withholds, on occasion, what he would like a believer to receive until she asks for it, she is then forced "to consider that the goods that accrue to her do so ultimately because of forces beyond human control." Specifically, she is "forcefully reminded that she is directly dependent on God for her provisions in life . . . that God is the ultimate source of all goods."[18]

On the other hand, Eleonore Stump argues, since God is so much more powerful and knowledgeable than us, it is also possible for us to become so dependent on God that we simply expect God to do everything for us. Thus, just as parents sometimes refrain from giving their children all that they would like to give them so as not to spoil them, it seems reasonable to assume that God at times refrains from automatically giving us all that he can and would like to give us so that we do not become overly indulged.[19]

Furthermore, Stump continues, it would be quite easy for an all-knowing, all-powerful God to impose his will on us to the point where we become simply slavish followers who lose "all sense of [our] own tastes and desires and will." Accordingly, just as a teacher might at times refrain from helping a student until requested, so as not to dominate the student, it seems reasonable to assume that God at times refrains from giving us all he can and would like to give us until petitioned, in order to preserve our autonomy as independent creatures.[20]

R. T. Allen offers us yet another reason why God might refrain in some cases from giving us all he can until petitioned: his desire to help us develop a concern for others.

> If we could not ask Him, in the straightforward sense which implies that we expect Him to do something and to do it because we ask, then the ways in which our moral concern could develop and express itself would be greatly restricted . . . One can at least help through prayer to direct the divine activity . . . (because God does, on occasion, wait for us to ask Him). If this were not possible, one would be helpless to act, which may lead

17 Michael J. Murray and Kurt Meyers, "Ask and It Will Be Given You," *Religious Studies*, 30 (1994), p. 319.

18 Ibid., pp. 313–14.

19 Stump, "Petitionary Prayer," p. 87.

20 Ibid., pp. 87–8.

to indifference, for there would be no practical point in concerning oneself with such problems.[21]

Finally, since answered prayer is often viewed as an observable display of God's power, some maintain that God refrains at times from intervening until requested in order to reaffirm the faith of those who already acknowledge his existence or to display his existence to those who do not yet believe.

4 Responses Critiqued

Some of these responses strike me as inherently problematic. Consider, first, Murray and Meyer's claim that God might at times withhold provisions so that we can learn more about his values (moral nature). We can learn about God's values from what occurs after our petitioning only to the extent that we can know with some degree of certainty that we are receiving (or not receiving) that which we have requested as a result of a decision made by God, and that this decision was made *primarily* because our request was consistent (or inconsistent) with his values – with how he would have us live. However, given any theistic perspective, it is always *possible* that, although that which is requested was perfectly compatible with God's moral nature, God decided for some reason – for instance, for the overall good of the petitioner or someone else – not to grant the request (at least at this time).

Furthermore, since free-will theists believe that God's decision to create a world in which individuals exercise meaningful freedom does in fact significantly (self-) limit his ability to intervene in earthly affairs, yet another *equally plausible* possibility for "unanswered prayer" always exists: that the request was perfectly compatible with God's moral nature or values, but that God was not able to intervene in this case.

Finally, a petitioner can learn something *new* about God's values or moral nature as a result of an answer to her prayer only if she is not certain when the petition is offered whether a request of this type is in keeping with God's general will. But it is my contention that a petitioner must already believe that a request is compatible with God's values before she can justifiably conclude that any specific "response" is from God. And if this is so, then the fact that a specific request has been granted can teach a petitioner nothing *new* about divine values.[22]

I also find the contention that God might at times wait to act until petitioned so as not to infringe on our autonomy (our freedom) to be inherently problematic when applied to one of the most common uses of petitionary prayer: intercession for others.

Let us assume that Tom is concerned with the marital problems being experienced by his friends Fred and Sally and asks God to intervene in some beneficial manner. A key assumption within free-will theism, remember, is that God so values significant freedom – the ability of individuals to maintain control over significant aspects of their lives – that he will not, as a general rule, force his created moral agents to

21 R. T. Allen, "On Not Understanding Prayer," *Sophia*, 11 (1972), p. 2.

22 For a more detailed discussion of this point, see my "Petitionary Prayer," pp. 478–9.

perform actions they do not desire to perform. Accordingly, it appears doubtful that the God of free-will theism would intervene in Fred and Sally's relationship primarily because he was requested to do so by Bill. For what sense can it make to say that God has upheld the integrity of significant freedom by withholding action until freely requested to intervene when the request, if complied with, requires that God in fact violate the very concept of significant freedom (personal autonomy) supposedly being preserved? Or as Stump, herself, puts this point, God can avoid the charge of oppressive meddling in the life of a person that God has been asked to help only if this person comes to the place where he "has willingly shared his thoughts and feelings and the like with God."[23]

The other reasons suggested for why God might wait until petitioned to intervene – to keep us from becoming too demanding of God or dominated by God or to help us recognize our dependence on God or to bolster our faith or to preserve our autonomy (in relation to self-directed prayers) – do not seem to me to be self-defeating. But I believe them to be "morally" unacceptable, given God's obligation with respect to our well-being.

There are, as I see it, four basic perspectives on the question of God's moral obligation to us:

1 God is under no obligation to attempt to ensure any specified quality of life for us.
2 God is obligated only to do all in his power to make our lives on balance worth living.
3 God is morally obligated to do all in his power to meet our basic needs – that is, to keep our long-term quality of life (both physical and mental) from being diminished significantly.
4 God is morally obligated to do all in his power to maximize our quality of life.

If either (1) or (2) is true, then prayer can clearly be efficacious in the sense in question. If God is under no obligation with respect to our quality of life – if (1) is true – then God can, simply because he so desires, always justifiably wait to give us what he can and desires to give us until we ask for assistance. Likewise, if God is obligated only to attempt to make our lives on balance worth living – if (2) is true – then God may well, at least at times, be in a position to wait justifiably to intervene until petitioned.

However, I personally reject both (1) and (2). The only initially plausible defense for either with which I am familiar is that offered by Robert Adams. Since a gracious God can love equally individuals of any given sort (for example, can love those who suffer as much as those who do not), he is not obligated, Adams argues, to create individuals whose quality of life has been maximized, or even whose basic needs are always met to the extent possible.[24] What gives this argument initial plausibility is

23 Since Allen's contention that God sometimes waits to respond so as to help us develop concern for others is clearly meant to apply primarily to intercessory prayer, his suggestion is also subject to this critique.

24 Robert Adams, "Must God Create the Best?," *Philosophical Review*, 81 (1972), pp. 317–32; *idem*, "Existence, Self-Interest and the Problem of Evil," *Nous*, 13 (1979), pp. 53–65.

Adams's accurate characterization of one aspect of divine grace. Just as a gracious parent can (or even ought to) love the child who is physically or mentally handicapped as much as the child who has no such condition, a gracious God can love a person in great need as much as a person whose needs have been met.

I do not believe it follows, though, from the fact that a gracious parent can (or even ought to) love all children equally that he or she can justifiably express love for (treat) a child in a manner that does not attempt to maximize this child's quality of life, or at least meet this child's basic needs. It seems to me, rather, that the truly good parent, even if gracious, is required not only to do all he or she can to meet a child's basic needs but in fact to help this child lead as productive and enjoyable a life as possible.

Likewise, I do not believe it follows from the fact that a gracious God can love equally individuals of any sort that he, as a perfectly good being, can express his love for them in a manner that does not attempt to maximize their quality of life or at least meet their basic needs. For example, I question whether it follows from the fact that a gracious God can love those who are mentally impaired as much as those who are not that he is not obligated, as a perfectly good being, to do what he can to help such individuals meet their basic needs. In fact, as I see it, a God who is perfectly good is required, even if "gracious," to do all he can to help them overcome whatever unnecessary barriers they face.

In short, I personally affirm (4). But even if we affirm only (3) – affirm only that God must do all that can be done to meet our basic needs – we encounter serious problems with the contention that God might at times refrain from acting until petitioned so that *we will better recognize our dependence on God* or *we will not become demanding of God* or *we will not become dominated by God* or *our faith will be bolstered or our autonomy will be preserved.*

It is true that we as human parents, for analogous reasons, on occasion refrain from helping until asked. We can, for example, easily imagine a parent not buying a toy for a child until asked so that the child does not become demanding or dominated, or so that the child comes to recognize the source of the desired item and thus increases her faith in her parent's goodness. But can we imagine any of these reasons justifying a parent's decision to refrain from giving a child enough food to develop properly or shielding a child from abuse until asked by the child to do so?

An analogous question arises with respect to requests made of God. We can (as I have already indicated implicitly) divide those things that God can, and would like to, give us into two categories: those *basic needs* which, if received, will keep our long-term quality of life – our long-term physical and mental well-being – from being diminished significantly, and those *discretionary needs* which, if received, will simply enhance our quality of life. For example, we can distinguish God's desire to protect a child from abuse (a basic need) from his desire to help a family determine how to secure financing for a new home (a discretionary need). And while it seems reasonable to assume that God might at times withhold discretionary provisions – the "little extras" – to keep the believer from becoming spoiled or dominated or to foster appropriate dependence or to increase faith or to preserve autonomy, is it reasonable to assume that God would withhold basic provisions solely or primarily for any of these reasons? For instance, while it may seem reasonable to assume that God will not help us achieve the "American dream" until petitioned, so as not to spoil us, is it reasonable to assume that God will not for any of these reasons do all he can to protect the lives of innocent individuals until petitioned?

If we assume, as I do, that (4) or at least (3) is true – if we assume that God is committed to attempting to maximize our quality of life, or at least to attempting to meet our basic needs – then the answer to such questions is obviously no. God will not wait to grant basic provisions until requested, and thus prayers requesting such activity cannot be efficacious in the sense normally assumed.

The problem here, it is important to reemphasize, is not one related to divine power. The God of free-will theism could intervene in the manner requested. The problem is moral in nature. If the God of free-will theism is as I envision him, then with respect to our basic needs and those of others, God won't refrain from doing what he can and would like to do until requested. God's moral nature requires rather that he simply intervene.

It might be argued (correctly, I believe) that nothing I have said rules out the possibility that God might at times refrain from granting *discretionary* provisions until requested. Moreover, I readily admit that most theistic traditions advocate or even encourage such prayer. But within all such theistic traditions with which I am familiar, it is held that believers should also petition for *basic* provisions. That is, it is held that it is important to pray when the "going gets tough," when something of real importance is on the line, when someone's "survival" is at stake. In fact, I believe it is safe to say that within the majority of theistic traditions (including Christianity) the desire to gain divine assistance with respect to our most basic needs is the most important purpose for petitionary prayer. And if this is true, then the contention that God is morally obligated to meet those basic needs he can and would like to meet even if not requested to do so becomes quite significant.

5 Counter-Response

My basic line of reasoning – that a good God would not withhold basic needs until requested – has not gone unchallenged. Murray and Meyers grant that "to withhold basic provision from those who do not believe, and who thus have no reason to pray for their daily bread, would be too cruel to be consistent with God's goodness."[25] But they disagree with my claim that for a perfectly good God to withhold *basic provision* – even occasionally – from believers *primarily* so that they will come to recognize from whom these provisions ultimately come is also "too cruel to be consistent with God's goodness."

God, they tell us, possesses middle knowledge – that is, he knows beforehand exactly what will actually occur in every conceivable situation. Specifically, he knew before creation exactly what petitions would be forthcoming in any world in which provisions are sometimes made dependent on petitioning. And a perfectly good God with this knowledge, we are informed, would not have chosen to

25 Murray and Meyers, "Ask and It Will Be Given You," p. 318.

actualize a world in which believers "will fail to petition for a good essential to their well-being."[26]

It is true, they grant, that *if*, as I and others have argued, God has no control over which voluntary choices he foresees are made in any possible world in which we are granted freedom of choice, then it may be that God, even with middle knowledge, will not be able to actualize a world in which no believer fails to receive basic provision because it was not requested. But even if this is so, they maintain, we need not conclude that any believer is unjustly denied provision because of lack of petition. Rather, it is then the believer's "failure to freely choose to pray that accounts for [her] un-met needs."[27]

However, I find such reasoning problematic on two counts. First, it is misleading for Murray and Meyers to imply that whether middle knowledge can ensure God's ability to actualize a world in which no believer ever fails to receive basic provisions because no request was made is an open question. Murray and Meyers are clearly discussing middle knowledge as it relates to creatures who possess libertarian freedom. And although a God with middle knowledge can *know* beforehand what each individual exercising libertarian freedom will freely choose in each possible situation in which such choice could occur, he cannot in any sense control what choice will be made. This in turn means that it is not the case, as Murray and Meyers imply, that only some proponents of middle knowledge must admit that God may not be able to actualize a world in which it is true both that some provisions are contingent on petitions and that no person fails "to petition for a good essential to [his or her] well-being." All proponents of middle knowledge must acknowledge this possibility.

Second, given my understanding of God's moral obligation to us, I obviously find any attempt to place the blame for unmet essential needs on believers themselves totally unacceptable. Just as I do not believe that a parent could justifiably withhold essential help – could justifiably fail to keep a child from permanent injury or death – even if a child purposely failed to ask for assistance, I do not believe that a perfectly good God could justifiably refrain from granting any believer's *essential* needs, even if she has consciously decided not to request God's help.

6 Conclusion

In closing, let me state once more what has and has not been argued. I have not argued that petitionary prayer is not in any sense a meaningful theistic activity. The question is whether the occurrence of certain states of affairs that God can and would like to bring about in our lives or the lives of others is dependent in part on whether we choose to request that he intervene.

Neither theological determinists – who deny that human choice can thwart God's will – nor process theists – who deny that God can unilaterally intervene in earthly affairs – can justifiably maintain that petitionary prayer is efficacious in this sense.

26 Ibid., p. 324.
27 Ibid.

On the other hand, since free-will theists believe that God can unilaterally intervene in earthly affairs but cannot unilaterally control that which is the result of free human choice, it is conceptually possible for such theists to maintain that God does at times wait to intervene until petitioned.

I have argued, however, that since God is morally obligated (at the very least) to do all within his power to ensure that our basic needs are met – to keep our long-term quality of life from being diminished significantly – God cannot with respect to such needs wait to grant that which he *can* and *would like to* grant us until requested to do so. Accordingly, since within most theistic traditions, this is perceived to be the most important purpose for petitionary prayer, I have no choice but to deny that petitionary prayer initiates divine activity in the sense that most theists believe. That is, with respect to our basic provisions, I have no choice but to deny that God will refrain from doing what he can and would like to do until requested. God's moral nature requires that he simply do it.

Reply to Basinger

In his essay, David Basinger raises a number of considerations against the efficacy of petitionary prayer. In this brief rejoinder I will offer a few remarks about three of them.

In an earlier essay by Kurt Meyers and myself, we argued that one good that can arise from petitionary prayer is that it at least sometimes allows the petitioner to gain insight into the divine nature and purposes. In his essay, Basinger responds that such insight is not available to the petitioner, since there is no way for the petitioner to know whether or not the event that one takes to be a "response to prayer" is *in fact* a response to prayer at all. For all the petitioner knows, the events that are taken to be "responses" might have occurred even if no petition had been offered, or, alternatively, might have come about (or been precluded) by events that have nothing to do with the petitioner's prayer at all.

While this reply is right to some extent, it is nonetheless clear that we often draw justified inferences about the nature and purposes of agents by taking note of states of affair that we have good reason to believe were brought about by them. We see such inferences being drawn, for example, in the case of Elijah and the prophets of Baal, a case I described in my essay (see section 3.4). When Elijah's prayer that God consume his sacrifice is answered by a flash of fire from a cloudless sky that vaporizes the offering he has prepared, the lessons are obvious to everyone.

Of course, few people claim to have experienced such immediate and dramatic responses to their petitions. But the point is important nonetheless. While it could be the case that some purely natural events explain the consumption of Elijah's sacrifice, the indirect evidence makes such an explanation highly implausible. The indirect evidence makes it clear that the consumption of the sacrifice was a response by God to Elijah's petition – a response brought about for the purpose (at least) of sending a message to the Israelites and the prophets of Baal about God's displeasure with idolatry. Many theists claim, similarly, that indirect evidence makes it plausible that particular events have occurred in response to their petitionary prayers. And while these judgments certainly will be false in some cases, there is no reason to think that they are always, or even often, *unjustified*.

Secondly, in his essay Basinger sets out four positions concerning God's "moral obligations towards us." Basinger argues that if God's obligations towards us are of the more robust sort described in either (3) or (4), then petitionary prayer can never change things when it comes to anything but "discretionary matters." The reason is obvious: if God were to withhold provision of basic needs because creatures fail to petition, he would fail to meet our "basic needs" or fail to "maximize our quality of life."

While I have serious reservations about the idea that God has moral obligations with respect to creatures (reservations shared by many Christian intellectuals who have addressed the matter), I must leave those aside here. Even if we adopt Basinger's framework, however, all that seems to follow from the stronger positions he favors on this question is that God cannot *consistently* withhold provision of basic needs because of failure to petition. But there is no reason to think that God might not have set things up in such a way that provision of even basic needs is only *sometimes* dependent on petition. And this, I have argued, is all that is needed to secure the sorts of goods that arise from making provision depend on petition in the first place. Unless Basinger can supply us with some (as yet unstated) reason for thinking that God must make *every instance* of a particular type of good depend on petition, there is no reason to think that he must.

Third, in the "Counter-Response" section of his paper, Basinger presents an argument that God's moral obligations towards creatures prevent God from providing for our "essential needs" in response to petitionary prayers. Specifically, Basinger says, "I do not believe that a perfectly good God could justifiably refrain from granting any believer's *essential* needs." If Basinger means to adopt this as a general principle which follows from the conceptions of God's obligations he endorses (3 or 4), then serious trouble looms. And the reason is simply that if (a) God exists, and (b) the principle is true, it would follows that (c) no believers would ever die from starvation, exposure, or, presumably, death on a cross. Since they do, we have an argument against not only efficacious petitionary prayer, but theism itself!

Surely Basinger does not mean to affirm this argument. Instead, he likely means to affirm only that God could never withhold such essential needs unless doing so was in some way required to secure certain outweighing goods. But if that is all he means to affirm here, we are back to the question we started with: are there any outweighing goods that permit God to make provision of goods sometimes dependent on creaturely petition? As a result, it is not clear that the remarks made in this counter-response get us any closer to the resolution of our question. Further discussion of the question must continue to focus on claims concerning outweighing goods of petitionary prayer and responses to those claims.

Reply to Murray

Is it ever justifiable for God to withhold that which he can and would like to give us (or others) until petitioned?

Murray and I agree that the answer to this question depends on whether there exist any goods that might result from a divine policy of making provision at times dependent on petitioning that could *outweigh* those goods that a person would not receive if she failed to ask for them. Murray clearly believes that such outweighing goods exist. In fact, he explicitly notes five: (1) to help us realize that "God is the ultimate source of all the goods we enjoy," (2) to help us come to a greater understanding of "God's nature and purposes," (3) to keep us from being overwhelmed or spoiled by God's gracious care for us, (4) to help us recognize our "interdependence and through this cultivate healthy mutual relationships within the community," and (5) to make us "better aware of each others' needs."

All of Murray's candidates for outweighing goods seem to me to be acceptable with respect to the "little extras" – those things that enhance our quality of life. For example, just as I agree with Murray that withholding toys from a child until they are requested is a justifiable way for a father to help the child appreciate who it is who is providing them, I agree that God could justifiably withhold help related to a better job or a new home until requested to foster proper appreciation for the fact that it is God who is our primary provider.

But I don't believe that any of Murray's candidates for outweighing goods are acceptable with respect to what I specify in my essay as basic needs: what we need to keep our long-term quality of life – our long-term physical and mental well-being – from being diminished significantly. For instance, just as I don't think that a parent could justifiably withhold basic health care or minimum shelter from a child until requested in order to foster appreciation of the parent as a provider, so I don't believe that God could justifiably withhold life-saving or life-sustaining intervention until requested primarily to foster better appreciation of God's role as provider or to teach us something about his nature or to keep from spoiling us.

Murray explicitly addresses my concern in his essay. However, I find each of his three attempted rejoinders unconvincing. First, Murray argues that I wrongly imply that God might withhold goods simply because someone "fails to pray," whereas the "ultimate reason" God might withhold basic goods is actually because the person "failed to pray in a situation in which there was an outweighing good that could be secured only if the provision were made in response to a petition." But it is exactly this "ultimate reason" that I am challenging. My claim is that with respect to *basic goods*, there exists no outweighing good that can be secured by not granting the provision unless requested.

Second, Murray offers what he sees as a successful counterexample to my claim that God would never withhold basic goods until requested. It may be true, he grants, that a parent (and by extension, God) "is never justified in withholding every instance of a type of basic good – for example, every instance of nourishment – but it is not at all clear that the same is true for some instances of a basic good – for example, one meal." But this challenge is based on a misunderstanding of my position. A basic good (need), as I am defining it, is that which we need to keep our long-term quality of life from being diminished significantly. Thus, to have one meal withheld is not to be deprived of a basic good, while to have enough meals withheld to diminish one's long-term physical and mental well-being is to be so deprived. So it seems to me that Murray's example actually supports my position.

Third, Murray argues that since a God with middle knowledge always knows exactly what will occur if he withholds basic goods until requested, we don't have to assume that this world is one in which God's "policy of making provisions (of even basic goods) hang on petition will have significantly bad consequences." Rather, we can assume that a God with middle knowledge "can make provision depend on petition selectively and thereby ensure that the outweighing goods are largely (if not completely) secured by such a policy" (p. 254). However, Murray's contention that a God with middle knowledge may well be able to ensure that basic goods will be withheld until requested only when to do so will result in outweighing goods simply begs the question. My argument again is that there *are* no such outweighing goods, and thus that to withhold basic goods will always result in "bad consequences."

So I remain convinced that my response to the issue at hand is correct: With respect to our basic needs (goods), it is never justifiable for God to withhold that which he can and would like to give us until petitioned.

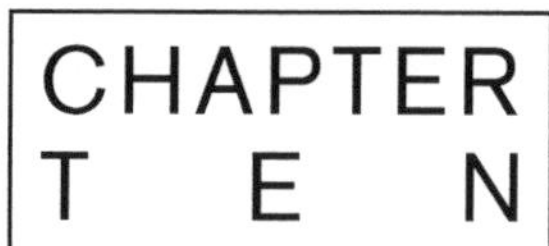

Is Eternal Damnation Compatible with the Christian Concept of God?

Jerry Walls and Thomas Talbott both agree that God is perfectly loving and that he desires the salvation of all the persons he has created. But they disagree as to whether God's desire will be fufilled. Walls argues that God has given human beings libertarian freedom and the opportunity to use it to accept or reject salvation. In so doing, God leaves open the possibility that some persons will freely and decisively reject him, a possibility which Jesus' own words lead us to believe will be actual. On the other side, Talbott contends that God's desire for the salvation of all will be fulfilled. He argues that it is not possible for one freely to reject God forever and that, even if it were, God's love would not permit anyone to do so.

Eternal Hell and the Christian Concept of God

Jerry Walls

Few ideas have gripped the human imagination more profoundly than the Christian doctrine of eternal hell, and few have been more culturally significant. The cultural significance of hell is reflected in the numerous works of art it has inspired. It has been graphically depicted in many paintings and has also been vividly described in poetry and literature, including classic works by Dante and Milton. And in our time, hell has appeared not infrequently in that most popular of art forms, the daily comics.

The reasons for our fascination with hell are obvious: it embodies claims of such extreme importance and urgency that no one could be human without caring whether or not those claims are true. In particular, the doctrine holds that all those who do not receive salvation through Christ will experience eternal misery in separation from God. No doubt the colorful way in which the miseries of hell have been pictured adds to our fascination. But the very possibility of eternal misery, however it is understood, is enough to assure our interest. One may reasonably not care about Helen of Troy and whether or not she really existed. One may rationally be indifferent about the legend of Helle and her ride on the ram with the golden fleece. But not to care, and care deeply, about whether hell exists is simply not to understand.

1 The Problem of Hell

Opponents of Christianity have responded to the extreme claims of hell with some correspondingly sharp criticisms of the doctrine. John Stuart Mill charged that the notion of hell implied that the Christian conception of God's character represented a "dreadful idealization of wickedness."[1] A century later, Bertrand Russell expressed similar thoughts: "There is one very serious defect to my mind in Christ's moral character, and that is that He believed in hell. I do not myself feel that any person who is profoundly humane can believe in everlasting punishment."[2]

These comments point up a potentially very serious problem for orthodox Christian faith: namely, that that faith includes a doctrine that is morally indefensible. This problem is complicated by the often observed fact that the bulk of New Testament passages which support the doctrine of eternal hell come from Jesus' own lips. Since the doctrine is rooted in the teachings of Jesus Christ himself, it cannot easily be eliminated from Christian belief without undermining the very foundations of Christianity. For Christianity is a religion based ultimately on revelation, rather than philosophical reasoning and speculation. And the doctrine of hell comes as part of what Christians accept as normative revelation. To put the point another way, the Christian believer faces a rather awkward dilemma if the doctrine of eternal hell is morally objectionable: he must either reject the normative status of the teachings of Christ or he must accept a morally intolerable doctrine.

Some Christian theologians have taken the extreme measure of simply rejecting the authority of Christ on this matter. More commonly, however, believers have responded to this dilemma in one of two ways: either they have argued that the doctrine of eternal hell is morally defensible or they have tried to show that Christ did not, in fact, teach it. To show that Christ did not teach eternal hell would require a persuasive alternative interpretation of the relevant New Testament texts. That is, it must be shown why the texts that have traditionally been understood to teach eternal hell really do not do so.

Such an approach can perhaps be successfully executed, but I want to insist that the burden of proof rests on those who take this view. The reason for this is simple.

1 John Stuart Mill, *Three Essays on Religion* (London: Longmans, Green, 1923), p. 114.
2 Bertrand Russell, *Why I Am Not a Christian* (New York: Simon & Schuster, 1957), p. 17.

There is a vast consensus in favor of those more traditional interpretations which understand Christ and other New Testament authors to teach that at least some persons will experience eternal misery as a result of their rejecting salvation. Although there is not the space to do so here, this claim could be easily documented from any number of classical theologians and normative creeds and doctrinal confessions in the various branches of the Christian Church.

That is not to say that the consensus is a unanimous one. There is a minority strand of teaching in the history of theology which affirms universalism, the view that all will be saved in the end. Sinners may be punished in hell for a limited time, according to this position, but eventually all will repent and receive salvation. The universalist tradition stretches all the way back to some of the early Church Fathers, so it can hardly be dismissed out of hand. Nevertheless, it has been rejected as a heresy by most theologians and official doctrinal statements. In view of this impressive tradition against their view, universalists must assume the burden of proof in this debate. They need compelling reasons, philosophical and/or theological, if their interpretation of the New Testament is to be preferred to more traditional readings.

In what follows I will argue that the doctrine of eternal hell is indeed compatible with the Christian concept of God. It is both morally defensible and logically coherent, so there are no compelling reasons to abandon the traditional understanding of Scripture in favor of universalist interpretations.

2 Universalism, Theological Determinism, and Libertarian Freedom

So, what arguments have universalists put forward to make their case against eternal hell? The most frequently cited argument is concisely stated in the following by John Hick, a prominent spokesman for the universalist position.

> For the doctrine of hell has as its implied premise either that God does not desire to save all His human creatures, in which case He is only limitedly good, or that His purpose has finally failed in the case of some . . . of them, in which case He is only limitedly sovereign. I therefore believe that the needs of Christian theodicy compel us to repudiate the idea of eternal punishment.[3]

If we take this argument at face value, it makes a very strong claim indeed: namely, that universalism follows by logical necessity from God's sovereignty and perfect goodness. If God is perfectly good, he wants to save all persons; if he is all-powerful, he can do so; therefore all will be saved. In other words, eternal hell is simply incompatible with the Christian concept of God.

What is immediately interesting about this argument is that it shares the same structure and essentially the same premises as another classic argument in the philosophy of religion. I am referring, of course, to the problem of evil as spelled out in terms of what seems to follow from the claims that God is omnipotent, omniscient,

3 John Hick, *Evil and the God of Love*, rev. edn (San Francisco: Harper & Row, 1977), p. 342.

and perfectly good. For centuries, critics have argued that if these claims are true, then there would be no evil in the world. Since it is apparent that there is evil, these critics conclude that there is no God, at least as traditionally understood. Or in other words, evil is incompatible with the Christian God.

What this points up is that the problem of hell is an aspect of the larger problem of evil. Indeed, it is arguably the most severe aspect of the problem of evil, for hell is by definition an eternal evil, so it holds out no reason to hope that it will eventually be redeemed.

What I want to argue is that if there is a solution to the problem of evil, there is a solution to the problem of hell. Indeed, the solution to both problems is essentially the same: namely, human freedom.

The appeal to human freedom has been a stock response to the problem of evil as long as the issue has been addressed. This remains true down to the present day. Indeed, the nature of human freedom and its importance for this debate have been articulated with considerable precision in analytic philosophy in the past few decades. No work has been more influential in this regard than Alvin Plantinga's "Free Will Defense."[4] Given the fact that this argument has been widely discussed, I will not provide a detailed summary of it here. But I do wish to point out its obvious relevance to the sort of argument for universalism given by Hick.

In the first place, Plantinga's argument assumes libertarian freedom: that is, freedom which is not compatible with determinism. If we are free with respect to a given action A, we have the power to choose to do A or to refrain from it, according to libertarians. Various factors may influence our choice, but a truly free choice is one that is not determined by prior conditions or causes and in which it is finally up to us how we choose on the matter.

This sort of freedom is necessary not only for morally significant choices, according to many philosophers, but also for genuine personal relationships. Without such freedom, we could not engage in real acts of love, trust, commitment, loyalty, and the like. This is why God values this sort of freedom and chose to create a world with creatures that are free in this manner.

Now, then, if God chooses to create such a world, it is possible that he may not have the option of choosing one that would be free of evil. For if we are really free in regard to morally significant actions, then it is possible that all persons will go wrong with respect to at least some of these actions. So even though God is omnipotent, he may not be able to create a world which has creatures who are free in the libertarian sense but which contains no evil.

Of course, if libertarian freedom is denied, and one assumes that freedom and determinism are compatible, things are altogether different. In this case, God could create a world in which people were "free" and in which there were no evil. God could determine everyone to "freely" choose the good in all situations. If we are free only in this sense, then it is reasonable to believe that if God is all-powerful and perfectly good, there would be no evil, at least no moral evil.

4 This work has been published and discussed in numerous forms since it first appeared in 1965. For a particularly clear statement, see Alvin Plantinga, *God, Freedom, and Evil* (Grand Rapids, Mich.: Eerdmans, 1977).

But the fact of pervasive and terrible evil is powerful reason to think that we are free in the libertarian sense. It is hard to imagine that an even moderately good God, let alone a perfectly good one, would determine the sorts of atrocities we have witnessed. If a perfectly good God chose to determine all things, including our actions, surely he would not determine such things as rape, child abuse, and world wars. It is much more reasonable to believe that such things happen because such choices are up to us, and we have chosen to do them against God's will.

Now the relevance of all this to the doctrine of hell is obvious. The ultimate free choice which God gives us is the choice to love him or not, to be rightly related to him or not. In our fallen condition, we need God's grace to be rightly related to him. God's grace comes to us in his offer of forgiveness and moral transformation. We are free, however, to refuse God's offer of grace and salvation.

Since we are free in this regard, God may not be able to save everyone, even though he is omnipotent and willing to do so. The same free will that accounts for much of the evil in the world also explains why universalism does not necessarily follow from the claims that God is both sovereign and perfectly good. The choice of hell and damnation instead of forgiveness and transformation is similar in nature to all other choices of evil. Indeed, the choice of hell is the climax and final outcome of the persistent choice of evil. Eternal hell is compatible with God's sovereignty and perfect goodness for the same basic reason that any other moral evil is.

By arguing that universalism follows from God's sovereignty and perfect goodness, the universalist is assuming that since God is sovereign, he can save anyone he wants to save. To bring this point into focus, it is worth noting that this assumption is shared by that theological tradition which holds that God has determined all things, including who will be saved and who will be damned. This tradition is generally called "Calvinism," after John Calvin, the great Protestant theologian who held this view. We can spell out the logic of Calvinism as follows:

1 Since God is sovereign, all he wills to save, and only those, will be saved.
2 God wills to save only the elect.
3 Therefore, only the elect will be saved.

Like Calvinists, universalists affirm premise 1. However, they diverge from Calvinists in their view of whom God wishes to save. We can spell out the logic of universalism as follows:

1 Since God is sovereign, all he wills to save, and only those, will be saved.
4 God wills to save everyone.
5 Therefore, everyone will be saved.

In contrast to both these views, let us spell out the logic of the Free-Will Defender who rejects universalism.

6 God has sovereignly chosen to create people who are free in the libertarian sense.
4 God wills to save everyone.

7 If we are free in the libertarian sense, we can reject salvation.
8 Therefore, all may not be saved.

Notice that while the Calvinist and the universalist agree that God can save anyone he wills, the universalist and the Free-Will Defender agree that God wills to save everyone. Moreover, the Calvinist and the Free-Will Defender agree that all are not saved (at least, they *may* not be), but they do so for very different reasons.

These differences point up the crucial importance of libertarian freedom in these matters. Clearly this is a point of contention between Calvinists and Free-Will Defenders. Philosophically informed Calvinists typically recognize that their view of God's sovereignty logically requires them to reject libertarian freedom.[5] If sovereignty means that God determines all things, then we can be free only in some sense that is compatible with such determinism. The heart of this "compatibilist" view of freedom is that one is free with respect to some action so long as he does that action willingly. One is determined to will as one does and to act accordingly. But so long as one acts in accordance with one's will – even though the will is determined – then one is free on this account.

Now what is significant here, and somewhat curious, is that many defenders of universalism also affirm libertarian freedom. One may tend to suspect that universalists would incline toward compatibilism, since they agree with Calvinists that God can save anyone he wills, with freedom intact. In fact, however, universalists characteristically argue that God can save everyone with libertarian freedom intact. Saving everyone with *compatibilist* freedom intact would be no great feat for an omnipotent God. For God could determine everyone to will to accept the offer of salvation and to act accordingly. Indeed, God could do even more, as suggested above. He could determine everyone to will only the good and to perform only good actions.

But saving everyone with *libertarian* freedom intact is another matter altogether. For if freedom is understood in such a way that it is really up to us whether we accept God's offer of salvation, then how can we be sure that everyone will do so? Interestingly, the universalist Hick concedes the force of this question. After noting that the actions of free beings cannot be predetermined, Hick comments: "It would infringe the nature of the personal order if we could assert as a matter of assured knowledge that all men *will* respond to God."[6] This concession is surely at odds with Hick's confident affirmation of universalism, cited above. Clearly there is a tension, if not a contradiction, in affirming both the certainty of universalism, on the one hand, and libertarian freedom, on the other. A clear commitment to libertarian freedom leaves open the possibility that not all will be saved.

3 Damnation, Life Orientation, and Divine Goodness

To this point, I have argued that the doctrine of eternal hell is compatible with the Christian concept of God. This is true for broadly the same reason that evil is com-

5 See John S. Feinberg, "God, Freedom and Evil in Calvinist Thinking," in Thomas R. Schreiner and Bruce A. Ware (eds), *The Grace of God, The Bondage of the Will* (Grand Rapids, Mich.: Baker Books, 1995), vol. 2, pp. 459–83.

6 Hick, *Evil and the God of Love*, p. 343.

patible with God's existence. But let us now turn to explore more fully what is involved in the claim that it is possible to choose damnation if we are free in the libertarian sense. Just how are we to understand this choice? Surely it is not the case that just any choice of evil is equivalent to choosing damnation. So what is the distinctive nature of the choice of hell?

I would suggest that the answer to this question lies along the following lines. The choice of damnation amounts to what I call *a decisive choice for evil.* It is a settled choice to reject the offer of salvation, a choice made with deliberation and understanding of what is involved. It is a choice that involves one's whole person in such a way that it is definitive with respect to one's beliefs, feelings, and desires. In other words, the decision is fully endorsed at every level of who we are, in terms of what we believe, feel, and want.

Not every choice of evil is like this. Sometimes evil is chosen with a deep sense of ambivalence. One may give in to temptation out of weakness of will, but regret the decision at some other level of one's being. Sometimes evil is chosen impulsively or out of a sense of obvious confusion or misunderstanding. The level of moral guilt or culpability involved in such choices is, of course, hard to assess. But one thing seems clear. The more deliberate and persistent one is in such choices, the more culpable one is.

The choice of damnation, is, I am suggesting, a deliberate and persistent choice to embrace evil and to reject salvation. But here an obvious question comes to mind. Is it not true that many people have little opportunity to receive salvation? Many people never hear about Christ at all, and many others have only a garbled understanding of the Christian offer of salvation. And many others suffer from various psychological maladies or cultural biases which make it difficult, if not impossible, for them to respond to the gospel in anything like an intelligent or deliberate fashion.

This is a difficult issue that must be taken seriously if the doctrine of eternal hell is to be defended from the charge of moral absurdity. For this objection raises the specter that God is profoundly unfair in the matter of eternal salvation. In short, many people do not seem to have a fair chance to receive salvation due to factors outside their control. Factors like the time and place of one's birth figure heavily here, as well as genetic and psychological factors. It seems unthinkable that the playing field should be so uneven in a matter of such magnitude as that of our eternal salvation.

The answer to this difficulty lies in spelling out more fully what is entailed by God's perfect goodness. For a start, let us consider the account of John Wesley, the great eighteenth-century theologian and evangelist. Wesley said that God's goodness is displayed "in offering salvation to every creature, actually saving all that consent thereto, and doing for the rest all that infinite wisdom, almighty power, and boundless love can do, without forcing them to be saved, which would be to destroy the very nature that he had given to them."[7] This reminds us that the Christian account of God's goodness is not merely a matter of cold moralism or legal righteousness. Rather, it is a matter of a personal God of boundless love who is willing to go to

7 John Wesley, *Works* (Grand Rapids, Mich.: Baker Books, 1979; reprint of the 1872 edn), vol. 10, p. 235.

extreme lengths to save us and restore us to a right relationship with himself. The Christian God is a God of overwhelming grace, whose love and goodness cannot be measured or limited.

Now if this is true, it is inconceivable that God would allow anyone to be damned through circumstances beyond their control. Rather, God will surely find a way to render the playing field even and give everyone a full and fair chance to choose the good and receive salvation. Following Wesley, it is reasonable to believe that God will do everything he can, short of overriding freedom, to elicit a positive response from everyone. Let us call this *universal optimal grace*. In view of this sort of grace, the choice of damnation would require just the sort of deliberate, persistent choice of evil I sketched above. Indeed, the notions of optimal grace and a decisive choice of evil mutually imply each other. One's choice of evil is not really decisive unless grace is optimal, and optimal grace is what makes it clear that one really prefers evil. In the face of optimal grace, one could not blame the choice of evil on misunderstanding, lack of opportunity, and so on.

4 Freedom, Optimal Grace, and True Happiness

But now that these matters have been made fully explicit, we face another difficulty. Does it really make sense to think that anyone would choose evil in the face of optimal grace? Is the notion of a decisive choice of evil such as damnation requires really an intelligible idea? This question has been pressed with considerable force recently by Thomas Talbott. It is easy enough, Talbott grants, to make sense of individual sins or evil choices. But what Talbott thinks is incoherent is the notion that anyone could persist in evil in face of the truth that evil is destructive of one's own happiness. The choice of hell is the choice of eternal misery, by definition. There simply is no intelligible motive for such a choice, Talbott insists. Such a choice would always involve ignorance, deception, or bondage to desire. But it is precisely the function of grace to remove these factors, and it is only when they are removed that we are truly free to choose.[8] Talbott elaborates on why the decisive choice of evil is finally impossible as follows:

> The more one freely rebels against God, the more miserable and tormented one becomes; and the more miserable and tormented one becomes, the more incentive one has to repent of one's sin and to give up one's rebellious attitudes. . . . We may think we can promote our own interest at the expense of others or that our selfish attitudes are compatible with enduring happiness, but we cannot act upon such an illusion, at least for a long period of time, without shattering it to pieces. So in a sense, all roads have the same destination, the end of reconciliation, but some are longer and windier than others. Because our choice of roads at any given instant is truly free in the libertarian sense, we are genuinely responsible for the choices we make; but because no illusion can endure forever, the end is foreordained.[9]

8 Thomas Talbott, "The Doctrine of Everlasting Punishment," *Faith and Philosophy*, 7 (1990), p. 37.
9 Ibid., p. 39.

Now Talbott's argument has considerable appeal and plausibility. However, I think it raises serious questions when we examine it carefully.

The main problem for Talbott's account is that it ends up denying libertarian freedom, despite its claim to do otherwise. We can see this if we reflect on what is involved in Talbott's claim that "because no illusion can endure forever, the end is foreordained." In particular, we cannot maintain the illusion that we can promote our own interest without submitting to God. Talbott insists that God always shatters this illusion in the end.

I want to argue that if this is true, then we are not really free in our relationship to God. For our freedom to be preserved, we must be able to resist the truth that God is the ultimate source of happiness. To resist this truth obviously requires that we must be aware of it. God gives us this awareness, I would argue, as a gift of grace. Indeed, one of the features of the optimal grace I mentioned above is that it helps us to see that our true happiness is found in a relationship of love and obedience to God. Moreover, optimal grace would encourage us to accept this relationship. But it cannot force us to do so if we are to remain free.

Our freedom comes into play in how we respond to the truth that our genuine happiness is found only in obedience to God. A positive response of faith is more than an intellectual or abstract awareness of this fact. Genuine faith is a matter of internalizing this truth in such a way that it shapes one's character through and through. It is about trusting God even when it does not seem to be the case that obedience to him serves one's interests.

For this response to be free, however, it must be possible to deny this truth, to put it out of our minds, and act as if it were not true. To do so, of course, is an act of self-deception. But when deception is chosen in this way, it cannot simply be removed without overriding our freedom, contrary to what Talbott suggests. For our freedom to be preserved, it must be possible to refuse to trust God in the face of adversity and to persist in the illusion that we can be happy without submitting to him. Indeed, it must be possible to maintain this illusion forever.

But Talbott's account will not allow this. In his view, God shoves down our throats the truth that he is the only source of happiness. He does so by making those who rebel against him ever more miserable and tormented, and thereby giving them ever more incentive to repent. Now if this is true, then no finite person could avoid repentance for the simple reason that no finite person can absorb *ever increasing* amounts of torment and misery. There is a limit to what any finite person can bear without simply being forced to give in and swallow the truth. So if God is to respect our freedom, there must be a limit to the amount of pressure he puts on us to move us to repent.

To be sure, optimal grace would make the consequences of sin and rebellion unpleasant, and thereby show the sinner that sin is hazardous to his happiness. But there are limits to what can be done without destroying freedom. It must be possible for the sinner to pay no heed to the warning that rebellion is hazardous to his happiness, just as the smoker can ignore the warning on his cigarette package that says smoking is hazardous to his health. Surely God's optimal grace will repeatedly put this truth before the sinner's eyes, but freedom requires that he have the ability to turn his eyes away and pursue happiness on his own terms.

But still, the question persists: Why would anyone do this? What could motivate anyone to choose eternal misery in the face of optimal grace and the offer of salvation? There is, I believe, a twofold motive which accounts for this choice. First, there is a perverse sense of satisfaction that the miserable can experience, a distorted kind of gratification that can motivate the choice to persist in their sin. This point is graphically illustrated in C. S. Lewis's fantasy novel *The Great Divorce*. Lewis describes a group of sinners who take a bus ride from hell to heaven and are given the option to stay there. But curiously, most of them choose to return to hell. They have persisted in sin for so long that they have grown comfortable in it.

One of Lewis's characters is a "Big Ghost" who is shocked to learn that one of his former employees, who was a murderer, is in heaven. The former murderer is sent to the Big Ghost to explain to him his need for grace and transformation. The Ghost finds this insulting and insists that he wants nothing to do with charity. Rather than accept instruction from his former employee, he decides to return to hell.

> "So that's the trick is it?" shouted the Ghost, outwardly bitter, and yet I thought there was a kind of triumph in its voice. It had been entreated: it could make a refusal: and this seemed to it a kind of advantage. "I thought there'd be some damned nonsense. It's all a clique, all a bloody clique. Tell them I'm not coming, see? I'd rather be damned than go along with you. I came here to get my rights, see? Not to go sniveling along on charity tied onto your apron strings. If they're too fine to have me without you, I'll go home." It was almost happy now that it could, in a sense, threaten.[10]

Notice that Lewis speaks of a "kind of triumph," of a "kind of advantage," and of the ghost's being "almost happy." This suggests that the damned cling to a shadowy, malformed sense of happiness that they will not relinquish. For them, hell is "home."

But there is a second motive as well. Moral transformation involves a degree of pain that must be embraced. The Big Ghost is painfully aware that it is unpleasant to humble oneself to repent and accept grace and transformation. In view of this, there is at least some advantage in holding onto one's own rights and sense of superiority.

Lewis makes the point about the pain in moral transformation in several other passages in *The Great Divorce* as well. He describes the grass in heaven as sharp and painful to the insubstantial feet of the ghosts from hell. The ghosts are assured, however, that if they stay in heaven and come to terms with reality, they will eventually become solid and "grow acclimatised."[11] In due time they will become fit for heaven and will experience it as pure joy. But becoming acclimatized is a painful process at first.

What this points up is that we are offered no option that is free of pain. The damned are those who choose the misery of hell rather than the pain of transformation. From their distorted perspective it is better to cling to the pleasure of evil rather than pay the price of giving it up to gain eternal joy.

10 C. S. Lewis, *The Great Divorce* (New York: Macmillan, 1946), p. 36.
11 Ibid., p. 55; cf. pp. 31, 42.

5 The High Value of Libertarian Freedom

Now to summarize. I have argued that the doctrine of eternal hell is compatible with the Christian concept of God for essentially the same reason that evil is compatible with God's existence. Human freedom not only accounts for the terrible reality of evil in this world, but also explains the remarkable possibility that evil will persist in the next world. Indeed, there are intelligible motives for why some may persist in sin and prefer hell to heaven.

Universalists like Hick and Talbott cannot consistently affirm libertarian freedom while also holding to the certainty of universal salvation. It is worth noting that Talbott is prepared to say explicitly that God should interfere with our freedom and even override it, if necessary, to save all persons.[12] This points up that a commitment to the value of libertarian freedom is a watershed between at least some universalists and those who believe that the doctrine of eternal hell is compatible with the Christian concept of God.

This is not the place for a detailed defense of the value of freedom. But one point is worth making in light of my general strategy of linking my defense of hell with the appeal to free will in theodicy. It is this. If God is prepared to override freedom, it is extremely hard to see why he ever allowed freedom in the first place. Why would God allow freedom with all its attendant evil and suffering if he is prepared to retract it in the end? If he is willing to force repentance in the end, why not determine everyone to obey from the beginning, and spare us all the suffering which disobedience has caused?[13]

In view of the fact that God chose to give us freedom, even at great cost, there is good reason to believe that he will continue to respect that freedom. Even if this means that hell is forever.[14]

No Hell

Thomas Talbott

According to traditional theism, God is a supremely perfect Being, and two of his essential properties are moral perfection and omnipotence. But the *Christian* concept of God – that is, the understanding of God that emerges from the Old and New Testaments of the Christian Scriptures – is a lot more specific than

12 Talbott, "Doctrine of Everlasting Punishment," pp. 38–9. Marilyn Adams also argues that God would override our freedom to prevent anyone from being damned in her book *Horrendous Evils and the Goodness of God* (Ithaca, NY: Cornell University Press, 2000); see esp. pp. 43–9, 157.

13 For more on these issues, see Charles Seymour, "On Choosing Hell," *Religious Studies*, 33 (1997), pp. 249–66; and Michael J. Murray, "Three Versions of Universalism," *Faith and Philosophy*, 16 (1999), pp. 55–68.

14 For further defense of these arguments, see my book *Hell: The Logic of Damnation* (Notre Dame, Ind.: University of Notre Dame Press, 1992); see also Jonathan L. Kvanvig, *The Problem of Hell* (Oxford: Oxford University Press, 1993).

that: more specific concerning the nature of God's moral character, and more specific concerning the nature of his power over human destiny and the ultimate course of history.

1 The Christian Concept of God

Concerning the moral character of God, the letter known as First John declares that God not only loves, but *is* love (1 John 4:8, 16b). It is his very nature to love. I interpret this to mean that God (logically) cannot harbor ill will towards, much less reject forever, any of those whom he has loved into existence.[15] To the contrary, as we read in 1 Timothy (2:4, NRSV), God sincerely "desires everyone to be saved and to come to the knowledge of the truth"; and in 2 Peter (3:9, KJV), "The Lord . . . is not willing that any should perish, but [wills instead] that all should come to repentance." This is, of course, just what one would expect from a perfectly loving God; furthermore, some of the clearest testimonials to the enduring and inexhaustible nature of God's love are to be found in the Old Testament. What, for example, could be clearer than this? "The steadfast love of the Lord never ceases, his mercies never come to an end . . . For the Lord will not reject forever. Although he causes grief, he will have compassion according to the abundance of his steadfast love; for he does not willingly afflict or grieve anyone" (Lamentations 3:22, 31–3, NRSV).

Concerning the nature of God's power over the ultimate course of history, a host of texts in the Christian Scriptures also declare that, although one may indeed resist God's will for a season,[16] no can defeat it altogether. In the book of Isaiah (46:10b; cf. 11b, RSV) the Lord thus declares, "My counsel shall stand, and I will accomplish all my purpose"; and in the story of Job (42:2, NRSV) we read that God's servant comes to the same conclusion: "I know that you can do all things, and that no purpose of yours can be thwarted." But no one insists more emphatically than St Paul does on the power of God to bring all things into subjection to Christ, to reconcile all things in Christ, and to bring acquittal and life to all persons through Christ.[17] Not only, says Paul, will God finally accomplish *all* of his redemptive purposes and bring the course of history to a foreordained end; his providential control over history includes even the power to transform the sinner's will and to bring about the desired free choices. For as Paul writes in his letter to the Philippians (2:13, NIV), "it is God who works in you to will and to act according to his good purpose."

From the primary sources of the Christian faith, then, we can extract two crucial ideas: first, that God is not only morally perfect, but also supremely loving; and second, that God is not only omnipotent, but also almighty in the sense that he exercises sovereign control over our human destiny. Each of these ideas seems deeply

15 I defend this interpretation in "The Love of God and the Heresy of Exclusivism," *Christian Scholar's Review*, 27/1 (Fall 1997), pp. 99–112.

16 In Luke 7:30 (NRSV), we read: "But by refusing to be baptized by him [John the Baptist], the Pharisees and the lawyers rejected God's purpose for themselves." This statement seems to imply that we can indeed resist God's will on particular occasions and over the short run, but it carries no implication that the Pharisees and the lawyers might resist God's will forever or defeat it altogether.

17 See 1 Corinthians 15:27–8, Colossians 1:20, and Romans 5:18, respectively.

entrenched in the writings that make up the Christian Scriptures; indeed, each is such that a dominant theological tradition has embraced it as a clear, obvious, and utterly central teaching of Scripture. The Arminian and Wesleyan tradition, as well as much of the Roman Catholic tradition, has thus embraced the idea that God is supremely loving and therefore *wills* the salvation of all sinners; and the Augustinian and Reformed tradition, as well as the Jansenist Catholic tradition, has embraced the idea that God is almighty and therefore sovereignly controls our human destiny. Of course, many who accept one of our crucial ideas will also reject the other. But no one can plausibly deny that, with respect to each of these ideas, many texts in the Bible appear to express it clearly and emphatically.

Now let us try to express these two ideas more precisely. As a first step, I shall simply stipulate that God's redemptive purpose for the world includes everything that he regards as *most* important; hence, it is by definition a purpose that overrides all others. If God regards it to be of utmost importance that he achieve justice in the end, for example, then that is part of his redemptive purpose for the world; and if he also regards it to be of utmost importance that he preserve human freedom, then that too is part of his redemptive purpose for the world. In the latter case, we might describe his redemptive purpose this way: It is his overriding purpose (and therefore his will) to achieve a state of affairs in which all sinners *freely* repent of their sins. Whether God has the power to achieve this purpose is, of course, a further question. But if God desires the salvation of all in *any* intelligible sense, and also desires to preserve human freedom in this matter, then his redemptive purpose for the world is simply a combination of the two. It is his overriding purpose of bringing it about (in Plantinga's weak sense[18]) that all are reconciled to him freely.

With this clarification in mind, we can perhaps now express our two crucial ideas more precisely:

1 Because God is perfectly loving, it is his redemptive purpose for the world (and therefore his will) to redeem all sinners and to reconcile all of them to himself.
2 Because God is almighty and sovereignly controls the final destiny of created persons, it is within his power to achieve his redemptive purpose for the world.

Insofar as these two propositions capture an essential part of the Christian concept of God, that concept logically excludes the traditional understanding of hell as a place of everlasting punishment or everlasting separation from God. For the conjunction of (1) and (2) entails

3 God will eventually redeem all sinners and reconcile all of them to himself,

and (3) is logically inconsistent with the traditional understanding of hell.

Accordingly, those Christians who accept the traditional understanding of hell must reject at least one of our premises above and deny that it captures an essential part of the Christian concept of God. Fortunately, few Christian philosophers writing today

18 See Alvin Plantinga, *The Nature of Necessity* (Oxford: Oxford University Press, 1974), p. 173.

seem prepared to reject premise 1; indeed, I am fully confident that Walls agrees with me concerning the loving nature of the Christian God. I shall confine my remarks here, therefore, to a defense of premise 2, which I take to be the more controversial premise in the context of our present discussion.[19] In particular, I shall examine a popular line of argument against premise 2, one that stresses the reality of human free will.

The argument begins with a claim that I am quite prepared to accept: namely, insofar as freedom and determinism are incompatible, free choice introduces into the universe an element which, from God's point of view, is utterly random in the sense that it lies outside his direct causal control. So in that sense our free choices, particularly the bad ones, are genuine obstacles that God must work around as he tries to bring his loving purposes to fruition. So far, so good. But the argument also includes the additional claim that we humans have the power to defeat God's loving purposes altogether. That is, we are free to reject God not only for a season, during a time when we are mired in ambiguity and subject to illusion; we are also free to reject him forever and thereby to defeat his love forever as well.

In what follows, however, I shall argue that any such picture of a defeated God rests upon a twofold error: a failure to appreciate the limits of *possible* freedom, on the one hand, and the limits of *permissible* freedom, on the other.

2 Free Will and the Concept of Damnation

Suppose that the parents of a young boy should discover, to their horror, that they must keep their son away from fire, lest he thrust his hand into the fire and hold it there. Suppose, further, that their son has a normal nervous system and experiences the normal sensations of pain; hence, the boy not only has no discernible motive for his irrational behavior, but also has the strongest possible motive for refraining from such behavior. Here we might imagine that when the boy does thrust his hand into the fire, he screams in agony and terror but nonetheless does not withdraw his hand. Nor does he show, let us suppose, any sign of a compulsion to get to the fire and thrust his hand into it; sometimes he just does it for no discernible reason and in a context in which nothing seems to force him to do it.

Is the story I have just told coherent? I doubt it, though perhaps more would have to be said to settle the matter decisively. But whether coherent or not, the story nonetheless illustrates an important point. If someone does something in the absence of any motive for doing it *and* in the presence of an exceedingly strong motive for not doing it, then he or she displays the kind of irrationality that is itself incompatible with free choice. A necessary condition of free choice, in other words, is a minimal degree of rationality on the part of the one who acts freely. Even on the assumption that nothing causes the boy to thrust his hand into the fire, his totally inexplicable act would be more like a freak of nature or a random occurrence than a choice for which he is morally responsible. Would his parents attribute to him some sort of moral guilt for his bizarre behavior? Not if they are thinking clearly. For moral guilt can

19 For a defense of premise 1 on exegetical grounds, see Talbott, "Love of God"; and for a defense on logical and theological grounds, see Talbott, "Doctrine of Everlasting Punishment," pp. 30–4 and pp. 40–1 (n. 30).

arise only in a context in which there are discernible, albeit selfish, motives for what one does. We have imagined, however, a case where the boy has no motive at all, not even a spiteful or a selfish one, for his bizarre behavior.

As our story illustrates, it is not enough merely to insist that a free choice requires indeterminism of a certain kind and then to leave it at that – as if there were no other necessary conditions for a free choice, which there clearly are. One additional necessary condition is a minimal degree of rationality; and this condition has the effect of limiting the range of possible free choice. For, as we have just seen, an utterly inexplicable and irrational choice – one for which there is no intelligible motive and the person making it has the strongest possible motive for choosing otherwise – will simply not qualify as a genuinely free choice for which one is morally responsible.

So with that understanding, let us now ask what it might *mean* to say that someone *freely* rejects God forever. Religious people sometimes speak as if God were just another human magistrate who seeks his own glory and requires obedience for its own sake; they speak as if we might reject the Creator and Father of our souls without rejecting ourselves, oppose his will for our lives without opposing, schizophrenically perhaps, our own will for our lives. But if God is our loving Creator, then he wills for us exactly what, at the most fundamental level, we want for ourselves; he wills that we should experience supreme happiness, that our deepest yearnings should be satisfied, and that all our needs should be met. So if that is true, if God wills for us the very thing we *really* want for ourselves, whether we know it or not, how *then* are we to understand human disobedience and opposition to God?

As a first step toward answering this question, let us distinguish between two senses in which a person might reject God. If a person refuses to be reconciled to God and the person's refusal does not rest upon ignorance or misinformation or deception of any kind, then let us say that the person has made a *fully informed* decision to reject God; but if the person refuses to be reconciled to God and the person's refusal *does* rest upon ignorance or deception of some kind, then let us say that the person has made a *less than fully informed* decision to reject God. Now no one, I take it, would deny the possibility of someone's making a less than fully informed decision to reject God; it happens all the time. Even St Paul, before his conversion to Christianity, presumably saw himself as rejecting the Christian God at one time. But what might qualify as a motive for someone's making a fully informed decision to reject God? Once one has learned, perhaps through bitter experience, that evil is always destructive, always contrary to one's own interest as well as to the interest of others, and once one sees clearly that God is the ultimate source of human happiness and that rebellion can bring only greater and greater misery into one's own life as well as into the lives of others, an intelligible motive for such rebellion no longer seems even possible. The strongest conceivable motive would seem to exist, moreover, for uniting with God. So if a fully informed person should reject God nonetheless, then that person, like the boy in our story above, would seem to display the kind of irrationality which is itself incompatible with free choice.

We thus confront the essential role that ignorance, deception, and bondage to unhealthy desires must play in any intelligible decision to reject God. But ignorance, deception, and bondage to unhealthy desires are also obstacles to free choice of the relevant kind. If I am ignorant of, or deceived about, the true consequences of my choices, then I am in no position to embrace those consequences freely. Similarly, if I suffer from an illusion that conceals from me the true nature of God, or the true import of union with God, then I am again in no position to reject God freely. I may reject a caricature of God, or a false conception, but I could hardly reject the true God himself. Accordingly, the very conditions that render a less than fully informed decision to reject God intelligible also render it less than fully free; hence, God should be able to remove these conditions over time – remove the ignorance, the illusions, the bondage to unhealthy desires – without in any way interfering with human freedom.

As a counter to this, philosophers sometimes argue in the following way: If God should shatter all of my illusions, remove all of my ignorance, resolve all of the ambiguities I face, and impart to me an absolutely clear revelation of himself, then that too would effectively remove any freedom I might have to reject him. William Lane Craig thus writes: "It may well be the case that for some people the degree of revelation that would have to be imparted to them in order to secure their salvation would have to be so stunning that their freedom to disobey would be effectively removed."[20] But if Craig is right about that, then the very idea of someone freely rejecting the true God forever is simply incoherent. If both ignorance and the removal of ignorance are incompatible with the relevant kind of freedom, then there can be no freedom of the relevant kind. So it seems that Craig is impaled upon the horns of a dilemma. Either I am fully informed concerning who God is and the consequences of rejecting him, or I am not. If I am not fully informed, then I am in no position to reject the true God, as we have seen; and if I am fully informed, then (as Craig himself insists) I am incapable of rejecting God *freely*. So in neither case am I in a position to reject the true God freely.

Perhaps this is but one more reason why, according to Paul, we do not choose our own destiny, which "depends not upon human will or exertion, but upon God who shows mercy" (Romans 9:16, NRSV). Indeed, quite apart from the incoherence in the idea of freely choosing to reject the true *God* forever, the very idea of choosing an eternal destiny seems remarkably queer and utterly unlike any other choice of which we may have had some experience. Just what kind of choice are we to imagine here? Are we to imagine a single choice that, unbeknownst to the chooser, seals an eternal fate? Or should we perhaps imagine a series of choices that, so to speak, "sneak up on a person" and seal an eternal fate? And does the chooser *know* that his or her fate is being sealed forever? Or does this come later as a surprise? If the chooser does know that, unlike a choice of career, *this* choice will seal an eternal fate, just what is it that renders the choice irreversible? Until one addresses questions such as these, any talk of freely choosing an eternal destiny will most likely conceal a lot of confusion.

20 William Lane Craig, "Talbott's Universalism," *Religious Studies*, 27 (Sept., 1991), p. 300.

3 Irreparable Harm and the Limits of Permissible Freedom

So far I have argued that the idea of someone freely rejecting the true God forever is deeply incoherent, in part because a person supposedly making such a choice would either lack some essential information about the true nature of God or lack the minimal degree of rationality necessary for freedom of choice. I shall now argue that, quite apart from the question of coherence, such a choice would also involve the kind of irreparable harm that a loving God could never permit.

Consider first the two kinds of conditions under which we humans feel justified in interfering with the freedom of others. We feel justified, on the one hand, in preventing one person from doing irreparable harm – or, more accurately, harm that no *human being* can repair – to another; a loving father may thus report his own son to the police in an effort to prevent the son from committing murder. We also feel justified, on the other hand, in preventing our loved ones from doing irreparable harm to themselves; a loving father may also physically overpower his daughter in an effort to prevent her from committing suicide.

Now one might, it is true, draw a number of faulty inferences from such examples as these, in part because we humans tend to think of irreparable harm within the context of a very limited time frame, a person's life on earth. Harm that no human being can repair may nonetheless be harm that God can repair. It does not follow, therefore, that a loving God, whose goal is the reconciliation of the world, would prevent every suicide and every murder; it follows only that he would prevent every harm that not even omnipotence can repair, and neither suicide nor murder is necessarily an instance of that *kind* of harm. So even if a loving God can sometimes permit murder, he could never permit one person to annihilate the soul of another or to destroy the very possibility of future happiness for another; and even if he can sometimes permit suicide, he could never permit his loved ones to destroy the very possibility of future happiness in themselves either. Just as loving parents are prepared to restrict the freedom of the children they love, so a loving God would be prepared to restrict the freedom of the children he loves, at least in cases of truly irreparable harm. The only difference is that God deals with a much larger picture than that with which human parents are immediately concerned.

So the idea of *irreparable* harm – that is, harm that not even omnipotence can repair – is critical; and if one fails to distinguish between that kind of harm and others, then one will miss the whole point of the above argument. Jonathan Kvanvig, for example, clearly misses the point when he writes: "Contrary to what Talbott claims, freedom is sometimes more important than the harm that might result from the exercise of freedom."[21] For of course I have never claimed otherwise. I have identified instead a *certain kind of harm*, such as the eternal loss of a loved one, that omnipotence could neither repair nor compensate for; such harm would outweigh not only the value of freedom, but also the value of any conceivable good that God might bring forth from the misuse of freedom. Suppose, by way of illustration, that God should know the following: If he should grant me the freedom to annihilate the soul

21 Kvanvig, *Problem of Hell*, p. 85.

of my brother and I should exercise that freedom, then thousands of people who otherwise would not freely repent of their sin would, under these conditions, freely repent of their sin.[22] We might imagine that the horror of such irreparable harm would induce these people to reexamine their own lives. Even so, God could not permit such irreparable harm to occur; an injustice such as I have just imagined – the complete annihilation of an innocent person – would outweigh any conceivable good that God might use it to achieve.

And this brings me to a final point. For the very reason that God could never permit some of his loved ones to do irreparable harm to others, neither could he permit them to do irreparable harm to themselves. This is a point that almost none of my critics seem to have appreciated. After conceding that one might justifiably interfere with someone's freedom to commit murder, for example, Jonathan Kvanvig goes on to criticize my analysis of suicide in the following way:

> Talbott has not . . . correctly analyzed the case of suicide. Sometimes interference in cases of suicide is justified, but it is not justified solely because suicide causes irreparable harm. . . . Rather, what justifies our intervention is the fact that the person will come, or will likely come, to see that his choice of death was not what he really wanted or would have wanted if he had reflected carefully. Alternatively, if we are fully convinced and it is true that the person is competent to choose, is rational in choosing suicide, and cannot be persuaded otherwise, then, from a purely moral point of view, interference is not justified (except insofar as the suicide has consequences for other persons such as dependent children).[23]

Observe, first, that Kvanvig here imagines a case where a "person is competent to choose" and "is rational in choosing suicide." Such a case is not difficult to imagine. If a person suffers from a terminal illness such as Alzheimer's disease, or suffers persistent and excruciating pain for which there is no treatment, or possesses information that an enemy could use against comrades in arms, then it may be quite rational to see suicide as the lesser of two evils. In at least some such cases as these, those who love the suicide victim may view the suicide with relief or even as a noble act; and in all such cases God would retain the power to reunite the suicide victim with his or her loved ones at some future time. The relevant cases for our purposes, however, are those in which the suicide is quite irrational, even as a fully informed decision to reject God would be quite irrational. In these cases, we can reason in one of two ways. We might insist that the decision to commit suicide, being irrational, is not truly free; or if we grant, for the sake of argument, that the decision is free despite its irrational character, we might then insist upon an obligation to interfere, where possible, with the freedom of others to harm themselves in a way that is both irrational and irreparable.

22 Of course, if the argument of the previous section is correct, then the supposition I make here – namely, that God could induce some people to repent freely only if my brother's soul should be annihilated – is deeply incoherent. But we are here granting, for the sake of argument, that there is no incoherence in such suppositions. For an example of someone who accepts the possibility that God could induce some people to repent freely only if he damns others eternally, see William Lane Craig, "'No Other Name': A Middle Knowledge Perspective on the Exclusivity of Salvation through Christ," *Faith and Philosophy*, 6 (April 1989), pp. 172–8.
23 Kvanvig, *Problem of Hell*, p. 84.

Observe, second, Kvanvig's final proviso concerning the consequences of a suicide for other persons. In conceding the relevance of such consequences, he in effect concedes the very argument he has set out to criticize. For no one is an isolated monad for whom supreme happiness, or the lack of same, is independent of other persons; indeed, wherever two people are united in love, their interests and the conditions of their happiness are so tightly interwoven as to be logically inseparable. If I should truly love my wife, my son, and my daughter, for example, and love them even as I love myself, then any harm that befalls them is harm that befalls me, and any good that befalls them is likewise a good that befalls me. So if any one of them were to commit suicide, that would indeed harm me; and if my daughter, say, were somehow to harm herself *irreparably* – even if by her own "choice" she were to make herself intolerably evil and thereby to damn herself eternally, so that she were to be lost to me forever – then my own happiness could never be complete, not so long as I continued to love her and to yearn for her redemption. For I would always know what *could* have been, and I would always experience that as a terrible tragedy and an unacceptable loss, one for which no compensation is even conceivable. Is it any wonder, then, that Paul could say concerning his unbelieving kindred whom he loved so much: "For I could wish that I myself were accursed and cut off from Christ for the sake of my own people, my kindred according to the flesh" (Romans 9:3, NRSV)? Nor is there anything irrational about such a wish. From the perspective of Paul's love, his own damnation would be no worse an evil, and no greater threat to his own happiness, than the damnation of his loved ones would be.

Every created person is an object of someone else's love (God's, if no one else's). So if God could never permit any of us to do irreparable harm to someone else, as Kvanvig appears to concede, then neither could he permit any of us to do irreparable harm to ourselves.

4 Conclusion

We have every reason to believe that an almighty and perfectly loving God would guarantee that everyone eventually comes to a good end. Paul calls this "predestination" and speaks confidently of a final victory over sin and death; he also presents a remarkable picture of how the end could be predestined even though our choices made in the present are genuinely free.[24]

As I would extrapolate and expand upon it, the picture is this: The more one freely rebels against God in the present, the more miserable and tormented one eventually becomes, and the more miserable and tormented one becomes, the more incentive one has to repent of one's sin and to give up one's rebellious attitudes. But, more than that, the consequences of sin are themselves a means of revelation; they reveal the true meaning of separation and enable us to see through the very self-deception that makes evil choices possible in the first place. We may think that we can promote our

24 See, e.g., Paul's discussion of God's kindness and severity in Romans 11. For an interpretation of Paul's universalism, see my own article, "Universal Reconciliation and the New Testament," *Christian Scholar's Review*, 21 (June 1992).

own interest at the expense of others, or that our selfish attitudes are compatible with enduring happiness, but we cannot act upon such an illusion, at least not for a long period of time, without shattering it to pieces. So in that sense, all paths have the same destination, the end of reconciliation, but some are longer and windier than others. Because our choice of paths in the present is genuinely free, we are morally responsible for that choice; but because no illusion can endure forever, the end is foreordained. As Paul himself puts it: We are all predestined to be conformed to the image of Christ (see Romans 8:29). That part is a matter of grace, not human will or effort.

Reply to Talbott

Talbott and I essentially agree on what it means to claim that God is perfect love. Because God is supremely loving, he genuinely desires the flourishing of all his creatures. Since human beings can only flourish when they are properly related to God, he desires that all persons receive his offer of salvation.

However, I would take exception to Talbott's interpretation of what is involved in God's "overriding purpose . . . to achieve a state of affairs in which all sinners freely repent of their sins." Talbott construes this in such a way that God is defeated if all persons do not freely repent of their sins and receive salvation. This claim is closely connected with his view of what follows from God's sovereignty: namely, that since God "controls the final destiny of created persons, it is within his power to achieve his redemptive purpose for the world."

By way of disagreement, I first want to reiterate that one of the fundamental differences between my view and Talbott's concerns whether the notion of a decisive choice of evil is a coherent one. I argued at some length in my essay that such a choice is possible, and that there are intelligible motives to account for it. So I will not repeat those points here. But whether the reader agrees with me or with Talbott on the possibility of eternal hell will turn largely on this issue.

The issue I want to focus on here is what Talbott calls God's "overriding purpose." Such a purpose, by definition, trumps all others, and a God who is sovereign in any meaningful sense would surely achieve it. What, then, is God's overriding purpose? In my view, it is to glorify himself by expressing his perfect love to all his creatures through his Son. Since God is glorified when he promotes the flourishing and well-being of his creatures, God's glory and human well-being are not at odds in any way. Rather, they readily converge.

However, I would insist, against Talbott, that the success of God's overriding purpose does not require that all persons accept his offer of salvation. The main reason for this is because God has chosen, in his sovereignty, to create us with libertarian freedom. As I maintained in my essay, such freedom is an essential component of our personal nature, the very nature that makes it possible for us to respond to God with genuine love, trust, and obedience. Indeed, genuine love and trust cannot be coerced or forced from us, but must be elicited in a manner that respects our personality and preserves our freedom intact. In view of this, God does not "control the final destiny of created persons" in such a way that all will inevitably accept his love, as Talbott contends. While he certainly desires that all created persons accept his offer of salvation, God's choice to create free persons in his image opens up the possibility that some of his creatures will choose not to do so.

The rhetorical force of Talbott's position turns crucially on his claim that God is "defeated" in the case that some persons forever reject his love, that his sovereign purposes would not be achieved. This is loaded language, of course, and no one who takes God seriously will accept the notion that he is vulnerable to defeat of any kind. Over against this claim, I would argue that God made the sovereign choice to create free persons knowing that some of them would exercise their freedom in ways he would not prefer. But he preferred a world with free creatures in which things happen against his will to a world without free creatures.

I am sure that Talbott agrees that many things happen in our world that God would prefer not to happen. World wars, rape, and child abuse are just a few examples that come quickly to mind. However, God is not defeated by these events, even temporarily; nor is he any less sovereign because he has chosen not to control things to the point of preventing them from happening. Likewise, God would prefer that none of his creatures finally reject his offer of salvation. But his ultimate purpose of glorifying himself by demonstrating his love to all persons is fully achieved even in the event that some persons persist in rejecting it.

The perfection of God's love does not depend on our response, nor does his glory hinge on our choices. However we respond to God's perfect love, he is glorified, and his overriding purpose is achieved. If we accept his love, he is glorified in our flourishing; if we persist in rejecting it, he is glorified when it becomes utterly obvious that we cannot be truly happy apart from him. Even in our misery, he continues to love us and to desire our well-being. Thereby his love is demonstrated and his sovereign purpose is achieved.

Reply to Walls

Walls and I agree concerning the loving nature of the Christian God, and that is a huge area of agreement. But we disagree on some important matters.

Whereas I regard hell, if it exists at all, as a forcibly imposed but temporary punishment, Walls regards it as a freely embraced eternal destiny. In support of his interpretation, Walls cites certain (unidentified) words of Jesus. But the words of Jesus, as recorded in the gospels, do not support the idea of a freely embraced destiny; they support instead the idea of a forcibly imposed punishment, even a torture chamber or a place of unbearable torment. In the parable of the sheep and the goats, those subjected to punishment not only do not choose their punishment; they are surprised to receive it. And in the parable of the rich man and Lazarus, the rich man's torment is hardly something that he has freely chosen to endure.

So, as I see it, Walls's account distorts the teaching of Jesus beyond recognition. It also requires that we swallow the idea of a *decisive choice for evil* – which, as Walls describes it, "involves one's whole person" and is "definitive with respect to one's beliefs, feelings, and desires." Does this mean that, given one's beliefs, feelings, and desires at the time of making a decisive choice for evil, choosing otherwise has already become a psychological impossibility? If so, then the choice is causally determined and not truly free in the libertarian sense. If not – if choosing otherwise remains compatible with these exact same beliefs, feelings, and desires – then the idea of the choice being *definitive* with respect to them carries no clear meaning. In any event, a decisive choice for evil could hardly be *definitive* with respect to anything but false beliefs (illusions) and unhealthy desires.

So it seems to me that Walls wants it both ways. He wants his imagined choice to be genuinely free in the libertarian sense, yet he wants it to be the kind of choice that only someone who is *already* in bondage to illusion and unhealthy desires could possibly make.

According to Walls, my universalism "ends up denying libertarian freedom." But that is just false. For on my view, libertarian freedom is an essential part of the process whereby God reveals himself to us and in the end saves us; indeed, how we encounter God's love in the future, whether we encounter it as kindness or as severity, may depend exclusively upon what we freely choose in the present.

So my account leaves plenty of room for libertarian freedom, as Walls understands it. But perhaps his contention is that I circumscribe such freedom in the wrong way. For I do deny that we choose (freely or otherwise) our own destiny, which is wholly a matter of grace, and I also deny that we have the power to maintain our illusions forever. All of which leads Walls to conclude that, given my view, "we are not really free in our relationship to God." But that is just false as well. If I am free right now either to obey or to disobey God, then I am also free right now in my relationship to him.

An important distinction I would draw here is between our free choices and their unintended consequences. As I see it, our free choices, particularly the bad ones, have real consequences in our lives, and these are often beyond our power to control. If I freely act upon the illusion that I can ski down a treacherous slope, for example, a fall and a broken leg may well shatter the illusion to pieces. Similarly, if I continue to act upon the illusion that I can benefit myself at the expense of others, the bitter consequences of such actions will over time shatter that illusion as well. Our free choices may be up to us, but their unintended consequences and the hard truths they sometimes reveal are not.

In short, I hold that God requires us, in the absence of repentance, to experience the full consequences of our sinful choices as we "smash our heads," so to speak, against the hard rock of reality; we are never free, in other words, to sin with impunity. But Walls seems to imply that we sometimes can sin with impunity. For, lest he shatter all their illusions and thereby undermine their freedom to resist salvation, God must protect the damned from the full consequences of their sinful choices. It is as if I should bring my hand near to a flame and God should protect me from the excruciating pain of the flame. In that event, my belief that I could so act with impunity would not be an illusion.

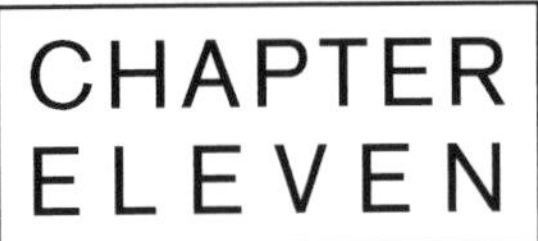

Is Morality Based on God's Commands?

This set of essays considers two major theistic views on the relation between God and morality. The first view, endorsed by Janine Marie Idziak, is known as the "divine command theory." It answers the above question affirmatively: an act is morally right because God commands it and morally wrong because God forbids it. Craig Boyd and Raymond VanArragon defend a view known as the "natural law theory." It answers the question negatively: human nature determines what is right or wrong so that, roughly, an act is morally right because it helps to fulfill human nature and morally wrong because it prevents this fulfillment. Idziak and Boyd and VanArragon draw out their theories and define them against popular objections.

Divine Commands Are the Foundation of Morality

Janine Marie Idziak

In Plato's *Euthyphro* Socrates raises the question, "Is what is holy holy because the gods approve it, or do they approve it because it is holy?"[1] This question is the beginning of a debate among philosophers and theologians about the *foundation of morality*. Is an action right (or wrong) *because* God commands or prohibits it, or does God command (or prohibit) the action because it is already right (or wrong)?

1 In Janine Marie Idziak (ed.), *Divine Command Morality: Historical and Contemporary Readings* (New York and Toronto: Edwin Mellen, 1980), p. 41.

A divine command ethicist takes the position that the standard of right and wrong *is* the commands and prohibitions of God. According to the divine command theory [DCT], "an action or kind of action is right or wrong if and only if and *because* it is commanded or forbidden by God."[2] This ethical theory maintains that "what ultimately *makes* an action right or wrong is its being commanded or forbidden by God and nothing else."[3] An ethics of divine commands is frequently expressed in terms of right and wrong being determined by the *will of God.*

While divine command ethics bases morality on *God*, an alternative approach to ethics bases right and wrong on *human nature*. This is natural law ethics. According to natural law theory, the basic principles of morals are objective, accessible to reason, and based on human nature.[4] An action is right if it serves to fulfill human nature, and wrong if it goes against human nature.[5] Our human nature includes various inclinations and tendencies. The task of reason is "to discover, sort out, and order these inclinations in accord with appropriate human fulfillment."[6] This essay will present the case that an ethics of divine commands provides a more plausible account of the foundation of morality than does natural law theory. It will do this by setting out a wide range of arguments providing positive support for the divine command theory, drawing comparisons with natural law theory. Several objections against the divine command position of particular appeal to natural law ethicists will also be answered.

1 Arguments for Divine Command Ethics

In the history of divine command ethics, formal arguments in support of this ethical theory are presented which draw from the realm of metaphysics. Various philosophers and theologians from the Middle Ages, the Reformation, and the Puritan era invoked the concept of God as *first and uncaused cause* in defense of an ethics of divine commands. One example is the Puritan theologian John Preston, who reasoned in the following way. God is the first cause. God's status as *first* cause implies that God is *uncaused*: that is, that God cannot be causally affected by anything. If God were to choose something because God perceived it to possess goodness or justice, then God would be causally affected by something external to himself, which is impossible. Therefore, it is not the case that God wills something because it is good or just; rather, something is good or just because God wills it.[7]

In the Middle Ages, Peter of Ailly took the familiar cosmological argument for the existence of God and constructed an analogue of it supporting an ethics of divine commands. "Just as the divine will is the first efficient cause in the class of efficient

2 W. K. Frankena, *Ethics*, 2nd edn (Englewood Cliffs, NJ: Prentice-Hall, 1973), p. 28.

3 Ibid.

4 D. J. O'Connor, *Aquinas and Natural Law* (London: Macmillan, 1967), p. 57.

5 Ibid., pp. 68–73.

6 Edward Collins Vacek, SJ, "Divine-Command, Natural-Law, and Mutual-Love Ethics," *Theological Studies*, 57 (1996), pp. 633–53: p. 639.

7 Janine Marie Idziak, "In Search of 'Good Positive Reasons' for an Ethics of Divine Commands: A Catalogue of Arguments," *Faith and Philosophy*, 6 (1989), pp. 47–64: pp. 48–51.

cause," so, Ailly contends, "in the class of obligatory law, it is the first law or rule."[8] Another medieval philosophical theologian, Andrew of Neufchateau, constructed an argument in support of the divine command position which draws an analogy between the metaphysical notion of God as "first being" and the ethical notion of God as "first good."[9]

These types of arguments in defense of an ethics of divine commands may leave the impression that this ethical theory belongs to the "God of the philosophers." However, divine command ethics has a solid foundation in the life of the religious faith community.

A *biblical* basis has been claimed for an ethics of divine commands. The twentieth-century theologian Emil Brunner remarks that the search for the basis of the Good "led us out of a eudaemonistic and anthropocentric definition of the Good – away from the Aristotelian and Thomist conception (that the Good is that which is adapted to human nature) – back to the truth of the Bible, namely, that only that which God wills is good; and that we are to will what God wills, because He wills it."[10] The same position is articulated by another twentieth-century Protestant theologian, Carl F. H. Henry: "This notion of an 'intrinsic good' is alien to biblical theology. The God of Hebrew-Christian revelation is the ground of ethics. He is the supreme rule of right. He defines the whole content of morality by his own revealed will."[11] Like Brunner, Henry contrasts biblical ethics with the natural law tradition: "The good in Hebrew-Christian theistic ethics is not that which is adapted to human nature, but it is that to which the Creator obliges human nature."[12]

Exactly what in the Bible serves as a grounding for an ethics of divine commands? In the Old Testament there are cases in which holy people perform actions which are normally regarded as morally wrong. These include Abraham preparing to kill Isaac, the Israelites despoiling (i.e., stealing from) the Egyptians on their way out of Egypt, the prophet Hosea committing adultery by taking a "wife of fornication," Samson killing himself, Jacob lying to deceive his father, the Israelites divorcing foreign wives, and the patriarchs engaging in polygamy. These are cases in which the action violates a prohibition laid down by God himself in the Ten Commandments, yet is performed *under a divine command* and is not considered morally wrong.[13] The most straightforward interpretation of these cases is to conclude that "divine commands can and do determine the moral status of actions."[14] Indeed, in commenting on these biblical cases, the fourteenth-century divine command ethicist Andrew of Neufchateau describes them as "actions which, *known per se by the law of nature and by the dictate*

8 Quoted in ibid., p. 57.

9 Ibid., p. 56.

10 Brunner, in Idziak (ed.), *Divine Command Morality*, p. 137.

11 Henry, in ibid., pp. 143–4.

12 Ibid., p. 141.

13 Andrew of Neufchateau, OFM, *Questions on an Ethics of Divine Commands*, ed. and tr. Janine Marie Idziak (Notre Dame, Ind.: University of Notre Dame Press, 1997), pp. xxii, 91; Philip L. Quinn, "The Recent Revival of Divine Command Ethics," *Philosophy and Phenomenological Research*, 50 (1990, suppl.), pp. 345–65: pp. 354–9; *idem*, "The Primacy of God's Will in Christian Ethics," in James E. Tomberlin (ed.), *Philosophical Perspectives*, vol. 6: *Ethics* (Atascadero: Ridgeview, 1992), pp. 499–503.

14 Quinn, "Primacy of God's Will," p. 501.

of natural reason, appear to be prohibited," contending that "it is possible that such actions not be sins with respect to the absolute power of God."[15]

Grounding for an ethics of divine commands can also be found in the New Testament. The contemporary philosopher Philip Quinn finds such a foundation in the well-known command of Jesus to love one's neighbor as one loves oneself:

> The love of neighbor of which Jesus speaks is unnatural for humans in their present condition. It does not spontaneously engage their affections, and so training, self-discipline and, perhaps, even divine assistance are required to make its achievement a real possibility. For most of us most of the time, love of neighbor is not an attractive goal, and, if it were optional, we would not pursue it. It must therefore be an obligatory love with the feel of something that represents a curb or check on our natural desires and predilections. Because the divine command conception holds that all obligations depend on God's will, such an obligatory love is properly represented as subject to being commanded by a divine lawgiver. It is, then, no accident that the love of neighbor the Gospels propose to us is a commanded love.[16]

Natural law ethicists base rightness and wrongness on human nature. Quinn essentially makes the point that the obligation to love all other people as we love ourselves (an obligation which natural law ethicists in the Christian tradition would not deny) *does not seem to be derivable from our human nature*. Quinn describes the love of neighbor which Jesus commands as "unnatural" for humans in their present condition, as something which does not spontaneously engage our affections, as something that represents a curb on our "natural desires and predilections." Since not all people "are alike in erotic attractiveness" to us, "nor are they all equal with respect to the charms of a virtuous character," Quinn infers that "a nondiscriminatory love of all alike is bound to go against the grain of our natural affections and their partialities." What is the case is that "it is God's will, made known to us by Jesus, that we humans love one another in this manner." In other words, Christians "seem to be committed to the view that the obligation to love the neighbor as oneself is a duty imposed by a direct divine command." And since "this commanded love is foundational for Christian ethics" and "what sets Christian ethics apart from all its rivals," Quinn proposes that we "find in what is most distinctive about the Christian ethics of the Gospels another reason for Christians to favor a divine command conception of moral obligation."[17]

When defining an ethics of divine commands, we stated that it is often expressed in terms of right and wrong being determined by the *will of God*. Down to the present day, *conformity to the will of God* is an important theme in Western spirituality. Hubert van Zeller, a monk at Downside Abbey in England, begins a book of popular spirituality with these words:

> There can hardly be a better practice in the spiritual life than that of meeting everything as an expression of the will of God. Phrases like 'if God wills' and 'it must be the will

15 Andrew of Neufchateau, *Questions on an Ethics of Divine Commands*, p. 91; italics added.

16 Quinn, "Primacy of God's Will," p. 504.

17 Ibid., pp. 506–7.

> of God' and 'may God's will go with you' come naturally to the devout. People in certain traditions of Christian life say these things all day long and mean them. *God's will becomes for them the standard of everyday decisions* and the background against which life happens. Nothing furthers the supernatural point of view so effectively as the cultivation of such a habit. It can be seen as an extension of the *Our Father*, as an identification with the disposition of Christ, as the application of 'I came not to do my own will but the will of my Father who is in heaven' to our own human concerns. It can be made to sum up the whole of our Christian service.[18]

Van Zeller goes on to say that "the merit attaching to any work is measured solely by its conformity to the will of God."[19] "I pledge myself wholly to the will of God" is the "attitude of mind which you would expect to find in a saint."[20] "The highest thing a human will can do," van Zeller claims, "is freely to will God's will."[21] In sum, an ethics of divine commands can be defended as the *philosophical formalization of an important theme of the spiritual life: namely, conformity to the divine will.*

Furthermore, this kind of spirituality is itself *biblically grounded.* Van Zeller calls our attention to the Psalms: "'In the head of the book it is written of me,' he says in the thirty-ninth psalm, 'that I should do your will. O my God, I have desired it, and to have your law in the midst of my heart.'"[22] Or again, we find "in the 142nd Psalm: 'Teach me to do your will, for you are my God.'"[23] Van Zeller traces the theme of doing God's will through the New Testament gospels and epistles:

> 'Not everyone who says to me, "Lord, Lord," shall enter into the kingdom of heaven,' Christ explains when pointing out that a tree is judged by its fruits, 'but he who does the will of my Father who is in heaven.' . . . Again there is that vivid scene given by St. Mark which shows our Lord so pressed with his work of preaching that Mary and some of his relations have to send messages to say they would like to speak to him: 'Who is my mother and my brethren? . . . whosoever shall do the will of God, he is my brother and my sister and my mother.'
>
> We could go through the epistles, combing them for references to the necessity for surrender to the Father's will. 'He who does the will of God,' says St. John, 'abides for ever.' 'That doing the will of God,' we read in Hebrews, 'you may receive the promise.' St. Paul to the Romans: 'Be not conformed to this world, but be reformed in the newness of your mind, that you may prove what is the good and the acceptable and the perfect will of God.' 'Not serving the eye,' St. Paul warns the Ephesians, 'but as servants of Christ doing the will of God from the heart.' He tells the Colossians how Epaphras is constantly praying for them that they 'may stand perfect and full in all the will of God.'[24]

Thus we have found yet another biblical grounding for an ethics of divine commands in the biblical theme of *doing the will of God.*

18 Dom Hubert van Zeller, *The Will of God in Other Words* (Springfield, Ill.: Templegate, 1964), p. 7; italics added.
19 Ibid., p. 18.
20 Ibid., p. 41.
21 Ibid., p. 58.
22 Ibid., p. 33.
23 Ibid., p. 76.
24 Ibid., pp. 109–10.

2 Critique of Natural Law Ethics

Natural law theory has been the dominant ethical tradition in Roman Catholicism. A criticism of natural law ethics which has come from the Protestant tradition is that "natural law is unbiblical."[25] Hence, the biblical bases we have found for an ethics of divine commands seem to provide an argument in favor of this theory in opposition to natural law ethics. However, natural law theorists might well retort that a biblical basis can likewise be found for their ethical system. They might cite Paul's letter to the Romans (especially 2:14), which speaks of persons who have not heard of the revealed law of God being "led by reason to do what the Law commands" and of a law "engraved on their hearts." Or again, they might point to the work of contemporary theologians like Josef Fuchs, who takes up the biblical concept of the *imago Dei* (that is, of human beings being made in the *image of God*) and incorporates it into natural law theory.[26] Thus, if a decisive case is to be made in favor of an ethics of divine commands, we must inquire further. Are there additional types of arguments which can be offered in support of an ethics of divine commands? Can we find any ways in which an ethics of divine commands is clearly superior to natural law theory?

Divine command ethics can be defended on the grounds that it follows from certain beliefs we have about God's nature and status and about the character of the relationship between God and human beings. John Locke saw following divine commands as a correlate of our dependency on God as *creator*. According to Locke, "it is proper that we should live according to the precept of His [God's] will" because "we owe our body, soul, and life – whatever we are, whatever we have, and even whatever we can be – to Him and to Him alone."[27] Since "God has created us out of nothing and, if He pleases, will reduce us again to nothing," we are, Locke proposes, "subject to Him in perfect justice and by utmost necessity."[28]

Moreover, theists regard God as *sovereign* over all. There cannot be anything which is independent of God, to which God might be subject and which would constitute a limitation on God.[29] God's dominion over the contingent has long been recognized. Everything which is contingent "depends on God's power for its existence whenever it exists."[30] Some philosophers have recently gone even further, to argue that necessary truths also depend on God.[31] An ethics of divine commands rightly extends God's sovereignty to the moral realm.[32] Indeed, "when human beings stake a claim to the independent validity of moral law, they deny God's supremacy as the only King and the only worthy object of devotion."[33]

25 James M. Gustafson, *Protestant and Roman Catholic Ethics: Prospects for Rapprochement* (Chicago: University of Chicago Press, 1978), p. 103.
26 Ibid., pp. 101–3.
27 Locke, in Idziak, *Divine Command Morality*, p. 182.
28 Ibid.
29 Idziak, *Divine Command Morality*, p. 9.
30 Quinn, "Primacy of God's Will," p. 495.
31 Quinn, "Recent Revival," pp. 359–61; *idem*, "Primacy of God's Will," pp. 495–7.
32 Quinn, "Recent Revival," pp. 361–3; *idem*, "Primacy of God's Will," pp. 495, 497–8.
33 Avi Sagi and Daniel Statman, "Divine Command Morality and Jewish Tradition," *Journal of Religions Ethics*, 23 (1995), pp. 39–67: p. 41.

Concomitantly, an ethics of divine commands satisfies the religious requirement that God be the supreme focus of our loyalties. As Robert Merrihew Adams has pointed out, "If our supreme commitment in life is to doing what is right just because it is right, and if what is right is right just because God wills or commands it, then surely our highest allegiance is to God."[34]

In basing ethics on a human nature common to all people and in using the human faculty of reason to discern ethical principles, natural law theory seems able to address "all people of good will" independently of the particularities of the various religious traditions.[35] Such universality would seem to be an advantage of the natural law approach to ethics. On the other hand, the anthropocentric focus of natural law ethics leaves open the possibility of *doing ethics without any reference to God.* This criticism has been forcefully stated by the contemporary ethicist Edward Collins Vacek, SJ:

> When Aquinas wrote, in an oft cited line, "We do not offend God except by doing something contrary to our own good," he himself opened the possibility of making our relationship with God superfluous for doing ethics. If the religious question of "offending God" depends on the prior moral question of "our own good," then the moral question may be settled independently.... Natural-law ethics can proceed under a rubric of "methodological atheism."[36]

Doing ethics in complete independence of God cannot be a satisfactory option for a theist. Such a stance ignores the centrality that God is supposed to have in the life of a theist. It fails to recognize God's sovereignty over all realms and flies in the face of the religious belief that God should be the supreme focus of human loyalties.

3 Criticisms of Divine Command Ethics Answered

On the other hand, divine command ethics has not gone without criticism from natural law theorists. For one thing, "natural-law ethicists criticize divine-command theory for distorting . . . the idea of God." Vacek continues:

> The intention behind this theory, as John Mahoney explains, is "to glorify the transcendence and majesty of God, and his supreme freedom of activity." The consequence, as John Reeder observes, has been that this voluntaristic theory "too radically separates God from his own creation." The idea of God behind this theory seems closer to that of an Oriental potentate issuing edicts accompanied by promises and threats than to that of a person who so loved the world as to become incarnate.[37]

This view of the divine command position is contradicted by the work of the twentieth-century theologian and divine command ethicist Karl Barth. Barth explic-

34 Robert M. Adams, "A Modified Divine Command Theory of Ethical Wrongness," in Gene Outka and John P. Reeder, Jr (eds), *Religion and Morality* (Garden City, NY: Anchor, 1973), pp. 318–47: p. 334.

35 Gustafson, *Protestant and Roman Catholic Ethics*, pp. 61–2; Vacek, "Divine-Command," pp. 640–1.

36 Vacek, "Divine-Command," pp. 640–1.

37 Ibid., pp. 639–40.

itly rejects the divine power as an adequate basis for adherence to divine command ethics,[38] and grounds the divine command position in *God's graciousness to us in Jesus Christ.* According to Barth, the basis of God's ethical claim on us lies in the fact that "God has given us Himself." In other words, it lies in the fact that "although He [God] could be without us – He did not and does not will to be without us"; in the fact that "He has taken our place and taken up our cause." [39] In sum, taking divine commands as defining what we ought to do is the fitting response to the way in which God has first reached out to us.

A frequent criticism of the divine command theory is that morality becomes an *arbitrary and capricious enterprise* if right and wrong are determined *solely* by God's commands or will. A corollary of this line of criticism is that God could will or command actions which intuitively seem abhorrent and wrong to us but which would have to be considered right because of the divine edict. These concerns about an ethics of divine commands have been voiced by the popular spiritual writer C. S. Lewis:

> To make this position perfectly clear, one of them even said that though God has, as it happens, commanded us to love Him and one another, He might equally well have commanded us to hate Him and one another, and hatred would then have been right. It was apparently a mere toss-up which he decided to do. Such a view in effect makes God a mere arbitrary tyrant.[40]

The contemporary philosopher Robert Burch has articulated the problem in the following way:

> One [objection] claims that theories like DCT make morality merely an arbitrary and capricious matter. For such theories seem to imply that anything whatsoever might be morally good if only it be willed by God. . . . Yet it is absurd, so the objection goes, to hold that such actions as the gratuitous infliction of pain, the breach of promise for no reason, and the termination of the life or freedom of the innocent are possibly morally good; and even God's willing could not make them so.[41]

A natural law ethicist might here claim superiority for his theory over an ethics of divine commands. On the natural law scheme there can be no question of arbitrariness, since rightness is determined on the basis of what is in accord with human nature and serves to fulfill it. Furthermore, the requirement of consistency with human nature would seem to preclude certain types of actions (for example, the gratuitous infliction of pain) from ever being considered morally right.

Divine command ethicists have developed several different replies to this line of criticism. In addressing the first objection, one approach takes issue with the idea that there is something reprehensible about making determinations through the will alone,

38 Barth, in Idziak, *Divine Command Morality*, pp. 126–7.

39 Ibid., p. 130.

40 Quoted in James G. Hanink and Gary R. Mar, "What Enthyphro Couldn't Have Said," *Faith and Philosophy*, 4 (1987), pp. 241–61, at p. 243.

41 Robert Burch, "Objective Values and the Divine Command Theory of Morality," *New Scholasticism*, 54 (1980), pp. 279–304: p. 289.

as the words "arbitrary" and "capricious" imply. In the Middle Ages the divine command ethicist Andrew of Neufchateau took over from Thomas Bradwardine descriptions of cases in which human beings perform just actions stemming not from a decision of reason, but from a sheer choice of will. Suppose, for example, that John has been given the power to pardon one, and only one, of two persons placed under a death sentence. Suppose further that no relevant differences can be found between the two condemned persons. In such a case, there is no better reason for pardoning the one than for pardoning the other. However, John justly frees the one whom he chooses to pardon, although reason did not move his will to make this choice. And from the very fact that John wills to free this particular one, the act of freeing him is just. The same sort of situation occurs when someone is in a position to bestow some gift or benefit on only one of two or more persons who are equally worthy of receiving it. The point of these cases is that, since we allow that justness can stem from sheer will in the case of human beings, there is surely nothing inappropriate or reprehensible about the same thing occurring in the case of the divine will.[42]

Another, very different type of reply to the first objection coming from medieval philosophical theology invokes the concept of the divine *simplicity*. Most basically, simplicity means that there are no parts distinguishable in God. Thus intellect and will are not separate faculties in God, as they are in human beings. Hence, when God wills something to be right (as the divine command ethicist claims), God's reason is also operating. Recognizing this takes away the sense of arbitrariness alleged to characterize the divine command theory. Heiko Oberman has developed this line of defense in his book on the medieval theologian and divine command ethicist Gabriel Biel:

> At this point, however, we must remember Boehner's defense of Occam . . . : the set order is for the *Venerabilis Inceptor* by no means a product solely of God's will; will and intellect are two different names for God's essence. This defense appears to be applicable also to Biel. Against the Thomistic emphasis on the priority of God's intellect, the priority of God's will is not stressed as much as the simplicity of God's being and the resulting unity of his intellect and essence. As the simplicity of God's being also implies a unity of essence and will, God's very essence guarantees the unbreakable relation and cooperation of intellect and will in God's *opera ad extra*. . . . Biel constantly tries to make clear that, whereas the will of God is the immediate cause of every act, these acts are certainly no arbitrary products of God's will alone. On the contrary, God's will operates according to God's essential wisdom, though this may be hidden from man.[43]

A third type of reply addresses both of the aforementioned objections. It consists in pointing out that what God wills and commands will be *consonant with and directed by God's nature and character*. God is "defined as perfect in knowledge, justice and love," and God will "by definition will in accord with these several attributes."[44] This means, first of all, that the commands of God in establishing moral right and wrong

42 Andrew of Neufchateau, *Questions on an Ethics of Divine Commands*, p. xvii.

43 Heiko Augustinus Oberman, *The Harvest of Medieval Theology: Gabriel Biel and Late Medieval Nominalism* (Cambridge, Mass.: Harvard University Press, *Divine Command Morality*, 1963), pp. 98–9.

44 Brown, in Idziak, *Divine Command Morality*, p. 250.

will be anything but arbitrary and capricious.[45] Second, if God wills in accord with the divine nature as *loving*, this means that God will not in fact command such acts as the gratuitous infliction of pain. Hence, God commanding such intuitively abhorrent and immoral actions reduces to a mere theoretical possibility which will never in fact be realized and, consequently, which need not trouble the divine command ethicist.[46]

4 Conclusion

In sum, what can be said in favor of adopting an ethics of divine commands as our account of the foundation of morality? First, an ethics of divine commands is biblically based. There are incidents recorded in the Old Testament in which an action normally regarded as immoral is made the right thing to do by a divine command. In the New Testament the central prescription to love our neighbor as we love ourselves goes against our natural inclinations and seems to be a duty imposed on us by a direct divine command. Further, an ethics of divine commands is grounded in the biblical theme of doing the will of God. Concomitantly, conformity to the will of God is an important theme in Western spirituality. In these respects an ethics of divine commands, as a theory of philosophical ethics, reflects the life and experience of the religious faith community.

An ethics of divine commands follows from beliefs we have about God's nature and status and from the character of the relationship between God and human beings. Specifically, it is related to our dependence on God as creator, to God's sovereignty over all, and to the religious requirement that God be the supreme focus of our loyalties.

Unlike natural law theory, an ethics of divine commands does not suffer from the defect of methodological atheism – that is, of making it possible to do ethics without any reference to God. Further, it is inaccurate to denigrate an ethics of divine commands on the grounds that it distorts our concept of God and makes morality arbitrary and capricious. It is likewise incorrect to portray an ethics of divine commands as entailing that intuitively abhorrent acts could be made the morally right thing to do by God. The beneficent and loving God who does the commanding would simply not give such commands.

Ethics Is Based on Natural Law

Craig A. Boyd and Raymond J. VanArragon

Most theists believe that God commands us to perform certain acts and forbids us from performing others. Those acts that God commands us to perform are morally

45 Ibid., pp. 250–1.

46 Adams, "Modified Divine Command Theory," pp. 320–4.

right; those that God forbids are morally wrong. But what exactly is the relation between God's commands and the rightness or wrongness of those acts? Is an act right because God commands it, or does God command an act because it is right? Conversely, does God's prohibition make an act wrong, or does God prohibit an act because it is wrong? These questions, first posed in Plato's *Euthyphro*, have long troubled theists, because each of the obvious answers carries with it unpleasant consequences. In other words, these questions appear to introduce a dilemma, as can be seen in the following argument:

1 If God's command *makes* an act right, then morality is arbitrary.
2 If God commands an act *because* it is right, then God's command is not essential to morality.
3 Either God's command makes an act right, or God commands an act because it is right.

Therefore,

4 Either morality is arbitrary, or God's command is not essential to morality.

This apparent dilemma forces theists to make the uncomfortable choice between God's sovereignty and a sturdy, objective foundation for morality.

Christian theists disagree on how to respond.[47] Those who subscribe to divine command morality (DCM) grab the first horn; they hold that the rightness of actions is determined solely by the commands of God. On DCM, God is not subject to some independent standard of moral rightness but is free to command whatever he wills. By contrast, those who subscribe to a natural law morality (NLM) take the second horn of the dilemma. They hold that God commands actions because they are right. They claim, further, that the rightness of actions is determined by various features of human nature rather than by God's commands. In this essay we will defend a version of NLM. In the first section, we will discuss DCM and set out three problems the theory faces. In the second section, we will explain NLM and argue that it is the moral theory that Christians should prefer.

1 The Divine Command Morality

According to the basic version of DCM, God's commands alone serve as the basis for rightness, wrongness, and moral obligation. As Janine Marie Idziak writes, "Generally speaking, a 'divine command moralist' is one who maintains that the content of morality (i.e., what is right and wrong, good and evil, just and unjust, and the like) is directly and solely dependent upon the commands and prohibitions of God."[48] Similarly, William Frankena summarizes the DCM as claiming that "what ultimately

47 In this essay we will be considering the issue primarily from the perspective of Christian theism. Theists of other religious persuasions may disagree on this issue too, and may do so for many of the same reasons that we will cite.

48 Idziak (ed.), *Divine Command Morality*, p. 1.

makes an action right or wrong is its being commanded by God and nothing else."[49] While some DCM theorists qualify this basic view in various ways, for this short essay our discussion will focus mainly on it.[50]

Proponents of DCM typically argue that their view preserves the tight connection between religion and morality,[51] and that it coheres best with the Christian ideas of divine sovereignty and freedom. They believe that a theory according to which morality is somehow autonomous and independent of God's will has unacceptable implications. Any such theory implies that God is compelled to command specific actions and forbid others, which threatens God's sovereignty and freedom and makes God subject to a standard of morality that is somehow above him. It implies further that we could come up with a complete and correct moral theory without appeal to the Christian faith, that the contents of our Christian faith add nothing to the content of morality. Thus, in order both to preserve the radical dependence of all creation (including the moral order) on God and to ensure that the tenets of our faith play an important role in our moral theory, DCM defenders claim that we must maintain that morality is determined by God's will.

But there are several critical problems with basic DCM. We will mention three of them.

First, as our initial dilemma suggested, on DCM what is right and wrong appear to be arbitrary because God has no prior reason for commanding or forbidding one act (or kind of act) rather than another. If God's command alone determines what actions are morally right, then it seems that God could have commanded *any* action, making the performance of that action morally right and the failure to perform it morally wrong. This feature of the view leads to the following unfortunate consequence: on DCM, God could have commanded that we torture innocent children for fun, and, had he done so, performance of that act would have been morally right. But obviously, as everyone knows, torturing innocent children for fun could not possibly be right, even if God commanded it. It follows that the rightness or wrongness of that act does not depend solely on God's command and that basic DCM is false.

Defenders of DCM may be tempted to respond to this difficulty as follows: It is not possible for God to command the torture of innocent children because God is perfectly good; and a perfectly good being would not issue such a command. Unfortunately, this response leads to a second problem for DCM: on DCM the claim that God is good is essentially meaningless. Norman Kretzmann discusses this problem in his critique of a variation on DCM which he calls "theological subjectivism":

> But do not suppose that the adherent of theological subjectivism can extricate himself from this terminal embarrassment [i.e., the problem that on theological subjectivism torturing children for fun could be morally right] with the pious rejoinder that God is good and can be relied on not to approve of moral evil. The only standard of moral goodness

49 Frankena, *Ethics*, p. 29.

50 Prominent recent defenders of DCM include Idziak, Philip Quinn, and Robert Merrihew Adams. See Idziak, "In Search of 'Good Positive Reasons'"; Quinn, "An Argument for Divine Command Ethics," in Michael Beaty (ed.), *Christian Theism and the Problems of Philosophy* (Notre Dame, Ind.: University of Notre Dame Press, 1990); and Adams, "Modified Divine Command Theory."

51 Idziak, *Divine Command Morality*, pp. 8–10.

> supplied by theological subjectivism is God's approval; and so to say within the context of theological subjectivism that God is good comes to nothing more than that God approves of himself – which is easy to grant but impossible to derive any reassurance from.[52]

We can put the point another way. What does it mean to say that God is morally good? A natural interpretation of this claim is that God always does what is right. According to DCM, this means that God always does what God commands, or perhaps what God approves of. Surely this is not much of an account of God's moral goodness; but it is difficult to see what resources DCM can use to come up with a better and more substantive one. And, to return to the first problem with DCM, nothing in this account of God's moral goodness precludes God's commanding the pointless torture of innocents or, for that matter, performing such acts himself.

The third problem for DCM is closely related to the first two. The problem is that on DCM we have unusual difficulty deciphering what it is that God actually commands.[53] We would perhaps not have such difficulty if all religious groups agreed about what God commands, if the content of God's commands was clear to everyone; but as a matter of fact, religious groups differ profoundly on this matter. Some believe that God commands that they feed the poor; others believe that God commands that they eliminate members of ethnic groups different from their own. How can we judge which group, if any, is correct? Of course, all of us think it obvious that the latter group is mistaken (we think it preposterous to suppose that God would command people to perpetrate ethnic genocide[54]); but we do not make that judgment by carefully determining which group has in fact received a revelation from God, or which group has correctly interpreted God's commands. It seems hard to know how we could make such judgments without in some way begging the question – without, that is, making certain assumptions about what God does in fact command.[55] And in fact we do not judge the latter group to be mistaken on those grounds: instead, we do so by implicit appeal to a standard of morality to which we believe that God himself conforms. We judge the latter group mistaken because we know that God would never command any group to perform actions which are so blatantly immoral. To sum up: as we have seen, basic DCM leaves open the possibility that God commands acts which we consider morally heinous; and given that some religious groups claim that God commands them to perform such actions, DCM does not give us strong grounds for rejecting their claims.

52 Norman Kretzmann, "Abraham, Isaac, and Euthyphro: God and the Basis of Morality," in Donald Stump et al. (eds), *Hamartia: The Concept of Error in the Western Tradition* (New York: Edwin Mellen Press, 1983), p. 35.

53 A similar issue is raised by Alasdair MacIntyre in "Which God Ought We to Obey and Why?," *Faith and Philosophy*, 3 (1986), pp. 359–71.

54 But what about the stories in the book of Joshua of the Israelites wiping out the Canaanites, apparently at God's behest? Perhaps it is stories like these that prompt Philip Quinn to remark that "[t]heists who take the Old Testament both seriously and fairly literally share religious reasons for sympathy with a divine command conception of ethics" ("An Argument for Divine Command Ethics," p. 289). The Bible also seems to provide considerable support for NLM, as we will argue in the next section.

55 A further complication is that on DCM it is possible that *both* groups are correct. There is nothing in the theory that entails that God gives the same commands to every group of people.

We have presented three problems for DCM, problems which seem quite serious. Unfortunately, some people who are inclined to accept DCM believe that these are problems they must simply learn to live with, because the alternatives to DCM are entirely unpalatable for Christians. If we suppose that morality has an objective basis in something other than the will of God, they think, then morality is autonomous, and God has no important role to play with respect to it. But this thought is mistaken. A properly understood NLM avoids the damaging problems that beset DCM while ensuring that God plays an essential role with respect to morality.

2 Natural Law Morality

2.1 Setting out the theory

Like DCM, NLM offers a theistic foundation for ethics. Also like DCM, NLM has the support of many in the Christian tradition both past and present. In fact, of the two theories, NLM may enjoy more support from the tradition, or at any rate more significant support. Historically, versions of NLM were endorsed and developed by such giants of the church as Augustine and Thomas Aquinas. More contemporary defenders of the theory include C. S. Lewis and Richard Swinburne. The version of NLM we will elaborate leans heavily on the natural law tradition that originated with Aquinas.

The following are central tenets of the version of NLM that we defend:

1 All human beings have a specific nature, with a specific end, in common.
2 Moral precepts are grounded in that human nature.
3 The basic moral precepts cannot change unless human nature changes.
4 These precepts are teleological in character – they direct human beings to their end.
5 All properly functioning human beings know what the basic moral precepts are.

This list makes reference to the notion of a "nature." As we are using the term (following Aquinas, who in many ways followed Aristotle), a nature is an ontological entity had by all created things. Each created thing has a nature specific to its kind; this nature makes it the kind of thing that it is. The nature of a thing directs it to its end, its *telos*. As (1) above states, human beings, like all created things, have a specific nature with its own specific end. We will say more about the defining features of human nature in a moment.

In order to understand points 2–5, we need to turn to Aquinas's account of natural law. This account can be found in his "Treatise on Law."[56] There he defines natural law as "the rational creature's participation in the eternal law." Roughly speaking, the eternal law specifies God's plan for all of creation. It includes specifications about the natures of created things, the end of each thing, and how that end is to be achieved (that is, how a thing's nature directs it to its end). The natural law is that part of the

56 Thomas Aquinas, *Summa Theologiae*, IaIIae, 90–7. For discussion, see Jean Porter, "What the Wise Person Knows: Natural Law and Virtue in Aquinas' *Summa Theologiae*," *Studies in Christian Ethics*, 12/1 (1999), pp. 57–69.

eternal law that human beings can grasp by the "natural light of reason." Part of the natural law encompasses our human nature, our end, and how we ought to behave in order to achieve our end.

On Aquinas's view, our *telos* as human beings is happiness. That is the goal to which we by nature strive. This view of the human *telos* is not unusual: Christians from Augustine to C. S. Lewis have affirmed it, and so have non-Christians, most famously Aristotle. But what is this happiness for which we strive? Happiness involves living well during our earthly lives, according to Aristotle; and in his *Nichomachean Ethics* he describes at some length what it is to live well. Christian thinkers have agreed that living well during one's earthly life is important; but they think that doing so is not sufficient for true happiness and genuine fulfillment. Christians claim that the only sort of happiness that is truly satisfying for human beings is found in communion with God. That is the happiness which we ultimately desire. As the *Catechism of the Catholic Church* puts it, "The desire for God is written in the human heart, because man is created by God and for God; and God never ceases to draw man to himself. Only in God will he find the truth and happiness he never stops searching for."[57] Claude Tresmontant makes a similar point:

> The purpose of creation was not merely to bring about a group of spirits living together peacefully before God in a just and happy society. The purpose of creation, the supernatural goal of creation, according to God's plan as it actually is, is a union, a marriage, a fundamental transformation, a divinization, of human nature.[58]

We seem, then, to have two ends corresponding to two types or levels of happiness: we have a natural end, the achievement of which comes from living a good earthly life; and we have a supernatural end, the achievement of which comes from union with the God who created us. So, by nature, we human beings strive to achieve our end, which is happiness. With our reason, we are able to grasp the natural law, which tells us how to achieve that end. (Or in any case, the natural law gives us significant guidance regarding our end. As will be explained in a moment, the natural law must be supplemented by the divine law.) How do we achieve our end? The natural law contains some of the general moral rules and principles by which we ought to live in order to do so. The most basic of these principles, Aquinas tells us, is that "good is to be done and pursued and evil avoided."[59] The natural law also specifies broadly which behaviors contribute to our end – which activities are good for us to participate in – and which do not. By virtue of our knowledge of natural law, we are able to distinguish between activities that are truly good for us and those that merely appear to be, between proximate ends that serve our true end and those that do not. For example, telling a lie may under certain conditions yield some good results – it may enable a person to get out of a difficult situation or land a football-coaching job that would otherwise be unattainable – but overall such an activity is not in fact

57 Profession of Faith, I, 26, in *Catechism of the Catholic Church* (New York: Image Books, 1997).

58 Claude Tresmontant, *The Origins of Christian Philosophy*, tr. Mark Pontifex (New York: Hawthorn Books, 1963), p. 108.

59 Aquinas, *Summa Theologiae*, IaIIae, 94, 2: "Bonum est faciendum et prosequendum, et malum vitandum."

good for us and does not serve our true end. It does not serve our true end, because lying does not satisfy our legitimate natural desire to live in community with others; it is instead a practice which helps to break down community. Hence, by virtue of our fundamental grasp of natural law, we are able to recognize that while lying may serve some reasonable proximate ends, it is nonetheless something that we ought not to do. In that way, natural law enables us to distinguish between good and bad ends, and dictates to us what sorts of rules and principles for living we ought to follow.[60]

Now, natural law does not give us a *complete* set of rules and principles to follow. In order for us to have a fuller awareness of how to achieve our end – and indeed, in order to know what our *supernatural* end is – we need another source. Reason must be supplemented by revelation; natural law must be supplemented by the divine law.[61] (Aristotle lacked revelation; that is why he had a reasonable grasp of our natural but not our supernatural end.) Fortunately, God has made the divine law accessible to some human beings. As we see throughout the Bible, for instance, God explicitly commands his people to perform actions and follow rules that no doubt they would not have settled upon without God's guidance. So the natural law has limits. Nonetheless, the natural law and the moral knowledge it contains is available to all properly functioning human beings: all of them naturally desire happiness and are capable of recognizing basic moral principles and distinguishing between actions that they ought to perform and actions that they ought to avoid.

To sum up, according to the version of NLM that we are defending, human beings share a common nature. Moral rules and principles are grounded in this nature; acting on them enables human beings to achieve their end. These rules apply to all human beings. Given that human nature is stable, the fundamental moral rules do not change. All human beings by nature strive for their end, which is happiness; and all have at least a rudimentary grasp of the moral principles contained in the natural law and revealed to us by reason.

We should now apply the foregoing to the dilemma posed at the beginning of this essay. Do God's commands make an act right, or does God command an act because it is right? NLM takes the second horn. God is the author and creator of human nature, so God knows which behaviors contribute to human flourishing and which do not. And here is the important point: *what makes an act right or wrong is whether it does or does not contribute to human flourishing.* God *knows* what acts are right and wrong, and God commands and forbids accordingly. To illustrate this point, Carlton Fisher offers the following analogy:

> Consider, if you will, the operation manual for a new car. In it we find instructions to guide our relationship to the car. Don't do this, that, or the other. Do this and that. Commands for behavior. These are the right things to do. Now, let's ask Plato's question in this context. Are these instructions right because General Motors commanded us to do them? Or did General Motors command us to do them because they are right? If you will allow me the assumption that General Motors knows what they are doing, I think you

60 Some of the forgoing was influenced by the natural law argument found in Mortimer Adler, *Six Great Ideas* (New York: Macmillan, 1981), esp. ch. 11.

61 Aquinas defends the need for the divine law in *Summa Theologiae*, IaIIae, 91, 4.

will agree that the answer is rather obvious. They are so commanded because these are the right things to do in caring for the car.[62]

Fisher applies the car analogy also to the commands in Scripture (to the precepts of the divine law): "The instructions which *are* in Scripture are there, not because God made them up, but because they *belong* in our instruction manual."[63]

Now God, being perfectly good, can only command us to perform acts that are morally right. On NLM this fact restricts what God can command. (On this point NLM differs from basic DCM.) In particular, the content of God's commands is restricted, based on what God has created: God can only command that we perform actions and follow rules that contribute to our flourishing. God cannot command creatures to fail to worship him. God cannot command any person not to direct herself to God. Given our nature and the good end to which it directs us, God must command that we perform certain types of actions and cannot command that we perform others. Thus, the nature which human beings have been given places constraints on God: it limits the actions that God can and cannot command.

2.2 Biblical support

It is true that the Bible does not present a fully developed account of NLM; but this is not surprising, since it does not present a comprehensive moral theory of any kind. No doubt, presenting such a theory is not the Bible's intent. Nonetheless, we can find biblical support for the central themes of NLM. In what follows we will briefly consider key passages from the book of Genesis, the Decalogue, the Sermon on the Mount, and Paul's Letter to the Romans.

2.2.1 The first Genesis creation narrative

Christians generally recognize that the story means at least to teach us that the cosmos is a contingent creation of a loving and wise God, and that human beings are a very important part of that creation. Here are two other points that the story makes which seem to fit in especially well with NLM.

First, the author of the first creation narrative tells us that at various points while creating the universe God looked at what he had made and saw that it was good. God *saw* that it was good. The author does not state that God *declared* that what he created was good, and that then it *was* good. It is not the case that what God created was neither good nor bad until God imputed to it a value that it did not previously have; instead, God created it and saw that it was good. God recognized the value it already

62 Carlton Fisher, "Because God Says So," in Beaty (ed.), *Christian Theism and the Problems of Philosophy*, pp. 361–2. Anthony Lisska makes a similar point when he says: "God too follows some version of rationality. Aquinas suggests that since God created human beings in a certain way – i.e., through divine archetypes in the eternal law, after which human nature is patterned – then it follows . . . that the moral principles commanded must be in accord with the moral principles derived from the dispositional analysis of human nature" (Anthony J. Lisska, *Aquinas's Theory of Natural Law: An Analytic Reconstruction* (New York: Oxford University Press, 1997), p. 113).
63 Ibid., p. 365.

had. Now no doubt we cannot base a theory of morality just on these words of the Genesis narrative. Still, the Christian tradition has made much of the fact that what God created is good. The position held by the tradition would lose much of its substance if we were to add that no matter what God had created, it would have been good provided only that God *said* that it was. And we should note that that addition would imply a view with respect to what we might call ontological value that is entirely in tune with the view that DCM takes of moral rightness. The first creation narrative, then, clearly suggests that it is not the case that the creation was good because God said that it was, but rather that God said that it was good because it was good. It does not seem much of a stretch to suggest that the same considerations that apply to ontological value also apply to moral rightness.

Second, the narrative implies that God has established an order to the creation. This implication is suggested by several passages, including the claim in the first chapter that God created each thing "after its own kind" (Genesis 1:12, RSV). This claim appears to support the Thomist view that all created things have stable, unique natures. More generally, the first creation narrative provides an account of the intelligibility and structure of the created order that fits well with the Thomist natural law tradition.

2.2.2 The Decalogue

Christians in the natural law tradition have often looked at the structure of the Ten Commandments as telling us a great deal about human nature.[64] The precepts listed there make clear that human nature involves not only a physical component, but a spiritual and social component as well. The first table of the Decalogue – the first four commandments – speaks to our spiritual nature, the part of us in virtue of which we are capable of sharing relationship with God. It claims, for instance, that we are to worship only God. The second table – the last six commandments – speaks to our social nature; it guides us in our relationships with other human beings. It orders us, for instance, not to commit adultery or to lie to others. It indicates a minimal kind of moral behavior we should exercise towards, and expect from, our neighbor.

2.2.3 The Beatitudes

The Beatitudes (Matthew 5:1–12) consist of Jesus' moral teaching to the disciples. The very name "beatitude" indicates that these are ways of being that lead to happiness. The disciples are taught that certain character traits like purity of heart, meekness, and mercy lead to a life of happiness. In short, the Beatitudes give us a blueprint of the kind of people we should be in order to achieve the abundant life with God that all of us seek, the life that is our end. Like the precepts of the Decalogue, the Beatitudes assume a human nature that is designed for relationship with both God and other people. There are important differences between the two, but together they point to complementary features of the moral life: there are certain actions that we ought not to perform, and there are certain traits of character that we ought to cultivate.

64 The Decalogue is given twice in the Bible, first in Exodus 20:1–17, then in Deuteronomy 5:6–21.

2.2.4 *The Epistle to the Romans*

In his Letter to the Romans, St Paul makes clear that there is a difference between natural and unnatural behavior for human beings. Natural behaviors and activities include worship of the Creator, monogamy, and benevolence; unnatural behaviors and activities include idolatry, promiscuity, and malice. Paul indicates that when humans act in accordance with their created natures, it is fitting and good; such behavior is no doubt morally acceptable. When they deviate from their created nature, the results are morally evil. So St Paul appears to tie what is morally right and wrong to what is natural and unnatural.

The first chapter in Romans makes an additional point that fits well with NLM, in particular with tenet 5 above. St Paul declares that God has made known to all humanity the truth about God and about the moral order. He says this: "For what can be known about God is plain to them, because God has shown it to them. Ever since the creation of the world his invisible nature, namely, his eternal power and deity, has been clearly perceived in the things that have been made" (Romans 1:19–20, RSV). Here Paul indicates that God reveals to human beings, without the aid of supernatural revelation, both theological and ethical truths.[65]

In summary, the Bible seems to make several claims about morality that fit well with NLM. The first creation narrative suggests that God does not make the creation valuable by valuing it, but instead that God values it because he sees that it is good. The narrative also tells us that God has established certain "kinds" of beings within an orderly universe. The Decalogue and Beatitudes tell us more about what are appropriate activities for human beings, and what sorts of character traits enable us to achieve our end. Finally, the Epistle to the Romans tells us more about natural and unnatural behavior, and suggests that all people are aware of the basic truths about God and the basic precepts of ethics.

2.3 The virtues of NLM

It should be clear, first of all, that NLM is not subject to the three criticisms faced by DCM that we mentioned above. God cannot command a person to torture an innocent child; performing such an action would obviously take the perpetrator (to say nothing of the victim) away from fulfilling his end. God's goodness is constituted of more than merely God's approval of himself. (We will say more about God's goodness in a moment.) Moreover, in order to determine what God commands, we need only consider whether the candidate action contributes appropriately to human flourishing. This may not always be clear, of course; but in cases where the proposed action is obviously heinous (from committing adultery to committing murder), there will be no question. Any properly functioning person will know in his heart, and can deter-

65 Josef Fuchs observes that in the first chapter of Romans St Paul is not developing a full NLM theory. Rather, St Paul is concerned with the pagan world's need for redemption in light of their rejection of what seem to him to be the obvious theological and moral truths available to all humans (*Natural Law: A Theological Investigation* (New York: Sheed and Ward, 1965), p. 15).

mine by reason, that such actions do not contribute to true happiness and that they are immoral.

Now, as we have seen, some Christians may be concerned that NLM breaks the connection between Christianity and morality by making the former essentially irrelevant to the latter. But such concerns are groundless. Christianity reveals to us our true (supernatural) end and how that is to be achieved. Christianity helps to fill in parts of the picture that natural law leaves unpainted. So NLM leaves the connection between Christianity and morality very much intact.

Christians may also be concerned that NLM places improper limits on God's freedom and power. To show that in fact the limits it places are not objectionable, we might follow Aquinas in making the distinction between God's *potentia absoluta* and *potentia ordinata*, between God's absolute and ordained power.[66] God's absolute power is his ability to create any possible order, while God's ordained power is his ability to do whatever can be done within the actual created order. In his discussion of this distinction, Aquinas says this:

> There is no reason why something should not be within divine power which God does not will, and which is no part of the present order he has established . . . as for what lies within power as such, God is said to be able to do it by his absolute power. . . . As for what lies within his power as carrying out the command of his just will, he is said to be able to do it by his ordinate power. Accordingly we should state that by his absolute power God can do things other than those he foresaw and predestined that he would.[67]

The point is this: God's power is restricted – the content of God's commands is limited; but it is restricted because of God's prior acts of will. God's freedom is restricted by his own actions. The acts that God can command – the acts that are morally right – are determined by the nature of the human beings God has chosen to create.

So God's freedom with respect to the content of his commands is constrained by what he has created. But there may be another sense in which God is *not* constrained: perhaps the mere fact that God issues commands *at all* is a matter of God's free choice and is, for that reason, extremely significant. In what way is that fact significant? In one sense, it may not be significant that God commands that we obey the principles of *natural* law, since, according to NLM, we are able to discern those principles without any special revelation from God. But the mere fact that God issues these commands at all indicates that God loves us and wants us to achieve the happiness that we are called to by nature. In any case, God's love for us is evidenced more clearly in the special revelation by which he reveals to us the *divine* law. For the divine law, as we have seen, is not accessible to human beings apart from special revelation. God's love and, indeed, God's *goodness* are made manifest in the fact that he longs for us to achieve our end, that he stoops to make clear to us what our true end is, that he tells us how to achieve it, and that he commands us to do so.

66 For a helpful discussion of the nature of God's power, see Lawrence Moonan, *Divine Power: The Medieval Power Distinction up to Its Adoption by Albert, Bonaventure, and Aquinas* (New York: Oxford University Press, 1994), esp. chs 6 and 7; also Craig A. Boyd, "Is Thomas Aquinas a Divine Command Theorist?," *Modern Schoolman*, 55 (March 1998), pp. 209–26.

67 Aquinas, *Summa Theologiae*, Ia, 25, 5, ad1.

So God is good partly in virtue of the fact that he commands us to be moral. God commands us to behave in ways that ultimately contribute to our happiness. Moral rules and principles are not arbitrarily imposed by God in order that we may prove our blind allegiance to him; instead, God commands us for our own good. In commanding us to be moral, God commands us to exhibit the same sort of self-giving love that he exhibited to perfection in the very act of creating us. Here it is worth quoting from the prologue of the *Catechism of the Catholic Church*: "God, infinitely perfect and blessed in himself, in a plan of sheer goodness freely created man to make him share in his own blessed life." Despite our sin, God calls us to participate in the divine life; he commands us to behave in ways that contribute to this end.

3 Conclusion

Of the two different approaches to the relation between God and morality, DCM and NLM, we believe that NLM should be the more attractive approach to Christians. NLM grounds morality in the human nature that God has created. In doing so, NLM avoids the serious problems faced by DCM, while at the same time affirming the deep dependence of the moral order upon divine activity.

Reply to Boyd and VanArragon

Boyd and VanArragon's essay in support of natural law ethics begins with the statement of a dilemma:

1. If God's command *makes* an act right, then morality is arbitrary.
2. If God commands an act *because* it is right, then God's command is not essential to morality.
3. Either God's command makes an act right, or God commands an act because it is right.

Therefore,

4. Either morality is arbitrary, or God's command is not essential to morality.

This dilemma is dissolved when it is recognized that the first premise is simply false. As my own essay points out, the position that God's command makes an act right does not entail that morality is arbitrary. First, God's attribute of simplicity assures that the divine intellect and will work together in issuing commands. Moreover, God's command will be consonant with, and directed by, God's nature and character as a being perfect in knowledge, justice, and love. Thus the commands of God will in fact be anything but arbitrary and capricious.

Similarly, another standard objection to divine command ethics raised by Boyd and VanArragon has already been answered. This is the contention that God could command and make right actions which are intuitively abhorrent from a moral point of view, such as the torture of innocent children. Because the God who does the commanding is beneficent and loving, this is a mere theoretical possibility which will never be realized, and hence it is not troublesome. However, Boyd and VanArragon raise two other objections which deserve further discussion.

One objection is that, on an ethics of divine commands, the claim that God is good is essentially meaningless. This is because saying that God is good comes to nothing more than saying that God approves of himself. Another way of stating the objection is this: If a person being morally good is explicated in terms of that person doing what God wills, then the claim that God is morally good reduces to the trivial claim that God does what God wills.[68]

A response offered to this criticism is that, when a divine command moralist calls God good, she is expressing a favorable emotional attitude towards God and ascribing to God certain qualities of character regarded as virtuous, such as kindness, benevolence, faithfulness, a forgiving disposition, and love. Further, these attitudinal and descriptive features are part of the ascriptions of goodness to human beings.[69] Thus there is a meaningful component to the claim that God is good, similar to what we mean in calling human beings good.

The second objection concerns the difficulty of deciphering what it is that God actually commands. This is a serious objection, for if we cannot reliably determine what God commands, then an ethics of divine commands becomes effectually useless as a guide to action, which is precisely the function that an ethical system is supposed to serve.[70]

Some advocates of divine command ethics from the Protestant tradition have placed heavy emphasis on the Bible as the source of our knowledge of divine commands.[71] It is noteworthy that Boyd and VanArragon themselves make recourse to the divine revelation contained in the Bible a necessary supplement to natural law:

> Now, natural law does not give us a *complete* set of rules and principles to follow. In order for us to have a fuller awareness of how to achieve our end – and indeed, in order to know what our *supernatural* end is – we need another source. Reason must be supplemented by revelation; natural law must be supplemented by the divine law. . . . Fortunately, God has made the divine law accessible to some human beings. As we see throughout the Bible, for instance, God explicitly commands his people to perform actions and follow rules that no doubt they would not have settled upon without God's guidance.

It is also noteworthy that here they slip into the language of divine commands.

68 Adams, "Modified Divine Command Theory," p. 337.

69 Ibid., pp. 338–41.

70 Janine Marie Idziak, "Divine Command Ethics," in Philip L. Quinn and Charles Taliaferro (eds), *A Companion to Philosophy of Religion* (Oxford: Blackwell, 1997), pp. 453–9: p. 458.

71 Richard Mouw, *The God Who Commands* (Notre Dame, Ind.: University of Notre Dame Press, 1990), pp. 8–10.

Other divine command moralists have looked to official Church teachings or to the possibility of personal revelation through prayer as legitimate sources of knowledge of divine commands.[72] Or again, Patterson Brown has suggested that "one can *infer* by means of reason alone . . . what God would command." For "we can presumably ratiocinate . . . what a supremely intelligent, loving, and just being would will; and this is by definition what God would will."[73]

Boyd and VanArragon argue that we ultimately discern what is and is not a divine command by implicit appeal to a standard of morality to which we believe God himself conforms (and hence which must exist independently of God). In deducing the content of divine commands from God's attributes, Brown's method for determining divine commands makes no appeal to an independent *moral* standard and thus escapes the criticism.

Finally, taking the offensive, a proponent of divine command ethics can point to two problems for natural law ethics which cut to the heart of this theory. First, is it really so clear what constitutes the "human nature" on which moral precepts are based? The post-Darwinian view of human beings is not the same as the traditional Judeo-Christian view. Or again, some emphasize the individual person and his autonomy, while others have a relational and communitarian view of being human.[74] Or again, some have argued that procedures such as artificial contraception and in vitro fertilization are inconsistent with human nature because they break the natural connection between the interpersonal act of sexual intercourse and the conception of a child.[75] Others have criticized this approach as too "physicalistic" and argued that human biological life is but one aspect of human existence.[76] In sum, the natural law ethicist is faced with the problem of negotiating competing views of human nature.

Moreover, the plausibility of a natural law approach to ethics can be challenged from a scientific point of view. Human beings no longer appear to be directly designed by God in all detail, but rather, "to be the outcome of spontaneous mutation, selective pressures, genetic drift, constraints set by the laws of physics, chemistry, and biology, as well as the effects of catastrophic events."[77] Since this is so, the question is seriously raised: Why should "human nature" be taken as morally normative at all?

72 Idziak (ed.), *Divine Command Morality*, p. 251.

73 Brown, quoted in ibid., p. 251.

74 Richard M. Gula, *Reason Informed by Faith: Foundations of Catholic Morality* (Mahwah, NJ: Paulist Press, 1989), pp. 63–74.

75 Jean Porter, "Human Need and Natural Law," in Kevin William Wildes, SJ (ed.), *Infertility: A Crossroad of Faith* (Dordrecht: Kluwer, 1997), pp. 96–7.

76 Gula, *Reason Informed by Faith*, pp. 220–49.

77 Kevin William Wildes, "Redesigning the Human Genome: Are There Constraints from Nature?," in *Germ-Line Intervention and Our Responsibilities to Future Generations* (Dordrecht: Kluwer, 1998), pp. 44–5.

Reply to Idziak

In her essay "Divine Commands Are the Foundation of Morality," Idziak raises two critical issues we wish to address. The first is the "arbitrariness problem" for DCM; the second is the idea that NLM operates as a kind of "methodological atheism."

With regard to the arbitrariness problem, it seems that Idziak, despite her protests to the contrary, is committed to the view that God's commands are arbitrary. She claims that since God is perfectly loving, "this means that God will not in fact command such acts as the gratuitous infliction of pain." But just as DCM presents problems for the claim that God is good (problems detailed in our essay), so it presents problems for the claim that God is loving. For what is it for God to be loving? Perhaps God is loving in virtue of the fact that he desires what is good for us. But if, as some versions of DCM claim, what is good is good because God approves of it, then to say that God desires what is good for us is just to say that God desires what he approves of for us. And here the arbitrariness problem again rears its ugly head: if God's approval makes something good for us, and God has no prior reason for approving for us one sort of behavior or treatment rather than another, then God could just as well approve that we be subject to gratuitous pain. If he did, then being subjected to such pain would be good for us, and God in his love would command that we inflict it on each other. So it seems that DCM cannot appeal to God's loving character to rule out the possibility of God commanding the torture of innocents.

A DCM theorist might reject this line of reasoning by asserting that while God by his commands determines what is morally *right*, he does not by his approval determine what is *good* for his creatures. That is determined by something else – perhaps by those creatures' natures. Such a DCM theorist would claim that God's commands are not arbitrary; they are determined by his love, which constrains him to command only what is good for his creatures. (And what is good for them is determined by their natures.) This position, however, is very close to the NLM theory that we defended in our essay, the main difference being that we believe that an act's contributing to creaturely flourishing makes it morally right, while this DCM theory claims that though God commands in accordance with what enables creatures to flourish, it is God's commanding that makes an act morally right. We leave it to the reader to decide how significant this difference is.

The most serious challenge that Idziak raises for NLM is the charge of methodological atheism, according to which NLM pursues ethical matters without any appeal to God. According to Idziak, "Doing ethics in complete independence of God cannot be a satisfactory option for a theist. Such a stance ignores the centrality that God is supposed to have in the life of a theist." She concludes that no Christian can advocate this approach to ethics, because it "flies in the face of the religious belief that God should be the focus of human loyalties."

Fortunately for us, this challenge misses the NLM theory that we defended. Idziak appears to be claiming that any moral theory that appeals to universal moral principles that can be known by the natural light of reason, apart from God, are operating under the "rubric of methodological atheism." But this is not true. Although our

Thomistic NLM theory does indeed appeal to the idea of universally knowable moral precepts, it also holds that the basis for these precepts lies in the creative activity of God.

So, while we agree with Idziak's contention that "Doing ethics in complete independence of God cannot be a satisfactory option for a theist," we also believe that not all versions of NLM are committed to this endeavor. Philosophers who assume that they are fail to distinguish properly between divergent streams of NLM. This mistake is understandable. Many of its recent proponents have portrayed NLM as providing an enlightened, reason-based alternative to religious ethics. And Hugo Grotius, seen by many as the father of modern NLM, believes that God is essentially superfluous to morality: he contends that even if there were no God, we would still have the natural law as a moral authority to guide us.[78]

We must, then, make an important distinction between different kinds of NLM theories. We must distinguish between those who appeal to natural law as an autonomous realm of ethics and those who see natural law as grounded in God's orderly activity in creation. The former theories adopt what we can call the "naturalistic autonomy thesis" (NAT): they see ethics as an autonomous sphere of inquiry that need not appeal to God. Many moral theories accept this thesis in one form or another; many make no appeal whatsoever to religion. All moral theories which accept NAT operate under the rubric of "methodological atheism." Insofar as some NLM theories accept NAT, Idziak's criticism is right on target. But we hope that it is clear from our essay that her criticism is not properly applicable to our Thomistic account of NLM.

78 Hugo Grotius, *Prolegomena to the Law of War and Peace*, tr. F. W. Kelsey (New York: Liberal Arts Press, 1957), p. 10.

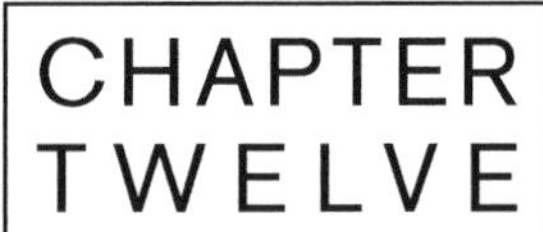

CHAPTER TWELVE

Should a Christian Be a Mind–Body Dualist?

Few questions in the philosophy of religion have received as much recent attention as this one. Many Christians answer it in the affirmative, believing that some form of mind–body dualism has the weight of Christian tradition on its side and that it is the view that makes best sense of the doctrine of life after death. Yet an increasing number of Christians reject mind–body dualism in favor of some version of materialism, claiming that dualism is an illegitimate import from Greek philosophy and that its place in Christian thought should be reevaluated. They argue, moreover, that materialism yields most of the advantages that dualism was supposed to provide while avoiding many of dualism's problems. In these essays, Dean Zimmerman argues in favor of mind–body dualism, while Lynne Rudder Baker defends a version of materialism.

Christians Should Affirm Mind–Body Dualism

Dean W. Zimmerman

1 Dualism and Christianity

Substance dualism is the doctrine that each human person is an immaterial substance, a soul – or at least, that each of us has a soul as a part of us. For nearly two millennia, dualism's defenders and opponents agreed that Christianity requires some form of this view. But many biblical scholars, theologians, and Christian philosophers now argue that dualism is not central to Christianity, that it is in fact a "Greek import."[1]

I believe that Catholics and most theologically conservative protestants have good reasons to resist this trend. Catholics have unequivocal pronouncements of ecumenical councils and the present-day teaching of the Magisterium: the soul is immediately created by God, it survives the dissolution of the body and enters into eternal life, awaiting reunion with its physical body.[2] And very many Christians of all sorts are committed to exegetical principles that *ought* to generate significant biblical support for dualism. Proving this is not a job for which I am at all qualified, so I leave it to others.[3] Here, I shall simply assume that the religious convictions of most Christians provide them with a reason to prefer dualism to materialism, other things being equal. (Many of the adherents of other religions are in a similar position.) Those whose faith is at least not *unreasonable*, not contrary to the evidence they have, may consequently have some genuine prima facie evidence, however slight, for judging dualism to be more probable than materialism. To such readers I offer a philosophical case for dualism. First, I articulate a version of "emergent dualism," and show that it is untouched by traditional objections to dualism. Second, I argue that materialism is at least as hard to believe as dualism, so that those with religious reasons to believe dualism cannot be faulted for letting them tip the scales.

For the structure of the argument of the second part (and for the fact that I have the guts to defend it, and for much else besides), I am indebted to the work and example of the late Roderick Chisholm.[4]

2 A Defensible Dualism

2.1 Emergent dualism

The empirical facts strongly suggest that human minds are dependent, both for their existence and many of their characteristics, upon brains. Some dualists have denied this. Descartes thought that: (i) no mere brain could produce conscious states without interacting with a soul; (ii) brains are not themselves capable of generating souls nat-

1 Peter van Inwagen speaks for many when he alleges that "the anthropology of the Fathers is the result of an unfortunate marriage between Athens and Jerusalem" ("Dualism and Materialism: Athens and Jerusalem?," *Faith and Philosophy*, 12 (1995), pp. 475–88). See also Warren Brown, Nancey Murphy, and H. Newton Malony (eds), *Whatever Happened to the Soul?* (Minneapolis: Fortress Press, 1998).

2 See, e.g., the catechism of the Council of Trent, and Pope John Paul II's Message to the Pontifical Academy of Sciences, Oct. 22, 1996.

3 John Cooper, for instance, makes a good case for the following claims: (1) The earliest Christians, including Christ himself, were substance dualists; (2) they (and not the Greeks, as so many claim) are responsible for the centrality of body–soul dualism within the Christian tradition; (3) their dualism is made explicit in the gospels and epistles; and (4) dualism in fact plays a crucial role in passages where *theological* points are being made *non-metaphorically*. See John Cooper, *Body, Soul, and Life Everlasting* (Grand Rapids, Mich.: Eerdmans, 1989; reprinted with a new preface, 2000).

4 See, e.g., Roderick Chisholm, "Which Physical Thing Am I? An Excerpt from 'Is There a Mind–Body Problem?'," *Philosophy and Phenomenological Research*, 41/2 (2002), pp. 291–309; and *idem*, *Person and Object* (LaSalle, Ill.: Open Court, 1976), ch. 3.

urally; and (iii) God does not care to work the miracle necessary to bring a soul into interaction with the brain of a nonhuman animal. But surely, at least the higher mammals *are* conscious; so at least one of these theses is false. Do all sentient creatures have souls, then? If (i) is true, they must. But, by (ii), each animal soul is specially created by God. Rejecting (iii) is a relatively minor departure from fully-fledged Cartesianism.[5] But wouldn't this be a rather sloppy way to make a world?

If the events in the brain of a chimp were causally sufficient to confer conscious states upon its *brain*, the similar events in my brain should do the same for *it*.[6] Denying that they do, the dualist should reject (ii). William Hasker,[7] Richard Swinburne,[8] and other contemporary dualists accept this conclusion, advocating a view sometimes called "emergent dualism: Organisms having nervous systems complex enough to generate conscious states automatically *also* generate nonphysical subjects for those states. Though brains and souls share no parts in common, each soul remains radically dependent upon one brain for its continued existence and for many, if not all, of its powers and dispositions. Since Hasker and Swinburne believe in an afterlife, they affirm that God could (and does) miraculously prevent the dissolution of the soul that would (or at least might) naturally occur when the nervous system upon which it is dependent ceases to function.[9] Hasker (but not, to my knowledge, Swinburne) also supposes that each nonphysical subject is located somewhere within the nervous system that generates it.

Some will say that emergent dualism is not *real* dualism, reserving the name for Cartesianism. But why should the particularities of Descartes's version be *sine qua non*? Emergent dualism deserves the label in at least the following sense: Its persons, unlike plants and the bodies of animals, are not made of the same kinds of stuff as ordinary inanimate objects. And that is what is needed if souls are to provide a pleasing alternative metaphysics of persons, one that is not itself open to the criticisms I shall shortly level against materialism.

Emergent dualism fares well against the usual anti-dualist arguments. In each case the objection either: (a) presupposes that the only viable form of dualism is the most radical kind (i.e., Cartesianism); (b) raises a problem that even materialists face; or (c) presupposes things that are incompatible with Western theism and that a Christian can and must reject.

2.2 Problems with body–soul interaction

Dualism's critics often ask: How can bodies and souls interact if they are so different from one another? Well, how can things so different as particles and fields interact? And anyway, why think that only very similar things can affect one another?

5 This is John Foster's response to the trilemma; see his *The Immaterial Self* (London: Routledge, 1991), ch. 6.

6 I suppose one *could* say that the presence of a soul in our case acts as a sort of "consciousness magnet," pulling mentality away from its normal subject, the brain.

7 William Hasker, *The Emergent Self* (Ithaca, NY: Cornell University Press, 1999).

8 Richard Swinburne, *The Evolution of the Soul* (Oxford: Clarendon Press, 1986), ch. 10.

9 Hasker, *Emergent Self*, ch. 8; and Swinburne, *Evolution of the Soul*, ch. 15.

There are, however, a couple of real problems about interaction.[10] The first turns upon the difference between the properties of the soul and the properties of matter. Since the conscious states of a nonphysical soul are supposed to be at once many, varied, and *fundamental*, how could they possibly enter into law-like relations with the kinds of states that figure in physics?[11] The laws governing fundamental physical properties such as mass, charge, and motion take the form of relatively simple mathematical relationships. It is unclear how the hoary host of conscious states, once construed as fundamental properties of souls, could enter into any such laws. The intrinsic states of souls would have to include phenomenal states, such as smelling an acrid odor or seeing a red after-image. It is not easy to see how the differences between phenomenal color, sound, smell, etc. could be represented as mathematically comparable, as would be required if laws linking the phenomenal and the physical were to be "in the style of contemporary physics."[12]

But there are powerful arguments to show that the "qualia" of phenomenal states (the felt redishness of the red after-image, the sharpness of the acrid smell, etc.) are not reducible to any physical or functional state of a body. Those of us convinced by them should be singularly unimpressed by this objection to dualism. We already *knew* there was trouble coming for the assumption that physics could catalogue all the fundamental causal relationships without *someday* having to allow for massive complications due to phenomenal qualia.

In any case, no Western theist is likely to be impressed by the claim that mental states cannot be fundamental, that they must always be identical with or otherwise dependent upon the complex physical states of complex systems, such as brains or perhaps computers. However true it may be that "His thoughts are not our thoughts," God's thoughts are thoughts, nonetheless. And Christian theology speaks with unanimity on this point: God does not need a body, not even a complex piece of ectoplasmic machinery, in order to think.

The second objection based on interaction, unlike the previous one, is a problem that only substance dualists face: How does my soul come to be paired up with just my body, when there could be *very similar* souls and bodies?[13] Here is an analogy. Suppose you have two similar guns and two similar targets, but each gun can only hit one of the targets. How does each gun come to be paired with its target? The answer inevitably invokes spatial relations among guns and targets. Perhaps one target is closer to one gun, and there is nothing in between them, while the other target is

10 An interesting question which I shall not discuss is whether dualistic interactionism is a coherent hypothesis on the supposition that all causation is a matter of the spatiotemporally continuous transfer of energy, or the transmission of a conserved quantity. See W. D. Hart, *The Engines of the Soul* (Cambridge: Cambridge University Press, 1988).

11 Cf. Richard Taylor, *Metaphysics*, 4th edn (Englewood Cliffs, NJ: Prentice-Hall), ch. 3; and Robert Merrihew Adams, "Flavors, Colors, and God," in his *The Virtue of Faith* (New York: Oxford University Press, 1987), pp. 243–62.

12 Cf. Adams, "Flavors, Colors, and God," pp. 251–8; Richard Swinburne, *The Existence of God* (Oxford: Clarendon Press, 1991); and *idem, Evolution of the Soul*, ch. 10. For a comprehensive case for the irreducibility of phenomenal qualia, see David Chalmers, *The Conscious Mind* (New York: Oxford University Press, 1996).

13 Cf. Jaegwon Kim, "Lonely Souls: Causality and Substance Dualism," in Kevin Corcoran (ed.), *Soul, Body, and Survival* (Ithaca, NY, and London: Cornell University Press, 2001), pp. 30–43.

farther away, or behind a fence. But the Cartesian can invoke no spatial relations holding between my soul and my body, Cartesian souls not being in space. Are there other, *nonspatial* respects in which my soul could be "closer" to my body than to other bodies? The Cartesian's souls are so cut off from one another and from the physical world that no answer seems available. But then it is as if there were identical guns paired with identical targets, each always hitting its own target *no matter how one points it*!

There are good reasons to think that the causal dispositions and powers of objects are, in a sense, *general* – that is, that they are propensities to react to certain *types* of objects, as opposed to *particular* objects.[14] If so, there couldn't be such guns, nor could Cartesian souls discriminate among similar bodies. The emergent dualist grants that souls are in space, presumably within the heads that generate them. She thereby disarms this argument against the possibility of interaction.

2.3 The difficulty of knowing who's who

We cannot keep track of souls by watching them closely, or grabbing hold of them. How do we know, then, that they are not constantly coming and going "behind the scenes," passing memories one to another like runners passing the baton in a relay?[15] The question leads to another well-known argument against dualism: If persons were identical with souls, it would be reasonable to be skeptical about whether we are dealing with the same persons from one minute to the next.[16] Since this is *not* reasonable, a person is not a soul.[17]

The objector assumes that we *can* know that we are dealing with the same *human bodies* from one minute to the next. But a determined skeptic can call the assumption into question for similar reasons: How do we know that God, or quantum-mechanical whimsy, is not playing similar tricks on the physical plane? Perhaps my body is periodically annihilated, replaced by a duplicate so quickly as to fool even the most careful observer. The right response is, surely, that although it's possible, it's not something anyone should lose sleep over. But then why can't the dualist say the same thing? So it's possible for souls to be periodically replaced by others, with the replacement seamlessly carrying on the mental life of the original. Why must the dualist *prove* that seamless replacement isn't happening in order to justify belief in sameness of soul, if it is not necessary to prove that seamless replacement isn't happening in order to justify belief in sameness of body?

14 John Foster and Peter Unger are willing to countenance radically non-general laws linking particular souls and bodies: Foster, *Immaterial Self*, ch. 6; and Peter Unger, *All the Power in the World* (forthcoming).

15 Cf. Kant, *Critique of Pure Reason*, trs. Norman Kemp Smith (New York: St Martin's Press, 1965), p. 342.

16 Cf., e.g., John Perry, *A Dialogue on Personal Identity and Immortality* (LaSalle, Ill.: Hackett, 1978).

17 The argument leaves open the possibility that, although not identical with a soul, a person might yet be *constituted by* a soul, as Locke thought. Perhaps one soul constitutes me now, but another one will constitute me tomorrow. To accept this would require that we say, with Locke, that my soul and I are distinct, but that the soul thinks whenever I do. The paradoxical result that there are "two thinkers" thinking my thoughts is hard to escape given standard materialism, as shall appear. Dualists can, and should, avoid it.

Perhaps the Cartesian need say no more. But the emergent dualist is not quite off the hook. The future states of physical objects depend to a great degree upon their present states. What shape an animal has after it has eaten depends not just on how much it eats but also on its original shape. What color it turns when exposed to sunlight depends in part upon how intense the sunlight is, but also in part on what color its skin was to begin with. In general, the intrinsic characteristics of a persisting physical object narrowly constrain its subsequent intrinsic characteristics (shape, color, mass, etc.). For one thing, they typically change *gradually*. Changes in weight, hairiness, shape, etc. are, in the normal course of things, nearly continuous.

These considerations suggest that our most basic evidence (without which we'd have none) for the persistence over time of individuals is this: observed continuities of intrinsic characteristics, the later ones generally evolving out of the earlier ones only gradually. But the emergent dualist has a hard time finding *any* intrinsic states of souls that can only change gradually. Phenomenal states (experiences of color, sound, etc.) often change radically, even discontinuously; what I've just been experiencing does not narrowly constrain what I might experience next. Emergent dualists admit that the content of my phenomenal experience is more dependent upon earlier states of my sense organs and brain than upon earlier states of my soul. So they are open to the following argument. (i) If the observable characteristics of a kind of thing do not display such continuities, it is impossible to acquire the most basic sort of evidence one can have for the identity over time of such things. (ii) If one cannot acquire the most basic sort of evidence for their identity over time, then it is impossible to acquire *any* evidence about their identity over time. (iii) The souls of emergent dualism do not display such continuities. Conclusion: It is impossible to acquire any evidence about their persistence from one time to another.

Premise (i) is false even for physical objects if it is supposed to mean that, for *all* observable states, the kinds of changes observed must be gradual. A two-sided mirror is a physical object. Its most readily observable states (mirror images) can change in what look to be discontinuous ways, and these states don't depend directly upon previous states of the same sort – that is, earlier images don't *cause* the later images. There are causal dependencies between *other* earlier and later states of ordinary mirrors. But this is not essential to our ability to know about their persistence. Here's a fairy tale. Double-sided "magic mirrors" are detectable only by their impenetrability and powers of reflection. They come into being only within a square formed by four magic wands. When the wands are separated, they disappear, although it is rumored that a powerful, deft wizard once passed a mirror from one set of wands to another. One could acquire good evidence for the presence of a persisting mirror just by noticing that there's a disposition to reflect that is exemplified continuously in a certain region. Analogously, the emergent dualist observes that there is (what she takes to be) a disposition to "reflect," in the phenomenal realm, what's going on in the brain; and she also observes that the disposition is exemplified continuously in the one "place" she can most directly observe. Apparently, the thing with these phenomenal states is dependent upon the presence of a properly functioning brain; but she may be allowed to hope that, perhaps only by a miracle, it could be preserved after the demise of this particular brain.

2.4 Are the emergent dualist's souls worth having?

What kind of afterlife could emergent souls look forward to? If they're completely dependent upon functioning nervous systems, then none, barring the miraculous. But even if God sustains them, and even if he creates bodies upon which they may once again come to depend, wouldn't they lack all memory of a past life? Perhaps, if they do not contain within themselves sufficient structure to ground the dispositions upon which memory is based. God could see to it that they *seem* to remember everything they did. Would that be *mere* seeming? Perhaps. But it could be *accurate* mere seeming, only failing as memory because it follows a devious causal route. And one might well wonder, why think that this route *is* devious?

Could such souls be justly rewarded or punished for characters they'd helped to create, even if the primary "carrier" of that character (the original brain) were long gone? I don't see why not. Some of us would hold a murderer responsible for what he did, even if brain damage has made him a relatively harmless amnesiac. And we wouldn't think that taking a pill that you knew would cause you to lose your memories and change your character would suffice to absolve you of guilt. Or is this just a hangover from Christian and dualistic ways of ascribing praise and blame? It's how I think about these matters, at any rate. And if emergent dualism is true, and God restores my memory (or quasi-memory) and holds me responsible for things I did, I'll appeal to his mercy rather than ask why he allowed me to remember them.

3 An Argument against Materialism

3.1 The varieties of "standard materialism"

Emergent dualism may not fall to any of the usual objections. But unless there are good reasons to doubt its materialist competitors, one should regard it as no more than a fanciful but unlikely empirical hypothesis.

Dualism and materialism are competing answers to the question that each of us may ask with the words: "What am I?" (spoken in a metaphysical tone of voice, with emphasis on the word "am"). The forms of materialism that can claim to be antecedently much more plausible than emergent dualism say that each human person is a material object that (i) includes among its parts *all* the bodily parts upon which the ability to think most immediately depends, and (ii) has more or less *natural* boundaries. Call any such view a version of "standard materialism." Obvious candidates for being me that fit the bill are the complete organism I refer to as "my body," the entire nervous system within it, the brain alone, the cerebrum alone, and perhaps even one or other single hemisphere of that cerebrum. My goal is to show that materialists must be *nonstandard* materialists or must hold some other views as doubtful as dualism.

3.2 Defending Chisholm's "entia successiva" argument

Elsewhere, I have defended a variation of Chisholm's argument against our being what he called *entia successiva*, "successive entities," things that gain and lose parts over time. All of standard materialism's candidates for being me are successive entities. New matter is constantly being assimilated by my body and my brain, and old matter being sloughed off, so that the matter of which each is constituted changes. Locke called a particular portion of the world's physical stuff a "mass of matter."[18] Right now, one mass of matter or heap of stuff "does duty for" the *ens successivum* that is my brain or body; and another will "do duty for it" later. These facts suggest an argument against standard materialism:

1 If I am a thing that gains or loses parts, such as a brain or a human body, then, each time I undergo a change of parts, there is another thing where I am, a mass of matter distinct from myself but having all the same intrinsic characteristics – e.g., size, shape, mass, and even mental states, like *feeling sad*.
2 But it is false that, where I am, there is something else with all the same intrinsic characteristics; there is only one thing here that feels sad, not two.

So I am neither a brain nor a human organism nor any other thing that changes parts.

If materialism is going to be significantly more plausible than dualism, then one of the premises of this argument must be false.[19] What would it cost the materialist to deny either premise? I begin with the second.[20]

3.3 Denying premise 2: problems with four-dimensionalism

There is really only one promising strategy for denying the second premise, and that presupposes "four-dimensionalism" – the thesis that things have "temporal parts."[21] The view can best be introduced by describing the way in which a spatially three-dimensional object is generally thought to fill the region it occupies: namely, by having a different part filling each of the many subregions in the region occupied by the whole. My body, for example, fills the man-shaped region it does by having a part filling the head-shaped part of the region, two others filling the arm-shaped subregions, two others filling the leg-shaped subregions, and so on. Four-dimensionalists claim that an object that lasts for a period of time is spread throughout that period in a similar fashion. For each instant, there is a distinct thing, a momentary "temporal part" of the object, something that exists then and only then; and for each longer

18 See John Locke, *An Essay Concerning Human Understanding*, ed. Peter H. Nidditch (Oxford: Clarendon Press, 1985), p. 330 (bk 2, ch. 27, §3); and my "Theories of Masses and Problems of Constitution," *Philosophical Review*, 104 (1995), pp. 53–110.

19 One could, of course, accept the conclusion and reject both materialism and dualism – but only by doubting one's own existence, something even most philosophers have found to be difficult.

20 I defend the claims of the next three sections in greater detail in the chapter on "Personal Identity," in Michael J. Loux and Dean W. Zimmerman (eds), *The Oxford Handbook of Metaphysics* (Oxford: Oxford University Press, 2002).

21 For a recent defense of this view, see Ted Sider, *Four-Dimensionalism* (Oxford: Oxford University Press, 2001). (Warning: In the writings of certain contemporary philosophers, "four-dimensionalism" sometimes means something other than the doctrine of temporal parts, something about the nature of truth – namely, that all truths are eternal truths.)

interval of time, there is a distinct *extended* temporal part of the object that exists just during that period and is composed of all the instantaneous temporal parts falling within the interval.[22]

How does four-dimensionalism help with the denial of premise 2? In some sense, there must be just *one* pain or pleasure located where I am, just one instance of each conscious experience I have. But how could that be if the mass of matter and I are intrinsically identical? Four-dimensionalism provides the only halfway plausible answer to this question. Strictly speaking, the four-dimensionalist says, there is only one thing located *just* here and now: my present temporal part. I am in pain only in virtue of *its* being in pain. And the mass of matter now making me up is in pain in virtue of its *sharing* this selfsame part with me. If First Avenue and Seventh Street each develop a pothole, this may not add two potholes to the number the city must fill – for it might be the same pothole, at their intersection. Just so with my pain and that of my constituting matter.

Four-dimensionalism may have cut down on the number of sadnesses and pains going on where I am. But the cost for the reduction in the number of *local* subjects of experience is a lavish outlay in *persisting* subjects of experience. Every whole that shares a temporal part with me shares my pains and pleasures. Consider: The temporal parts from my first 37 years constitute a persisting thing that will cease to exist sooner than I; likewise for my temporal parts from this last year, or month, or day. In fact, there is a great host of beings here, each equally sad in virtue of sharing the one temporal part. Many strange consequences follow. It is hard to see how I could be sure which one of them *I* am. And it is odd that so many of the thinkers behave in seemingly irrational ways. When I make a small sacrifice now for a greater benefit to myself later, there are ever so many others who make the sacrifice with no hope of reward.[23] On top of these sorts of objections, there are more general problems with four-dimensionalism that have led many philosophers to reject the view.[24]

Four-dimensionalism is, I said, the only feasible way to deny premise 2. But which is harder to believe, four-dimensionalism or emergent dualism? Having survived the usual objections unscathed, the latter seems to me to be at least no *less* plausible than four-dimensionalism has turned out to be – though that might not be saying much.

3.4 Denying premise 1: coincidentalism and two-category theories

There are two radically different, initially plausible ways to deny the first premise. One might deny either that there are two things where I am, or that both are sad if one is. I begin with theories that take the latter approach.

22 Though nothing here turns on the issue, one can be a four-dimensionalist while denying the existence of literally instantaneous parts; see my "Persistence and Presentism," *Philosophical Papers*, 25 (1996), pp. 115–26.

23 For objections along these lines see Eric Olson, *The Human Animal* (New York: Oxford University Press, 1997), pp. 162–8.

24 See my "Temporal Parts and Supervenient Causation: The Incompatibility of Two Humean Doctrines," *Australasian Journal of Philosophy*, 76/2 (June 1998), pp. 265–88.

The person who recognizes two things here, the one thinking, the other not, has a choice. She *may* say that each is a physical object composed of microphysical particles. Then I call her a "coincidentalist": one who posits coincident physical objects made, at some level, of all the same parts arranged in the same way, but differing in their characteristics. But she may say instead that either the human being or the matter is not *really* a physical object in the full-blooded sense of the word – that it does not have particles as literal parts, but "contains" or 'includes' them in some other sense. Theories along these lines I will call "two-category theories," since they imply that the coincident matter and person are really very different, belonging to radically different "ontological categories" – for example, one but not the other might be said to be really an event or process, or a mathematical function from times to physical objects, or a set of particles. Two-category views are adopted to help make the coincidence of matter and person easier to swallow; the two things have properties that go by the same names but are really quite different. I criticize coincidentalism first.

On the coincidentalist view, the matter and the person do not share all their intrinsic characteristics. But, at the microphysical level, the two are intrinsically just alike. One might point out that one is a (mere) mass of matter while the other is a person or an organism. But why does the one get to be the one, the other the other, when they are so similar in every observable respect? What I find most puzzling is how things so alike in their *construction* could differ so radically in their *powers* and *potentialities*. The matter constituting a living body can survive being squashed by a steamroller, while the body cannot. The body can survive the gradual replacement of all its present constitutive atoms, while the mass of matter itself surely cannot. What explains these differences in abilities? Nothing other than the fact that the one is an organism, the other a mere mass of matter; but this is a fact one could never discover by examining their construction.[25]

Furthermore, it is unclear how the one can be thinking and the other not, given their structural similarity. Certainly both the matter in my body and the organism itself are disposed, right now, to produce the same observable behavior in the same circumstances – to emit the same sounds when my skin is burned, for instance, and to cause the same motions of molecules. If the one is in pain while the other is not, it is hard to see how pain could in any sense be "realized in" microphysical states, since these are shared. The pain must be some further, nonphysical property of the organism, caused by microphysical events (located inside my head) that happen to both matter and organism. But these events somehow fail to cause pain in the physically indiscernible mass of matter, within which they also occur. Again, why don't they, since the two are intrinsically exactly alike and are located at the same place? No wonder some have dubbed this view "The New Dualism."[26] I find it at least as incredible as the old.

25 Cf. Michael B. Burke, "Copper Statues and Pieces of Copper: A Challenge to the Standard Account," *Analysis*, 52 (1992), pp. 12–17.

26 See Michael B. Burke, "Persons and Bodies: How to Avoid the New Dualism," *American Philosophical Quarterly*, 34 (1997), pp. 457–67.

Two-category views are meant to explain away the problems associated with distinct but coincident entities by treating the matter and the human being as very different kinds of things – so different that, for any property we should be loathe to attribute to *both* of them, only *one* of them could have it in the most fundamental way, the other one either lacking it altogether or possessing it only derivatively. The most popular theory along these lines is due to Peter van Inwagen.[27] His view implies that when we talk about the matter making up a living body, we're really talking about the particles that are now parts of the body. Although van Inwagen is officially agnostic about whether plural terms like "the particles" denote sets, the implications of his theory are more easily explained on the assumption that they do.[28] Van Inwagen says that "the matter constituting my body now" is a name for a collection of particles – the set containing all the ones in my body now. This collection existed before all its members were parts of my body, and it will continue to exist as most leave my body. Why distinguish between this collection and the matter now constituting my body? Why suppose that masses of matter are physical *objects*? Van Inwagen says that only one object now has these particles as parts: my body (which, according to him, is identical to me). The matter is (at best) just a set or collection with the particles as *members*.

The problem with this clever response to premise 1 is that it depends upon a contingent empirical assumption: that matter consists of partless particles, ultimate simple atoms. If there were persons whose bodies were superficially like ours, but made of infinitely divisible matter (of the sort postulated by Aristotle, Descartes, and, arguably, even Newton[29]), the matter constituting one of them at a moment could not be identified with any particular set of tiny bits of matter. Such a body could continue to be made of the same matter even if the *set* ceased to exist due to the breakup of some tiny bits, as long as the scattered parts remained within the body. On the assumption of infinite divisibility, no particular set of objects will serve as the matter; the matter must be an object in its own right.[30] So the body of a creature just like me but with "electrons" and "quarks" that turn out to be tiny extended solids (with parts inside of parts inside of . . .) will be constituted by a mass of matter that is a physical object in its own right. If I am identical to *this* body, he must be identical with a physical object of the same size. Van Inwagen agrees that there can be at most one physical object made of the matter in this creature. So the poor thing would be a briefly conscious, usually scattered mass of matter. I say that if he is, I am. And maybe I am. But one can be forgiven for hoping that this crazy version of materialism is false, and that emergent dualism, though possibly equally crazy, may be true instead.

27 Peter van Inwagen, *Material Beings* (Ithaca, NY, and London: Cornell University Press, 1990).

28 Those who find set theory unproblematic are not likely to have any complaints about this assumption, and it makes no difference to my criticisms.

29 Newton probably held that matter is infinitely divisible stuff that takes the form of extremely tiny extended spheres that cannot be divided by any *physical* force. This was Boscovich's interpretation, at any rate.

30 For detailed argument, see my "Theories of Masses and Problems of Constitution" and "Personal Identity."

Other two-category theories lead much more quickly to bizarre conclusions. They are seldom discussed, and I can think of no *living* philosopher who holds one of them (at least not as a theory about how *persons* are constituted). I consider them in detail elsewhere.[31]

3.5 Denying premise 1: the case of the disappearing matter

The other way to deny premise 1 is to say that there is only *one* thing here, a human organism that feels sad, say. There is no such thing as a mass of matter distinct from myself but present in the same location, threatening to feel sad if I do.

But surely there is matter in the universe, in this room, in my body. At least there are "fundamental" (so far as we can tell now) particles (which may or may not persist "identically" through time). To be made of some of this world's matter is, if these particles are ultimate, to be made of some batch of such particles; if they are not ultimate, but are in turn made of smaller, *truly* fundamental particles, then to be made of our kind of matter is to be made of a batch of these smaller things; and if what we *call* "fundamental particles" are made instead of some infinitely divisible stuff that comes prepackaged as tiny solids, then to be made of some earthly matter is to be made of some portion of *that* stuff. Consider, again, a living body like mine but made of such stuff. Since it is like mine, the matter that comes together to form it at a given moment was once scattered. As shown earlier, matter of this sort must be treated as a physical object in its own right, not a mere set or collection of particles. How could there be just one thing where the creature is? There would seem to be just two options: Either there are not two things here, because the living body *is* the mass of matter and was scattered a short time ago and will become scattered again (an option I said was no easier to believe than emergent dualism); or the once scattered matter that comes together to form the body literally *ceases to be* when, as we would normally say, "it" constitutes the body.

The second alternative was suggested by Chryssipus and is defended by Michael Burke.[32] According to Burke, there are such things as masses of matter – physical objects that can survive scattering and arbitrary rearrangement of parts, but not any changes in matter. But he denies that there is one *here*, where my body is. When one of these masses of matter is about to take on the shape of a human being, it suddenly ceases to be, replaced by an organism that *can* survive the gain and loss of stuff, but that *cannot* survive scattering or arbitrary rearrangement of parts.

Many objections can be raised against this sort of picture. Where did the matter go? The change it undergoes when it comes to constitute a human organism seems to be merely a rearrangement of its parts, something a mere portion of matter can easily survive; why should taking on a new shape destroy it? And is it not an undeniable truism that the matter now constituting me was once scattered? But if the matter *now* constituting my body is not the same as the matter that ceased to be

31 Zimmerman, "Personal Identity."

32 See Michael Burke, "Dion and Theon: An Essentialist Solution to an Ancient Puzzle," *Journal of Philosophy*, 91 (1994), pp. 129–39; and *idem*, "Preserving the Principle of One Object to a Place: A Novel Account of the Relations among Objects, Sorts, Sortals, and Persistence Conditions," *Philosophy and Phenomenological Research*, 54 (1994), pp. 591–624.

as it came to constitute me, what is it? Either there is really no such thing as the matter now constituting me; or else "the matter now constituting my body" is just another name for my body, this human organism that can survive the gain and loss of parts.[33] On either alternative, to make something out of some matter is really to cause the matter to be replaced by something that is *not* made of that matter. Neither alternative does justice to the obvious facts: that there is some matter constituting my body now, and that this very matter does not have a human form at every time it exists.[34]

Each premise of the *entia successiva* argument is, then, quite defensible. If either one is false, then one will have to say some hard things about persons or matter, or else make some rather unintuitive, a priori claims about the nature of the physical world. So I conclude that dualism – emergent dualism, at any rate – deserves to be taken seriously, given the alternatives. Those who, like most Christians, have independent reason to think that it is true, can hardly be blamed for believing it.[35]

Christians Should Reject Mind–Body Dualism

Lynne Rudder Baker

Through the ages, Christians have almost automatically been mind–body dualists. The Bible portrays us as spiritual beings, and one obvious way to be a spiritual being is to be (or to have) an immaterial soul. Since it is also evident that we have bodies, Christians have naturally thought of themselves as composite beings, made of two substances – a material body and a nonmaterial soul. Despite the historical weight of this position, I do not think that it is required either by Scripture or by Christian doctrine as it has developed through the ages. So, I want to argue that there is a Christian alternative to mind–body dualism, and that the reasons in favor of the alternative outweigh those in favor of mind–body dualism.

The version of mind–body dualism that has attracted Christians is substance dualism. Substance dualism is the thesis that there are two kinds of finite substances:

33 This is, I believe, Burke's official view. See Michael Burke, "Coinciding Objects: Reply to Lowe and Denkel," *Analysis*, 56 (1996); and my "Coincident Objects: Could a 'Stuff Ontology' Help?," *Analysis*, 57 (1997), pp. 19–27.

34 Perhaps, due to the ephemerality of particles obeying quantum statistics, this matter exists only for an instant; but then, once again, it is not at all like the body it constitutes.

35 I thank Ted A. Warfield for his contribution to a joint presentation defending dualism (at the April 2000 Pacific Regional Meeting of the Society of Christian Philosophers) that included elements of this essay; the present paper is better than it would have been in numerous ways due to my collaboration with Warfield. I am grateful to the Council for Christian Colleges and Universities, the Calvin Center for Christian Scholarship, and the Christian Scholars Program for support of my research on personal identity while this essay was being written.

material (e.g., bodies) and nonmaterial (e.g., souls). On this view, we human persons are fundamentally, at least in part, nonmaterial substances. A substance dualist holds either that a human person is identical to a nonmaterial soul or is identical to a composite of a nonmaterial soul and a material body.

From Plato on, a soul or mind has been conceived of as something that can exist apart from any material substance at all.[36] Recently, philosophers have proposed a modification of this idea, so that a mind may be thought of as an emergent substance – perhaps not able to exist apart from any body, but made of a different sort of "stuff" from ordinary material objects.[37] The "stuff" that the nonmaterial soul is supposedly made of is undetectable – or at least it has not been detected – by physics. Nor (in contrast to, say, "dark matter") is there any theoretical need for physics to postulate such nonmaterial "stuff." On both the Platonistic conception and the revised conception, the soul or mind is a nonmaterial substance unlike substances that make up the rest of the created world. According to all versions of substance dualism, a mind is a unique kind of substance, fundamentally different from ordinary material substances. When I speak of mind–body dualism, I have in mind Substance Dualism in either its traditional or revised form.

Mind–body dualism is a philosophical thesis about the nature of human persons. I deny mind–body dualism, because I do not think that it is the correct account of the nature of human persons. I shall argue that human persons are material beings. But notice two things. First, my denial that human persons have nonmaterial souls is perfectly compatible with the view that God is an immaterial being. Although I deny mind–body dualism, I do not deny all dualism. In particular, I do not deny a dualism between the natural and the supernatural realms. My materialism pertains only to the natural world. Like most Christians, I think of God as an immaterial being. Second, the fact that mind–body dualism is a *philosophical* thesis about human persons is important. Christianity has almost no specifically philosophical commitments. When Christians seek a philosophical outlook congenial to their faith, the door is open to a wide variety of positions. Mind–body dualism is one position compatible with Christian faith, but it is not the only such position.

One reason why Christians have been attracted to mind–body dualism is that mind–body dualism has seemed to be the only alternative to taking persons to be identical to animals. People have assumed that there are only two possibilities: We are just like all the other animals, or we differ from the other animals by having nonmaterial souls. The overlooked possibility here is that we differ from the other animals, but not by having nonmaterial souls. This is the possibility that I shall explore. We, like the other animals, are material beings; but, unlike the other animals, we are essentially persons. To be a spiritual being does not require having any nonmaterial soul. One and the same thing – a human person – is *both* a material being and a spiritual being.

36 Thomas Aquinas did not think of a soul as a substance; rather, a rational soul was the form of the human body. However, since he thought that the rational soul was "subsistent" and could exist apart from any body, I count him as a mind–body dualist.

37 See Hasker, *Emergent Self.* Dean Zimmerman and Ted Warfield presented a version of this kind of dualism at the Society of Christian Philosophers at Fuller Theological Seminary, March 2000.

I want to show here that there is a kind of materialism that is congenial to Christian believers and that, on balance, this materialism is preferable to mind-body dualism. On my view – I call it "the constitution view" – something is a *person* in virtue of having a first-person perspective, and a person is a *human* person in virtue of being constituted by a human body (or human animal). So, I need to explain what I mean by a "first-person perspective," and what I mean by "constitution" when I say that a person is constituted by a human body. Let's start with the first-person perspective.

1 The Idea of a First-Person Perspective

The first-person perspective is a very peculiar ability that all, and only persons, have. It is the ability to think of oneself without the use of any name, description, or demonstrative; it is the ability to conceive of oneself as oneself, from the inside, as it were. Linguistic evidence of a first-person perspective comes from use of first-person pronouns embedded in sentences with linguistic or psychological verbs – for example, "I wonder how I will die," or "I promise that I will stick with you."[38] If I wonder how I will die, or I promise that I'll stick with you, then I am thinking of myself as myself; I am not thinking of myself in any third-person way (e.g., not as LB, nor as the person who is thinking, nor as her, nor as the only person in the room) at all. Anything that can wonder how it will die *ipso facto* has a first-person perspective and thus is a person.

A being may be conscious without having a first-person perspective. Nonhuman primates and other higher animals are conscious, and they have psychological states like believing, fearing, and desiring. They have points of view (e.g., "danger in that direction"), but they cannot conceive of themselves as the subjects of such thoughts. They cannot *conceive of* themselves from the first person. (We have every reason to think that they do not wonder how they will die.) So, having psychological states like beliefs and desires, and having a point of view, are necessary but not sufficient conditions for being a person. A sufficient condition for being a person – whether human, divine, ape, or silicon-based – is having a first-person perspective.[39] So, what makes something a person is not the "stuff" it is made of. It does not matter whether something is made of organic material or silicon or, in the case of God, no material "stuff" at all. If a being has a first-person perspective, it is a person.

Persons, defined by first-person perspectives, are a genuine novelty in the world. What one thinks from a first-person perspective cannot be adequately translated into

38 Hector-Neri Castañeda developed this idea in several papers. See "He: A Study in the Logic of Self-Consciousness," *Ratio*, 8 (1966), pp. 130–57, and "Indicators and Quasi-Indicators," *American Philosophical Quarterly*, 4 (1967), pp. 85–100.

39 Gallup's experiments with chimpanzees suggest the possibility of a kind of intermediate stage between dogs (which have intentional states but no first-person perspectives) and human persons (which have first-person perspectives). In my opinion – for details see my *Persons and Bodies: A Constitution View* (Cambridge: Cambridge University Press, 2000), pp. 62–4 – Gallup's chimpanzees fall short of full-blown first-person perspectives. See Gordon Gallup, Jr, "Self-Recognition in Primates: A Comparative Approach to Bidirectional Properties of Consciousness," *American Psychologist*, 32 (1977), pp. 329–38.

third-person terms. To wonder how I will die is not the same as wondering how LB will die, even though I am LB. This is so, because I could wonder how I will die even if I had amnesia and didn't know my name. A being with a first-person perspective not only can have thoughts about herself, but she can also conceive of herself as the subject of such thoughts. I not only wonder how I'll die, but I realize that the bearer of that thought is myself.

Person is an ontological kind whose defining characteristic is a capacity for a first-person perspective. A first-person perspective is the basis of all self-consciousness. It makes possible an inner life, a life of thoughts that one realizes are one's own. The appearance of first-person perspectives in a world makes an ontological difference in that world. A world populated by beings with inner lives is ontologically richer than a world populated by no beings with inner lives. But what is ontologically distinctive about being a person – namely, the capacity for a first-person perspective – does not have to be secured by a nonmaterial substance like a soul.

2 The Idea of Constitution

If something is a person in virtue of having a capacity for a first-person perspective, what distinguishes human persons from other logically possible persons (God, Martians, perhaps computers)? The answer is that human persons are constituted by human bodies (i.e., human animals), rather than by, say, Martian green-slime bodies.

Constitution is a very general relation that we are all familiar with (though probably not under that label). A river at any moment is constituted by an aggregate of water molecules. But the river is not identical to the aggregate of water molecules that constitutes it at that moment. Since one and the same river – call it 'R' – is constituted by different aggregates of molecules at different times, the river is not identical to any of the aggregates of water molecules that make it up. So, constitution is not identity.[40] Another way to see that constitution is not identity is to notice that even if an aggregate of molecules, A_1, actually constitutes R at t_1, R might have been constituted by a different aggregate of molecules, A_2, at t_1. So, constitution is a relation that is in some ways similar to identity, but is not actually identity. If the relation between a person and her body is her constitution, then a person is not identical to her body. The relation is more like the relation between the river and the aggregates of molecules.

The answer to the question, What most fundamentally is x?, is what I call "x's primary kind." Each thing has its primary-kind property essentially. If x constitutes y,[41] then x and y are of different primary kinds. If x constitutes y, then what "the thing" is, is determined by y's primary kind. For example, if a human body constitutes a person, then what there is, is a person-constituted-by-a human-body. So you – a person constituted by a human body – are most fundamentally a person. Person

40 I am assuming here the classical conception of identity, according to which if a = b, then necessarily a = b.

41 Here and elsewhere I'll omit reference to times.

is your primary kind. If parts of your body were replaced by bionic parts until you were no longer human, you would still be a person. You are a person as long as you exist. If you ceased to have a first-person perspective, then you would cease to exist – even if your body was still there.

Whether we are talking about rivers, human persons, or countless other constituted things, the basic idea is this: When certain things of certain kinds (aggregates of water molecules, human organisms) are in certain circumstances (different ones for different kinds of things), then new entities of different kinds come into existence. The circumstances in which an aggregate of water molecules comes to constitute a river have to do with the relation of the water molecules to each other; they form a stream. The circumstances in which a human organism comes to constitute a human person have to do with development of a first-person perspective. In each case, new things of new kinds, with new kinds of causal powers, come into being. Since constitution is the vehicle, so to speak, by which new kinds of things come into existence in the natural world, it is obvious that constitution is not identity. Indeed, this conception is relentlessly anti-reductive.

Although not identity, constitution is a relation of real unity.[42] If x constitutes y at a given time, then x and y are not separate things. A person and her body have lots of properties in common: the property of having toenails and the property of being responsible for certain of her actions. But notice: the person has the property of having toenails, only because she is constituted by something that could have had toenails even if it had constituted nothing. And her body is responsible for her actions only because it constitutes something that would have been responsible no matter what constituted it.

So, I'll say that the person has the property of having toenails derivatively, and her body has the property of being responsible for certain of her actions derivatively; the body has the property of having toenails nonderivatively, and the person has the property of being responsible for certain of her actions nonderivatively.[43] If x constitutes y, then some of x's properties have their source (so to speak) in y, and some of y's properties have their source in x. The unity of the object x-constituted-by-y is shown by the fact that x and y borrow properties from each other. The idea of having properties derivatively accounts for the otherwise strange fact that if x constitutes y at t, x and y share so many properties even though $x \neq y$.

To summarize this discussion of the idea of constitution, constitution is a very general relation throughout the natural order. Although it is a relation of real unity, it is short of identity. (Identity is necessary; constitution is contingent.) Constitution is a relation that accounts for the appearance of genuinely new kinds of things with

42 Some philosophers have held that the idea of unity without identity is incoherent. In *Persons and Bodies*, I give a completely general definition of "constitution" that is coherent. Moreover, since the Christian Trinity is supposed to be three Persons in one Being, a Christian who believes in the Trinity is in no position to claim that the general idea of unity without identity is incoherent.

43 For a technical account of "having properties derivatively," see Baker, *Persons and Bodies*, ch. 2. Not all properties are subject to being had derivatively. Excluded properties are (a) properties expressed in English using "essentially" or "primary-kind property" or variants thereof; (b) properties expressed in English using "is identical to" or "constitutes" or "exists" or variants thereof; (c) properties rooted outside the times at which they are had; (d) properties that are the conjunctions of two or more properties that either entail or are entailed by two or more primary-kind properties.

new kinds of causal powers. If F and G are primary kinds and Fs constitute Gs, then an inventory of the contents of the world that includes Fs but leaves out Gs is incomplete.[44] Gs are not reducible to Fs.[45]

3 Human Persons

Putting together the ideas of a first-person perspective and of constitution, we get this:

> HP: An entity x is a human person at t if and only if (i) x has a capacity for a first-person perspective at t and (ii) x is constituted by a human body at t.

An entity x is a person in virtue of satisfying (i), and x is a human (rather than a divine or Martian) person in virtue of satisfying (ii). If x is a person constituted by a human body at t, then x is essentially a person. That is, there could be no time at which x existed without being a person. But x is not essentially a *human* person. An entity x is a human person only if x is constituted by a human body, and it is possible that x is constituted by a human body at one time but constituted by a non-human body (a bionic body, a resurrection body) at another time. Even though it is possible that we come to have different bodies, anything that begins to exist as a human person (i.e., begins to exist constituted by a human body) is essentially embodied.[46]

In HP, I mean "capacity" in a very narrow sense. An object x has a capacity for a first-person perspective at t if and only if x has the relevant structural properties required for a first-person perspective, and either (i) x manifests a first-person perspective at t or has manifested a first-person perspective at some time prior to t or (ii) x is in an environment at t conducive to development and maintenance of a first-person perspective. For human persons, the relevant structural properties for a first-person perspective are those of a normal brain of an infant.[47] We may never know

44 There is much more to be said about the idea of constitution. See Baker, *Persons and Bodies*, esp. ch. 2, and *idem*, "Unity without Identity: A New Look at Material Constitution," in Peter A. French and Howard K. Wettstein (eds), *New Directions in Philosophy*, Midwest Studies in Philosophy 23, (Malden, Mass.: Blackwell, 1999), pp. 144–65.

45 Note that this is a completely general claim. It is not "property dualism."

46 I put it this way because of the Incarnation. I want to allow for saying that the Second Person of the Trinity essentially has a human nature, but is not essentially embodied. The Second Person of the Trinity, with a human as well as a divine nature, existed as an immaterial being before he came to be constituted by the body of Jesus of Nazareth. Since the Second Person of the Trinity did not begin to exist at all, he did not begin to exist as a human *person* (*à la* HP). His being fully human does not require that he be essentially embodied. (I don't know whether this is the right thing to say, but I do not want to rule it out by my account of human persons.)

47 The relevant structural properties for a first-person perspective are nonderivative properties of a brain, and hence are nonderivative properties of the human animal. But the capacity for a first-person perspective is a nonderivative property not of the human animal but of the person. So, when a human animal has the requisite structural properties, a new being comes into existence – a person – at the moment that the animal manifests a first-person perspective, or is in the requisite environmental and organismic circumstances.

the exact moment when a person comes into being.[48] On the other end of earthly existence, this understanding of human persons allows that a person can go into a coma without ceasing to exist. If x has manifested a first-person perspective before going into a coma (and hence was a person), then x continues to exist (and hence continues to be a person) as long as x's brain still has the physical endowment to support a first-person perspective.

The animal that constitutes a person has developed from zygote to embryo to fetus. Then, when that organism develops the capacity for a first-person perspective, a new being comes into existence – a person constituted by the organism. The organism does not go out of existence, any more than the piece of marble that constitutes Michelangelo's *David* went out of existence when Michelangelo finished his piece. The statue is constituted by the piece of marble, but is not identical to it. Similarly, the person is constituted by the body, but is not identical to it. But to say that the person is not identical to the body does not mean that the person is identical to the body-plus-some-other-thing (like a soul).[49] *David* is not identical to a piece-of-marble-plus-some-other-thing. If x constitutes y and x is wholly material, then y is wholly material.[50] The human body (= human animal) is wholly material, and the human body constitutes the human person. Therefore, the human person is wholly material. A human person is as material as Michelangelo's *David* is.

Let me illustrate two ways in which a human person and the body that constitutes her are a unity. First, my body has good digestion nonderivatively; I have good digestion derivatively, in virtue of being constituted by a body that has good digestion independently of its constitution relations.[51] But it is still the case that I do have good digestion. On the other hand, I have a right to sit in a certain seat at the opera nonderivatively; and my body has a right to be there derivatively in virtue of the fact that my body constitutes me, and I have the right to sit there regardless of any properties of my body. If x has a property derivatively, then x does have the property.[52] Second, I am a person nonderivatively, and my body is a person derivatively. That is, my body is a person solely in virtue of constituting me, and I am a person independently of my constitution relations to my body. Thus, the idea of having a property derivatively explains two things about the unity produced by constitution: (1) the fact that my body and I, though nonidentical, have so many properties in common, and (2) the fact that I am a person and my body (now) is a person (now) does not imply that where I am there are two persons. My body is not a separate or different person from me.[53]

48 Developmental psychologists agree that from birth a first-person perspective is under way. See, e.g., Jerome Kagan, *Unstable Ideas* (Cambridge, Mass.: Harvard University Press, 1989), and Daniel N. Stern, *The Interpersonal World of the Infant* (New York: Basic Books, 1985).

49 Someone may ask: If a human person is not identical to a body or to a soul or to a body-plus-a-soul, what is she identical to? This question is a red herring. A person is identical to herself and not another thing.

50 For details, see Baker, *Persons and Bodies*, ch. 2.

51 The expression "having a property independently of constitution relations" is a technical locution, defined in ibid., p. 48. It is not a causal term.

52 As I mentioned earlier, not every property is subject to being had derivatively: e.g., "being a person essentially" or "being identical to a person" is always had nonderivatively (if at all).

53 For details, see Baker, *Persons and Bodies*, pp. 173–5. See also my "Materialism with a Human Face," in Kevin Corcoran (ed.), *Body, Soul and Survival* (Ithaca, NY: Cornell University Press, 2001), pp. 159–80.

Underlying the constitution view is the idea that what something is most fundamentally is often determined by what it can do – its abilities and capacities – rather than by what it is made of. This is obvious in the case of artifacts: What makes something a clock has to do with its telling time, no matter what it is made of. Similarly, according to the constitution view, what makes something a person has to do with its having a first-person perspective, no matter what it is made of. The traditional field of answers to the question "In virtue of what is something a person?" (a body? a brain? a mind? some combination of these?) is misleading. A person is a basic kind of thing, and one is a person not in virtue of what one is made of, but in virtue of what one can do.

4 Why a Christian Should Endorse the Constitution View of Human Persons

I shall set out a simple, valid argument to prefer the constitution view of human persons to mind–body dualism, and then I shall defend each premise. Here is the argument:

1 The constitution view of human persons is preferable to mind–body dualism unless there is some overriding reason – either philosophical or religious – to accept mind–body dualism.
2 There is no overriding reason – either philosophical or religious – to accept mind–body dualism.

Therefore,

3 The constitution view of human persons is preferable to mind–body dualism.

4.1 First premise

The basic reason for accepting premise 1 can be expressed as a slogan: "Don't introduce a bifurcation unless you need to." Christians already have the bifurcation between nature and grace, between the Creator and the created. But nature itself is a unified whole with its own integrity, and human persons are a part of nature. We make better sense of the integrity of the world if we do not bifurcate nature. The constitution view, an anti-reductive materialism, construes nature as an integrated whole.

A second reason to accept premise 1 is that the constitution view of human persons fits into a comprehensive metaphysical view of the natural world. Since constitution is a very general relation in the world, and not specific to persons and their bodies, there is no special pleading for human persons. So, on this score, the constitution view is less *ad hoc* than mind–body dualism.

A third reason to accept premise 1 is that the constitution view bypasses all the well-known problems of interactions between nonmaterial and material substances. After 350 years, mind–body interactions remain as mysterious as they were in Descartes's time. Although I reject "scientism" root and branch, empirical investigation of the natural world has produced an amazing body of knowledge with no end in sight. Nonmaterial substance simply does not fit in with what we know about the natural world. Thus postulation of a nonmaterial substance, which seems closed to empirical investigation, should be a last resort.

Even if these three reasons provide good support for premise 1, as I think they do, premise 1 is still no good without premise 2.

4.2 Second premise

There are two kinds of support for premise 2, philosophical and religious. First, the philosophical: One motivation for mind–body dualism is that it takes persons seriously in a way that reductive materialism does not. But this motivation is equally a motivation for the constitution view. Dualism has nothing over the constitution view in terms of taking persons seriously, as the following examples show.

(1) Persons *qua* persons have ontological significance. According to the constitution view, the property of being a person is not just a property of nonpersonal things. Anything that is a person either constitutes or is identical to something that is *essentially* a person – that is, to something that could not exist without being a person. Any time the property of having a first-person perspective is instantiated, something (a person) has it essentially.

(2) Human persons do not have the bodies that they actually have necessarily. It is logically possible that a person have a different body from the one that she in fact has. The constitution view admits the logical possibility of waking up in a different body – as did Gregor Samsa in Kafka's story "The Metamorphosis." (Neither proponents of the constitution view nor mind–body dualists have any idea how such a thing could happen.) Slightly more realistically, a person would change bodies if her organic parts were replaced one by one with synthetic parts until the organism no longer existed, but the person (defined by a particular first-person perspective) continued to exist.

(3) With respect to questions of survival, we care about identity, not just qualitative similarity. I want to know if I will be around, not just if some future person (or persons!) psychologically similar to me will be around. According to the constitution view, there is a fact of the matter about whether a particular future person is I. A future person is I if and only if she has my first-person perspective. As a "criterion of personal identity," this condition is circular; but that is not surprising. All it means is that there is no way to define what a person is in nonpersonal terms. Personhood is irreducible to anything else.

So, I see no overriding *philosophical* reason to accept mind–body dualism – especially in light of the availability of the constitution view.[54] But perhaps there is some

54 For an illuminating discussion of philosophical arguments for substance dualism, see Hasker, *Emergent Self*, ch. 5. Hasker has searching criticisms of arguments by Swinburne and Talliaferro. Hasker's own "unity-of-consciousness" argument for dualism relies on a Principle of Reducibility that I think ought to be rejected for reasons unrelated to issues concerning persons. I regret that discussion of the Principle of Reducibility here would take us too far afield.

overriding *religious* reason that ought to pull the Christian to dualism. For example, someone might claim that the Bible gives overriding reason to accept mind–body dualism.

A thorough discussion of biblical reasons to be a dualist is given by John W. Cooper.[55] Although I cannot do justice to the rich arguments here, I will give a summary assessment. The arguments that Cooper presents in favor of soul–body dualism (as he calls it) do not tell against the constitution view. For example, he points out several things that must obtain if the Christian doctrine of life after death is true – for example, "The being that I am must continue to exist [after physical death]," and "I must somehow be aware of myself as the same person who formerly lived on earth." Then, as if in conclusion, he says, "All this must be possible without my bodily organism." Notice that on the constitution view, all this *is* "possible without my bodily organism." Thus, Cooper's "unpacking of biblical teaching" here gives no reason at all to accept mind–body dualism over the constitution view. The constitution view does not allow that we cannot exist unembodied; it does allow that we cannot exist without the bodies that constitute us now.

Cooper's main argument for soul–body dualism is from the doctrine of an intermediate state between death and a general resurrection. Cooper argues that "the doctrine of the intermediate state [between death and the general resurrection] logically requires the possibility that persons can exist without earthly bodies."[56] Again, this is no problem for the constitution view, which entails the logical possibility of our existing without *earthly* bodies. (To say that we can exist without earthly bodies is not to say that we can exist without any kind of body.) Moreover, there is no reason to think that the intermediate state must be a disembodied state. For all we know, persons in the intermediate state are constituted by intermediate-state bodies. So, Cooper's arguments provide no reason to prefer mind–body dualism to the constitution view.

Other kinds of biblical evidence – such as the language used in discussions of anthropology in the Old and New Testaments – may be adduced for one position or another. But that's the problem. The Bible is not a philosophical text; its language does not point unambiguously to any philosophical position.[57] Indeed, given the kind of document that I think the Bible is, I do not think that it can fruitfully be mined for philosophical theories; the best that we can do is to formulate philosophical theories that try to be faithful to Scripture as a whole, not to "proof texts." Biblical evidence for mind–body dualism as opposed to the constitution view is inconclusive, as we should expect, given the kind of document that the Bible is.

Christian doctrine may provide another motivation for a Christian to be a mind–body dualist. Again, I think that the constitution view does as well as mind–body dualism in making sense of Christian doctrine. Let me all too briefly mention two doctrines. First, consider the doctrine of Christ as being one Person with two natures, "of one substance (*homoousios*) with the Father as regarding his Godhead,

55 Cooper, *Body, Soul, and Life Everlasting.*

56 Ibid., p. 179.

57 Ibid., chs 2–8.

and at the same time of one substance with us as regards his manhood."[58] Christ is fully human and fully divine. The mind–body dualist would have to say that Christ consists of three substances – one infinite and two finite. On mind–body dualism, Christ is immaterial in his divine nature, and partly material and partly immaterial in his human nature. By contrast, on the constitution view, Christ is immaterial in his divine nature and material in his human nature. The mind–body dualist's construal seems to me clumsier than the constitutionalist's construal; in any case, there is no overriding reason here to accept mind–body dualism.

Another doctrine that might motivate a Christian to be a mind–body dualist is the resurrection of the dead.[59] The doctrine entails bodily resurrection. According to the constitution view, we are essentially embodied; so, if the constitution view is correct, there is an obvious explanation of why life after death would be embodied life (since, according to the constitution view, we cannot exist unembodied). Mind–body dualism would provide no obvious explanation of why resurrection should be bodily (since, according to mind–body dualism, we can exist unembodied). So, I don't think that the doctrine of resurrection gives overriding reason to endorse mind–body dualism.

Finally, consider the idea that we are made in the image of God. A mind–body dualist might say that since God is immaterial, he made us in his image by giving us an immaterial part, a soul. But a proponent of the constitution view could say with equal justice that since God is self-conscious, he made us in his image by giving us self-consciousness (i.e., first-person perspectives). Being made in the image of God does not favor mind–body dualism any more than it favors the constitution view.

I conclude that premise 2 is true: There is no overriding reason – either philosophical or religious – to accept mind–body dualism over the constitution view. Since, by premise 1, the constitution view is preferable to mind–body dualism unless there is some overriding reason – either philosophical or religious – to accept mind–body dualism, a Christian should endorse the constitution view of human persons.

5 Conclusion

What the constitution view of persons shows is that there is a way to be a materialist about human persons and still be an orthodox Christian. Like the constitution view, mind–body dualism also conceives of human persons as distinct from organisms, since according to mind–body dualists, human persons "have two parts linked together, body and soul."[60] What the constitution view offers is a *materialistic* way to conceive of human persons as distinct from organisms.

58 Definition of the Union of the Divine and Human Natures in the Person of Christ, Council of Chalcedon, AD 451, Act V; quoted in *The Book of Common Prayer*, p. 864. I should note that the definition also says "truly man, consisting also of a reasonable soul and body." It is not obvious that we should take "reasonable soul and body" to imply two substances, since the definition also says "of one substance with us as regards his manhood" rather than "of two substances with us as regards his manhood."

59 For a fuller discussion of how the constitution view can handle the idea of the resurrection of the dead, see my "Material Persons and the Doctrine of Resurrection," *Faith and Philosophy*, forthcoming.

60 Swinburne, *Evolution of the Soul*, rev. edn (1997), p. 145.

Christian tradition is largely dualistic. I take tradition seriously and depart from it only when I think that the Christian community has made a mistake, and when I have an explanation for how Christians could have made that mistake. Although I think that mind–body dualism is consistent with Christian doctrine, I also think that mind–body dualism is a philosophical mistake. It is easy to see how Christians could have made this mistake if they assumed that the only way to distinguish us sufficiently from organisms is by postulating nonmaterial souls. But the constitution view shows that the dichotomy – either we are identical to animals or we have immaterial souls – is a false one. The constitution view offers a third way. Since the constitution view is also consistent with Christian doctrine, and since the constitution view fits better with what we know about the natural world, I think that, on balance, it is a better philosophical bet than mind–body dualism.[61]

Reply to Baker

Lynne Rudder Baker's materialism is a version of the view I criticized under the heading "coincidentalism." She says that there are (at least) three material objects in the space my body occupies: an aggregate of matter, a human organism, and a person. Although each is made of the very same atoms, arranged in the very same way, they are quite different. The person can survive the death of the organism; the organism can survive a brain trauma that "kills" the person; only the lump of matter can survive being run over by a steamroller. Because of these differences, they have different careers. Apparently the powers and potentialities of a physical object are not determined by its physical structure alone – an odd conclusion. But there are further problems.

Zimmerman (the person), the organism that is his body, and the aggregate of matter that now constitutes it are very similar, at present. Being made of the same atoms, they had better have the same shape, weight, spatial location, etc. But what about the conscious mental states I enjoy? Are they shared, too? Are there three pains when I step on a tack, three things feeling sad whenever I am sad? If so, how do I know which one *I* am? These questions (driven home forcefully by Eric Olson[62]) generate the "too many minds" objection.

Here is my own way of pressing one part of this objection.[63] Consider a defective human organism, a feral child perhaps, that is conscious but incapable of ever acquiring a "first-person perspective." Compare this creature with a full-fledged human person who, though minimally conscious, is heavily sedated and so temporarily unable to take on a first-person perspective. Suppose blood of their common type is needed; one or the other must be the donor and endure a jab in the arm. You know that, in their present conditions, neither one would remember the pain. According to Baker,

61 I am grateful to Katherine A. Sonderegger for reading a draft of this essay and discussing it with me.

62 See, e.g., Olson, *Human Animal*, ch. 5.

63 For a more thorough presentation, see my "Material People," in Loux and Zimmerman (eds), *Oxford Handbook of Metaphysics*, pp. 491–526.

if you stick the person, there are three things (person, organism, aggregate of matter) each feeling pain; stick the other, and only two (organism and aggregate) feel pain. So, in the absence of other moral considerations, you *must* jab the feral child, so that there will be one less creature in pain. But that's ridiculous.

Some coincidentalists say that, in each case, only one thing is really subject to pain, the others remaining completely insensate.[64] I criticize this response elsewhere.[65] Baker seems to have a different response. She allows that there are three subjects of pain in the one case and two in the other; but insists that, in both cases, *one* of the entities is in pain in a more direct or robust fashion than the others. Only one of the coincidents is in pain "nonderivatively." The extra entities are only "derivatively" in pain. Feeling pain is a property they "borrow" from the thing that has it in the more robust way. In the case of the drugged person, there are two pain-borrowers; in the case of the feral child, only one. But borrowers of pain do not increase the amount of pain in the world.[66]

Another part of the "too many minds" objection is the allegation that, if coincidentalism were true, I could never be sure of such things as whether I have the persistence conditions of the person, the organism, or the aggregate. Baker's response again invokes the idea that some coincident entities merely borrow properties from others. First-person thoughts, such as one might express in English using "I," refer nonderivatively to the person, and only derivatively to the animal or aggregate. No skepticism about who one is should arise, since each coincident entity asks the same question: "Do I have the persistence conditions of a person, organism, or aggregate?" with "I" referring (nonderivatively) to the person. If the three answer, "I have the persistence conditions of the person," no one is wrong. Each coincident entity thereby thinks (derivatively or nonderivatively) that *the person* has these persistence conditions.[67]

If Baker's strategies are to work, derivative exemplification must be a matter of having a property only "by courtesy," in virtue of standing in an especially close relationship ("constitution") with something that *really* has the property. If it were more than this, extra coincident entities feeling pain derivatively *would* increase the number of creatures in pain; jabbing the feral child rather than the drugged person *would* be mandatory in virtue of its causing less suffering. Similarly, derivative reference must not be *real* reference. If derivative reference were *a species of reference*, the fact that a first-person thought derivatively refers to the animal and aggregate would be enough to generate first-person thoughts with the animal and aggregate as subject, thoughts with the content "I (i.e., *the animal*) have the persistence conditions of a person" and "I (i.e., *the aggregate*) have the persistence conditions of a person." If these thoughts were *also* being thought, *even derivatively*, then two out of three things thought are false – the wrong persistence conditions are attributed to organism and aggregate.

64 This is the line taken by Sydney Shoemaker, "Realization, Micro-Realization, and Coincidence," *Philosophy and Phenomenological Research*, forthcoming.

65 Dean Zimmerman, "Shoemaker's Metaphysics of Properties, Mental Realization, and Constitution," *Philosophy and Phenomenological Research*, forthcoming; and *idem*, "Material People."

66 See Baker, *Persons and Bodies*, p. 102.

67 Ibid., pp. 203–4.

When confronted with "too many minds," Baker makes derivative having of properties sound very second-class: "the fact that y has such properties at t [derivatively] is not a different fact from the fact that x has them at t and x constitutes y at t."[68] The animal constituting me thinks the same thought that I do "solely in virtue of constituting something that has the thought nonderivatively."[69] But if such use of the derivative–nonderivative distinction lays to rest the "too many minds," it turns her view into substance dualism. If nonderivative having of properties is *real*, and derivative having of properties is merely borrowing them in virtue of intimate ties to things that *really* have them, then persons are not really physical or biological beings. Aggregates of matter are nonderivatively heavy, made of particles, spatially-located, etc.; organisms nonderivatively digest food, grow, etc. Persons only have these properties or do these things "by courtesy." They may truly be said to be heavy, or growing, "solely in virtue of" constitution relations to things that are heavy or growing; but only in something like the way a hermit crab may truly be said to be white or beautiful in virtue of its intimate relations to the white or beautiful shell it happens to have borrowed at the moment. A Cartesian dualist will typically allow that, although I am a nonphysical soul, in ordinary contexts I may truly be said to be heavy or growing in virtue of being united with a body that is heavy or growing. Wherein lies the difference between Baker and the dualist?

John Cooper argues, persuasively, that Christians should be committed to an "intermediate state" between death and resurrection. And Baker says that her materialism is not inconsistent with the doctrine. On her view, although I must be constituted by *some* kind of body, the utter annihilation of this physical body in a nuclear explosion, say, is consistent with my continuing to exist – albeit constituted by a body made of completely different stuff.

This reinforces my suspicion that her view is dualism-in-disguise. Organisms and aggregates of matter cannot, presumably, lose all of their physical parts at once; and there are limits on the ways in which the subsequent physical states of organisms and aggregates may evolve out of earlier ones. Baker's persons are free of such constraints. They can, miraculously, jump from one body to another, losing the shape and size and so on of the one body, and instantaneously acquiring those of the other, whatever they might be. Not even a miracle could allow mere hunks of matter or organisms to perform such feats. I would say that, if the current size and shape and physical makeup of an object puts no necessary constraints upon the immediately subsequent size and shape and physical makeup of that object, then the object does not *really* have that size, shape, or makeup – however appropriate it is to ascribe them to it in ordinary contexts on the basis of relations to things that really have them. Persons that can pass instantaneously from organic matter to ectoplasm (or whatever intermediate-state bodies are made of) are "physical" in an attenuated sense at best, able to pass from one body to another like shadows or spirits.

To sum up: Baker uses the derivative–nonderivative distinction to respond to the "too many minds" objection and allows for the doctrine of an "intermediate state."

68 Ibid., p. 58.
69 Ibid., p. 102.

She thereby becomes a Cartesian dualist with a complicated theory of the relation ("constitution") that unites nonphysical persons and bodies. If she decides *not* to use the derivative–nonderivative distinction to respond to this objection, she is left with too many minds.

Reply to Zimmerman

Dean Zimmerman defends a version of substance dualism – emergent dualism – as a view for Christians. Is there any reason – philosophical or religious – to prefer emergent dualism to the (nondualistic) constitution view?

Zimmerman advises Christians to resist the trend toward holding that "dualism is not central to Christianity." He cites (1) tradition, (2) present-day teaching of the Roman Catholic Magisterium, and (3) "exegetical principles that *ought* to generate significant biblical support for dualism."

With respect to (1), Christian thinking on the topic of an afterlife is rich in its variety. The tradition does not seem to speak with the single voice of substance dualism.[70]

With respect to (2), emergent dualism is obviously at odds with the Roman Catholic view that "the soul is immediately created by God." The incompatibility is twofold. According to emergent dualism: (i) the soul is not created by God, but is generated naturally by the brain (or body); and (ii) there is no "immediate animation," since the soul cannot emerge until there is a brain (or body) for it to emerge from.

With respect to (3), Zimmerman does not mention which exegetical principles he has in mind, but the Bible is a compendium of testimony by various witnesses to God's activity, and not a plausible source of philosophical theses. Many different competing philosophical theses are compatible with Christian doctrine.

So, I do not see any religious reasons to prefer emergent dualism to the constitution view. Are there any philosophical reasons to prefer Emergent Dualism?

(A) According to emergent dualism, what is a person? Is a person identical to a soul by itself, or is it identical to a composite of the emerged soul and the brain (or body) from which it emerges?

On the one hand, if a person – you, for instance – is identical to a brain/soul (or a body/soul) composite, then you could not exist in heaven or anywhere else without the same brain (or body) that you have now. In that case, if you exist in an afterlife, your soul must be "attached" to the same brain that you had during your earthly existence. But brains (and bodies) are often destroyed – either violently at death, or by

70 See Caroline Walker Bynum, *The Resurrection of the Body in Western Christianity, 200–1336* (New York: Columbia University Press, 1995), and Jeffrey Burton Russell, *A History of Heaven: The Singing Silence* (Princeton: Princeton University Press, 1997).

cremation, or by decay – yet one's prospects for an afterlife are not subject to such contingencies.[71] Moreover, the same argument that Zimmerman mounted for the conclusion that "I am neither a brain nor a human organism nor any other thing that changes parts" (Zimmerman's defense of Chisholm's *entia successiva* argument) would lead to the conclusion that I am not a brain-soul (or body-soul) composite. Brain-soul (or body-soul) composites have parts that change just as bodies alone have. So, I think that it is untenable to hold that you are identical to a brain-soul (or body-soul) composite.

On the other hand, if you are identical to a soul by itself, then, as I mentioned earlier, you did not come into existence until you already had a brain (or body) from which you (i.e., your soul) emerged. Moreover, Zimmerman says that each soul is "radically dependent upon one brain for its continued existence." In that case, emergent dualism forgoes one supposed advantage of traditional dualism – namely, that souls could exist separated from any body. If there is no possibility of "separated souls," then emergent dualism has no advantage over nondualistic positions like the constitution view.

(B) According to Zimmerman, souls are "in space, presumably within the heads that generate them." This claim is supposed to counter an objection to dualism – Why *this* soul with *this* body? Again, it seems to me that emergent dualism avoids an objection to traditional dualism by giving up an advantage of traditional dualism. If – as traditional dualists hold – souls are not in space at all, then it is unsurprising that neither physics nor neuroscience has found any. But if – as at least some emergent dualists hold – souls are located in space, in our heads, then it is odd in the extreme that neither physics nor neuroscience has seen any signs of them. I think it methodologically unwise to postulate substances *in our heads* that are invisible to physics and neuroscience.

So, I see no philosophical reason to prefer emergent dualism to the constitution view. I would like to conclude by commenting on Zimmerman's criticism of "coincidentalism" – a view that is in some ways similar to the constitution view.

Zimmerman defines "coincidentalism" as the view that where a person is, there are two things, "one thinking, the other not," where each is a physical object composed of microphysical particles. Note that this is not the constitution view, according to which some animals – human and nonhuman – can reason and, therefore, can think. We human persons are constituted by human animals, to which we are not identical. But thinking is *not* what distinguishes me from my body (the human animal that constitutes me now). I am not identical to my body, because I have a first-person perspective necessarily, and my body has a first-person perspective only contingently – in virtue of constituting me. Even though the constitution view is not a version of coincidentalism, as defined by Zimmerman, some of Zimmerman's objections to constitutionalism also apply to the constitution view. Here are two such objections.

71 See Peter van Inwagen, "The Possibility of Resurrection," in Paul Edwards (ed.), *Immortality* (New York: Macmillan Publishing Co., 1992), pp. 242–6; reprinted from the *International Journal for Philosophy of Religion*, 9 (1978); Dean Zimmerman, "The Compatibility of Materialism and Survival: The 'Falling Elevator' Model," *Faith and Philosophy*, 16 (1999), pp. 194–212.

First, what Zimmerman finds puzzling is "how things so alike in their *construction* could differ so radically in their *powers* and *potentialities*." This is puzzling only in the context of an assumption – namely, that the identity and the nature of a thing are determined by its construction. This is clearly a question-begging assumption.

I explicitly hold the following two views. (a) What a thing most fundamentally is, is often determined by what it can do – its causal powers, its functions, the roles that it plays – rather than by what it is made of. (b) The properties that are essential to something may be intentional, where intentional properties entail that there are people with beliefs and desires. (Both (a) and (b) seem obvious in the case of artifacts.) In the context of (a) and (b) – as opposed to the question-begging assumption – there is nothing at all puzzling about "how things so alike in their construction could differ so radically in their powers and potentialities." A non-question-begging argument should refute (a) and/or (b) – not just presuppose that they are false.

Second, Zimmerman says of the coincidentalist that "it is unclear how the one [an organism] can be thinking and the other [the matter in my body] not, given their structural similarity." Zimmerman's objection seems to be aimed at either (i) the view that my body thinks, but the mass of matter making it up does not, or (ii) the view that I think, but my body does not. Since I hold neither (i) nor (ii), no argument against either (i) or (ii) is an argument against the constitution view. Moreover, as (a) and (b) suggest, structurally similar things may differ in kind if they have different causal powers or different functions.

So, I still see no reason – religious or philosophical – for a Christian to prefer substance dualism (even in its emergent dualist version) to the constitution view. Hence, a Christian still should not be a mind–body dualist.

Index